P9-CNB-636

3 0379 10075 3625

L4 303.34092
F91

Duns Scotus Library

LOURDES
UNIVERSITY

6832 Convent Blvd.
Sylvania, OH 43560

Robert K.
Greenleaf

Robert K. Greenleaf

A LIFE OF SERVANT LEADERSHIP

DON M. FRICK

BK

BERRETT-KOEHLER PUBLISHERS, INC.
San Francisco

Copyright © 2004 by Don M. Frick

All rights reserved. No part of this publication may be reproduced, distributed, or transmitted in any form or by any means, including photocopying, recording, or other electronic or mechanical methods, without the prior written permission of the publisher, except in the case of brief quotations embodied in critical reviews and certain other noncommercial uses permitted by copyright law. For permission requests, write to the publisher, addressed "Attention: Permissions Coordinator," at the address below.

Berrett-Koehler Publishers, Inc.
235 Montgomery Street, Suite 650
San Francisco, CA 94104-2916
Tel: (415) 288-0260   Fax: (415) 362-2512   www.bkconnection.com

ORDERING INFORMATION

Quantity sales. Special discounts are available on quantity purchases by corporations, associations, and others. For details, contact the "Special Sales Department" at the Berrett-Koehler address above.

Individual sales. Berrett-Koehler publications are available through most bookstores. They can also be ordered direct from Berrett-Koehler: Tel: (800) 929-2929; Fax: (802) 864-7626; www.bkconnection.com

Orders for college textbook/course adoption use. Please contact Berrett-Koehler: Tel: (800) 929-2929; Fax: (802) 864-7626.

Orders by U.S. trade bookstores and wholesalers. Please contact Publishers Group West, 1700 Fourth Street, Berkeley, CA 94710. Tel: (510) 528-1444; Fax (510) 528-3444.

Berrett-Koehler and the BK logo are registered trademarks of Berrett-Koehler Publishers, Inc.

Printed in the United States of America

Berrett-Koehler books are printed on long-lasting acid-free paper. When it is available, we choose paper that has been manufactured by environmentally responsible processes. These may include using trees grown in sustainable forests, incorporating recycled paper, minimizing chlorine in bleaching, or recycling the energy produced at the paper mill.

Library of Congress Cataloging-in-Publication Data

Frick, Don M.
    Robert K. Greenleaf: A life of servant leadership / Don M. Frick.
      p.   cm.
    Includes bibliographical references and index.
    ISBN 1-57675-276-3
     1. Greenleaf, Robert K. 2. Executives—United States—Biography. 3. Business consultants—United States—Biography. 4. Leadership. 5. Management.
    6. Organizational effectiveness. I. Title: Servant-leadership. II. Title.

HC102.5.G73F74 2004
303.3'4'092—dc22
[B]   2003063741

First Edition
09 08 07 06 05 04   10 9 8 7 6 5 4 3 2 1

To Ann McGee-Cooper.
Friend, mentor, servant-leader to so many,
and especially to me.

Contents

PART III

Leader: 1964–1990   249

Foreword

Peter M. Senge

In *The Great Learning*, Confucius said "To become a leader one must first become a human being." I believe Confucius's statement means little today because we have lost the sense of our life's journey as one of becoming a human being. And, with that loss, we have lost the foundation of lived experience for developing as leaders.

As much as anything, I believe it is this loss that has motivated the extraordinary interest in Robert Greenleaf's work around the world in the past two decades. When Greenleaf wrote his essay, *The Servant as Leader* in 1970, he could hardly have imagined the growing interest the next 30 years would bring. Initially, the essay predictably attracted a small group of ready converts from religious organizations, from organizations, like some in the military, where values-based approaches to leadership were well established, and from people already drawn to a developmental approach to leadership. But today, the interest is far broader and more diverse, and it has spread well beyond the US, even beyond the Judeo-Christian tradition that was so important for Greenleaf's inspiration. *The Servant as Leader* has been translated into more than a dozen languages, and the Greenleaf Center for Servant Leadership in Indianapolis is now a global hub for operations in Australia/New Zealand, the UK, Canada, the Netherlands, the Philippines, Singapore, Japan, Korea, and South Africa.

But there are many reasons for the growing interest in leadership, and it is easy to force-fit Greenleaf's work to fill needs for which it is ill-suited. Much of what is written today on the subject focuses on power, either explicitly or implicitly. This occurs because leadership has, in its colloquial use, become a synonym for "boss-ship"—as when we use the word "leader" to refer to a person in the position of greatest authority. This is tragic and undermines progress in developing real leadership. If the word "leader" is a mere synonym for boss or positional authority, it has no meaning at all. Two words to describe the same phenomenon mean that one is redundant. Moreover, being a boss hardly guarantees being a leader. Many occupy positions of great authority and contribute little leadership. I believe much of the contemporary fascination with leadership reflects our obsession with positional power, and with the wealth we expect to accompany it. This is why so much of what is written about leadership focuses on presidents and CEOs —and why this writing contributes so little.

Still, despite frequently misusing the word as a marker for positional authority, it also points at issues we all sense as crucial. Indeed, leadership, or the lack thereof, seems to relate to many ailments that we see everywhere in the modern world—abuse of power, obsessive focus on the short term over the longer term, and a profound loss of purposefulness.

These problems sit much closer to Greenleaf's concerns, but I think it is a mistake for people to look to "servant leadership" as a kind of formulaic solution to them. Many seem to treat the recent corporate malfeasance witch hunt catalyzed by the Enron, Worldcom, and Tyco scandals as a singular occurrence. But it followed by only a decade the infamous "junkbond" scandal in the U.S. that put Michael Milliken and other highly successful dealmakers into jail. I recall much chest thumping by business schools about integrating ethics into their programs in the early 1990s— and even a few endowed professorships on the subject. Yet it would take some pretty strong rose-tinted lenses to assess any real progress in business practice that resulted. As concerns with abuse of power rise to the surface once again, it is a mistake to look to Greenleaf as a dispenser of an ethical antidote. Ethics became a kind of moral window dressing on MBA programs in the 1990s because these programs still held to premises that remain unchallenged—such as unquestioned views that *the* purpose of business is to make money and that those most successful at it are those whose passion for this purpose runs deep. Challenging such assumptions lays closer to Greenleaf's real concerns. For above all, Robert Greenleaf's writings were concerned with what motivates us and how we might cultivate deeper sources of motivation.

I first read *The Servant as Leader* in 1982, and although there are many ideas I keep rediscovering when I return to the essay, there is one that I have never forgotten from that first reading.

At the end, Greenleaf relates a vignette from the Herman Hesse story, *The Journey to the East*, around which he weaves many key points of the essay. The scene comes at the end of Hesse's story, after the narrator has found the secret spiritual order for which he had searched for years, and after discovering that his servant Leo, without whose physical and spiritual ministrations he would have succumbed during his odyssey, is the head of the order. As he ponders a small sculpture of him and Leo, he notices that "it seemed as if my image was adding to and flowing into Leo's . . . It seemed that in time . . . only one would remain: Leo." Hesse then adds, "As I stood there and tried to understand what I saw, I recalled a short conversation I had had with Leo during the festive days at Bremgarten. We talked about how the creations of poetry become more vivid and real than the poets themselves."

I will never forget reading that last line. I can remember vividly where I was when I read it—sitting in an airplane window seat on a nighttime flight to Houston—and what I was doing—traveling to conduct an opening workshop for the new American Leadership Forum organized by Joseph Jaworski, who had asked people to read the essay as background. I can feel how it moved me even now. It simply took my breath away, and brought simultaneously an immense sadness and a profound sense of calm and clarity. As I look back on this, this simple thought, "The poem becomes more vivid and real than the poet," seems to have signaled three awakenings for me.

Firstly, it confirmed the essence of the work we had started to do on the nature of vision. Although the word later became widely used, and indeed overused, its meaning was rarely appreciated. Although it functions as a goal, a vision is more than just a goal. It is a goal that comes from our deepest sense of purposefulness. It also becomes a vehicle for living purposefully, because a sense of purpose is only as real as the effort one gives to bringing it into reality. A vision focuses that effort. Greenleaf seemed to understand all of this profoundly, and reading his words was an enormous encouragement.

Secondly, although we understood the spiritual significance of this work, we rarely talked about it. Yet, here stood such a simple and direct acknowledgement of the essence of a spiritual undertaking: when we truly give ourselves to creating what springs from our deepest source, who we are disappears. There are many ways to define spirituality but one of

my favorites is simply seeing that who we are transcends—transcends
what we do, transcends what we believe, transcends our personal history,
transcends our physical form, and ultimately transcends all thought, including our images of who we are. Being genuinely committed means
knowingly taking action that shifts the locus of my attention toward what I
seek to create, and away from my self and what my creating will bring me.
This represents a radical departure from self-serving goals that preoccupy
most of us. Years later, I discovered Robert Frost's admonition on creating,
"All great things are created for their own sake." It is no wonder he was
one of Greenleaf's favorite poets.

Lastly, Greenleaf had the courage to say all of this—that your individuality will burn in the fires of creation—so directly, in a culture that often
seems to value the worth of the individual over all else. To the extent we give
ourselves to be truly generative, we will be less real than what we create.
These are not the rules of sacrifice, but the principles of generativity, and
they transcend culture.

As I look back at this now, I understand that Greenleaf was also reminding us of the profound paradox of leadership; simply put, who is the
"we?" On the one hand, vision and leadership are intimate and deeply personal matters. On the other hand, our normal sense of self may be diminished in the undertaking. In this simple reminder about what becomes
"most vivid and real," Greenleaf was subtly reminding us that leadership
ultimately calls forth a different 'self.'

For those like me who have found *The Servant as Leader* to be a deep
well of continuing insight and inspiration, knowing better Robert Greenleaf
the man and how he grew his gifts is an extraordinary opportunity. For
example, it is fascinating to discover Greenleaf's own approach to using
the power of "boss-ship"—such as how he influenced AT&T's eventual
adoption of a radical new approach to personnel assessment through
slowly, gradually influencing many people's thinking rather than using
his positional authority, or how he engaged those far from the centers of
power in his 'study teams' when he was asked to develop new recommendations (chapter 12). Similarly, it becomes much clearer how Greenleaf's understanding of the power of genuine vision grew during his
years at AT&T (chapter 7), when the company was still energized by the
dream of universal telephone service and "the spirit of service" established by founder Theodore Vail.

Lastly, it comes as no surprise that Robert Greenleaf had little interest in drawing attention to Robert Greenleaf. Through mutual friends, I had some small sense of Greenleaf the Quaker, but it is reassuring to discover him here as a person struggling—to both find his distinctive voice (chapter 14) and then have to live with the personal attention his writings brought (chapter 20). It is easy to see Greenleaf's discomfort with being the center of attention as modesty, but I think that motivation is secondary. On the other side of the doorway of giving up the self in creating, what is created develops a life of its own. Attention on one's self is simply a distraction from what really matters— what is emerging. As Gibran said, "Your children are not your children. They are the sons and daughters of life's longing for itself."[1] Even to the end of his life, Greenleaf struggled to help people understand the problem of misplaced attention on him as "the creator" versus their own work as servants.

Confucius said that the first two "meditative spaces" in becoming a leader are "knowing how to stop," and "stopping." Gradually, the meaning of these words was lost, until they became reinterpreted during the Ch'ing dynasty, China's last dynasty, as that one should know how to be respectful and subservient in the presence of authority. But, their original meaning was quite different: one must learn how to stop the flow of thought and then, when needed, do so.[2] If this capacity is lacking, then we can only see what our past experience prepares us to see. We cannot see a situation freshly.

Becoming a human being, and preparing a foundation for leadership, starts with developing the capacity to see what we have not seen before. If this capacity is absent, actions taken in the face of novel circumstances will actually be reactions from our past rather than appropriate for the present. As the capacity to stop becomes developed, our actions start to emerge from a broader field, the field of the future that is seeking to emerge. Then, we attain what Lao Tzu called "non-action action, where nothing is done and yet nothing is left undone." Or, as Greenleaf would have said, we become a "channel" for what is seeking to emerge.

The future taking shape today seems to be making Robert Greenleaf's work more and more a channel for what might emerge—but only as we continue discovering what his life and thoughts mean for the servant in each of us.

Peter M. Senge

Peter M. Senge is founding chair of SoL (Society for Organizational Learning) and senior lecturer at the MIT Sloan School of Management. He is author of *The Fifth Discipline* (1990), and co-author of three related fieldbooks: *The Fifth Discipline Fieldbook* (1994), *The Dance of Change* (1999), *and Schools that Learn* (2000). He is co-author of *Presence: Human Purpose and the Field of the Future* (SoL 2004).

Preface

One day in 1986 a manila envelope postmarked Dallas, TX arrived in the mail. I opened it eagerly because it was sent by the author Ann McGee-Cooper, my friend and long-time mentor. Inside was a thirty-seven page essay bound in a plain orange cover with the title *The Servant as Leader*. The first paragraph hooked me: "Servant and leader. Can these two roles be fused in one real person, in all levels of status or calling? If so, can that person live and be productive in the real world of the present? My sense of the present leads me to say yes to both questions. This paper is an attempt to explain why and to suggest how."[1]

I spent the rest of the day reading and re-reading this piece by Robert K. Greenleaf, a man whom I had only heard about through Ann, and experienced a shock of recognition: "Yes. I've always believed that," I said to myself, "but could never put it into words." There was something about the way the essay was written that stopped my world. Its unusual organization and Emerson-like epigrams, its fusion of hopefulness, clear-eyed pragmatism, wisdom, and transcendence—all of this stunned me. At the end of the day I called a friend and said, "I want to work with these ideas for the rest of my life."

In many ways I was not a good candidate to be captured by the writings of a man from my grandfather's generation who had spent his life studying organizations and thinking about leadership. Seven years earlier I had fled organizations and gone into business for myself, frustrated by the injustices and spirit-draining events we all experience in the workplace. Perhaps the move was inevitable. I had grown up in a parsonage and experienced first-hand the effects of my denomination's exercise of a tight pyramidal power structure, at least as it was practiced during my childhood. I spent four years in seminary to think through my own theology and considered ordination, but I never once heard a discussion about how soaring theological ideas would apply to the way a minister treated employees in the church office. In my work at broadcast television and radio stations, a museum of art, and a university, I met some wonderful people and learned a great deal, but I was unable to experience the sense of meaning and community I yearned for at work. So I made up my own job.

My new role as a free-lance consultant and producer of communications projects gradually gave me entry to a few spirit-*sustaining* organizations nurtured by authentic servants, and I developed a perspective I never had as a captive employee: Maybe the workplace *could* be a forum for personal evolution and meaningful contributions. Perhaps my problem with organizations was also a problem with me. Was it possible that my eagerness to do a good job, fit in, and please the bosses had caused me to give up my essential self, thereby robbing the organization as well as frustrating me?

Then I read *The Servant as Leader* and ran across lines like this: "Evil, stupidity, apathy, the 'system' are not the enemy. . . *The enemy is strong natural servants who have the potential to lead but do not lead, or who choose to follow a non-servant.*"[2] Greenleaf had found me out.

In 1988 I attended the first Symposium on Servant Leadership in Atlanta and met some brilliant people who knew and had worked with Bob Greenleaf. Greenleaf himself attended the gathering by speakerphone. Then, in 1990, the year Bob died, the Robert K. Greenleaf Center for Servant Leadership not only moved to Indianapolis but set up shop in an office next to one where I worked part-time. I called this event "synchronicity squared" and was certain that lightning would strike me dead if I did not get more deeply involved with servant leadership. I met the Center's director, Larry Spears, and worked part-time with the organization for more than four years. I pored over archives and edited a book of Greenleaf's unpublished manuscripts.

The more I read Greenleaf's private and public writings, the more convinced I became that one could not fully appreciate the *juice* of servant leadership without some understanding of Greenleaf the person. In fact, he once told an interviewer, "My writings are all autobiographical."[3] As I met trustees of the Greenleaf Center who had known Bob and listened to their stories, I found myself drawn to this quiet eccentric. I wondered how he had lived his own life as a servant-leader, especially while working in a top job at AT&T, one of the world's largest bureaucracies. As powerful and positive as Greenleaf's writings were, I also wanted a better understanding of his personal challenges. Somehow, that would make him real, a human being more interesting than the icon he was becoming, and more accessible as a role model.

The idea of a biography popped into my consciousness and would not go away. The impulse seemed to come from beyond my small self and had nothing to do with personal ego. I finally decided I had better write the book so I could get on with my own life. Now, six years later, the book is finished and I know I can never "get on" with the life I once had. I have spent too much time with Robert Greenleaf for that luxury and must now move on to a different kind of life.

We all are wounded healers, seeking to teach that which we need to learn. Perhaps one thing I needed to learn from Robert Greenleaf was that it is acceptable to live life in a slightly unconventional way, choosing to respond to one's inherent personal genius and destiny.

Robert Greenleaf had his own strategies for living a life of achievement and excellence but claimed he never had a blueprint, and his overarching purpose was neither recognition nor wealth—which reminds me of a radio interview I did some years ago with Bruce Joel Rubin. He had written a screenplay that would later be made into the movie *Brainstorm*, and he would eventually write blockbuster films like *Jacob's Ladder*, *Ghost*, *Deceived*, and *My Life*. Bruce had traveled the world seeking truth, studying various religions. When I asked what he was doing with his life, what he really wanted to accomplish, he replied, "I want to introduce progressively higher notions of *being* into the common consciousness."

I believe the same could be said for Robert Greenleaf, even though he chose the print medium and his own life as the modes of communication rather than film. His "higher notion of *being*" included the possibilities of harnessing personal and organizational potentials for what can only be described as the expression of love. It sounds too trite to even mention, and seems nearly impossible to accomplish in many of our inhuman systems. Still, that is what a servant-leader chooses to do, using his or her flaws, shadows, inadequacies and paradoxes as key tools.

There is no master plan for living as a servant-leader, but it certainly involves learning from those who have tried valiantly to do so in their personal and organizational lives, as Robert K. Greenleaf did. If the phrase "servant-leader" strikes an odd chord of resonance with you as it still does with me, if it stops your own world for a moment, gently challenges and lures you forward, read on. The stories of Robert Greenleaf's life may give you clues about what to do next.

Don M. Frick
November, 2003

Acknowledgements

Until I wrote this book, I never fully understood the importance of the Acknowledgements section. There are so many to thank, deeply and profoundly. First is the Greenleaf family. Bob and Esther's children—Newcomb, Lisa, and Madeline—shared hours of conversations, allowed full access to personal items, and helped me understand the spirit of both of their remarkable parents. Thanks also to the Greenleaf Center board which got the ball rolling on this biography some years ago. Besides contributing the Afterword, Greenleaf Center President and CEO Larry Spears has generously shared his personal deep knowledge of Robert Greenleaf, allowed access to interviews he conducted with those who knew Bob, put me in touch with key contacts, and offered helpful suggestions on the manuscript.

This book would not exist but for the nurturing of a remarkable servant-leader, Dr. Ann McGee-Cooper, who first introduced me to Robert Greenleaf. Since then, she has inspired, encouraged, contributed, read drafts, and put up with my craziness. Thank you forever, Ann.

The biography would have taken years longer without the diligent work of Anne Fraker, my friend and colleague at the Greenleaf Center who, for four years, deciphered Bob Greenleaf's handwritten scrawl on hundreds of documents and showed me how a professional researcher and scholar should go about things.

We are all indebted to Dr. Joseph J. Distefano for conducting a series of wide-ranging, biographical interviews with Robert Greenleaf in December, 1985. The transcripts of those sessions, along with Dr. Distefano's essay, *Tracing the Vision and Impact of Robert K. Greenleaf* and his personal papers were valuable source documents. Diane Cory (formerly Diane Bullard) and Fred Myers also contributed a wealth of biographical information to the Greenleaf legacy by conducting multiple "open discussions" with Bob during the last years of his life. Diane and Fred were both AT&T employees at the time and were able to get Bob to kick back, relax, and reveal details of his work which would otherwise have been lost to history.

I was fortunate to have access to scores of people who knew and worked with Robert Greenleaf and who graciously submitted to interviews for this book. There are too many to list here, but their enthusiastic conversations made all the difference in the research and writing.

TDIndustries in Dallas is the country's longest-running experiment in servant-leadership, and certainly one of the most successful. Special thanks to TDI's Jack Lowe, Jr., Ben Houston, and Bob Ferguson—heroes all, in my humble opinion—but I have yet to meet any TDI Partner who did not teach me something about the real-world practicality of servant-leadership.

Sandra Fisk and her Leadership Greater Galesburg (Illinois) classes taught me more than I could possibly share with them during sessions over the course of four years. Sincere appreciation to Ginny Duncan of Fond du Lac Wisconsin and members of her Spirituality and Leadership group who allowed me to join them for eighteen months while staff and faculty from Marian and Ripon Colleges grappled with the deepest issues of leadership and spirituality. Debbie Bonnet of the Lumina Foundation and Morton Marcus of the IU Business Research Center also offered strong encouragement along the way.

I offer deep appreciation to my doctoral committee: John Adams, Gary Boelhower, Lawrence J. Lad, Jan Mooney-Smith, Michael Q. Patton, and Deborah Vogele-Welch. Intrepid peers in my Union Institute and University doctoral adventure—we modestly call ourselves "The A-Team"—offered belief in this project when none was warranted, cheers for successes and condolences for failures. Thank you, Tina, Greg, Gator Bob, Thomas, Paige, Haley, and Ashford, for the kind of friendship which trumps mere Ph.D. degrees. Old friend Mike Sullivan offered brilliant insights which could only come from an Addy Award-winning producer, and Dr. Hamilton Beazley helped me keep the vision while he sharpened my thinking and writing. Profound thanks to Karin who paid a personal price to support my Greenleaf biography obsession. Then, there is my family, especially Linda and Jack, my mother/musician/author Rene, cousin Janet Bleck, Aunt Ruth and Uncle J.T. Seamands, and cousins from the whole Seamands clan, writers all.

Supporters of this book include a list of impressive people and organizations who have enriched my life and work. The Lilly Endowment, Inc., and especially Susan Wisely, supported primary research and travel, ably administered by Indiana State University's irrepressible servant-leader Jan Arnett. Southwest Airlines contributed tickets to visit far-flung archives. The book could not have been completed down the final stretch without the support of The Circle of Servants, a wonderful group of people and organizations who believe in the Greenleaf legacy. The Circle of Servants includes:

Bill Bottum
Ann McGee-Cooper & Associates (AMCA), Dallas
First United Methodist Church, Vandalia, Illinois
Linda and Chris Linn
Rene Frick
The Schneider Corporation, Indianapolis
Sterling College, Sterling, Kansas
South Side Lumber, Herrin, Illinois
Synovus, Columbus, Georgia
TDIndustries, Dallas
Virginia Duncan
Centex Construction Company, Dallas, Texas
Gift from friends in honor of Dr. Ron Anderson, CEO, Parkland Health and Hospital System, Dallas, Texas

Finally, sincere appreciation to all archivists and special collection librarians who, I am convinced, are destined to save the heritage of American democracy as we know it.

Introduction

I t is entirely possible you have heard the phrase "servant leadership," read a few essays on the subject, or even worked in the management or organizational fields for years, but know little or nothing about Robert Greenleaf and his contributions. Bob wanted it that way. All his life he avoided promoting himself, partly because he was a natural introvert and the world's best listener, but mostly because it was a better strategy for him to get things done. The question then arises:

WHY READ THIS BOOK?

If this were a biography of Winston Churchill or Mother Teresa, the introduction would not need to answer this question. Those people and their contributions are already well-known to the general public. Not so for Robert Kiefner Greenleaf (1904–1990), the gifted, paradoxical man who first defined the term "servant-leader" and wrote about its implications for individuals, organizations, and societies. Greenleaf was willing to promote his writings in a conventional way, but he abhorred the idea of becoming a cult-like figure and even forbade the showing of a modest videotape about his life at the first Symposium

1

on Servant Leadership held in Atlanta in 1988. Greenleaf wanted his work to stand on its own and for readers to apply it in personal ways without the benefit of final "answers" from him.

Perhaps because of Bob's success in avoiding the spotlight and a general lack of knowledge about his historical role in inspiring scores of people and organizations during his lifetime, various experts insisted for years that no one really wanted to read about the life of Robert K. Greenleaf, a relatively obscure figure in leadership and management circles. They were right, of course, until recently. Today, through the work of the Greenleaf Center for Servant Leadership in Indianapolis, there is growing interest in Greenleaf's ideas, with Centers in ten countries—and counting. As you will read in the Afterword, a number of prominent, successful corporations use servant leadership as a guiding philosophy, and these are joined by numerous religious, not-for-profit, and even government organizations. Interest in servant leadership has reached a critical mass through scores of books and hundreds of magazine articles. "The servant leadership concept is a principle, a natural law," writes Stephen Covey, "and getting our social value systems and personal habits aligned with this ennobling principle is one of the great challenges of our lives."[1] You may wish to read a biography of Robert Greenleaf simply to understand more about a powerful movement afoot on the international scale. There are other reasons, though:

- Readers familiar with any of Greenleaf's writings will be curious about the inspiring and complicated person behind the philosophy. Here they will find dozens of previously-unpublished excerpts from Greenleaf's letters, journals, essays, autobiographical notes, and a clear presentation of the basics of servant leadership.

- Readers who devour leadership and management literature, especially titles which emphasize value-based approaches to management and leadership, will be interested in knowing more about a person whose work is an inspiration to many of their favorite thinkers and writers. Warren Bennis, author of the leadership classic *On Becoming a Leader*, says, "Servant leadership is a counterbalance to the glorification, deification, and lionization of leaders who have neglected or forgotten what they are there for. Greenleaf's work is like a superego conscience prod to remind leaders of why they are there. It is so easy for organizations to get totally consumed with the bottom line, with financial stakeholders, and not with the workers, not with all the clawed cartography of people whose lives are affected by the organization."[2]

- Although this is not a "how-to" book, organizational practitioners who are weary of the latest fads and are looking for more timeless principles upon which to base the evolving greatness of their institutions will find help and solace here.

- Religious leaders who seek to understand servant leadership and apply it to their faith traditions; educators who care about transformative, experiential learning; historians interested in filling in a few holes about twentieth-century history; consultants who understand the importance of pragmatism *and* reflection—all will find readable stories and practical ideas from the life of Robert Greenleaf.

- Finally, anyone who wishes to have a life of meaning and service or has asked, "How can I live as a servant-leader at work, at home, and in the community?" will find inspiration in these pages. In Greenleaf's life hope, meaning, joy, and fulfillment of one's greatness arise from the *process* of being a servant, a seeker and a leader. It starts with oneself but is only real when it results in congruent, strategic action in the world, right through old age.

Having said all that, readers will recognize that Bob Greenleaf was not perfect, but that is part of what makes him inspiring, at least to me. He was both darker and lighter than his writings. He faced and made friends with his inner demons, charted his own eccentric course, and cared deeply about improving American and global society. Young Robert began with all the limitations and prejudices of his time, but the arc of his life was one of emergence into greater consciousness— from a nineteenth-century male, to a thoroughly modern and enlightened twentieth-century business executive, to a twenty-first century visionary and practitioner.

Greenleaf's first published essay reached the world when he was sixty-six years old and his first book when he was seventy-three, giving high hope to aging baby boomers (like me) who wonder where the time has gone and when they will finally make a lasting difference in the world.

Bob lived his life without following the advice one would find in traditional self-help books. He heeded inner promptings of intuition, prepared himself without always knowing the goal of his preparation, gained much of his learning from astonishing people whom he sought out and befriended, and always, always remained a *seeker*. He lived servant leadership before he ever defined it, negotiated the complex bureaucracy of AT&T, survived good and bad bosses, had a second career as a writer and consultant, and left an influence that has not yet reached its peak.

Predictably, not all the questions about Robert Greenleaf have been fully answered here. Still, studying his life teaches the value of listening, patience, reflection, study, heeding intuition, *and* engaging in strategic action. His work triggers fresh ways of thinking about leadership and ultimately poses ancient questions about transcendent meaning, personal shadows, and possible glories.

It is easy to read Greenleaf's writings and project him as a kindly Quaker icon, a wise sage who urged a more humane way of leading, managing and directing organizations, a prophet-preacher in the temples of organizations who invited us to replace money and egotistical power with active servanthood on the altar of ultimate meaning. There is partial truth in those projections but it all sounds soft, mystical, even religious. A kindly icon would have little of importance to say to organizations that practice a modern form of Darwinian capitalism, to adrenaline-driven workers who must stay wired to challenges of the global economy, or to disciples of the latest theories of leadership that use war, sports, and machines as their underlying metaphors.

Greenleaf *does* have much to offer in fact, to individuals and businesses, educational and religious organizations. His way is not soft, but hard—hard in the way it is hard to accept that our personal answers are not always right, hard to believe that organizations really are breathing organisms, hard to understand that we are capable of projecting our shadows onto the world and believing the problems are "out there," and hard to embrace the truth that we each have it in us to engage in outrageous manipulation *and* brilliant, ethical genius. The *easy* way to personal and organizational effectiveness is to dwell on externals; the hard way is to first go inside—the path Robert Greenleaf chose.

WHAT IS SERVANT LEADERSHIP?

The core idea of servant-leadership is quite simple: authentic, ethical leaders, those whom we trust and want to follow, are servants first. This is a matter of intent, action, skills, capacities, and being. A servant-leader stands in sharp contrast to the person who wants to be a leader first and then, after clawing his or her way to the top, decides to perform acts of service. Servant leadership is about "the nature of legitimate power and greatness," to quote the subtitle of Greenleaf's groundbreaking book *Servant Leadership*, and it all begins with the individual. Servant leadership goes beyond individuals, however. To build a more caring society, organizations and their trustees can—and should—also function as servants. Those who are unfamiliar with Greenleaf's ideas may want to read the Servant Leadership Primer in the Appendix and consult several of the titles in the Bibliography.

ORGANIZATION OF THE BOOK

Three themes define Greenleaf's life and work: servant, seeker, and leader. Those same themes organize this book in a more-or-less chronological fashion, even though Greenleaf acted in all three roles in every era of his life. He uses none of these terms in their traditional sense. For him, a *servant* is not a "service provider," a martyr or a slave, but one who consciously nurtures the mature growth of self, other people, institutions, and communities. This is done in response to the deepest guidance of spirit, not for personal grandiosity. Servanthood is a function of motive, identity and right action. A *seeker* is different from a mere achiever—one who sets goals and attains them in a straightforward fashion. A true seeker is open to experience from all quarters and follows a path without always knowing the destination. For Greenleaf, an authentic *leader* is one who chooses to serve, and serve first, and then chooses to lead. This kind of leader—a servant-leader—employs reflection, listening, persuasion, foresight, and statesmanship to act ethically and "go out ahead and show the way." A servant-leader may operate quietly or publicly, but his or her title—President or CEO—is not the point. The janitor of a school may be a more powerful servant-leader to students than the principal.

The Servant section traces young "Rob" Greenleaf's experience from childhood through graduation from Carleton College. He first learned about servanthood from his father, a man worthy of his own biography. By the time he graduated from Carleton in 1926, Bob had embraced *servant* at the core of his identity.

The Seeker section tracks Greenleaf's career with AT&T, ending in 1964 when he took early retirement. During this period, Bob and his wife Esther learned from an incredible variety of famous and not-so-famous ministers, writers, thinkers, doctors, theologians, activists, business luminaries, psychiatrists, and even psychics. The theme of *seeking* was formalized when Greenleaf became a Quaker and when he realized he should prepare for usefulness in old age. During this period, Greenleaf made significant contributions at AT&T, was present at the founding of National Training Laboratories, began teaching at MIT and other schools, traveled for the Ford Foundation, and struggled to accept his own destiny as someone other than an AT&T executive.

The Leader section begins with Greenleaf's retirement and founding of the Center for Applied Ethics (now the Robert K. Greenleaf Center for Servant Leadership) and tracks his peripatetic travels and consultancies as his ideas brewed and matured. The servant-leader philosophy emerged into public view with the publication of his first essay on the subject in 1970 and continued evolving through numerous writings until his death in 1990. Robert Greenleaf, a dyed-in-the-wool introvert, did not seek to become a public figure, but now the fat was in the fire. His life would not come full circle until he chose a more aggressive leadership role in advocating his own ideas. To paraphrase Kant, Greenleaf might have said that leadership without servanthood is empty; seeking without leadership is dead.

Robert K. Greenleaf's influence did not end with his death. In important ways, it simply took on new life. In the Afterword, Larry C. Spears, President and CEO of the Greenleaf Center in Indianapolis, tells the remarkable story of what has happened with Greenleaf's ideas since 1990.

LIVING LIFE FORWARD, READING LIFE FORWARD

We live our lives forward as a grand adventure, striving to accomplish that which we were born to do. Rarely does the journey proceed with linear simplicity. Although I have tried to give context for major people and events when they are introduced and some sense of their influence, this biography is written more-or-less as Greenleaf lived it, without knowing all the answers beforehand. Indeed, at the end of his life Bob admitted that even he did not always understand the full impact of certain people and ideas in his life. Readers who are familiar with Greenleaf's writings will spot ideas and phrases he may have borrowed from one or more of his friends and intellectual mentors, but simultaneity is not causality. Unless Greenleaf made the connection or reported it to others, I do not.

Rest assured that the accumulated, colored threads of Bob's living did come together in a gift to the world during the last twenty years of his life: the tapestry of his servant leadership writings. (For those who wish to see a visual representation of Greenleaf's life and ideas, a timeline of his life and mindmaps of his servant writings are offered in the Appendix.)

When Robert Greenleaf was born in 1904 he inhabited a world radically different from the one we live in, and the same could be said for the world he left when he died in 1990. I have sought to present the times of Bob's life through vivid details so the reader may not only have knowledge of then-contemporary events and worldviews but also develop a *feel* for them. In like manner, one cannot assume that today's readers are familiar with some of the people whom Bob befriended, even if they were famous in their day. For that reason I have included short sketches of the lives and/or ideas of people like Sir Laurens van der Post, Gerald Heard, Alfred Korzybski, Rabbi Joshua Heschel, Ira Progoff, and Nicolai Gruntvig, along with snapshot views of Quaker history, the human relations movement in business, the Hawthorne studies, and other historical and intellectual trends.

No details, quotes, or thoughts are invented. From George Greenleaf's 1904 musings about his home town of Terre Haute, Indiana to the weather in New York on the October day in 1929 when Bob started work at AT&T headquarters, I have sought to be accurate, crosschecking multiple sources where possible. Speculations—and there are very few of them—are clearly labeled. Any mistakes are my responsibility alone.

Readers may have questions about some events. Why, for example, did Greenleaf's parents learn about his marriage by reading of it in the paper? I don't know, and Bob did not write about it. If a life is a work of art, and this one is, there are always tantalizing unanswered questions about the meaning of things. Without that lure, art is merely decoration, and a life is merely an existence.

A WORD ABOUT WORDS

Throughout this book, you will see a hyphen between the words "servant" and "leader," because that is how Bob Greenleaf wrote it. He omits the hyphen in the phrase "servant leadership." Many other writers have left out the hyphen in both usages, but it is not a trivial matter. Like so much of Bob Greenleaf's thinking, his usage does not quite fit standard rules. "Servant" and "leader" are not two adjectives connected by a hyphen to form a compound adjective, nor are they two words which are in the process of becoming one word—as far as we know. Both of these usages were suggested by Bob's intellectual mentor E. B. White in his classic *The Elements of Style*.[3] Generations of college students have learned another rule from Harbrace: "Hyphenate words chiefly to express the idea of a unit or to avoid ambiguity."[4] The idea of a unit comes closest to Greenleaf's usage, but his phrase purposely does *not* avoid ambiguity.

Servant and leader are two nouns which usually describe two quite different roles. The hyphen holds them together in paradox, creating a Zen-like *koan* which stops the reader as he or she considers how two such dissimilar words could go together. Greenleaf was fully aware of this effect and wanted the reader to complete the meaning.

He wrote that he was comfortable with paradox in his own life, and even welcomed it:

> I believe in order, and I want creation out of chaos. My good society will have strong individualism amidst community. It will have elitism along with populism . . . Yet, with all of this, I believe that I live with as much serenity as do my contemporaries who venture into controversy as freely as I do but whose natural bent is to tie up the essentials of life in neat bundles of logic and consistency. [5]

The phrase servant-leader points to a whole that is greater than the sum of the two parts. The joining evokes the presence of a third force, one which is as ancient as Buddha, Lao-Tsu, and Jesus, and as fresh as the latest book on organizational behavior—the transformative power of serving.

Although Greenleaf never wrote about it, he may have omitted the hyphen in the phrase "servant leadership" because that phrase describes a *philosophy* of leadership, one among several possible, and refers more to the strategic actions taken by a servant-leader. Although it is a topic beyond the scope of this discussion, I consider servant leadership a *philosophy* rather than a *theory* of leadership, when the word *theory* is used in its traditional academic sense.

Greenleaf often uses the words "man" and "he" as generic indicators of humankind and people. This does not mean he was sexist, but that he was a product of his times. Part of his story is how he evolved into greater consciousness about such matters. Toward the end of his life, for example, he wondered aloud, "Why *do* we use the word 'chairman' when it could be 'chairperson'?" In most cases, I have left his original language intact.

Servant: 1904–1926

IN MY VIEW OF THE WORLD THERE ARE PEOPLE WHOM I WOULD call "spirit carriers." Servants who nurture the human spirit are spirit carriers. They serve to connect those who do the work of the world, or who are being prepared for that role, with vision from both past and contemporary prophets. Those servants find the resources and make the intensive effort to be an effective influence. They don't just make speeches or write books as the prophet does. They are spirit carriers; they connect the prophecy with the people so that it changes their lives. The spirit is power, but only when the spirit carrier, the servant as nurturer of the human spirit, is a powerful and not a casual force.[1]

Robert K. Greenleaf

Breakthrough to a Paradox

Great ideas, it is said, come into the world as gently as doves.
Perhaps, then, if we listen attentively, we shall hear, amid the uproar
of empires and nations, a faint flutter of wings, the gentle stirring of
life and hope.[1]

ALBERT CAMUS

No one knows what triggers a revelation, or even an insight. Some say it is a mechanical combination of existing ideas. Others argue that inspiration comes from beyond, a luminous gift of God. Many believe dreams conspire with the non-conscious mind to dramatize fresh possibilities. Breakthroughs often come when the mind is relaxed and the doors of perception are open.

Bob Greenleaf had the revelation of his life while driving an Arizona highway, his wife at his side, with a sense of frustration gnawing at him. It happened in the unsettled October of 1968. America's university campuses were in an uproar because of the Vietnam war, racial unrest, riots, assassinations, and the alienation and fierce idealism of youth. College presidents were worried; faculties were divided.

The charter class of Prescott College in Prescott, Arizona was entering its junior year. The school had been founded in 1966 as an experiment in the advanced educational theories of the time: experiential learning, personal development through independent living (no residence halls), open classrooms that welcomed adults with established careers and recent high school graduates, opportunities for independent study, and shared governance. Ronald Nairn, a teacher in his first administrative job, was the school's president. He invited an unlikely consultant—sixty-four-year-old Robert K. Greenleaf—to facilitate ten days of voluntary afternoon seminars with freshman students on the subject of leadership.

Before beginning a career as consultant, Greenleaf had served as head of management research at AT&T. He retired in 1964 to found the Center for Applied Ethics and begin a peripatetic journey among the leaders of America's universities, corporations, and foundations. Greenleaf had gray, thinning hair and a certain severe look that was softened by his devilish wit and a habit of listening intently, often responding with a twinkle in the eye rather than with words. Bob's wife Esther was with him in Arizona. She was a first-rate visual artist, Bob's intellectual equal, and his lifelong teacher about the practical uses of intuition.

The consultancy did not go well. Even here, in the fresh Arizona air full of possibility, there was conflict in 1968. The faculty, up in arms about the very idea of student seminars, exerted influence to sabotage the project. When the misadventure ended, Bob and Esther began the drive to their next destination in California. Bob was frustrated. He accepted the lion's share of the blame. A natural introvert, he always welcomed the opportunity to be alone with Esther, with whom he could be quiet or think out loud. He told Esther the experience was "a total failure. I couldn't get over to young people the notion of their opportunities to lead. Maybe I should just start to write and let it go where it wants to go."[2]

Earlier that year, Bob had given a series of lectures to the Dartmouth Alumni College on the topic "Leadership and the Individual." In them, he criticized universities for fostering anti-leadership attitudes.[3] By Bob's reckoning, universities had lost sight of their purpose, which he believed was to serve the needs of students. Worse, they tended to kill *spirit*, the deep impulse of the soul, the gift of ultimate mystery. Without *spirit*, which made life worthwhile, and without overarching goals to direct the energy of *spirit*, universities could be coercive, staff and students cynical, and consultants irrelevant.

The car droned westward, following the weaving the roads that would take the Greenleafs from the mile-high town of Prescott, which was experiencing its driest season in twenty years, to the moist, sea-level city of San Francisco. Both sat in quiet reflection. For Robert Greenleaf, reflection was not so much an active process of thinking about details of an issue as a mental emptying to make space for his whole self to contribute. He trusted the deep nudgings of intuition. For him, this was not a mystical approach to problems, but a practical one. Then, as had happened so many times before in his life, Bob had a flash of insight that changed things forever. He remembered the Hermann Hesse book *Journey to the East*, and the story of Leo. The narrator of the book described how Leo, who began the tale as a menial servant to a traveling band of seekers, was in fact the leader of the mystical order the group was seeking. Suddenly, a two-word phrase popped into his mind: servant-leader. That said it all. It described what he was trying to communicate to the people at Prescott; they should all lead by serving each other. True servants operate out of love. True leaders seek to serve those who are led. People who serve *are*, in fact, leaders and followers. This one paradoxical phrase seemed to sum up the goal of his entire career: to lead through service and encourage people and institutions to serve first. In fact, it described—in spite of all his personal foibles and internal contradictions—the underlying theme of his whole life.

Esther knew that this idea, like so many proposed by her unusual husband, would steep in his mind until it found the right time for expression. He treated ideas like she treated the visual images of her art, using them to strike out in certain directions to see what happened. Even though an end result is in mind, one does not block the gifts of inspiration by planning each detail in advance.

The servant-leader idea matured more quickly than most. Soon after they returned to their home in Cambridge, Massachusetts, Bob's internal clock told him it was time to sit down and write. He let the words flow with little concern for academic methods of linear outlining or exposition. He called his little essay, *The Servant as Leader*.

Robert Greenleaf didn't know it at the time, but from the date that seminal work was published in 1970 until his death in 1990, he would continue to write more essays—and a novel—on the servant theme. He would do more than write, though. He would teach, encourage, listen, reflect, and disseminate ideas like a bumblebee on a life-sustaining pollinating mission. Bob Greenleaf's work was destined to directly affect religion, education, government, and for-profit and not-for-profit organizations and foundations. His thinking would inspire efforts as diverse as the Center for Creative Leadership in North Carolina; the Yokefellow Institute in Richmond, Indiana; the Lilly Endowment in Indianapolis; and the TORO Company in Minneapolis-St. Paul. Before his death, Bob's ideas would advance the disciplines of management theory, organizational development, service learning, assessment theory, and leadership studies, to name just a few.

None of this activity was part of a master plan when he sent two hundred copies of *The Servant as Leader* to selected friends and colleagues around the country for their thoughtful responses. He was simply doing what he had always done—responding to the promptings of an inner gyroscope. He knew he had hit upon a catchy phrase—servant-leader—but could not suspect that it would allow him to turn his life's experiences into a practical philosophy of service, excellence and inspiration for others.

His own life had embraced all the elements of a servant philosophy, plus a few darker themes. It had done so since his earliest days in Terre Haute, Indiana, a city and a state that offered glory and paradox that paralleled his own inner struggles.

First Light

*This is a most peculiar state. Almost invariably, on
so-called clear days in July and August out here, an indescribable
haze over everything leaves the horizons unaccounted for and the
distance a sort of mystery. This, it has always seemed to me, is
bound to produce in certain types of mind a kind of unrest. In such
light, buzzards hanging high above you or crows flying over the
woods are no longer merely the things that they are but become the
symbols of a spiritual, if I may use the word, or aesthetic,
suggestiveness that is inescapable. . . .*[1]

FRANKLIN BOOTH, quoted in
A Hoosier Holiday,
by THEODORE DREISER

In the early morning hours of July 14, 1904, George Greenleaf settled
and opened the *Terre Haute Morning Star*. Medical matters were on his
mind today, and that's why the story about Carl Kitchner caught his eye.
It said that Kitchner, "a patriotic little American lying on a bed of pain"
had been diagnosed with lockjaw [tetanus]. The four-year-old was hurt on

July 4 when he was injured by wadding from a toy pistol. Unfortunately, tetanus was not one of the diseases treated by Dr. Ward, "The Old Reliable Specialist," who advertised cures for rheumatism, nervous disability, stammering, and diseases of men. His ad boasted that "he does not treat all diseases but cures all he treats."[2] Mr. Greenleaf was relieved that his family physician was Dr. Charles F. Gerstmeyer, an able man who was admired in the community both for his medical skills and his untiring efforts in promoting technical education. George's wife Burchie was already showing signs of labor, so today was likely the day when his good doctor friend would be called to the Greenleaf home.

George Greenleaf was intensely interested in politics and noted the *Star's* report that well-known Hoosier author Booth Tarkington had written from Europe saying he'd like to be nominated as a state senator from Indianapolis—as if he could have the nomination just for the asking! There was a story that Terre Haute was eagerly awaiting the visit of labor leader Mother Jones, "The Angel of the Mines," who was scheduled to speak on Saturday evening.

As if on cue, distant whistles interrupted George's reading, announcing the beginning of a coal mine's morning shift. Good! Lord knows coal miners needed all the work they could get. With six mines near the city, and coal running the steam engines that gave primal energy to the factories and locomotives, King Coal's future in Terre Haute was unlimited.

George took a moment to reflect on the growth of the city of his birth, a model of Midwestern industry. Terre Haute (French for "high ground"), located on the western edge of Indiana and the eastern bank of the Wabash river, sat at the intersection of two of the country's most important highways: the east-west National Road (now U.S. 40), and the north-south Dixie Bee Highway (U.S. 41). Swift electric streetcars and interurban lines moved people cheaply and efficiently between destinations. Horses pulled carriages and delivery trucks through the raucous streets, but they had to avoid the new horseless carriages, like the one bought that year by Dr. George L. Dickerson, a physician who listed office hours in George's morning paper as, "every day in the year from 8 to 12, 1 to 5, and 7 to 8 o'clock."[3] Nine railroad lines radiated from Terre Haute to all parts of the state and country. Seventy-five years of industrial development had attracted a polyglot population with heritages as diverse as German, Irish, African-American, Jewish, Syrian, French, Italian, Hungarian, and other Southern and Eastern European nationalities.[4] It was a city of factories and tradespeople and robust working men—laborers and craftsmen who knew how to use their hands, muscles, and machines to make a living and forge a future. Men of common sense and hot, sweaty work. Men whose hard lives were leavened by the civilizing influence of their women and a few public-minded community stewards. George Greenleaf understood these men. He was one of them, with experience as a grocer and skills gained working as a machinist and steam-engine mechanic.

George returned to reading the *Star* and noticed a story that made him wonder whether the growing prohibition movement would affect Terre Haute's largest industries—her distilleries. His city was home to some of the largest whiskey distilleries in the world.[5] The front page story, in its entirety, read:

CARRIE NATION SPOKE
(By Star Special Services)
MADISON, Ind., July 13 - Carrie Nation addressed a large audience here tonight.
During the day she destroyed several liquor signs.[6]

George heard the rooster cock-a-doodle in his back yard and looked up to see dawn breaking over Terre Haute, drenching his beloved city with the yellow-white light of progressive optimism that would banish shadows all across this great land. Yes, Terre Haute was booming, and Indiana was humming. Teddy Roosevelt was in the White House, and America was on the move. Mr. Greenleaf believed every person in America could make a difference, so he expected the world to shift imperceptibly when a new Greenleaf appeared on this fine summer day, joining older sister Lavinia June Greenleaf, who had been born four years earlier.

Later on that cloudy Thursday of July 14, 1904, Dr. Gerstmeyer delivered a blue-eyed boy into this seemingly ordinary Terre Haute working family residing at 1810 North 11th Street. Mother and son were both healthy. The child was promptly named Robert Kiefner Greenleaf, Kiefner being his mother's maiden name. On the day of Bob's birth, George Washington Greenleaf was thirty-four years old, and Burchie Mae Greenleaf was twenty-seven.

George stepped out of the house into the humid July air, leaving behind the cries of a small life astonished to be part of a new and confusing world. Mr. Greenleaf was a man of high integrity and deep beliefs but not one who gushed emotions. He was, in fact, a person who trusted his interior life, who pondered before he spoke and meant what he said. Still, his emotions were running high today. He had a son! A son to teach and mold. A son who would tag along with him on work and community activities that only a male could enjoy in this enlightened time. A son who would grow up to live nearby, give him grandchildren, and be there for him in his old age. George looked forward to getting to know this new life, this son. Would he have the temperament of his father or of his mother? Time would tell, but George hoped for the best. He did know one thing: a son changes a man's life in ways that are different than the changes wrought by a daughter.

Back in the house, something was also changing for Burchie Greenleaf. Mrs. Greenleaf was an attractive but volatile woman. Her ways were often mysterious and troublesome to her soft-spoken husband. For four years, she had dutifully stayed home with her daughter June, caring for her adequately. On the day of Bob's birth, Burchie Greenleaf oddly began to lose interest in June. This disaffection went beyond the usual family dynamic of focusing more attention on the newest arrival; it was simple neglect. No one knew why this dynamic evolved, and young Bob would not realize that it had happened until after his mother's death. In later years, Bob would find a family picture that told the whole sad story. It was taken when he was about four years old. His reflections on it yielded a surprise:

> The two children were seated in front of the parents. In front of Father, I was well dressed and looked happy. My sister, in front of her mother, looked sad, was poorly dressed, hair unbrushed—a shocking contrast. I marvel that she was a constructive contributor to society and lived such a long life. [7]

George Greenleaf's intuitive genius with machines provided the prospect for his family's long-term security during this zenith of the Industrial Age, but the family was not yet secure, either physically or emotionally. For one thing, the Greenleafs did not live long enough in any location to feel settled. Soon after Bob's birth, they moved to an old one-story house on Washington Avenue. Bob's first faint recollection was of that home.

Mr. Greenleaf was a gentle, soft-spoken man with a steel backbone when it came to matters of principle. Still, he could be angered. For the rest of his life, Bob would remember two times when his father spanked him. The first was when Bob called him "a redhead." The second occurred when Bob popped a cracker into his father's mouth while he was taking a nap and snoring. In those days, even mild-mannered fathers expected more than a modicum of respect from their children.[8]

Within several years, the Greenleafs moved to 1021 South 21st Street, which must have seemed like an estate to young Bob and June Greenleaf. The three-room house sat on an acre of ground. An attached shed served as a kitchen, but there was no central heat or plumbing. Water was drawn and hauled from a well. Kerosene lights provided illumination, and the outhouse provided a place for relief of bodily functions. A small barn on the property housed the Greenleaf's horse and carriage. Nearby was a pigeon cote. George caught pigeons in the old bell tower at Rose Polytechnic Institute and sold them to supplement his income.[9]

When Bob was four years old he had his first ride in an automobile, provided by his Uncle John and Aunt Anna Parkhurst, who drove a Rambler to Terre Haute from their home in Marengo, Illinois. The car looked like a horse-drawn, single-seat carriage. The putt-putt engine under the seat was connected to the rear axle with a beefed-up bicycle chain. Bob liked to squawk the horn by squeezing its bulb. Anna, his father's sister, had married John in 1888, soon after John had graduated from Rose Polytechnic. Uncle John was Assistant Professor of Astronomy on the first staff of the University of Chicago's Yerkes Astronomical Observatory at Williams Bay, Wisconsin, which opened in 1897. John Parkhurst would play a critical role in Bob's life, introducing him to a wider world beyond Terre Haute.

George accepted a job at Rose Polytechnic a few years after Bob's birth. Rose Poly (renamed the Rose-Hulman Institute of Technology in 1971) opened its doors in March 1883. Its mission was to provide men (and they were all men in those days) a rigorous program of training in science and multiple technologies—thus the prefix *poly*—needed to design and maintain the muscular machines that were carrying America forward. Terre Haute had need for such men. Railroads and mines needed them. The local distilleries, paper mills, glass factories, and utilities needed them. The companies that manufactured 123 different products in the city by 1925 required trained men who could talk the language of steam, gears, and pulleys.[10] George W. Greenleaf never had the benefit of formal training in these areas; he gained his knowledge through old-fashioned apprenticeships. Yet, he was a man who seemed to not only understand but *feel* the sweet emotions of well-oiled, perfectly functioning machinery. Over time, he became invaluable at Rose Polytechnic.

George worked 54 hours a week at the Rose Poly job. He was a machinist in the "Practice Shops" where students could help with the construction and repair of machines for commercial accounts. From an early age, young Bob, or "Rob" as his father called him, would tag along and watch his father in action. When George had to work late on an emergency repair, Bob would simply curl up in the corner and sleep.[11]

In addition to his Rose Polytechnic job, George was active in local politics and the Machinist's Union. He first ran for a seat on the Terre Haute City Council in 1910. Six-year-old Bob helped by binding together pages of campaign literature with string. Mr. Greenleaf won the election and served a four-year term that paid $200 per year. He enjoyed sharing his life with his son, so he took him along to evening City Council meetings. Terre Haute was not a genteel city in those days, and neither was its Council, at least not in Bob's memory:

> I remember attending evening meetings of the City Council, where I would stay awake as long as I could because the meetings were very exciting—tumultuous is a better word—and Father was usually in the heat of the action. When I could no longer stay awake, I would curl up in his coat behind his chair and go to sleep, to be carried home at the end of the meeting.[12]

To spend so much time with his father, little Bob had to stay on the move. In his role as an officer in the Machinists Union, George Greenleaf became a friend of the pioneer union leader Eugene V. Debs, the Terre Haute native who founded the American Railway Union and the American Socialist Party. Debs was a savvy politician and made an indelible impression on young Bob Greenleaf:

> I recall attending a labor rally as a young child on a Sunday afternoon when Eugene Debs spoke . . . Father knew him quite well and met him frequently on the campaign trail. Since Father was an officer in the Machinists Union, he was a part of the labor officialdom and sat on the stage behind the speaker. I sat with him. At the conclusion

> of Debs' speech, a crowd of reporters and others gathered around
> him and Father took me up to meet him. When Debs spotted me, he
> broke away from the crowd and came to me, went down to his
> haunches on my eye level, put his hands on my shoulder and talked
> to me for maybe 45 seconds . . . The impression of those intent,
> kindly blue eyes, lighted by the fire of the revolutionary, left their
> mark on me and remain vivid to this day. I think I caught a little
> spark from that.[13]

The bald, bow-tied, distinguished Mr. Debs was a major political figure of the day. Under the Social Democratic party (later the Socialist
party) banner, he ran for President of the United States five times, beginning in 1900. In 1918, Debs gave an antiwar speech in Canton, Ohio, ar-
guing against American participation in the great European War. The
speech was not wildly radical. It was "merely a restatement of what
Debs had said for years, with only one vague statement about capitalism
declaring wars for profits while the workers fought them and died."[14]
For his efforts, Debs was charged under the wartime Espionage Act,
convicted, sentenced to ten years in prison and stripped of all citizenship rights. While Debs was home on bail before surrendering to the
District Attorney in Cleveland, a Terre Haute barber commented, "Well,
it's coming along to Easter time, and we're getting ready for another
crucifixion."[15]

Debs wound up in the Atlanta Federal Prison, where his cell door was
never locked. In 1920, the ailing Socialist Party, with a membership of five
thousand, again chose him for their presidential candidate. It was the last
time he would run for the presidency. Campaigning from his cell, Debs
garnered 919,000 votes. He was not released until the Senate ratified the
peace treaty. Finally, he was sent home on Christmas day, 1921, but his
civil right to vote was never restored.[16] A few days later, seventeen-year-
old Bob had his final encounter with Eugene Debs, again in the company
of his father. They joined a small group that met Debs at the train station
and walked with him to his home. The home is now a national monument, sitting in the middle of the Indiana State University campus. In later
life, Greenleaf called it "a touching memorial to one of the nation's great
men."[17]

Even though most Terre Haute residents may not have agreed with
Debs' socialist leanings, they respected him as a caring reformer and

greatly admired the compassion sensed by young Bob Greenleaf. Poet James Whitcomb Riley, an unlikely friend of Debs, wrote:

> And there's Gene Debs—a man 'at stands
> And jes' holds out in his two hands
> As warm a heart as ever beat
> Betwixt here and the Jedgment Seat.[18]

One evening in 1910, Bob, June, and their parents went outside to watch Halley's Comet make its brightest appearance of the century. The wonder of the spectacle remained with him, and he later considered a career in astronomy like his Uncle John's.

The occasional awe at 1021 South 21st Street was mixed with anxiety, however. Young Bob suffered several childhood injuries there. His first memory of Christmas was punctuated by a painful burn from the stove. Another day, his high chair fell over backwards. He hit his head on the baseboard, resulting in a bump at the base of his skull that lasted until his death.

He never forgot another incident that one could see as a metaphor for his increasingly out-of-control mother. Bob was in the buggy with Burchie when the horse bolted and became a dangerous runaway. No one was injured, but young Bob was frightened. His worst memory of that place, however, was of a fight between his parents. Kitchen pots flew. A kerosene lamp was overturned.[19]

Marital relations did not improve, but living conditions did when the family moved to South 18th Street soon after the comet appeared. The Greenleafs rented a house for a year and then bought a new five-room bungalow next door. This home had electricity and gas but no running water, although a handy pump on the kitchen sink drew water from a rain water cistern. A small coal shed at the rear of the lot also housed the privy, a modern two-holer. They lived there through Bob's elementary school years at Montrose grade school and his first year of high school. Bob's health was good through those years, interrupted only by a case of German measles.

Meanwhile, George and Burchie continued their fights. After one tumultuous confrontation, Mr. Greenleaf took his children to spend the night at the home of his sister, Olive Couche. George told his children that he might have to get a divorce.[20]

There were several villains in this family drama. Alcohol was one, and Burchie Greenleaf was the alcoholic. Alcoholism was a shameful thing in those days. It was seen as a moral failure, not a disease. There was no twelve-step program, no Alcoholics Anonymous for sufferers or Al-Anon support network for families. Instead, there were the condemnations of evangelists like Billy Sunday, the militant acts of prohibitionists like Carrie Nation who demonized all alcohol, and the personal shame of painful family secrets.

A second bad actor was Burchie's emotional temperament. She had what might have then been called a "nervous condition." Volatile, unpredictable, by turns attentive and distant, Burchie must have been unfathomable to her children.

After Bob left home, Burchie's elderly, indigent father moved in with the Greenleafs. He required constant attention, but Burchie quickly ran out of patience. One day she impulsively packed him up and dumped him with her older sister in Anderson, Indiana. George was not amused:

> When Father came home that evening and learned what had happened, he jumped right on a train to Anderson, Indiana, and brought Grandfather back. No nonsense about it. Grandfather was going to stay with us, and he did for the few remaining years of his life. . . . When my turn came, there was no question as to what my responsibility towards family was.[21]

In later years, Robert Greenleaf wrote extensively about the effect his father had on his development but seldom mentioned the influence of his mother:

> My mother was adequate. That is the best I can say for her. She fed and clothed me and took care of me when I was sick. But she was a deeply flawed person—the product, I suspect, of a highly neurotic mother. From my earliest memories she was both contentious and tempestuous with her neighbors, relatives and everyone.[22]

By Bob's high school years, the worst of the family fights had subsided. Burchie let June and Bob go their own way, although Bob still saw his mother as "an uncertain quantity," and with good reason. After ten years in the South 18th Street house, Mrs. Greenleaf again entered into what Bob called "her restless period." Through the remainder of his high school and college years, the family moved every year or two, finally buying several adjacent homes in the suburb of East Glen, which they owned until the end of their lives. George and Burchie lived in two different houses, and June lived in the third until her death in 1989.

June Greenleaf was a companion during Bob's growing-up years. She was attractive and smart, the scholar of the family. She and Bob went to concerts and plays and sang together in the church choir during his high school years, but he never considered their relationship to be close.[23]

After graduation from Wiley High School, June attended the Indiana State Normal School in Terre Haute and then Teachers College of Columbia University, where she received a masters degree. She returned to her Terre Haute high school to teach Latin and French until she was fifty, when an illness forced early retirement. June never married.

Robert Greenleaf was not one to dwell on how the negative aspects of his early family may have affected his life, even if they did introduce a certain melancholy to his already introspective nature. In one set of autobiographical notes, he wrote, "I would not say that I had either a happy or an unhappy childhood. I was loved by both parents. Mother was tempestuous and erratic but she loved me and cared for me."[24] What Bob focused on was the positive way his father handled the situation:

> All of her life she was a terrible burden to Father. At times he thought of divorcing her, but the temptation really did not last. One of my father's claims to sainthood is that he took his marriage vows seriously and stayed with his wife and cared for her to the end (she died at age 70). In the contemporary mode, if Father had not been a gentle, peaceful man, she would have been a battered wife. The provocation was ample.[25]

When Burchie Greenleaf died in 1946, Bob went home to be with his father. George told his son that he simply wanted to be rid of all the furniture and other items his wife had collected through the years. Bob could have sold them to an antique dealer and given the money to his father, but he did something that was more symbolic and emotionally valuable: "I made a big fire out behind his house and burned the whole lot."[26]

George Greenleaf: Community Steward

*Father felt a deep commitment to his city, and I believe he left it a bit
better than he found it, especially its school system. In his old age he
confided his unhappiness with how the city's leadership had evolved.
"Our city once had a great people, and it no longer has them," he
complained. As he saw it, its business and professional people, its
newspaper owners, the board of institutions, were all mediocre. In the
heat of one of Father's political battles, the town's leading citizen, in
money and prestige, tried to buy him off. It may be that I inherited
from him my critical view of our institutions generally, large and
small, for profit and not-for-profit.[1]*

ROBERT K. GREENLEAF

George Washington Greenleaf was, by every account, a remarkable
man. He was also Bob Greenleaf's original template for a servant-leader.
A tall, slim gentleman with an angular face and wire rim glasses, he cut a
fine figure in turn-of-the-century Terre Haute. Bob described his father as
"bright, lean, spare, gentle, soft-spoken."[2] He followed politics avidly, was
involved in his community, worked long hours, and sang baritone in The
Rusty Hinge Quartet.

George was descended from people who, to use the words of Hoosier poet Sarah Bolton, "paddled their own canoe."[3] John and Margaret Feuillevert were French Huguenots (Calvinists) who fled to England in the 16th century, some of the earliest refugees from religious persecution in their home country. In 1634, their son Edmund Greenleaf ("Feuillevert" translates to the English "Greenleaf") packed up his wife Sarah and their nine children and sailed to America, settling in Newbury, Massachusetts. Their descendents were famous doctors and fighters and not-so-famous merchants and shopkeepers. Edmund and Sarah's son Stephen (1628–1690), the eighth of nine children, married Elizabeth Coffin, the daughter of Tristram Coffin, who formed the company that purchased Nantucket Island for "20 pounds and two beaver hats." Stephen and Elizabeth's oldest son, Captain Stephen Greenleaf, Jr. (1652–1743), became known as "the great Indian fighter" for his brave but injury-ridden service battling Indians and the French. Captain Stephen's son, Rev. Daniel Greenleaf, (1679–1763), got into trouble with his Congregational Church in Yarmouth when he "talked of worldly matters on the Sabbath." His great offense occurred after a second Sunday service when he asked for the loan of a horse so he could hurry to Boston and see his oldest son who was near death with smallpox. The patriarchal lineage included another doctor, a shipping merchant and farmer who built the first house, sawmill, and gristmill in the town of Brattleboro, Vermont; an ancestor who died at sea in 1803 while on "a coasting voyage for his health;" and other fine men who led good lives and served their militias when duty called. And so it went through the years.

At least two luminaries sprouted from branches of the Greenleaf family tree. Famed Quaker poet, pamphleteer, abolitionist and suffragist John Greenleaf Whittier (b. 1807) was a descendent of Edmund Greenleaf's grandson Tistram, who had come to America with his parents at the age of six. Poet T. S. Eliot was two generations closer to Bob's line than Whittier. Eliot claimed descent from the same "illustrious" Rev. Daniel Greenleaf who not only had quarrels with his church members at Yarmouth but, apparently, also with his wife. At one point she moved twelve of their children to Boston, where she opened an apothecary and grocery so she could earn enough to send several of the children to college.

Samuel Knight Greenleaf established a Midwestern branch of the family when he moved to Ohio in 1832. After his death, his wife Olive, two of her children and their families moved to Paris, Illinois, a small town across the state line from Terre Haute. Olive lived to the age of ninety and was known around Paris as "Grandma Greenleaf," a pillar of the Baptist Church who took a lively interest in all current events. She was Robert K. Greenleaf's great-grandmother.

Bob's grandfather, William Knight Greenleaf, enlisted with the Illinois Volunteers in 1862, was wounded at the battle of Lookout Mountain, and spent the next eighteen months in captivity at the Andersonville Prison in Georgia, where more than 49,000 prisoners died after enduring terrible suffering. He spent his time productively, however, by apprenticing to a Confederate doctor. After the war he moved his family to Terre Haute, where he seems to have had a sort of medical practice.[4]

George Washington Greenleaf, born in 1870, was the youngest of a large working-class Terre Haute family and a lifelong resident until his death in 1950. George had a distaste for war and zealous patriotism, maybe because of his father's stories about his Civil War experiences. Bob never knew his paternal grandparents, but he reflected all his life on his own father's life experience:

> Father left school and went to work in a [wagon wheel] factory at age 11, after completing only five grades. His father and two older brothers also worked there. A few years later he apprenticed as a machinist and worked at that trade until he was 48. The earliest part of that career was with The Standard Wheel Works in Terre Haute. This company tried to make a manager of Father and dispatched him on two occasions to open branches, one in Brooklyn, New York (where I was conceived), and one in East St. Louis. Both of these attempts failed. I have often wondered whether Father, bright and hard-working as he was, really didn't have it in him to be a manager. And I have wondered whether I inherited that from him, except that I knew early that I didn't want to be a manager and resisted efforts to make me one.[5]

When he returned to Terre Haute, George ran a grocery store. Most of his customers were employed by a nearby glass-blowing plant, and George extended them credit during the hot summer months when the plant was closed. One fall, the workers returned to find their plant permanently shut down without notice. That ended the Greenleaf grocery business, but the workers never forgot his kindness. "I recall the old ledgers being up in our attic," remembered Bob, "and, through the years, one of these old glass blowers would occasionally run up to pay his bill."[6]

Mr. Greenleaf next worked in a hardware store until he got the job as machinist at Rose Polytechnic's Practice Shop. Somewhere along the way he acquired an expensive set of mechanical drawing instruments, which may have indicated aspirations to be a draftsman. Bob eventually inherited these instruments, along with his father's personal machinist's tools, and passed them along to his own son.

George Greenleaf was active in politics because he saw himself as a community trustee—one who took responsibility for the wider affairs of his city. He started as a precinct committeeman, serving four years on the City Council and eight years on the school board. He was not without personal ambition but consistently put principle above pragmatism, as he proved in his fight against Donn Roberts.

Donn Roberts was elected mayor of Terre Haute in 1912. He quickly gained control of the city's officialdom: police, judges, prosecutor, and sheriff. Then he made a fatal mistake. He tampered with the federal election in 1913. "Tampered" may be too mild a word. The mayor and his cohorts flat-out hijacked the election, according to the account of one historian:

> On Election Day, 1913, gamblers, gunmen, and local "undesirables" were supplied with phony police badges, and drunken bruisers were made election officials. In every precinct ballots were tampered with and each experienced its share of false registrations. Taylorville, on the west bank of the Wabash River, cast more votes than there were men, women, children, cats, and dogs living there![7]

Dogs were special favorites for Roberts. His minions registered the names of dogs as voters in every precinct, then hired men to visit each precinct and vote under the appropriate canine's name. One such "worker" bitterly complained because he voted twenty-one times and was paid for only twenty. He received 25 cents per vote.[8]

A local grand jury said the election was "the most appalling condition of lawlessness that could possibly exist in a civilized community," but Mayor Roberts was acquitted in what was called a farce of a trial.[9] He and his Democratic machine continued to steal money from the city treasury, engage in construction swindles, and control the city's red light district. Two years later, George Greenleaf—a Republican on the City Council— and a few other like-minded citizens decided to go to the Feds. In March, 1915, one hundred sixteen people were indicted on charges of conspiracy to defraud the United States government. Among them were most of the elected power structure of Terre Haute. It was called the biggest election fraud in American history.

During the trial at the U.S. District courtroom in Indianapolis, the manufacturer of the voting machines used during the election claimed they were tamper-proof. On the stand, George Greenleaf, the wizard mechanic and machinist, demonstrated that the voting machines could, in fact, be tampered with. His son recalled the incident seventy-three years later. "[Father] later said to me that he didn't think they had tampered with the machines. 'They weren't smart enough. Besides, they had enough control over the tabulation process (they had bought off some Republicans) that they didn't need to tamper with the machines.'"[10]

The whole scene reminds one of a line spoken by Abe Martin, a cartoon character drawn and syndicated by humorist Kin Hubbard of *The Indianapolis News*: "Now an' then an innocent man is sent t' th' legislature."[11] This time, Terre Haute was lucky that a few innocent men remained to clean up the city.

On April 18, 1915, Vandalia Railroad train number seven stopped a few minutes at Terre Haute's Union Station. It was transporting Donn Roberts and fourteen of his cohorts to the federal penitentiary in Leavenworth, Kansas. Fifteen thousand residents, many of them cheering, came to watch their former mayor smile, bow, and wave as the train chugged westward.[12]

Even after the steel door clanged shut on his Kansas cell, Roberts would not resign as mayor. The City Council moved to impeach him. During the debate Roberts' attorney was asked, "Do you believe that a city of 60,000 inhabitants should be governed by a man who is serving sentence in prison on conviction of a felony?" The attorney replied, "It is not the question at issue. I do not think that this Council should deliberately kick him out of office."[13] That comment drew huzzahs from many die-hard Roberts supporters.

Unbelievably, Roberts later ran for Governor of Indiana from prison. He was released in 1919, returned to Terre Haute, and almost won another term for Mayor. Then, he dropped out of sight. Young Bob Greenleaf saw him one more time and learned the kind of respect granted his father by his toughest enemy:

> I was about 19 and a student at Rose Tech, then a new campus located a couple of miles east of town. I had missed my ride to school late one afternoon and thumbed my way. I was picked up by a workman in his soiled clothes in a battered jalopy. As we jogged along, he asked me my name. When I told him, he said, after a pause, "I'm Donn Roberts." There was a moment of awkward silence. Then he put his hand on my knee and said, "I want you to know that I have great affection for your father." Father was deeply moved when I reported this to him. Then he said, "I have often wondered why this rough, tough gang didn't rub me out, and I concluded it was because I was always friendly with them and respected them as persons. We had heated differences, but we were not enemies.[14]

Several years before Donn Roberts' trial, George Greenleaf showed his practical compassion after a great tragedy. Around 9:30 p.m. Easter Sunday night, March 24, 1913, a killer tornado hit Terre Haute and leveled a six-block-wide strip across the south side of town, just a few blocks from the Greenleaf home. At 1906 South 9th Street, a house and barn were blown away but a horse was found uninjured in the cellar of the house. The storm wiped out the Root Glass Company, designer and supplier of the original Coca Cola bottle. Twenty-five people eventually died.[15]

Rev. Benson, the Greenleaf family's pastor at Montrose Methodist Episcopal Church, woke Mr. Greenleaf in the middle of the night and asked him to take over relief efforts at the church. George got dressed, moved into the church for the next few days, and performed admirably. Bob later noted, "That pastor, at that time, would not have rated Father as a pillar of his church. But when he had that kind of problem, he knew where to take it."[16]

Four days after the tornado, 5,000 Midwesterners had died from the accompanying flood, and few parts of Terre Haute were spared the water or the misery. George took his nine-year-old son along to inspect the damage, a trip Bob remembered vividly:

> Terre Haute, as its name implies, is on high ground on the east bank of the Wabash River and well above flooding. There is a bridge across the Wabash River at the foot of Main Street, and a two-mile causeway connects the city to West Terre Haute that is also on high ground. The intervening land was regularly flooded and on this land was a shanty town of squatters called Taylorville. This town was not in the city but was a problem because the squatters were largely indigent people and a source of trouble and expense. After the big flood in 1913, there was a move for the city to buy this land and make a park of it in order to keep the squatters out. One Sunday afternoon shortly after the flood had subsided, Father was one of a committee of three from the City Council who was dispatched to look over this flood land and make a recommendation. I went along.
>
> It was a desolate place. Short rivers ran here and there as a result of the flood. But as we made our way through it, we walked by one shanty that had been propped up again and was occupied. From the open door came the strains of an accordion playing, "Be it ever so humble, there's no place like home." That settled it. The committee returned to recommend that the city neither buy nor try to control this land.[17]

Besides taking his son to City Council meetings, the Rose Poly practice shops, and visits for official business, George made sure Bob was exposed to as much of the real world of work as there was to see in Terre Haute. Bob remembered it all:

> During all the years of my childhood, Father devoted many of his Sundays to me. These were the days before so much [plant] security, and we could visit local industries. We made many excursions to the water works, the gas works, the electric generating plant, and the big locomotive repair shops of the Pennsylvania Railroad (Terre Haute was a division point where engines were changed—before diesel), and I have vivid recollections of those places after 70 years.[18]

It was the kind of father-son relationship that was more common in America when the family worked together on the farm, a closeness that tended to disappear after most dads went to work in offices and factories and left their sons at home. Even in Terre Haute during the first twenty years of the century, most fathers probably did not spend as much time with their sons as George Greenleaf did, especially if they had as many responsibilities as this man. Young Bob learned lessons from his father that he would later apply in his own life and pass along to others, especially in his writings on servant leadership. Specifically, Bob described several memorable events where his father demonstrated the power of withdrawal, accessing intuition, and "seeing things whole." It was a vivid learning experience:

> In the era in which I grew up, factories were still powered by stationary steam engines. The driving of individual machines by electric motors was just beginning. Factory power was often distributed to small machines by an elaborate network of overhead shafts, pulleys and belts, and big machines were usually driven by their own individual engines. By this time, Father had acquired the reputation as an expert on the maintenance of these stationary steam engines, and the occasional Sunday venture would be to respond to a call for help with an ailing engine. Two of these visits stand out in my memory.
>
> The first was a paper mill that made heavy brown craft paper. This big long mill produced paper in large wide rolls. The mill was powered by an enormous engine. Its flywheel (as I recall it) was about 15 feet in diameter and the shaft a foot through. The problem with this engine was that when it started or stopped, it vibrated heavily and really shook up the place. Once carrying its load, it ran fine.
>
> I recall Father just standing there looking at the engine and saying "start 'er up" or "shut 'er down," not listening to the chatter of the folks who were trying to tell him all of the analytical approaches they had taken to try to solve this problem. After about five minutes of watching intently as this engine was started and stopped, he asked for a sledge hammer. When this was brought, he crawled in beside this big flywheel and gave a few sharp cracks to the keys that locked the wheel to its shaft. He crawled out and asked them to start 'er

up—and she purred. All that was wrong was that these keys had worked loose so that whenever the engine started or stopped, that big flywheel shifted a little bit on its shaft and really shook up the place.

On another Sunday Father was called to a dairy that had a new steam pump with an engine problem. This pump had a small engine that had come from the factory in a crate and had been connected to the live steam by a local plumber. When the steam was turned on, the engine made no response at all—a curious reaction for a steam engine that would be expected to make some movement, even if it did not work well. I remember Father just standing there and looking at that engine for several minutes and, again, not listening to the chatter of the operators of the dairy. Finally he said, "Unless somebody has invented an engine the likes of which I have never seen, this is the first steam engine I ever saw that had a bigger intake than it had exhaust." All that was wrong was that they were putting the live steam into the wrong end of the engine.

Seventy years later I wrote an essay acknowledging my debt to E.B. White, the great writer who made the New Yorker magazine. I noted that he had the gift of seeing things whole; moreover, he had alerted me to the importance of that gift at age 25 when it was a most valuable learning. In my tribute to White, I noted that my father also had that gift, but he didn't have White's writing expertise to make an idea memorable. But my awareness of that gift in my father when I was quite young, reinforced by White whom I read and reread for 50 years, has been a bastion of strength to me all of my adult life.

In the course of my formal education, I don't recall ever having heard anything about this essential idea of "seeing things whole." But then, for the most part, my teachers were not artists. White and my father stand out clearly in my memory as being artists—very different kinds of artists, but true artists, both of them. And together, their models have been powerful influences on my cutting out distractions, and withholding conclusions or actions until a clear insight emerges out of the wholeness.[19]

George Greenleaf used his personal political ambitions as a vehicle for service. In 1916 he made a run for County Clerk of Vigo County, an election that he lost. Bob suspected the effort put him in debt, even though his father never mentioned it. It was a major loss, because the position held more political power and paid more money than George's previous elected positions. In his later years, George told his son, "If I had won my last big contest for office, that would have put me in the big money, and I would not be here today. I am lucky that I lost."[20]

George returned to his role as a school board trustee. Then, in the fall of 1918, he accepted an appointment to the office of Inspector of Factories, Buildings, and Workshops for the State of Indiana at a salary of $2,000. On October 14, school board attorney Henry Moore gave an opinion that Greenleaf's new position disqualified him to remain on the board, because it would violate a state law disallowing any person to hold more than one lucrative office. The newspapers were already speculating about who his replacement might be.[21] They were premature.

George Greenleaf was out of town when the move was made against him. He returned two days later and vowed to fight for his job. Indiana's Attorney General issued an opinion in Greenleaf's favor, but the local folks didn't seem to think this mattered. The board insisted that the fact that Attorney General Stansbury even *gave* an opinion upheld their view that he was a state employee (Greenleaf was actually an appointee) and was no longer a member of the school board.[22]

One can understand their nonchalance. By law, the Terre Haute School Board was limited to five members. Mr. Greenleaf, who had been elected to the board by the largest majority in history, often questioned the board's leaders and voted against them. In response, the majority "machine" on the board allowed a trustee whose term had expired to remain on the board—as chairman!—and then seated an additional unelected person as a voting trustee. As a result, two "members" of the board were unelected and illegally empowered. No matter. This was Terre Haute.

On October 18, Greenleaf went to court and got a temporary restraining order to prevent the board from unseating him. In response, the board held a secret meeting and ousted Greenleaf anyway, appointing one of their buddies as his successor. Judge John Cox held board members in contempt. The case dragged on for weeks, while school board attorneys sought and were granted four postponements. The judge's final judgment was to hold board members in contempt, scold them, and instruct them to go home and "straighten out this mess."[23] It was a lenient sentence by any standard.

The board was still not impressed. A week later, they had done nothing. Finally, on February 12, four months after the brouhaha began, Judge Cox ordered Greenleaf reinstated as trustee. Board members received no punishment for their actions.

Through all this, George Greenleaf continued to attend every board meeting. He was not recognized by the Chair, but he spoke anyway, an early version of Jimmy Stewart in *Mr. Smith Goes to Washington*, a common man speaking and acting with dignity in the face of corrupt officials who had violated his profound notions of fairness and decency.

George traveled in his state position. He had an office in the Indiana Capitol building and kept a room in Indianapolis. He came home on weekends, but Bob often visited him in the big city. George kept this job for two years. Bob later wrote about his father's tenure:

> I recall that near the end of his tenure, he observed that his greatest difficulty in enforcing the building code (exits, fire escapes, etc.) was with churches and church-related institutions. It seemed to him that because their purposes were noble (as they saw it), the laws did not apply to them. Some of his long-held negative ideas about churches may have been showing. When he resigned, he saw Governor Goodrich and thanked him for not interfering with him in the enforcement of these laws. The Governor replied, "It was not because I wasn't asked."[24]
>
> After two years as a state inspector, Father resigned in order to accept the position of Superintendent of the Practice Shops at Rose Tech where he had worked as a machinist for so many years. A faculty title went with this: "Assistant Professor of Shop Management." The supervision of buildings and grounds was also his responsibility. He kept this position until he retired at age 77, in 1947. I am sure that he would never have gotten that appointment had he remained as a machinist in those shops. His political effort ultimately paid off in personal terms."[25]

George Greenleaf continued to be an inspiration to his son until his death at age eighty. Even though Bob seldom traveled back to Terre Haute, he continued corresponding with his father and often reflected on his father's life, especially after he and Esther moved into a retirement home.

Few old people I have known—and I live among a lot of them—could match the peace and serenity of Father's last years. I believe he looked back on his life with satisfaction of a life well lived and obligations (including care of Mother and family) well met. I have thought much about those final three years—from retirement at age 77 to his death at age 80—as I have moved into my own old age. But the immediate cost of that last big political loss (in 1916), as I see it now in perspective, was high. I suspect that during his two years of illness after that loss, he accepted the reality that he was not going to make it into the big time. But when he worked it out, as he clearly came to see it, he was better off than if he had succeeded in his last big try. I judge his life, in total, as one of profound success . . .

Just a few days ago, my wife and I recalled our first meeting with him after we were married. We were married in September of 1931 and visited him that Christmas. During our conversation with him, only one short sentence came through, "In the course of your relationship I urge you both to keep sweet."

In the course of his life, whether dealing with the man he put in the penitentiary or with his erring wife, he kept sweet. There were probably other instances in which his ability to keep sweet made a difference. Somehow, during his life, he may have had other mottos to follow—but I suspect that this one characteristic of his, probably acquired early in his life, seemed to him wholly sufficient for leading a good life. And it was something the two of us would remember after 56 years—right to the very end.[26]

The last essay Robert Greenleaf wrote before his death was *My Life With Father*, a tribute to the man who embodied so much wisdom, courage, responsibility, and calm during his lifetime. In it, Bob acknowledged the grounding afforded him by a father who served his community and cared for his son:

Father lived by an ethic that prompted him to work to leave the world better than he found it. He knew there were forces that were constantly working to tear it down. They could not be checked by preachment alone. Only people, individual people, who exerted constructive influences within life situations (like his labor union and political party) could offset the destructive influences and help shape a better future. He did not share Eugene Debs's revolutionary ideas, although he respected Debs as a person. In fact, he respected all persons.[27]

As I enter my 84th year, I now see my life with my father as the years of my formation. These years are the rock on which I stand as I sum up my life . . . In my last talk with Father in the hospital a few days before he died, I sat holding his hand and there was a boom of a salute somewhere. Father heard the noise and asked, "What was that?" I said, "This is Veteran's Day and that was a salute somewhere." Father replied after a pause, "I don't like war." This was about the last thing he said to me.[28]

Religious and Hoosier Heritages

*I treasure the Judeo-Christian tradition. I do not value it above other
traditions, but it is the one in which I grew up. The great symbolic
wisdom of this tradition grows on me day by day. I regret the dogma
that people have built around this tradition, which limits access to it.
I cringe when I think of the wars that have been fought and may yet be
fought because of the human tendency to forge hard doctrine out of the
stories by which the wisdom of people and events, which make our
tradition, have been handed on to us.... Much as I value the tradition
in which I live, I feel a compelling obligation to leave it a mite better
than I found it.[1]*

ROBERT K. GREENLEAF

T hrough the years, interest in the spiritual component of Robert
Greenleaf's writings has been growing. Organizational development pioneer Peter Vaill says that Greenleaf was one of the first to openly bring
spirituality into formal thinking about organizations and management.
"There are a number well-known leadership theorists, psychologists, and
communications experts who are personally quite spiritual and religious,"

he explained, "but the face they present to the world is a face of science, of reason, of the technical skill dimension. All of that skill goes out the window when the going gets tough unless there is a spiritual dimension behind it, a deeper valuing, and a more profound sense of mission and vision."[2]

Bob Greenleaf's own views on religion and spirituality were iconoclastic. They evolved through the years, but their first anchors were his father and a dynamic Methodist minister with a muscular, social-activist brand of Christianity.

George and Burchie Greenleaf were not particularly religious, but their South 18th Street house was near the Montrose Methodist Episcopal church at 17th and College Avenue, and the whole family joined in 1912.[3] The Methodists were among the first to evangelize the Terre Haute mission field in the 19th century. They were still strong during Bob's boyhood, boasting four churches in the city.[4]

The attraction of Montrose Methodist to the Greenleafs was its minister, twenty-nine-year-old John G. Benson. Benson was a handsome, brown-haired man with gifts of oratory. He was minister at Montrose from 1910 to 1913. By all accounts, Rev. Benson kept the excitement going with a men's chorus, youth activities, social functions, outreach programs, and social activism. When Rev. Benson left Montrose Methodist in 1913, the church had 176 baptized adults, 46 baptized children, and 37 children under instruction for baptism and membership.[5] Reflecting back on these times at the end of his life, Bob Greenleaf judged preacher Benson "a remarkable young pastor."[6]

For the three years of Benson's pastorate, Bob and June were involved in a range of church activities. They lost interest when Benson left, but during Bob's last two years of high school and first two of college, he and his sister joined the Centenary Methodist Church in downtown Terre Haute, where they were active in the choir, Sunday School, and some of the church's social programs.[7]

Although Robert Greenleaf never referred to his experiences with the Methodist Church as important to his own ideas about organizations, the Methodists exposed him to a denomination with a "genius for a methodical approach to religion," a community of believers that engaged in the kind of pragmatic service that was echoed in Greenleaf's later, mature approach to organizations.[8]

Rev. Benson and the Terre Haute Methodist churches were grounded in the deep traditions of founder John Wesley's "Social Gospel." Methodism emerged during the painful human upheavals that attended the birth of the Industrial Revolution in 18th-century England, where Wesley saw the same kinds of wretched people who were profiled by Charles Dickens. After a personal experience that transformed his academic religious interest into the burning fire of a true believer, Wesley not only preached the necessity for personal salvation, but emphasized the importance of Christians uniting to improve society. He thought that believers should take practical steps to help the needy *and* directly address the structures of society that caused such misery—all for the sake of making Christ's Kingdom on earth a here-and-now reality. In short, he pulled off the trick of combining personal piety and social activism. For his efforts, he was ostracized by his own Episcopal church.

Believing the Gospel's mandate to transform all of society, Wesley had a big problem: how (in God's name) could he do such a thing? Organization! He gave compulsive attention to disciplined beliefs and organizational structures that, operating together, might make the Gospel a social reality. The name "Methodist" was originally a derogatory term applied to these peculiar people who had a method for everything. Wesley and his brother Charles wrote hundreds of hymns that grounded the movement in common ritual. In America, Frances Asbury organized both the connections between separate churches ("connectionalism") and the "itinerancy" of traveling preachers who braved storms, bandits, and Indians to bring the Gospel to unbelievers.[9] Historian John Baughman further explains: "All the societies were tied together by Circuit Riders, Quarterly Meetings, Annual Conferences, and every four years, a national General Conference. Procedure was succinctly spelled out in the *Book of Discipline* prepared and revised by General Conferences of the Methodist Episcopal Church."[10]

Methodist organization was a brilliant approach for America's untamed frontier and worked especially well in Indiana, proving Greenleaf's maxim that "organizations are how you get things done." The Methodists had the muscle to launch mission efforts to start new churches and provide support to failing ones. All the Methodists in the state—or the country if necessary—could rally behind a disaster relief effort in a local community or a massive political effort. Furthermore, there was able leadership in the church. By the turn of the century, the overwhelming majority of Methodist clergy were college educated, most with advanced seminary training in theology and homiletics ("preaching").[11] In Indiana, the church concerned itself with furthering higher education through universities like DePauw in Greencastle, alleviating suffering through institutions like Methodist Hospital in Indianapolis, and upholding personal morality, the hot issues being temperance and secular temptations. Methodists also took positions on current social issues, as outlined in their 1908 Social Creed which called for "industrial arbitration, factory safety, abolition of child labor, protection of women workers, reduction of hours of labor, and a guaranteed living wage—the application of the Golden Rule to the whole of society."[12]

George Greenleaf, the labor officer and city council member, would have been impressed by such positions to the extent that they were acted upon, and Rev. Benson did work diligently to apply the Social Creed to Terre Haute life. In 1912, Benson's immediate superior in the church, Greencastle District Superintendent James Campbell, reported on a Terre Haute "Labor Parliament" which was led, in part, by Rev. Benson. Twenty thousand copies of the Labor Creed were distributed in the city. Ministers of other denominations were enlisted to devote weeks of sermons to the labor issues of the day, which can be seen in some of the titles: "One Day's Rest in Seven," "Brotherhood, the Social Solvent," "The Crime of Child Labor," and "The Religious Significance of the Labor Movement." Ministers spoke in factory shops and labor union meetings. The climax came with a three-day rally in May, highlighted by a speech by Dr. H. F. Ward, Secretary of the Methodist Federation for Social Service.[13]

The following year, the Methodist Annual Conference heard how Rev. Benson and others were moving beyond rallies and directly into the social structures.

> Some Terre Haute sinners still defy the militant hosts of the Kingdom. Here the cauldron of political and social poisons boils and bubbles. Our pastors there are fearless leaders and have won some victories . . . J.G. Benson, A.E. Monger and other pastors were within the last two weeks called before the grand jury to testify concerning certain charges reflecting on men high in authority and on conditions involving the morals in some educational institutions in the city . . . This is a field of activity very inviting to the brave and judicious pastor, but no place for the coward or time server.[14]

Superintendent Campbell was not exaggerating the corruption in Terre Haute's city government. At that time, the shenanigans of mayor Roberts and his political machine were coming to light. In 1913, taking a stand was a dangerous thing to do.

In the Methodist Church, young Bob Greenleaf saw both the glories and the shadows of a highly structured organization. Unlike Baptist churches, which were "congregational," with ultimate power residing in each local congregation, the Methodist church was organized like a corporate pyramid. Every Bishop held the power of appointments—deciding where each minister would serve—and appointments were decided each year during the Annual Conference.[15] Because of its clear lines of authority *and* its flexibility, the church could quickly rally the necessary resources to meet emergencies like floods and tornados. On the other hand, because of its internal needs, the church could also lose sight of its true mission, at least in the eyes of Mr. Greenleaf. After Rev. Benson moved on to another church, the Greenleafs dropped active participation in Montrose Methodist. This withdrawal raised a few eyebrows with the congregation, especially when Mr. Greenleaf's financial pledge to the church's Every Member Canvas dropped accordingly. Bob remembered the day the issue came to a head:

> Father's attitude toward the church, except for the brief period [when Benson was pastor] was quite distant; we remained members and Father continued to make a very nominal contribution. I recall a conversation in our home with members of a church committee who had come in the hope of persuading Father to raise his contribution. Father listened patiently and then said, "No, I think our contribution is about right. I am glad the church is there, but as an instrument for doing good in the world, I rate it well below my labor union and my political party." The committee left in a huff![16]

George Greenleaf's judgment of the church was based on outcomes. Doing good was doing good, whether it was accomplished by labor unions, political parties, or churches. For him, commitment to an abstract theological position was not enough to justify involvement in any church. This working man liked to see concrete results and was willing to invest his scarce resources in the people, institutions, and systems that produced them. His attention to results was echoed decades later in Robert Green-leaf's formulation of the "best test" for a servant-leader, which judged the actions of the servant by both motives and outcomes.[17]

Another interesting parallel exists between Bob Greenleaf's later thinking and Methodist belief. In *The Servant as Leader* Greenleaf wrote, "Everything begins with the initiative of an individual."[18] He goes on to say that one chooses to serve and lead.[19] The Methodist Church of his youth also believed that everything began with a personal "conversion experience"—*metanoia*—a clear moment when one's priorities are re-aligned because of a personal choice to follow God's will and live out an intimate relationship with God through Jesus. This concept echoed the ex-perience of John Wesley, whose heart was "strangely warmed" at Alders-gate Church in London. William James wrote about the conversion experience, and it is still a cornerstone of admission to membership in the traditions of many Protestants.[20]

Bob's friend Peter Drucker noticed this emphasis when they became friends years later. "Bob was always out to change the individual, to make him or her into a different person. I was interested in making people *do* the right things, in their actions and behaviors."[21] While Greenleaf never reported having a conversion experience in the Methodist tradition, he did experience a series of luminous moments at critical junctures, which changed his life forever, and he consistently urged people to change them-selves first before embarking on plans of action.[22]

Along with the emphasis on a conversion experience, Methodist the-ology stresses personal introspection before engaging in ministry or social action. In Methodist language, one is "called" to action or a "burden" is placed on one's heart to become involved in clergy or lay ministries. In other words, the Holy Spirit will speak in the quiet of one's inner, sacred space: guiding, directing, luring, giving inspiration when required. Bob often wrote about inner guidance as the deepest source of effective lead-ership, both religious and secular:

> As I read the record of the life of Jesus, I do not believe that his great leadership rested as much on his knowledge of the theological roots of his tradition as it did on his belief in the dependability of the inspiration that was available to him as he faced the crises of his ministry.[23]

As an adult, Bob would not usually employ the kind of confrontational activism he saw in the Methodism of his youth. His temperament and strategies tended to be more subtle. He would, however, always remember the social vision that guided the Methodist mission and the integrity that moved its leaders to action.

Bob noted that the root of the word "religion" comes from *re ligio*—meaning to "rebind."[24] Here is his full definition of religion: "Any influence or action that rebinds or recovers alienated persons as they build and maintain serving institutions, or that protects normal people from the hazards of alienation and gives purpose and meaning to their lives—is religious. Any group or institution that nurtures these qualities effectively is a religious institution, regardless of the beliefs it holds."[25] Many, if not most, theologians would dispute this definition since it omits the content of beliefs and fails to confront the ultimate source of the religious impulse; in other words, there is no theology of God. Bob's definition is operational rather than philosophical, but he came by it honestly—from his father.

Using his own definition, one could argue that Bob's earliest and strongest "religious" influence was George Greenleaf acting as servant to his community. Bob concluded that his father's actions were more important than his doctrines:

> When Father was approaching 80, he told me that he realized he was in his twilight years, and he thought he should read something in the Bible. "I tried," he said, "but I quickly gave it up because it made no sense." Yet in my perspective upon the essential meaning of the word "religion," Father was deeply religious and would be seen as such in any peace-loving culture.[26]

By the time he reached high school, Bob's outlook had been molded by another powerful shaping force—his identity as a Hoosier. Throughout his life, Bob embraced his Hoosier heritage with pride. It is easy for non-Hoosiers to dismiss this attachment as a quaint but unimportant detail of one's early history. Discarding that heritage, however, would be as big a mistake for a Hoosier as it would be for, say, a native Texan. Like Texans, Hoosiers have a strong sense of place. It means something *different* to be from Indiana rather than from New England, the West, or even another Midwestern state like Illinois or Iowa. Robert Kiefner Greenleaf absorbed the identity of "Hoosier" in his bones, and it helped shape the servant theme that became his lasting legacy. Understanding Indiana also helps us understand Greenleaf's grounding as a writer, his preference for evolution over revolution, his use of humor, his lifelong affinity for working men and gadgets, his interest in cooperatives, and his sometimes-bemused attitude toward those who held formal leadership positions.

So, who's a Hoosier? The origin of the word is lost to history. By some accounts, the term came from a call that pioneers made when a stranger approached an isolated cabin. With their distinct nasal twang, which one can still hear today in southern parts of the state, the settler yelled, "Who's yere?" Another story is that the word was adapted from the word "husher," because early residents of the state, especially the brawny rivermen on the Ohio, liked to "hush" their opponents. In the early days of statehood (Indiana was the nineteenth state, admitted to the Union in 1816), a German contractor named Hoosier set up shop on the Indiana side of the Ohio river opposite Louisville. One authority believes his workers came to be called "Hoosiers" and took the name north with them as they settled other parts of Indiana. Yet another possibility is that the term came from "husar," a Celtic word that means, "uncultured hill people" or an "uncouth rustic."[27] The term reached national consciousness in 1839 when John Finley published his poem, "The Hooshier's Nest."

Later, the Hoosier mythology was further defined by numerous works of literature, including Edward Eggleston's *The Hoosier Schoolmaster*, George Cary Eggleston's *The First of the Hoosiers*, James Whitcomb Riley's dozens of poems describing a sentimental, rural Indiana, and Meredith Nicholson's book, *The Hoosiers*. The quintessential Hoosier of literature was a person of the land. In northern Indiana, Gene Stratton Porter found success in 1909 with her first sentimental "Limberlost" novel, celebrating the natural glories of a dense swamp near Porter's home.

Bob Greenleaf was born in a period when it was never hotter to be a Hoosier. Indiana was at the height of its political, literary, and industrial powers. It could be argued that he left the state when it was in decline. Historians have identified Indiana's "Golden Age" as the period from about 1880 to 1920. Hard as it is to believe now, national politicians coveted the state's support during those years because it was both a bellwether state and a swing state. From the end of the Civil War until 1920, Indiana voted for the winning presidential candidate in every election but two. Furthermore, in every election but two from 1868 through 1920, a gentleman from Indiana appeared on the national ticket seeking the presidency or vice presidency.[28]

For all its rural mythology, Indiana was industrialized rapidly between 1880 and 1920. Because the Ohio and Wabash rivers enfold the bottom third of the state, commerce developed earliest in these areas. The Old National Road, running east-west, and the Michigan Road, going north-south, intersect in Indianapolis, a capital city that was chosen by sticking a pin in the exact center of the state, an area that proved to be a wilderness swamp. (The White River, which runs through Indianapolis, was never fully navigable.) Because of its location on the Wabash, Terre Haute is one of the older industrial cities in the state. One hundred twenty miles north, Lake Michigan was the attraction for U.S. Steel, which built its mills in Gary between 1906 and 1908. During Bob Greenleaf's time in Indiana, the state was a major manufacturer of automobiles. Over two hundred makes were produced there, including marques widely considered America's finest: Duesenberg, Cord, and Auburn. Light and heavy industries attracted and kept a large population of skilled craftsmen. Knowing something about machines was simply expected of red-blooded Hoosier males during Bob Greenleaf's childhood.

In literature, Indiana authors were all the rage. Robert Underwood Johnson, editor of *Century Magazine*, wrote George Ade in 1911 that "it is difficult to fire off a shot-gun in Indiana without injuring a large section of the literary class of America."[29] An entire generation of Indiana writers made their mark as scribblers of sentiment, evoking nostalgia for a past that was fast disappearing with the industrialization of the state. With the publication of his book of poems *The Old Swimmin'-Hole, and 'Leven More Poems* in 1882, James Whitcomb Riley helped popularize the style and also gave the world a record of the Indiana dialect of the day, discerned by his keen ear while traveling the state as a sign painter, dramatist, and pitchman-entertainer for patent medicine traveling shows.

In 1880, Lew Wallace of Crawfordsville, about forty miles east of Terre Haute, gained instant fame with *Ben Hur*, the best-selling novel of the nineteenth century. Other popular Hoosier authors included Gene Stratton-Porter, Mary Hartwell Catherwood, Maurice Thompson, Meredith Nicholson, Charles Major, George Ade, and Booth Tarkington, the latter being one of Bob's favorite authors. Some Hoosier natives blossomed outside their state: Ambrose Bierce, Theodore Dreiser, Edward Eggleston,

William Vaughn Moody, and David Graham Phillips. The poet Max Ehrmann, author of "Desiderata," was a Deputy Prosecuting Attorney in Terre Haute whom George Greenleaf would have known. This curious proliferation of authors has never been fully explained, but the identity of "Hoosier" does give a writer a place to stand. Bob Greenleaf was always in good literary company.

Sentimentality has always been joined by a parallel emphasis in Indiana's literature—humor. Hoosiers don't like pretense, and humor is one way they deflate it. It has always been so. Lafayette's George Ade, a popular author and playwright when Bob was a young pup in Terre Haute, put an appropriate edge on the rustic Hoosier. In *Fables in Slang* and other books, Ade profiled Hoosiers who appeared to be country rubes but outsmarted the city slickers every time. His contemporary, Frank McKinney, a cartoonist for the *Indianapolis News* under the pseudonum of Kin Hubbard, gave the world Abe Martin, a cracker-barrel philosopher who stood for common sense and good-natured insight into the borders of darkness and grandiosity within each of us.

> "We're all purty much alike when we git out o' town."
> "We'd all like t' vote fer th' best man, but he's never a candidate."
> "It's th' good loser that finally loses out."
> "It's no disgrace t' be poor, but it might as well be."[30]

Bob's close friends often commented on his ability to be wry, funny, serious, and hopeful at the same time. You can find people like that on the street corner of any small town in Indiana. Hoosiers are sometimes suspicious, but are not thoroughly cynical. The Hoosier ethic is to give ordinary people the benefit of the doubt and most politicians the doubt of many benefits. They have been, and remain, hospitable to strangers, deeply patriotic, convinced of the essential goodness of people, and more open to eccentricities than outsiders might suppose. Furthermore, they dearly love the geography of their land, which has few astounding vistas but offers instead an abundance of fertile, rich soil in the north and lovely, rolling hills in the south. William Hershell, a well-known reporter for the *Indianapolis News*, wrote a poem called "Ain't God Good To Indiana?" which praised the state's virtues. It is widely quoted in the state, and even inscribed on a plaque in the Statehouse rotunda.

In later life, Bob Greenleaf wrote, "As a theoretician, I'm an idealist. As a practitioner, I'm a gradualist." That position is right out of Hoosier history, revealing parallel strains of conservatism and populism. The state learned gradualism the hard way, and canals were the teachers.

In 1836, the Indiana legislature, in a sincere effort to lift Indiana out of the mud and isolation of pioneer days, voted to spend millions of dollars to build canals. Their timing was wretched. Railroads were the up-and-coming transportation technology, and the state went broke. Hoosiers, profoundly embarrassed, vowed it would never happen again in their state. In 1851, citizens ratified a new constitution that forbade the state from ever going into debt for either capital or maintenance items. Until the last years of the twentieth century, Indiana was the only state in the union to have such an iron-clad provision.[31]

This single event goes a long way toward explaining how Indiana became a state of gradualists rather than agents of bold change—they had been burned once. In his book *The Indiana Way: A State History*, Indiana historian James H. Madison explains how the "Indiana way" is the middle way—the way of moderation, not radicalism. While the state has changed (sometimes slowly) with the times, it has continued to affirm the bedrock lessons of its past.[32]

To this day, the lessons Hoosiers learned from the canal fiasco can be seen in public policy and everyday attitudes: state government should be watched and limited. Local action is best. Evolution is better than revolution. Take your time and think things through. If you can't afford it, don't do it. (The pioneer phrase was: "Use it up, wear it out, make it do, or do without.") The best public officials are those who save money. Healthy suspicion of power is part of good citizenship. Think about goals and outcomes before you act. All of these themes can be seen in Greenleaf's mature theories about power, leadership, and management.

Greenleaf always considered himself an idealist rather than a dreamer, but Hoosiers have always had room for a few dreamers. New Harmony, Indiana, a hundred or so miles down the Wabash from Terre Haute in the southwest part of the state, hosted two major communities of visionaries. In 1814, George Rapp and his German band of "Harmonists" created a commercially successful settlement in the Indiana wilderness. The Harmonists, believing themselves God's chosen people, renounced personal property and sex in exchange for farming, manufacturing, and communal living made civil by schools, a library, a printing press, and the pleasant sound of French horns to awaken them each morning. In 1824, they were bought out by the wealthy Scotsman Robert Owen. Owen was focused on this world, but no less of a dreamer than Rapp. To his mind, private property was only one of many evils impeding the establishment of ideal human communities. He believed that religion and the traditional family structure brought out the worst in people. Hundreds of Europeans, including many of the leading intellectuals of the day, agreed. The keelboat *Philanthropist* that brought Owen to New Harmony also brought William Maclure, father of American geology, and Thomas Say, a giant in American zoology. Indiana was going to be home to the first model community! Historian James Madison summarized the community's vision:

> All were to be equal, including women (but not "persons of color"); extensive and sustained education was provided for children and adults. All would contribute as they were able to the life of the community; all would receive an equal share of its material and cultural rewards.[33]

Unfortunately, the seamier aspects of human nature got in the way. Not everyone wanted to work, or was capable of it. Bad management was exacerbated by ideological disputes. Owen's New Harmony community, an economic failure, lasted two years, but it gave the nation its first kindergarten, an approach to education based on understanding concepts and integrating them into everyday experience rather than rote memorization, and an early seeding of the idea of equality. It also gave the state the Owen children, who distinguished themselves in various ways in nineteenth century Indiana life.

Stories of the accomplishments and failures of the New Harmony experience were well known in Bob Greenleaf's youth. It was a good grounding for later life when he would develop an interest in the Cooperative Movement in America and abroad.

Lovely landscapes also have shadows, and Indiana is no exception. The word "Indiana" means "land of the Indians," but Native Americans were treated as abominably there as anywhere else in America.[34] After the War of 1812, settlers felt safe to live in the state and began repeating the old American story of taking lands by force or forced treaty and moving out the Indians. Chief Menominee and his fellow Potawatomi were forced to leave Indiana for Kansas in 1838. Even then it was called "The Trail of

Death." The Miami faced a similar fate. By the year 1850, commonly called the end of the Pioneer Period, only a few hundred native Americans remained in the state that has a name that honors them above that of any other state.

Indiana has a mixed history on race relations, much of it shameful. Indiana was a free state that went with the North during the Civil War, but many people south of what is now Route 40, which bisects the state geographically and, in many ways, culturally, weren't overjoyed about it. The General Assembly became so contentious that Governor Oliver Hazard Perry Throck Morton—better known as Oliver P. Morton—ran the state government during the war with a military autocracy. The state treasury was a strongbox in the corner of his office, filled with borrowed money. Seventy-four percent of Indiana's males capable of bearing arms fought with honor in the Civil War, most as volunteers but many as conscripts. Those who were drafted and did not report were promptly jailed unless they could pay the state $300 or provide a human substitute.[35]

By the end of the war, the high-handed Morton had arrested civilians and tried them in military court, scared the free speech out of many opponents (especially Democratic newspaper editors), supported Lincoln in his suspension of the writ of *habeas corpus*, and succeeded himself as governor, the latter act probably as illegal as all the others. Today there is a prominent statue of Morton at the entrance to the Indiana Statehouse, praising him as Indiana's great war governor.

Morton's vilification and subsequent glorification reveals an interesting facet of the Hoosier character that persists to this day. Indianans admire a strong-willed person, but they also want to limit damage. They savor an old-fashioned political scrap as a high form of Midwestern entertainment but equally enjoy judging and denouncing it. This ambivalence toward public policy and personages directly affected George Greenleaf's role as a public servant fighting political corruption in Terre Haute. It probably helped Bob Greenleaf to not be overly impressed by top executives or the country club crowd he encountered in the higher echelons of AT&T.

The end of slavery did not mean the end of racism in Indiana. By 1924, the year Robert Greenleaf moved away to finish college, the Ku Klux Klan claimed a *half-million* members in the state. D.C. Stephenson, the Grand Dragon of the Realm of Indiana, controlled state government, as well as most local municipalities. The Klan's power began to unravel the following year when Stephenson was sentenced to life imprisonment for second-degree murder, but it is fair to say that Indiana has never been a conspicuous leader in promoting race relations. Bob Greenleaf, like his father, seems to have escaped the worst of the racial prejudices that were so common during his childhood that they were barely given a second thought.

Greenleaf's home town of Terre Haute may have the juiciest history of any city in the state. Because of its location on the Wabash river and its intersecting roads and railroads, Terre Haute for years claimed the slogan "Crossroads of America," a phrase that Indianapolis rudely stole and uses to this day. It has also been known as "Prairie City" and "Pride City." City fathers once tried out the slogan "Terre Haute Gets My Vaute!" but wisely discarded it.[36] Through the years, informal sobriquets gained greater fame: "Hogalopis" (after the pork packing plants), and "Sin City," a name slapped on Terre Haute by *the Saturday Evening Post* in 1961.[37]

The city sits in the middle of a large bituminous coal field that has been home to generations of tough miners and even tougher labor disputes. From the days of the French *voyageurs* to the years of massive European immigration, Terre Haute's location made it more cosmopolitan than the more isolated Indiana hamlets and more diversified in its industry. It also had more than its share of saloons and houses of ill repute.

When Bob was five years old, Mayor Bidwell was impeached for not enforcing laws regarding saloons and prostitution. The political and legal fun continued with a succession of scandals until Bob left the state. Apparently the geographic "high ground" did not always apply to public life. Fortunately for the city, however, most of her citizens held to those stable Hoosier values of home, hearth, and decency. George Greenleaf was one of the more important of those community stewards.

Robert Greenleaf's later views on the need for trust between leaders, managers, and employees were not modeled on the Terre Haute of his youth. Or maybe they evolved partly in reaction to his experience of endless confrontations in Terre Haute. Coal miners, bricklayers, railroadmen, construction workers, electricians, and pork packagers—all had their rugged unions. Labor leaders had to be tough enough to tackle owners and managers on the issues of safety, working conditions, child labor, and benefits. Eugene Debs often led the charge. Labor tension continued in Terre Haute after Bob Greenleaf moved away. In 1939, the city was the scene of America's last general strike. The militia was called in to handle

23,000 workers who were convinced that local industrialists were "unscrupulous and fascistic."[38]

The Terre Haute of Greenleaf's youth was a microcosm of Indiana's parallel impulses. It was a site of growth and prosperity, a cauldron of unrest and tension. It was home to thousands of Klan supporters and friends of the socialist Debs. It was, at the same time, rural and agricultural in mindset, urban and industrialized in commerce. It was a wide-open town whose majority supported the temperance movement. In the arts, Terre Haute was home to musician "Scatman" Crothers (born in 1910) and Paul Dresser, composer of the state song, "On the Banks of the Wabash." On the other hand, it was also the birthplace of Dresser's brother, Theodore Dreiser, whose harsh realism in novels like *Sister Carrie* and *An American Tragedy* was anything but idyllic.

In Terre Haute, Bob Greenleaf had plenty of practice with paradox.

Awe of the Stars

He studies hard,
And recites easy.
No matter what's up,
He's always busy.

Poem about BOB GREENLEAF
from the 1921 WILEY HIGH
School yearbook, *The Red Pepper.*

When Bob's Aunt and Uncle Parkhurst visited Terre Haute again in 1917, they took a renewed interest in their 13-year-old nephew, and invited him to ride back to Marengo, Illinois to spend the summer. He immediately accepted, and this time he got to ride in a "modern" automobile that carried him north to exposure to another universe:

> This was my first venture into the "educated" world, a radical break
> from the working class environment that had surrounded me up to
> that time. With the introduction of photography, astronomy was

> burgeoning at that time and the Yerkes [Observatory] community [in
> Wisconsin] was alive with graduate students working for their Ph.D.
> degrees. It was a strange picture to me. The director, Edwin Frost,
> had a master's degree. Uncle John was an engineer. Barnard, the best
> known member of the staff had, I believe, no college degree. I recall
> asking Uncle John, "How come that none of you folks has a PhD and
> you're giving them to other people?" But his answer was, "How do
> you suppose the first fellow ever got a Ph.D. degree?"[1]

John Parkhurst, a man widely admired by fellow astronomers, was a
healthy role model for his nephew. One of his favorite sayings was,
"There are a thousand wrong ways of doing a thing, and only one right
way."[2] His notebooks of celestial observations were meticulous, and his
published papers—averaging three per year—were concise and lucid. He
drove a spotless car at a steady twenty miles per hour and kept it in top
mechanical condition. "The car was a 'consecrated' one, at the service of
the whole neighborhood," according to a eulogy in *Popular Astronomy*
magazine.[3] As a youngster, Parkhurst was ill with tuberculosis and spent
years on crutches. "One likes to imagine that this quiet lad had thought
things through, had seen that life held little for him if he wasted his resources as did his companions . . ." wrote astronomer Storrs B. Barrett.
"He could hardly be drawn into giving an opinion not backed by previous careful consideration."[4] These traits mirrored those of his brother-in-
law George Greenleaf and his nephew Bob. Throughout his life, Bob
Greenleaf would be concerned with doing things the right way, and would
not waste time with activities he considered trivial, like card games.

Yerkes observatory was on high ground overlooking Lake Geneva. At
the foot of the hill, on the shore of the lake, stood College Camp, a major
conference center owned by the YMCA College in Chicago. The camp
could accommodate 1,000 people, although most were required to sleep in
tents. Greenleaf would later work at College Camp for three summers.

During that summer of 1917 young Bob was living in a peaceful cocoon,
isolated from a world ablaze in The Great War. He was allowed to peer
through the big 40-inch refracting telescope at Yerkes, watch astronomers
take pictures with their bulky 8 × 10-inch negatives, and learn to drive.

The summer ended too soon. Bob returned to Terre Haute to finish
the eighth grade and found it difficult to readjust to the mundane ways of
Indiana. The Parkhursts, through their genuine interest in this young

nephew and their willingness to introduce him to the wider world, had set forces in motion that would eventually lead Bob to separate from his home on the Wabash and his loving father. George Greenleaf sensed this sea change well before his son did:

> I think Father looked somewhat askance at this new influence in my life because, as I later concluded, the seeds were planted for the moves that would ultimately separate my way of life and my residence from his. Father occasionally made some disparaging remark about the impracticality of astronomy; but he did not press the point, and when the inevitable consequence came, he accepted it. [5]

In the fall of 1918, Bob entered Wiley High School. It was a large school for its time, with an enrollment of nearly 1,100 students. "School was an awful bore until I got to high school," he recalled years later.[6] In high school, he was Committee Chairman for the Hi-Y Club, a member of the Sophomore Executive Committee, a writer for the school paper, *The Pep Staff*, Treasurer of his junior class, and President of his senior class. He was happy, admired, and accepted by his peers:

> In retrospect, I would say that they were my best years because I felt that I "fitted the world." For one thing, I fitted socially. I was active in the usual roles. I went to parties and escorted girls, though I did not "date" otherwise. (I have never danced after high school) . . . I have never since felt as "in group" as I did in high school. Ever since leaving high school I have been somewhat out of step. I'm not sure how or why it happened . . .
>
> These were some remarkable people (in retrospect) and some great dedicated teachers. I was not at the top of my class academically but was always in the top 10%.[7]

The principal of Wiley High School was an older man named Orville Conner, a person of serious and severe disposition who walked with an uneven step. Bob and the other students called him "old step-and-a-half." Principal Conner learned not to venture onto the wooden floors of the hallways during classes because hundreds of toes would pick up the cadence of his offbeat gait. By all accounts, he was not loved.

Then, a remarkable thing happened, something that taught Bob the power of affirming people rather than judging or ridiculing them. It all came about because of a big jovial Irish boy named Jerry Fitzgerald, whose father owned a bakery in Terre Haute. Bob always remembered Jerry's lesson:

> At a Hi-Y meeting Jerry brought up the subject of our attitude toward Mr. Conner. He said, in effect, "Our negative feelings toward this old man are going to cast a shadow on our memories of this place. What do you say that we decide to like him and show it." There was some discussion of this and the group bought it. We had the "establishment" in this group, including those who edited the school paper and the yearbook. The first thing we did was to decide that we would dedicate the next year's yearbook (class of 1921) to him and that in other tangible ways we would show our good feeling for him.
>
> The effect of this was spectacular. The old man changed in attitude and appearance. Perhaps it was our attitude, but he seemed to mellow. There was often a smile on his face. It was a good year.[8]

The dedication page in the 1921 yearbook, *The Red Pepper*, does indeed show Professor Orville E. Conner with a slight smile on his face.

Bob did not grow up with many books around him at home. The family owned a set of the *Encyclopedia Britannica*, which his mother never consulted, and a few books of poetry, mostly by Burns and Scott. His father loved poetry, though, and often quoted Burns from memory. Wiley High School expanded his literary exposure. The curriculum strongly emphasized the basics: mathematics, science, English grammar, reading, and writing. *The Red Pepper* yearbook devoted much space to award-winning short stories and poems written by students. Bob left with a solid grounding in reading, writing, and arithmetic. The school also reflected the changes in society following World War I. Bob's senior year, for example, was the first for a girl's basketball team. "A call was issued for candidates and about 50 real, live girls responded," reported the yearbook.[9]

Always inquisitive, Bob found his world enlarged by exposure to the working world. As a freshman, he began working on Saturdays in a downtown store that sold men's clothing and a full line of shoes. The store was owned by the Kohn brothers—Joe, Louis, and Eddie—who gave

Bob his first look into Jewish family life, something he later recalled as a valuable part of his early experience.

Early in his work life, Bob showed a shrewd but quiet sensitivity in serving the needs of others. One Saturday in the fall of 1918, a small, elderly man entered the store complaining that he could not find shoes that fit. His feet were small, and all the men's shoes were big, stiff, and heavy. His clerk was 14-year-old Bob Greenleaf.

Bob disappeared into the back room and returned with a pair of very light, soft shoes with flat heels and wide toes. They were wonderful. Each year for the next six years, the man sought out young Bob to fit him with a new pair of shoes. What the man did not know, and what Bob never told him to protect his pride, was that he was wearing shoes designed for old women.[10]

For a different kind of work education, George Greenleaf found his son a summer job as an apprentice at Buettuer & Shelfrugue Machine Company, a firm of about 100 employees. "He wanted me to get educated which, of course, I wanted also. Yet he wanted me to have a taste at least of the benefits of his way of growing up."[11] Bob was able to work with various craftsmen in this versatile little company that did machining, forging, electrical work (mostly motor and control rebuilding), and foundry. While he never acquired high skills in any of these areas, he appreciated the experience. "I really had an exposure to the work of the world which few of my age and generation received," he wrote later.[12] "I think I learned what [father] valued."[13]

The summer after his high school graduation, Bob again worked at College Camp at Lake Geneva. This stint kept his relationship with the Parkhursts alive and also gave him time and distance to think about what he would do next. His sister June had just graduated from Indiana State Teachers College in Terre Haute and was headed to Columbia Teachers College in New York. Rose Polytechnic was a possibility for Bob. Years earlier, his Uncle John had graduated from there and, of course, the school was his father's employer. Bob did not have the money to go away to school and had no clear aim for his life, so he decided by default to return to Terre Haute and attend Rose Poly. He enrolled in the electrical engineering program.

Rose Poly was a small but rigorous school. There were only about thirty seniors out of two hundred fifty students in the student body, reflecting a brutal weeding-out process. In this demanding environment,

Bob again scored in the top ten percent academically, in spite of his struggles with a drafting class. He soon realized he did not want to be an engineer but still had no clear direction. At Rose Poly, he joined in few school activities. "There were fraternities, but I did not join one. I have never had much attraction for exclusivity, something I learned from Father."[14]

In his freshman year, Bob learned a lesson about leadership. He was part of a group of students who got rid of the Rose Polytechnic president and the chair of the school's board of trustees. Over sixty years later, Bob remembered the excitement:

> This was shortly after World War I, and this fellow had (according to him) done great things during the war. I recall that some past sage had written, "And wars, like mists that rise against the sun, make men but greater seem, not greater grow." This new president was one of those guys. Unfortunately for him, he taught a senior course in which he bragged a lot about his past exploits and gave names and places.
>
> These seniors began to take notes, caucused, and concluded that this guy was a fake. They collected a fund and dispatched some fellows to check into these stories. As a result of this investigation, they quietly confirmed their suspicions. Also, there was some faculty rebellion about the president's high-handedness, and two or three, including Father, were quite vocal about it. Then one day the president announced that Father and two key faculty members were fired. Promptly, the seniors called a meeting of the entire student body and revealed the document containing the information they had collected on the president. The students voted unanimously that if he was not gone in two weeks, they would close down the school. The seniors gave their data to the press—juicy stuff—and the fat was in the fire.
>
> There was a great uproar during which the president threatened to sue the students. The trustees of the school came alive. Within two weeks both the president and the trustee chairman, the head of a local steel company who had hired and backed the president, were gone. Nobody was fired. This was the closest I ever came to being party to a revolution. And Father came out a hero.[15]

The coup at Rose Poly showed Bob the value of solid information, strategy, timing, and consensus in effecting organizational change. He may not have considered himself a revolutionary, but many years later the president of AT&T would call him the company's "kept revolutionary."

———————

Excitement of a different kind awaited during the summer and fall of 1923. Bob got a job as a dishwasher at the YMCA camp in Wisconsin next to Yerkes Observatory. Shortly after Bob arrived, his Uncle John invited him to go with a group of Yerkes astronomers to Catalina Island off the coast of California to observe a total eclipse of the sun. In return for helping as a handyman, all expenses would be paid. The price was right, so the adventure was set.

Catalina Island was lovely, but the eclipse was a bust. It rained all day on September 23, the first time that had happened in memory. Bob made some useful contacts during the experience however, including two astronomers from Carleton College in Northfield, Minnesota, who had arrived a few weeks before the eclipse.

On the way home, Bob spent a day in the "monastery" at the observatory atop Mount Wilson, the world's largest observatory, where he was able to look through the 100-inch mirror of the big reflecting telescope. He wasn't expecting a primal religious experience, but that is what he had when he focused on a great nebulae. "What a sight!" he said. "I shook with awe and wonder at the majesty of all creation. This primitive unstructured feeling, the powerful sense of awe and wonder, is to me the source of religious feeling at its greatest depth."[16] The spectacle and the feeling remained with him to the end of his life. In typical Bob Greenleaf fashion however, he was not content to leave his literal "mountaintop experience" on a mental shelf. From that mystical Mount Wilson event, he extracted practical guidance on how to act in the world. In the last decade of his life he wrote, "Experimentally, I have found that my own sense of ethical sureness follows from an intensity of this feeling. (I submit as the ultimate test of the efficacy of religious feeling whether it nourishes the insight and the resolve that are the root and ground of creative ethics. Does one, because of it, act responsibly and with greater rightness and determination in the outside world?)"[17]

Bob met several world-class astronomers at Mt. Wilson. Like him, these men were thrilled by the infinite beauty of the heavens, yet they were also practical scientists—dreamers and doers, cosmologists and pragmatists. Astronomy was a field that continued to lure young Bob, a natural introvert who was given to both cosmic reflection and practical outcomes.

From California, he traveled alone and stopped to see the Grand Canyon. By the time he got back home, his outlook had broadened far beyond the bounds of Terre Haute, Indiana. It would take only one more push to move him away for good, and it came during the 1923 Christmas break when Bob attended the ninth quadrennial International Convention of the Student Volunteer Movement in Indianapolis. The Student Volunteer Movement was organized in 1891 as an offshoot of the YMCA and YWCA clubs. Bob joined 7,000 Christian student leaders from more than 1,000 colleges, universities, and seminaries in the United States and thirty-nine foreign countries to hear the speeches, sermons, and business sessions in Cadle Auditorium.

Bob grumbled that this was a "pretty conservative bunch" but reveled in the intellectual stimulation and exposure to students with divergent ideas. Years later, he could not even remember the focus of the conference. Whatever the stimulus, his response was to make a fateful decision:

> I cannot recall how it happened, but in the course of the days there several things came together in my mind. I was doing well at Rose Tech but I knew I was there because it was handy and cheap. I was sure at that point that I did not want to be an engineer. . . . I decided there in Indianapolis that I would leave Rose Tech at the end of the semester in January, get a job to earn some money and hope by the next fall to take off in some other direction.[18]

When Bob announced his decision, his father was stunned and saddened. He had expected his boy to live and die in Terre Haute, near his parents. As Bob later put it, "He knew that this was probably the end of that dream, and it was." [19] Bob did not yet know what school he would attend or what he would study there. He could live with those uncertainties. For now, he was comfortable knowing that he was responding to a prompting of spirit and intuition.

In February Bob started a job with North Ruffin's Construction Company, which was building a new stadium on the old Vigo County fairgrounds. The site was on East Wabash Street at the edge of town, close to the Greenleafs' home. Bob was a generalist for the company: time keeper, office man, surveyor, and general roustabout. He was immediately thrown into the realities of life in a tough union town. Late in the spring the carpenters struck, and all the trades but bricklayers went out with them. Bob's company decided to go ahead with non-union help to complete the stadium and got away with it, but not before they were threatened and occasionally sabotaged by angry union members. During this six-month job, Bob saw first-hand both the violence and touching humanity of working men:

> This was my first exposure to life in the raw. I had seen many kid fights, and had been in some, but not grown men in fist fights. Some were patrons of brothels, and there was one near. We worked till noon on Saturday and paid for the week—through Thursday—at that time. There were usually some crap games after closing on Saturday and occasionally some would lose their whole week's pay. Then they were likely to come looking for me to see if they could draw their Friday and Saturday morning pay so they would have something to take home to feed their families.
>
> One morning in late winter we had been snowed in and I was alone in the shanty with a warm stove fire doing my office work when one of the laborers, a crude, rough man, came in, red-eyed. A child had died during the night. Could he draw his pay for the days he had worked so he would have some money to bury his child? Etched in my memory after nearly 60 years is the view through the window of my shack of that poor man trudging off in the snow to a hovel somewhere to bury his child.
>
> But there were heroic moments too, like the Monday morning when I was checking over my last week's accounts and discovered that I had made an overpayment of some hundred dollars. But I did not know to whom. I was sitting there thinking about how I was going to explain this to the office when one of these rough fellows came in and looked at me and said, "You look worried kid, what's the matter?" I told him my problem. He said, "Let me see what I can do about that." In a few minutes he came in with two men who paid me $50 each. I have no idea how he found them so quickly. But these fellows had a network of relations that I never understood. I was an outsider. Fortunately I knew it.
>
> There were lighter moments too. One of the big black laborers was a Sunday preacher. I tried when I could on Monday morning to get a shovel and go up with the labor gang and we would lean on our shovels a bit to get this fellow to deliver parts of his sermons. They were wonderful.

> And there were rewarding moments like the close of my last day
> when I left to return to college in the fall. This large group gathered
> around the shanty and presented me with a nice gold watch which I
> still treasure. It was a touching ceremony.[20]

Bob was impressed by the people he came to know and admire on this job, but the management role he occupied dulled any remaining ambitions he had to "run things." Years later he reflected on the irony that, even though he became director of management research for the world's largest corporation, he thought he was a lousy manager. (People who worked for him disagreed.) He was hard-wired as a "conceptualizer" who enjoyed the big picture, not an "operationalizer" who saw to daily details.

During the spring of 1924, Bob kept in close contact with John Parkhurst. Bob chose to at least explore astronomy. After he reached that decision, Uncle John recommended Carleton College in Minnesota because it had one of the best undergraduate programs in astronomy at that time. Carleton conducted research and published the *Journal of Popular Astronomy*. Furthermore, two of the school's professors had been at Catalina, and a third was a close friend of Bob's Uncle John. Through these connections, a job as a "computer" in the observatory was arranged. (In those days a "computer" was not a machine but a person who made mathematical calculations.)

Bob picked up several summer credits at Indiana State Normal School (now Indiana State University). Finally, the day arrived for him to leave his city and his family. It was a bittersweet parting:

> This was a sad moment for father. We had been close. And he knew
> that the chances of my ever coming back to Terre Haute were small.
> He had been born there, and while as a young man he had made a
> couple of excursions away, at this point he intended to die there, and
> he liked the idea of a continuity of family interest in a community.
> But he accepted my going.[21]

Bob got on the train still not knowing exactly where he was going in life, a seeker without a goal. He was fortunate to be taking with him a Hoosier identity, and the experiences and inner resources given by a remarkable father.

A Willingness to Venture

"In my last two years at Carleton I had a hell of a good time, but there wasn't much intellectual enjoyment in it. I simply was not designed to be taught in schools, and I have often said that I am glad that I received what passes for a respectable education before all of this was taken so seriously." [1]

ROBERT K. GREENLEAF

Drive through the rural Minnesota prairie where Route 19 meets Route 3, about forty-five miles south of Minneapolis-St. Paul, and you will enter Northfield. A sign at the city limits welcomes visitors to a place of "Cows, Colleges, and Contentment." The cows can be seen just outside of town, where they presumably munch their way inside city limits when no one is looking. The colleges include St. Olaf and Carleton, and contentment seems to be pretty much everywhere. Today, the town retains much of the charm it had when Bob Greenleaf arrived there in 1924, and probably more than in 1876 when the Jesse James gang robbed the First National Bank on Division Street, shooting and killing Joseph Lee Heywood for refusing to open the safe.

In 1924, Carleton College was a church-related, liberal arts institution. Bob's Uncle John picked the right school for a young man interested in astronomy in the 1920s. Astronomy had made Carleton famous from Chicago to Seattle.

In 1871, only five years after its founding, Carleton hired William Wallace Payne as Professor of Mathematics and Natural Philosophy. Payne stayed at Carleton for nearly forty years. He demanded much from his students and inspired the most famous pun in Carleton history: "He never knew pleasure who knew Payne."[2] Payne's real interest lay in astronomy, which was probably the most popular science of the day. In the first of several shrewd moves, he began buying astronomy instruments with his own money and in 1876 convinced the school to build and equip the first Goodsell Observatory, named after Carleton College's founder.[3] Payne found a practical niche for the school's astronomy program—time and weather services.

In the 1870s, an accurate, widely distributed time standard was important to the nation's railroads. Punctual departures and arrivals built the trust of riders, and exact timing was critical to switch tracks and avoid collisions. Coincidentally, Goodsell Observatory also needed a precise system for measuring time. Payne saw the opportunity. In 1878, the Carleton time service sent out the first time signals west of the Mississippi to railroads in the Twin Cities and Chicago. In 1883, the observatory provided a time ball service in St. Paul. Every day at noon, a sphere was dropped down a pole atop the Fire and Marine building so that all residents could set their watches and clocks. A similar service has been preserved in the New Year's Eve celebration in New York's Times Square. By 1888, Carleton College, a tiny school on Minnesota's plains, was known as the timekeeper for the entire Northwest, a distinction it held until World War II. The Goodsell Observatory also became the site of the first weather monitoring station in the state, established by the U.S. Signal Corps in 1881. The college sent free weather reports and forecasts to newspapers within a 200-mile area, which were happy to include the Carleton College byline in each report.[4]

In 1886, the school built a new Goodsell Observatory, where Bob Greenleaf was destined to spend many late hours. It is a splendid Romanesque structure that has since been placed in the National Registry of Historic Places. By the time Bob Greenleaf arrived in 1924, the school had graduated—and hired—a number of distinguished astronomers, including Herbert Couper Wilson, who had organized the trip to Catalina Island that had so impressed Bob.

Northfield was smaller than Terre Haute, but the campus culture was positively cosmopolitan compared to Rose Poly. This was the Jazz Age, the postwar era of world-weary sophisticates. Bob was not cynical like his distant relative T.S. Eliot, whose *Love Song of J. Alfred Prufrock* was the bored battle cry for the disillusioned of the time, but he was also not immune to the saucy insouciance that had infected even the Carleton community. The student newspaper, *The Carletonian*, tracked the times in a typical piece by the editor, whose pen name was Jake. It was called "Confessional."

> We are the young intellectuals.
> We possess the gray hairs of youth.
>   We mouth half-truths learnedly and when called to account reply:
> All is relative.
>   We scoff at religion as superstition; at faith as a sign of ignorance; at hope as delusion; at love as self-deception.
> We criticize that we may seem to be above criticism.
> We are pseudo-radicals, pseudo-philosophers, and pseudo-cynics; our logic is faulty and our premises unsound . . .
> We are the young intellectuals.[5]

A few days later a student wrote a reply to the editor; "Outside of the classrooms I have seen among the most of us nothing that might legitimately earn for us even the 'pseudo-' part of (Jake's) definitions. Our classroom thinking will be of small benefit to us if it is not carried over into the larger fields of human action and thought."[6]

Bob Greenleaf, ever the pragmatist, might have replied, "Exactly!" He was not one who indulged in abstract philosophical speculations for fun; they had to be connected to action. In that sense, he was a serious student. His majors were mathematics and astronomy, with minors in economics and English.[7] He quickly became disillusioned with what he saw as lack of rigor, at least in mathematics. "I daresay that very few of my Carleton classmates would have survived the regime at Rose," he once wrote. "At Rose, mathematics was something everybody had to learn to use. At Carleton it was something that one played around with."[8]

A student discussion group in Bob's first year at Carleton would have supported his observation. In answer to the question, "What are we in college for?" students outlined four reasons: ". . . for culture, because our parents want us to be here, because the period just following high school is a transitional age and, in the perplexity of most boys and girls in deciding what they wish to do—the idea of college seems the simplest solution and (finally) men come to college for athletics."[9]

Bob's criticism extended to some faculty members. He had a paying job with the astronomy department, keeping track of a thousand or so asteroids in the solar system. Most students would have simply done the work and collected the paycheck, but that was not good enough for Bob.

> The method of locating (the asteroids) and calculating their positions had been worked out by the older of the three professors I worked with. It was a self checking procedure and not too difficult to follow. But I was curious about how the formulae had been derived. The old professor was amused by my questions, but he could no longer work it out. When I went home for Christmas I stopped to see Uncle John and he couldn't work it out either. So here I was grinding away with the primitive hand-cranked calculator of that day on a procedure that nobody around could describe. I gave up. That was not the way I wanted to spend my life. So I finished out the year with this work and got another college job for the next year and left astronomy behind.
>
> If any one of these professors had been a dedicated researcher, I might have caught some inspiration. But they weren't. They were quite friendly folks and good to me. But there was no challenge.[10]

Still, astronomy left its mark on the young stargazer.

> I did some thinking during those long quiet hours of darkness. What was out there? Space without limit; time without a beginning; staggering masses and distances; old stars blowing up; new stars being born; all in motion. I got an idea of a great cosmic force, magnificent order beyond the power of a little man's mind to grasp. I feel small and insignificant, yet as important as any other part. I am a part. Maybe a big part; maybe a little part. Maybe I "only stand and wait." I don't worry about it. Whatever it's going to be, it's going to be. I just watch for *my* signals. [11]

Bob may have been intellectually curious, but he was not an egghead. For one thing, he was sweet on several girls. In the 1925 yearbook *Algol*, Robert Greenleaf and "Babe" Lockin were mentioned as one of the couples that shared "Adventures in Friendship." One stanza of the poem introducing the couples illustrates the sweet innocence that survived at Carleton, even during the Roaring Twenties.

Everything is wonderful
　　On a night in June,
Walking home the longest way,
　　Getting there too soon.[12]

Claudia M. Bray Hyde, class of '25, was asked by her grandchild years later, "What was it like at Carleton when you were there? What did you do? Where did you go on dates?"

"I told her of ice-skating on the (Cannon) river, of tobogganing on one of the campus hills, of canoeing, of hikes and picnics and an occasional dance."[13]

Dancing was a fairly new activity at this Christian college. The first Junior-Senior Formal was not held until 1921, and the first all-college dance in December of 1924. Still, the faculty restricted where and when students could dance, and the college catalog reminded students that "social activities of the College are under the supervision of the faculty, and every effort is made to provide a natural and wholesome social life."[14]

There may not have been many hip flasks and Stutz Bearcats among students, but the Twenties were still seen in fashions—"short skirts with belt lines at the hips for women and turtle-neck sweaters, coon-skin coats, and knickers in the spring and fall for men." Bobs and bangs were the rage in women's hair styles.[15]

In his first year at Carleton, Bob got involved in school plays, working behind the scenes as stage manager or lighting director. Sometimes he received more kudos than the actors. The review of *Twelfth Night* is but one example:

> Robert K. Greenleaf deserves special congratulation upon the work which he did with the lighting and scenery. Seldom does an amateur production have the artistic play of light which he gave to this with

> mobile blending of color such as one expects in Theatre Guild pro-
> ductions. The set for the Duke's palace with stars visible in the night
> sky outside the window was the most effective. Mr. Greenleaf de-
> signed and made the three piece window used in this set, as he did
> the bunch lights, proscenium strips, and switchboard used for the
> lighting. He was assisted by Edward Ouelette.[16]

Ed Ouelette was one of the first friends Bob made at Carleton. Ed, a
Minnesota native, was a bright freshman, one year younger than all the
others in his class. Ed had what he called an "inferiority complex" when
he met Greenleaf on the top floor of Willis Hall, constructing scenery for a
play.

> He took me and kind of put me under his wing . As we did things, I
> think his instinct was to bring me out. It was during that time that I
> began to realize that I could serve. But, he also had this instinct to
> serve me.[17] On reflecting on it, I can see that he had more maturity
> and more skill in these things he did with his hands and was helping
> me to feel good about doing that kind of thing myself, which I
> wanted to do. Working with him, I could feel that I did a good job
> and we could rejoice in it together.[18]
> I was amazed at his knowledge of electrical stuff because he
> fixed it so you could turn on this and that light, and he made fix-
> tures. We made an electric sign that spelled out the college yell that
> we hung on the front of the dormitory.[19]

Ed and Bob were involved in a few college hijinks. Because of his
other responsibilities, Ed had keys to many of the buildings on campus.
He and Bob went into the music building one night, located the breakers
for the girl's dormitory, turned off the power, and high-tailed it out of
there.[20] That episode and several others landed him in the office of the
"Prexy," college president Dr. Donald Cowling. In the privacy of Prexy's
office, Bob discovered a man who was warmer than his image as an aloof,
reserved intellectual whose main interest was raising money for Carleton.
In a tribute to Dr. Cowling forty years later, Greenleaf recalled how he
"discovered the man few knew, a man with deep and dependable

understanding and compassion and with an unequivocal belief in freedom for the human spirit to flower. I was too young to understand it all at the time, but it is an influence that has grown through the years and continues to grow."[21]

Ed Ouelette said that one thing that would surprise most people about Bob was his capacity for creative mischief. It was not a trait Greenleaf denied or even regretted.

> After I was through with astronomy I didn't fit. I didn't want anything in particular except to get my sheepskin and get the—out of there. So I became a hell raiser. Not the noisy rough kind of hell raising, but the more orderly kind where something went boom on one side of the campus while I was quietly studying in my room on the other side." [22]
>
> I am sorry for those who have never gotten into trouble because they really cannot share my experience. It is one thing to understand compassion intellectually, or even to give it. It is quite another thing to receive compassion when one knows that all one is entitled to is justice. There is no one best way to live a life, I have concluded. There are penalties and compensations for being 'good' as well as for being 'bad'. Paradoxically, one must be both good and bad to enjoy this life to the full or to comprehend its meaning.[23]

Ed says that, "Bob was always looking slightly over the horizon someplace."[24] The two of them remained lifelong friends, with Bob generally serving as the older mentor. On matters of theology, though, Bob often learned from Ed, who grew into a well-read theologian and respected pastor.

Near the end of his first semester at Carleton, Greenleaf became a leader in an unlikely arena: the Men's Glee Club. Since the 1880s, the Glee Club had been a prominent musical fixture at Carleton, but it had recently fallen on hard times. The college wanted to regain the Glee Club's luster because the popular group could tour during semester breaks, bringing positive attention to the school. The women had a Glee Club too, but they were not allowed to give concerts out of town. Bob sang rumbling bass, and his pal Ed sang tenor during rehearsals for just such a tour. But things were not going well.

> With the (musical) leadership we had, we were getting absolutely
> nowhere and we were coming up on a January trip. So, Bob took it
> upon himself to go to the president of the college and just tell him
> what was what with our men's Glee Club. The result was that Cowl-
> ing said, "Is this for real? Because if I act, I want it to be the right
> thing."
>
> So he fired the one guy and put in another one and we had an
> intensive three weeks of rehearsal. We were able to make the trip. But
> it was Greenleaf who, for the good of the college and everybody in
> the group, saw that something was done. If that's not leadership, I
> don't know what is![25]

Where others may have grumbled about the situation with the Glee
Club, Bob Greenleaf acted. His decision was not likely to make him popular with the music director or the school administration, but he did it anyway. He had the example of student leaders who had confronted the
president of Rose Polytechnic, the memory of his father's many battles
with powerful political authorities, and an abiding ethic that was already
in place: to serve first. It would not be the last time Bob would confront
school authorities at Carleton.

One day in philosophy class, the professor noticed that most students
were drowsy and inattentive, undoubtedly because of a late-night social
function the previous evening. Bob, who called himself "a night owl by
nature," seemed to be the only alert student in the class. The professor
stopped speaking to gain attention, then said slowly, "You know, there is
only one person in this room who is paying any attention to what I am
saying." "Then [he] directed his eye at me with something of a half cynical smile." Bob recalled years later, "whereupon my classmates turned
and regarded me with that malevolent countenance reserved for those
who give the teacher an apple. Then the professor added, 'And he doesn't
know what it is all about,' thus relieving me of the odium of being the
teacher's pet, but implanting the seal of interdiction irrevocably so far as
any scholarly aspirations on my part were concerned."[26]

If an academic life was not in the cards, what was? Bob was eager to
hear any vocational suggestion that would fit his unusual temperament as
an insider/outsider. The direction came from an unlikely source: Dr. Oscar
C. Helming, the goateed chairman of the Economics Department. Ed

Ouelette said Professor Helming made his students read some "awfully dull" textbooks, but that he could make economics interesting in the classroom.[27] Helming was destined to be a prophet to the young man by suggesting the course and meaning of his career.

Helming, an ordained Congregational minister, believed in a version of the social gospel that Bob Greenleaf had learned from the Methodists. In a pamphlet titled *The Church and the Industrial Problem,* written for the Chicago Church Federation the year he came to Carleton, Helming stated:

> The Christian gospel stands for the moral growth of the individual, for personal salvation. It also stands for social salvation. We now realize that these two things are in the end inseparable.[28]

Furthermore, Helming taught that one's Christian duty was to serve—not just neighbors, but organizations. In a 1924 vesper service at Carleton, he spoke on a scripture that many clergy would later choose to explain servant-leadership: "He who would be great among you will be your servant." Devoting one's life to service and sacrifice, even unto death, was the highest calling.[29]

Most of the Reverend Doctor Helming's work in economics was about understanding and humanizing capitalism. He was a realist who wished to see things as they were, not as they should be, but argued for the central role of ethics in American business life.

> Ethics is not a substitute for economics; it is not a substitute for any kind of accurate knowledge. On the other hand, knowledge is dead unless it is somehow related to action . . . But if ethics must yield to knowledge, knowledge must in turn be responsive to moral impulses . . .[30]

To Oscar Helming, the moral or ethical impulse was as concrete as labor and capital. It was simply *there,* and it was powerful.

> [Ethical impulse] is revolutionary, breaking the bonds of outworn traditions and customs. It allows no stagnation, no inertia, no crystallization of special privilege which robs the mass in the interest of the

> few. It is a vital force which stirs the spirit and will of man, touching
> his power to do, as well as his knowledge of what ought to be done.
> As such it has an essential part to play in economic life as well as in
> education, in politics and in religion.[31]

In this context, the role of faith communities was to "help create an atmosphere in which good will and fair play shall thrive . . . It must keep
the human factor to the front as against the insidious temptation to pursue profits at the expense of human well-being." [32] Helming foresaw a day
when America's economic system would hasten a kind of heaven on
earth, provided people of good will—that is, ethical servants—did their
jobs.

> If in our homes, schools and churches, a new generation of people
> were trained to appreciate the various values attainable in a civilized
> country, public opinion would cease to estimate men by their posses-
> sions and learn to estimate them by their qualities as persons. Able
> business men would still handle large sums of money; but they
> would reckon with capital resources as means to carry out projects to
> enrich society . . . The distinction between the public servant in busi-
> ness and the selfish profiteer would be clear and unmistakable."[33]

In some ways, Helming was an intellectual version of Bob's father,
more vocal but equally dedicated to social action. He was involved in the
exciting events associated with the progressive labor movements of the
day, had taken stands in favor of strikers at US Steel in Gary, and persist-
ently questioned the methodology of industry leaders, especially their attitudes towards their own workers. The response from management was
predictable: abuse and rejection.

In June, 1921, Helming wrote a polite letter to the Minnesota Steel
Company in Duluth asking permission to tour the plant, explaining that
he was a newcomer to the northwest and wanted to "know the conditions
in Minnesota as thoroughly as possible" to enhance his teaching at
Carleton.[34]

In response, Mr. S. B. Sheldon, Vice President and General Manager at
Minnesota Steel, fired off a letter to Carleton president Dr. Cowling. "The
information that Mr. Helming asks for and the privilege requested is that

which is not ordinarily granted in manufacturing plants. I would be glad to hear from you personally as to what purpose Mr. Helming proposes to put his information to."[35] There is no evidence that Mr. Sheldon knew of Helming's pamphlet *The Church and the Industrial Problem*, but he probably suspected another do-gooder was on the loose, looking for problems to preach against. There were plenty of those pesky people around in 1921, especially in the church.

Cowling wrote back in firm support of Dr. Helming, explaining that the information would be used in the Professor's classes, but he went even further.

> I feel that it is exceedingly important that the educated people in the country understand thoroughly the conditions which exist in our great industrial centers. I also believe that complete publicity on the part of our great manufacturing centers would do much to help solve some of our labor problems . . . I do not believe that any proper and legitimate policy in industrial or commercial undertakings will be injured by publicity.[36]

Two days later, Mr. Sheldon wrote both Doctors Helming and Cowling that the Minnesota Steel Company would be delighted to have the good professor visit; he would find them a "startling example of what the Corporation is trying to do and in most cases succeeding, for its employees." Unfortunately, the only people who could explain matters properly, including himself, would be out of town next week when the professor wanted to visit.[37] It must have been a hastily scheduled trip. In any case, there is no evidence that Dr. Helming ever had the opportunity to tour the plant.

As a result of this and other encounters, Helming eventually decided that the fulcrum for changing large organizations must be positioned *inside* institutions like Minnesota Steel, not outside. Bob Greenleaf was ready to hear that insight, which was prophetic for 1926. It was communicated in a course on the Sociology of Labor Problems.

> Helming was not a great scholar nor an exciting teacher. But he was, to me then, different from my other teachers. He had been around; he was wise. We were *simpatico*.

One day, in the course of a rambling lecture, he made a statement like this: "We are becoming a nation of large institutions . . . Everything is getting big—government, churches, businesses, labor unions, universities—and none of these big institutions are serving well, either the people whom they are set up to serve or the people who staff them to render the service. Now, you can do as I do: stand outside and suggest, encourage, try to bring pressure on them to do better. But nothing happens, nothing changes, until somebody who is established inside with his hands on the levers of power and influence, and who knows how to change things, decides to respond. These institutions can be bludgeoned, coerced, threatened from the outside. But they can only be changed from the inside by somebody who knows how to do it *and who wants to do it*. Some of you folks ought to make your careers inside these institutions and become the ones who respond to the idea that they could do better."

There was not much response to this suggestion that morning. I had a short talk with Professor Helming later, but he didn't have much more to say about his suggestion. I have no idea what other students got from this statement, and I regret that I had no further communication with Professor Helming. But, really, it was many years, and Professor Helming was long since dead, before I realized the full significance of what was said that morning. I am not sure that I fully realize it yet because it is still a growing idea.

My doors of perception must have been open wider than usual that morning because that remark set the course of my life. I did not think of it in those grandiose terms at that time. I have never been one to set big idealistic goals. I just work along from day to day and let inspiration guide me. Not much of the current "futures" talk moves me. I am much more concerned with what I am doing right now, and what is now visible on the horizon, and at this time I decided to follow this advice from Professor Helming, I was thinking only of what I could do next after graduation.[38]

Bob was offered a fellowship to stay and take a Masters degree in Astronomy, but it was too late.

Clearly, at that point, I was through with school. In fact, I had arrived at a rather low opinion of education. I was glad that I had my

> experience at Rose, glad that I left when I did, glad that I had my
> experience with the construction company, glad that I had taken a look
> at astronomy and rejected it, glad for the experience at Carleton—
> particularly for that one piece of advice from Professor Helming. But
> I knew I wanted no further education in terms of pursuing a degree.
> I even toyed with the idea of packing my bags, saying goodbye to
> my friends, and leaving after my last class, skipping the final exams.
> The degree lacked meaning and still does. I guess that I didn't have
> the guts to act on that idea. It would, of course, have hurt my parents
> and probably would have been only an act of bravado. But I did think
> about it enough to ask that none of the family come to graduation,
> and a negative attitude toward "degree hunting" persists to this day.[39]

Carleton College almost saved Bob the trouble of leaving on his own without a degree; the Dean was prepared to withhold his sheepskin for other reasons. When he arrived at Carleton, Bob had been pleasantly surprised to learn that, due to his Indiana State work and the rigorous nature of the Rose program, more credits transferred to Carleton than he had expected. As he neared the end of his senior year however, he was informed that, upon recalculating the transferred credits, the school decided he still did not have enough for graduation. He would need to return the following year. Bob disagreed. He thought the school's record keeping was inaccurate. Besides, in his mind, the right credits in the right categories were not the point of education. If the school decided not to graduate him, that was fine. He would simply be on his way. He was not about to do something to meet someone else's expectations.

The school backed down and justified his degree by giving four hours' credit for a course at Rose Polytech in which Bob had earned a grade of D+. The school decided he could graduate in 1926, but his views on higher education were soured forever.

> One of the darkest days of my life was the day I graduated from
> college. Being given somewhat to emotional speculations on my own
> capacity for development, I had gone to college with high hopes. I
> emerged without distinction (on the verge of disgrace, in fact), disil-
> lusioned, with a diploma that I promptly lost. Equilibrium was re-
> stored only after years of speculation when I concluded that my role
> was to know nothing.[40]

> I did not have the questioning attitude toward the adequacy of
> undergraduate education that I now have. But the seeds of question-
> ing were laid then, and they have kept germinating for these nearly
> fifty-five years.[41]

Still, Bob got the degree, without which he would probably have
never enjoyed the career he did. In the final tiff with Carleton, his fierce
integrity of purpose had shown itself again. Ed Ouelette knew Bob would
win the fight either way.

> When crisis incidents like this came up, there was just no question
> about which way he was going to go.
>   I think he connected that with something I would call "adven-
> turesomeness," which is a kind of act of faith. It's a hunch that you
> go into this thing somehow believing that things will reorient them-
> selves as people have the integrity to act. Things reorient themselves
> around that. This may be where we connected without ever stating
> it . . . a willingness to venture.[42]

In later years, Greenleaf sometimes faulted Carleton as a place that
lacked "spirit." It was not that way for Ed Ouelette or many other classmates like John Nason, who eventually served as the school's president.
By Bob's own account though, his Carleton days were pleasant, even if he
did feel that familiar, poignant sense of being an outsider.

> I enjoyed my two years at Carleton. I made some lifelong friends, got
> involved in dramatics, raised a little hell, fell in and out of love, and
> generally fit the role of the not-too-serious college boy of the twen-
> ties. But I did not "fit" the way I did in high school. I was, in a sense,
> "outgroup." I was my own group. And have been ever since.[43]

He may have been "outgroup," but the in-group noticed Bob's quiet,
behind-the-scenes services. After praising his feat of raising a huge electric
Carleton sign atop West Hall for Homecoming, the 1926 Carleton yearbook, the *Algol*, said, "Time and again, Bob has been the man upon whose

shoulders fell the responsibility for making a dance or a play a success from the electrical and mechanical standpoint. This is always an arduous and unappreciated job but Bob has functioned royally."[44]

As he and one-hundred thirty five classmates walked across the stage to get diplomas, Robert K. Greenleaf's destiny was in motion. The only thing he needed was an arena big enough in which to play it out.

PART II

Seeker: 1926–1964

ALL OF THIS SUGGESTS TWO KINDS OF SEEKERS: THOSE WHO seek to find and those who seek to seek. The first see the search as a path toward finding something they want. When they find it, they hope to settle down and enjoy it. The search will be over. The others are interested in the search. They don't want anything but opening vistas for the search.

The search gives them joy. They do not expect ever to settle down. Instead, they hope to grow.[1]

Robert K. Greenleaf

7

Adventure in Spirit

*I chose the American Telephone and Telegraph Company because it
was the biggest at that time . . . I tried to get into a position from
which I could learn about that company in depth and influence it
with ideas. . . . I never announced my vision within the company.
I probably would not have been hired in the first place or survived
long if I had done so. I always tried to the best of my ability to do
well the job at hand, but I also always had my own agenda, from my
first day to my last.*[1]

ROBERT K. GREENLEAF

T he summer after graduation, Bob again worked at the YMCA College Camp. Professor Helming's comments haunted him during the bright days at Lake Geneva. Something had shifted within him, something big. Nevertheless, he did not respond by formulating a full-blown plan of action for his life. He was too practical to believe that any such scheme would hold up over the years and too open to ongoing, inner guidance to expect that a concrete timetable would have power for him.

As he had done before and would continue to do throughout his life, Bob Greenleaf launched into a new adventure without knowing the exact outcome. He did know two things: he wanted to work for the largest possible organization, and he wanted to be in a position to effect change from within that organization.

His beloved Uncle John had died the previous year, and the young man missed his counsel during this period. After College Camp, Bob went to Chicago to visit with Milton H. Wright, the father of Bob's classmate Robert T. Wright. Mr. Wright was impressed with the young man and immediately offered him a job in his own small business. Bob thanked him but said, "No, I wanted to get into the largest business there is, and I am not concerned about what field they are in."

"That's easy," said Mr. Wright. "AT&T is clearly the largest."

"I'm not sure I've heard of that company," said Bob. (The Terre Haute phone company was an independent.)

"It's American Telephone and Telegraph. I know a man in their Ohio subsidiary. I will talk with him."[2]

Bob went home to Terre Haute and received a letter in a few days offering him a job as a laborer—called a "groundman"—with an Ohio Bell line construction crew in Youngstown, Ohio. He quickly accepted.

Unlike so many young men who look to big business as a road to success and wealth, Bob Greenleaf had different motives. For him, a large organization was a platform for living out a peculiar destiny. After working for a construction company, he had no desire to be a building contractor. After three years as an apprentice in a machine shop, he had no drive to manage a factory. He was class president in high school, but that role seemed to satisfy any desire to be the top dog. "By the time I got to college," he said, "I was through with running things. That was not the way I wanted to live my life."[3]

George Greenleaf made a final plea for his son to find a job in Terre Haute, but it was too late. Young Rob had grown up into Robert, his adult son, and had been captured by the idea of making an impact on society from within a large organization. There simply weren't any organizations big enough in Terre Haute. It was a sad parting, one that taught Bob Greenleaf an important lesson. "I learned from that not to have any expectations from my own children. You raise them, start them on their way. Then, go your own way."[4]

And so, in the fall of 1926, the year Henry Ford initiated a five-day work week, a year after *The Great Gatsby* appeared and the first Bell Labs opened for business, Bob Greenleaf checked in at the YMCA in

Youngstown, Ohio and reported for work at the Ohio Bell Telephone Company. He would be a Buckeye for three years.

His first job was with a crew of six men who rode around in an old pickup with solid tires at a top speed of eighteen miles per hour. Their task was repositioning telephone poles to make way for a road-widening job. Each pole had four cross-arms carrying short haul and long distance lines, plus a few local circuits. The work involved disconnecting the wires, digging a new hole, jacking the old pole out of the ground, sliding it across the ground to the new hole and reconnecting the wires. Bob's foreman was Jim Harris, a strapping, brawny, rough-hewn product of the farm, about eight years older than his newest employee.

Jim found the perfect task for this green college kid's first day of work: carrying the two-hundred pound jack and digging holes in swampy ground. It was an initiation to test the resolve of any young man, the kind of task the old pros liked to throw at the rookie to see what stuff he's made of. An older groundman digging the next hole came over to pass the time of day and casually mentioned that Bob's hole quota for the day was three.

Bob survived, and even thrived. He knew these men. They were like the laborers he worked with in Terre Haute; men of heart and hands and muscle; men of practical wisdom. To the end of his life, Greenleaf remembered a bit of the homespun wisdom passed on by Jim Harris. Puffing on his pipe during a philosophical moment, Harris said, "You know, if a fellow is a S.O.B., deep down inside, he had just better go ahead and be one, because if he tries to be something else he will likely be seen as both a hypocrite *and* an S.O.B., and that's worse!"[5]

Bob spent two months with the line crew, an improvement over the six months' initiation period his father guessed would be necessary. As usual, Bob had his own goal, which was to "get off the poles before Christmas."[6] His reassignment was no accident. In his short time at AT&T, he had worked hard to prove his ambition and caring. In his first days on the job Bob enrolled in the Telephone Reading Course in the Bell System and completed it in record time with a grade of 97.4 percent. He continued taking every available AT&T course, as well as several at local colleges. Within a few weeks of joining the line crew he offered to tutor his colleagues in the Fundamentals course. W. L. Eastman, the Director of Instruction, corresponded with Bob several times during this period, complimenting him on his "exceptionally good record" and determination.

"I am pleased with your attitude of helpfulness," he wrote in one letter, "and believe that you will not only get much personal satisfaction out of the help you will give others but that it will prove to be a help to you as well."[7]

Bob sent his father a copy of one of Mr. Eastman's letters. Beginning with the affectionate greeting, "Dear Rob," Mr. Greenleaf wrote back, "I am especially pleased to learn that you have been helping the boys who never had a chance. 'Whatever you do for one of the least of these my brethren, you do for me.' If you still think you owe me something, just continue to pay in that kind of coin."[8]

During the last hours of his final day with the line crew Bob was perched atop a pole in the darkness, fighting a driving sleet storm. A "corner pole" (where the line made a sharp turn) had been moved earlier in the day. The crew could not leave until slack was taken out of each live wire attached to this pole. Bob climbed the pole to "tie in" each line as it was properly tensioned. Darkness fell—total darkness—and light rain turned to sleet. Bob, thoroughly soaked and half-frozen, endured electric shocks every time a ringing signal went through one of the lines. When the job was done, he was too numb to climb down, so he loosened his safety strap and slid to the ground. It was his last time atop a pole.[9]

At the beginning of December, he was transferred to the office of the Division Toll (long distance) Engineering office in Akron. This was one of four divisions of Ohio Bell Telephone Company, whose general offices were in Cleveland. His new boss looked at Bob's qualifications and told him to help with the backlog of drafting projects. Bob refused. He said, "I quit an engineering school partly because of my distaste for drafting, and I'm not going to do it now."[10] This was an unusual response from a new employee, but the boss accepted Bob's resolve and assigned him the job of uncovering the reasons why the office consistently underestimated the cost of projects.

In the course of that assignment, Bob learned something about how large organizations function. Using a slide rule, he made his own calculations on a major project. His numbers were checked and rechecked by six or more offices. Later, Bob discovered that he had made an error that resulted in a discrepancy of several thousand dollars. No one had caught it. The lesson: bureaucracies can easily perpetuate errors.[11]

From his first months on the job, Bob sensed that AT&T was an extraordinary company with an unusual determination to serve. Signs reading

"The Spirit of Service" were plastered everywhere, but more importantly, average employees seemed to have a sense of excitement and mission. He asked himself, "How did this company get to be this way?" and began a decades-long investigation of AT&T's history.[12] Greenleaf would eventually be recognized as the company's most knowledgeable historian. What Bob learned about AT&T taught him the importance of a grand dream of serving, the coaching and statesmanship to make it happen, and the ennobling power of a sustaining spirit.

Greenleaf's readings of AT&T history and his conversations with the company's old-timers led him to examine the partnership between two remarkable men: J.P. Morgan the Elder and Theodore N. Vail. Morgan, the statesman and mentor, ran interference so that Vail, a far-sighted operator and able manager, could build the structure of America's modern phone system and introduce service as an abiding ethic. Greenleaf's later writings on trusteeship had their origin in the relationship between Morgan and Vail.

By the time he controlled AT&T in 1907, James Pierpont Morgan was the most powerful financier in America. Morgan was able to wrest control of AT&T from the group of conservative Boston owners who had been buying up independent competitors, creating what was called "a ruthless, grinding, oppressive monopoly."[13] Several states had passed laws mandating interconnection between local independents and AT&T's long-distance lines, but the Bell companies fought them and usually won. Darwinian capitalism still trumped the notion of service for the public good, according to author John Brooks.

> Indeed, the Bell policy against interconnection could reasonably be attacked only under a public-utility concept of the telephone business that would put service equal to or ahead of private profit. And such a concept had not yet gained the ascendancy at AT&T, or in the courts, or in the federal government in 1907.[14]

On May 1, 1907, Morgan chose Theodore Vail as the new president of AT&T. Vail was no stranger to the organization. Twenty-nine years earlier, he had signed on as the first president of the Bell Telephone Company, which at that time—only two years after the invention of the telephone—boasted a total of 10,755 phones in service.[15] He served until 1886 and built the Bell System with hard-headed efficiency.

In his second stint as president, Vail continued the policy of buying up independent phone operations, aided by Morgan's ability to freeze their credit. Both men believed that, *for the sake of the public good*, competition did not fit the phone business. In the first of his famous annual report essays, reminiscent of contemporary annual report musings by Warren Buffet, Vail introduced the notion of "Public Relations," by which he literally meant the corporation's relationship with the public, not what we would today call "spin." In that same 1907 report, Vail shocked traditional business thinkers with a radical idea.

> Vail introduced the concept—all but new to American industry, and indeed outright heresy to its leading thinkers then—that maximum private profit was not necessarily the *primary* objective of private enterprise. Profit was necessary to ensure the financial health that made possible renovation and innovation of facilities but it was only one element in an equation. The problem was to achieve a proper balance. It was a new concept of the corporation.[16]

A few years later, Vail committed another heresy. He suggested that management should be honest. "If we don't tell the truth about ourselves, some one else will," he wrote in 1911, challenging the traditional secretive attitude of corporations of the day.[17]

Back at the company, Vail invited small groups of managers to sail up the Hudson on his yacht *Norna*, where he treated them like princes and listened to their concerns. He established a meritocracy system for promotion, combined the research and development departments, watched pennies at headquarters, and installed people with strong conceptual talent in a central staff. Vail looked for people who were more than technical managers. John Brooks wrote that Vail sought "men capable of the vision to look beyond the immediate problems of installing telephones and making them work, to the larger questions, such as the relations of the company with the communities it served, the relations between people within the company, and the relations of the company with government—men with a touch of the thinker in them, whose thought and instinct would cause them to avoid decisions that might seem right today but prove to be disastrously wrong tomorrow."[18]

A potentially lethal challenge loomed for the company however, one that instructed amateur AT&T historian Bob Greenleaf on the value of business statesmanship. The government was turning up the heat on big monopolies like AT&T. In January 1913, United States Attorney General George W. Wickersham and the Interstate Commerce Commission advised the company it was being investigated for, among other things, violation of the Sherman Antitrust Act.[19] The new U.S. President, Democrat Woodrow Wilson, was likely to raise the temperature even higher. J. Pierpont Morgan had the bad timing to die in March of that year, but his death may have freed Vail for what was hailed as one of the most statesmanlike acts in American business history—a compromise called "The Kingsbury Commitment." It was named after AT&T Vice President Nathan C. Kingsbury, who sent a letter to the government proposing the settlement, but the strategy was all Vail's. With the Kingsbury Commitment, AT&T promised three actions: (1) AT&T would dispose of Western Electric, making that company "entirely independent"; (2) AT&T would purchase no telephone independents without the approval of the Interstate Commerce Commission; (3) the Bell System would make its long-distance lines available to all telephone companies.[20] The arrangement cost AT&T ten million dollars, but it also bought the company seventy-one years of additional life.

The Kingsbury Commitment, Vail's insistence on honest accounting, his focus on the public good, and his view that profit was not the only goal of business transformed AT&T into a covenantal company. A covenant is a "formal, solemn, and binding agreement" that carries more weight than a legal contract or a handshake business deal because it involves the honor and identity of covenantal partners.[21] Yahweh made a covenant with the people of Israel; a man and woman become husband and wife by entering into a covenant. Early in the twentieth century, AT&T made a covenant with the American public: "We will be allowed to operate as a monopoly, but we will do so in the public interest." Perhaps the motives were mixed, but by the time Bob Greenleaf joined the company, the abiding vision to provide cheap, universal telephone service was quite real for each employee, and so was the personal obligation to provide outstanding service to every subscriber.

Greenleaf lived long enough to see AT&T finally dismantled. He believed that by the 1980s, AT&T had no visionary statesman like Vail to rescue it from its own short-sighted policies, because the organization did not tend to value or promote people who were "conceptualizers," statesmen and historians of their own company. History would have told them how AT&T had weathered earlier challenges and given clues for survival.[22]

Years later, Greenleaf summarized his views on Morgan and Vail:

> (Morgan) was a powerful, intelligent and creative man who would be out of style today.[23] Morgan was a tycoon! He was a very rich man; he lived lavishly, had a lot of money and wanted more, which was a source of power. But he also cared for the quality of the institutions that he controlled, cared in a way that was very different than what people in his kind of position held at the time, or even in our time.[24] The Morgan companies were the first to issue financial statements with a certified public accountant's attest . . . these are commonplace today, but in 1903 the idea was revolutionary.[25]
>
> At the age when most people today have started their countdown, Vail built the modern business in the thirteen years between 1907 when he was sixty-two, and 1920 when he was seventy-five, when he died in the harness . . .[26] But all that I can gather about that crucial period is that, really, Morgan was the primary institution builder. Vail could not have existed without Morgan and would not have become the statesman that he ultimately did in that position without the nurturing of this extraordinary owner-trustee. Vail emerged from that not only a great manager and builder, but a statesman, a statesman who had the foresight and creativity to adapt this large institution to changing social conditions.[27]

The relationship between Morgan and Vail laid the first brick of the foundation for Greenleaf's later ideas about the role of trustees, the importance of foresight and a sense of history, and that elusive thing he called *spirit*. Morgan, for all his faults as judged by today's standards, was a nurturing trustee-coach who cared about building an institution of excellence and allowed his people to get on with the job. Vail was an able manager who was also a "conceptualizer"—a big-picture thinker—who could adapt strategic plans to meet changing conditions. In 1913, Vail saved AT&T from antitrust actions by using foresight, which meant that he understood the present trends so deeply he could see just over the horizon and exercise startling statesmanship to preserve the core business.

Greenleaf also saw personal and institutional *spirit* in Morgan and Vail—a sustaining vision of what AT&T could be. Morgan nurtured it in

Vail, and Vail embedded it in AT&T's institutional culture. When Vail died in 1920, there was no Morgan to choose another person of spirit to replace him. From that time on, AT&T generally promoted managers, whom Greenleaf saw as possessing mindsets different from visionaries or statesmen.

Finally, AT&T's history taught Bob that institutions, for all their faults, could function as servants to employees and to the wider society.

During his time in Akron, Greenleaf was visited by Henry L. Mead, the friend of Milton Wright who had arranged for Bob's first job with AT&T. Mr. Mead was in charge of personnel for the Plant Department (construction and maintenance) at Ohio Bell, based in Cleveland. His department was an organization of about 4,000 employees. Bob was offered, and accepted, a transfer to the Cleveland office. While living in Cleveland, he joined the Unitarian Church.[28]

In the late spring of 1927, Bob became involved in what he later called, "the most formative experience of my adult life."[29] He was asked to go to St. Louis for training as a leader of "foreman conferences." This was AT&T's first formal attempt at management training. It was modeled after an approach devised by Charles R. Allen, who developed it during World War I as a way to improve efficiencies in war industries. The leader of the St. Louis conference was Michael J. Kane, a New York AT&T staff member who had been part of Charles Allen's team during the Great War. The training procedure was simple. For two weeks, Kane conducted the conference as if the twelve attendees were foremen. For the next three weeks, each person took turns conducting the conference. That was it. Bob was now trained.

Back in Cleveland, he was promoted to Supervisor of Training. He spent a year conducting two-week courses with foremen. There were no lectures, no reading assignments, and no published agendas. Greenleaf was twenty-three years old. His "students" ranged in age from 30 to 63. The teacher was smart enough to realize that he was the real student here.

> I learned much from these men. They were in the spot where the buck stops. The elaborate executive hierarchy above them thought their great thoughts about what ought to be done. What actually got done was what these fellows were able (and, to some extent, willing) to do. This was my graduate education. And, for the kind of career I had, I cannot imagine a better one. The language of 'getting things done' has stayed with me.[30]

The next summer (1928) Bob went to New York for six weeks to learn from Mike Kane how to conduct a course for foremen in the on-the-job training of craftsmen. When he returned, he was made Supervisor of Technical Training. To expand the effectiveness of his efforts, Bob decided to teach the teachers rather than directly instruct the thousands of people who worked in skilled and technical crafts. As a control, he added an interesting innovation to each two-week "train the trainers" class—one new employee hired for craft work was chosen to go through each class with the experienced veterans. The neophyte would quickly point out areas that were difficult to grasp and served as a ready-made audience for other class members. Greenleaf also organized a faculty that could teach those skills (called "crafts" by AT&T) that were best taught in a central school.

During the year of crafts training, Bob was given an interesting challenge by the foreman in charge of the long-distance test board. This man's staff performed routine tests and troubleshooting. The problem was that with the new transmission technologies, his men were faced with doing elementary algebraic computations, which none of them could do. Could Bob Greenleaf teach an evening class in algebra? Certainly!

At the first class, Bob discovered that these men not only knew no algebra, they barely knew any arithmetic. He developed a simple pedagogy that was wildly successful. At the end of each session, he gave ten problems to drill the men in arithmetic processes. One of the ten questions was a ringer, though. It required elementary algebra for a solution. By the next session, the students had solved every problem but that odd algebra stumper. Bob reasoned it through with the class but—and this is critical—did not answer their questions by giving the appropriate rule of algebra. He asked them how a person would have to *think* to solve such a problem. Class members formulated the rule themselves, which Bob then helped them generalize. At the end of this session they were given nine problems that required them to apply the new rule that they helped reason out, and then there was another problem that pushed them to the next level. Within a few weeks, Greenleaf's nascent mathematicians covered material that took a year to cover in high school, and they wrote their own textbook to boot. As an instructor, Greenleaf honored his students and saw them as partners in the adventure of learning.

Bob Greenleaf was in the right place, with the right company, at the right time. He enjoyed extraordinary freedom and was imbued with the spirit of AT&T's earlier, exciting, institution-building years of 1907–1920.

Furthermore, he enjoyed a warm, mentoring relationship with his bosses, who were not only competent but earthy in the ways a boy from Terre Haute could appreciate:

> The late 1920s in Cleveland were great years. We were building a cathedral, not just laying bricks. I worked with great people. My immediate boss, Henry L. Mead, and his boss, the department manager Robert P. Bunyan, were both extraordinary people. I recall one day going into Bunyan's office as one of his three division superintendents was leaving. Bunyan was sitting there puffing on his big meerschaum pipe and chuckling. I asked him what was funny. He said that his Division Superintendent whom I saw leave was getting a little restless and had come in to ask what a fellow had to do to get to be a General Plant Manager around here. 'What did you tell him?' I asked. 'I said I guess you will have to shoot the son of a bitch that's got the job.'[31]

Ironically, in Cleveland Bob directly supervised more people than at any time in his later career, even when he was in charge of developing managers in an organization of over one million people. He made wonderful friends, one of whom he helped avoid bankruptcy by working with a third friend to take over the hapless man's affairs. His native belief in the wisdom of everyday people—those sensible, practical, unpretentious folks who got things done—was reinforced by wide experience, and he held a growing belief that individuals could work within large organizations to nurture learning, growth—and yes, profits. Bob Greenleaf was finding his niche within the company without violating his persistent mission to get into a position where he could change things for the better.

Mike Kane knew talent when he saw it. In 1929, he invited Bob to join his staff in New York and offered a broad portfolio in the Operations and Engineering (O&E) department. Bob described his job as "an engineer on the general staff in a consulting and research capacity on all phases of personnel."[32] It was an opportunity that a plucky *seeker* could not let pass.

Crash and Rush

*My habits of work are not such that carefully analyzed progressive
steps from the present to the remote future have much appeal. Most of
the tasks which confront me are not susceptible to such analysis . . .
I am content to be on my way. Once over the first rise of ground I
can appraise the casualties thus far and set my eye on the next
objective. One veers and tacks under this procedure and sometimes it
seems that ground is being lost. But on an unexplored terrain I
know no other method.[1]*

ROBERT GREENLEAF

Monday, October 14, 1929, dawned a beautiful fall morning, with
highs expected to reach the mid-60s. New York was in the middle of a
fourteen-day dry spell, but no one was complaining, especially not Bob
Greenleaf, who was reporting for his first day of work at the headquarters
of the world's largest corporation. Bob strode through the cacophony of
the Manhattan morning and stepped into the hush of his new office at 195
Broadway, just a short walk from Wall Street. AT&T's twenty-nine-story
neoclassical building reminded him he was at the center of corporate
power. Sculptured Oriental maidens with turbans supported drinking

spouts along the marbled corridors. Doric columns and heavy draperies adorned the board room where "the Cabinet" met, including AT&T Board men such as William Cameron Forbes, the former Governor-General of the Philippines and grandson of Ralph Waldo Emerson.[2] Bob's ambitions for influence in this building were unusual. He had no desire to be one of the Cabinet, but he wanted to eventually affect company policies from his small corner of the big AT&T world, 450,000 employees strong at the time.[3] The company would need all the help it could get in the immediate years ahead.

The summer of 1929 had been one of spectacular, but illusive, performance on the New York Stock Exchange. From June 1 to September 3, AT&T stock had soared from 209 to 304.[4] That was as high as it would go, because that day, the bull market ended.[5] It would take seven weeks for it to slide into a bear market, an incipient recession, and finally crash into a full-blown depression on Black Thursday, October 24. At sunrise on the Monday following the crash, thousands of blackbirds mysteriously descended on Wall Street, ate every available scrap of food and suddenly departed, leaving scores of dead and dying birds who were too sick or weak to escape.[6] The event was both an omen and a proclamation of fact; by July of 1932, AT&T's stock sold at 72, and most of the country's businesses and financial institutions were weak, dead, or dying.[7]

While the country sank into its financial and psychological Depression, Bob's personal life took an upswing. In June 1931, Maron Newcomb, an AT&T colleague based in Chicago, made a trip to New York where he visited his talented and beautiful niece Esther Hargrave and asked if he could introduce her to a young man named Bob Greenleaf. "He's not much to look at, but he's the most considerate young man I have ever met," he told Esther.[8] She agreed to meet Bob at the 125th Street Ferry for a first outing at the Palisades, the forested cliffs on the western banks of the Hudson.

Bob was waiting when she arrived at the rendezvous site. His bright blue eyes must have lit up when he saw her, a slim, five-foot-two beauty with brown eyes, brown hair, a confident walk, and an aura of elegance and style. As for Esther, from a distance she saw a twenty-six-year-old man just one-quarter inch shy of six feet tall. As she drew nearer, the artist in her noticed his long face constructed of low planes, held in serious demeanor. The sun was shining, backlighting his brown windblown curls.

He greeted her and she thought, "He's not even as good-looking as Uncle Maron promised!"[9] Still, there was something about him, something about her response to him, that transcended all that. As they stood looking across at the New York skyscrapers, she must have sensed that this was her one man of destiny, because events progressed rapidly after that day. Three months later, on September 6, they were married. For years, Bob joked that he "picked up Esther on the 125th Street Ferry."[10]

The wedding was performed quietly in the pastor's study of the church Bob had been attending, the Community Church of New York. The famous Unitarian minister John Haynes Holmes presided over the short ceremony. One of Esther's friends came along as witness, but two were needed, so Holmes recruited his wife Madeleine for the duty.

If the wedding was not a big deal, neither was its announcement to the world. George and Burchie Greenleaf first learned that their son was married by reading about it in a Terre Haute newspaper, which had reprinted the announcement forwarded by a paper in New York. Esther was close to her mother and probably wrote or called before the ceremony, because "girls talk."[11] Neither set of parents would meet their new in-laws until the following Christmas, when the young Greenleaf couple took a train trip west. That was when George Greenleaf gave his advice that they both "keep sweet."[12]

There was to be no Greenleaf honeymoon for three years after the wedding, and even then it would be a learning trip to Europe. On the day of his marriage, Bob could not have known how important Esther would be to his work, his intellectual development, or his personal evolution into full maturity, but he would have fifty-eight years with her to find out.

Esther Hargrave was born on October 17, 1904 in Ripon, Wisconsin and grew up in Roberts, Wisconsin as a middle child sandwiched between Bill, one year older, and Eleanor, two years her junior. She received a degree in architecture from the University of Minnesota, where she earned a *Phi Beta Kappa* key. After graduation, she studied painting at the Art Institute of Chicago, then got a job in New York, where she earned enough money to live in Paris for six months and study with André Lhote, one of a group of artists who contributed to the development of Synthetic Cubism and has been judged by one art historian as "the official academician of Cubism."[13] At the time Bob met her, Esther was a fully independent woman, living at the Evangeline Hotel for Women, supporting herself by teaching at Cooper Union and working for interior designer Elsie Sloan.

Esther was a light-filled Mozart to Bob's brooding Beethoven, an airy, optimistic Libra to his complicated Cancer.[14] She was not tumultuous or Bohemian but light, rational, friendly, sociable, absolutely fair, and not inclined to share her sufferings with many people. Esther had an abiding sense of style, design, and loveliness. She was imbued with the sensibilities of not just an artist, but of *Artist*. Art was not simply something she did, but something she lived, and she was brilliant at it. She was also a woman in touch with her modernist times. Frank Lloyd Wright was a powerful influence on her thinking about architecture. Modern art was one of her passions, and she adored Matisse. By contrast, Bob liked "realistic" paintings and preferred time alone, even though he was gracious, thoughtful, and wryly funny to friends and colleagues. At the young age of twenty-six, he already presented an intense mien, showing little interest in sports, card games, or cocktail parties. He was lured by *ideas*, big ideas about religion, organizations, the social order, and the endless complexities of one's inner life. That attraction was balanced by the sheer pleasure he got from working with his hands.

By outward appearances, Esther was the more unconventional of the two. She painted abstract art, wore striking outfits, came from a family that believed in homeopathy and fresh, organic food, and was willing to walk up to strangers and start conversations. Bob presented himself like a typical early twentieth-century male executive. He was cautious about how he dressed and how much he revealed to others. He was a natural introvert, still a captive of Midwestern provincialities, but time would reveal—and their daughter Lisa would agree—that, although Esther was highly creative and intuitive, Bob was the more thoroughly unconventional one *inside*.[15]

In old age, Bob and Esther saw a psychic who told them, "You two have been one before. Now you are two, but you will be one again." Their daughter Lisa thought that was odd, but ten years later, after both parents had died, Lisa showed their pictures to another psychic who said, "Old. They are essence twins. They actually share one essence but, for the fun of it, they did a mitosis; they separated. Actually, they completely fit together as one large being."[16]

For a week following the wedding, Bob and Esther continued to live apart until they could make arrangements to set up house together. They then took a small, two-room apartment with a kitchenette in Greenwich Village, near the Rand School for Social Science (devoted to worker education and socialism) and the New School for Social Research. "New York is a great place for young people to be," said Bob. "There is so much going on all the time."[17] The Greenleafs took advantage of the action, attending nearby lectures by thinkers like John Dewey. One weekend, they attended four performances of the London String Quartet playing all six of Beethoven's complex, almost avant-garde Later Quartets.[18]

Bob's provincialism was evident early in the marriage when he pronounced modern abstract art "a bad joke."[19] One day Esther asked him what kind of art he would prefer she create, and he said, "Something more realistic." Esther then decided she would experiment with more "representational" art. It was an accommodation she was willing to make—for the time being—for the sake of the marriage. Bob did not order her to change what she painted; she offered.[20] Still, when Esther's younger sister Eleanor (Nora) heard about the decision, she was furious. To the end of her life she claimed Bob had "Beat Esther down! Just beat her down!"[21] Nora, a feisty and powerful woman, was Bob's harshest critic throughout the marriage, believing he dominated Esther, prevented her from having an independent life, and ruined her chances for fame as an artist. Bob and Nora never reconciled.

Shortly after they were married, Elsie Sloan cut Esther's salary, because the Depression was taking its toll on interior design clients. Esther understood the reason for the cut and wanted to keep her job at reduced wages. Bob, however, disagreed. He wanted her to quit the job, and he won this battle. In his mind, the husband was supposed to be breadwinner and king of the castle; the wife, keeper of domestic order.

Bob's attitude was typical of men of the day, but something more personal was at work here. Bob desperately wanted—and needed—stability in his own home. He remembered his mother's erratic episodes, her raised voice, the barely adequate housekeeping and inadequate nurturing, pans flying through the air. It was all scary then, and the prospect of a repeat was terrifying now. A wife who gained public recognition for her work was likely to be drawn away from the nurturing and order-keeping essential for Bob to indulge his lifelong love of deep silences.

Years later one of their daughters reflected on this dynamic. "Bob had to build some order in his [home] life, and Esther had to give it to him. But she was capable of it—peace, order, reliability. She had to remain rational and calm even if he was not . . . Once, as I was leaving college, he asked, 'Well, what do you want?' I said, 'I would like recognition.' He looked away, his face fell and he said, 'Oh dear.' I think he really thought that that would not bring a woman happiness; it would sow seeds of dissension and create disharmony in her personal life. And, of course, it does."[22]

New York City may have been the epicenter of the catastrophic Wall Street meltdown, but it was still the place to find world-class thinkers and doers, many of whom Bob met personally. The first luminary who influenced him was *New Yorker* magazine writer and humorist E. B. White. Greenleaf discovered White's writing his first week in Manhattan, and White's outlook was to have a "very great . . . remarkable" influence on his ability to "see things whole."[23] To understand White's effect, which one can see throughout Bob's career, one must fast forward to a 1987 essay summarizing White's influence on his thinking, *My Debt to E. B. White*.

> My career as an organization man and a bureaucrat in a huge institution, where I was very much at home, was radically different from White's who never was an administrator and who had great difficulty keeping regular office hours. Yet, across that great gulf of temperament and experience, he was able to communicate to me his great gift of seeing things whole, and it has proved to be an asset all my life.[24]

My Debt To E. B. White lifted up four of White's themes that support wholeness. First was ethical conduct, as illustrated by White's poem about Nelson Rockefeller destroying Diego Rivera's fresco that contained the head of Lenin, and White's fight with Xerox over corporate sponsorship of a journalist's article. Second, determination to show life as it is, a work in progress that does not always tie up loose ends, like the "unfinished" ending of White's *Stuart Little*. Third, love of the sheer beauty of this world, as illustrated by this passage from *Charlotte's Web*:

> It was the best place to be, thought Wilbur, this warm delicious cellar, with the garrulous geese, the changing seasons, the heat of the sun, the passage of swallows, the nearness of rats, the sameness of sheep, the love of spiders, the smell of manure and the glory of everything.[25]

Finally, wholeness required direction: "'*The right direction*'," said Bob, "that White also attributed to Harold Ross in his obituary, is central to

White's concept of wholeness. One often does not know the precise goal, but one must always be certain of one's direction. The goal will reveal itself in due course."[26]

Seeing things whole is not always comfortable, because it causes a person to turn and squarely face the Big Questions: life, death, human frailty, the lies we tell ourselves, the meaning of inner struggles. In that same essay, Greenleaf quoted White's essay on *Walden*.

> Henry went forth to battle when he took to the woods, and *Walden* is the report of a man torn by two powerful and opposing drives—the desire to enjoy the world, and the urge to set the world straight. One cannot join these two successfully, but sometimes, in rare cases, something good or even great results from the attempt of the tormented spirit to reconcile them.[27]

From his earliest days at AT&T, Bob had the "urge to set the world straight" in his quiet way. While he would have his moments of play and joy, he would contain them in a larger, almost world-weary context of one who knows the inadequacies of himself and others. He did, however, have faith that something "good or even great" would result from his work.

It could be argued that Bob Greenleaf already had a tendency to "see things whole," going back to the days when he watched George Greenleaf's reflective strategy for fixing steam engines and his ability to work through political messes in order to build a better, more whole community. Bob lamented that formal education did not teach seeing things whole, but he had this advice for others: "When you look at *anything* or consider *anything*, look at it as 'a whole' as much as you can before you swing on it."[28]

Always the pragmatist, Greenleaf believed the efficacy of ideas was proven through their application. He consciously tried to "see things whole" throughout his career, and encouraged others to do so in order to break their limiting assumptions. There are many examples, but one occurred in September of the tumultuous year of 1969, when Carleton College invited him back to Minnesota to meet with a group of students, administration, and faculty a few days before classes began. The group gathered in the Language House lounge to consider "issues affecting the student's position in society and the college, especially as they relate to career decisions."[29] It was an open-ended agenda that could have failed unless the group found focus. Greenleaf had them read E.B. White's short story, *The Second Tree From the Corner,* in which Trexler, the story's main character, is asked by his therapist, "What do you want?" Trexler is forced to think about unattainable goals and finally decides to accept himself as he is and not make himself over. Greenleaf did not say another word for the next two hours, while students discussed the story.

Years later, Greenleaf remembered, "Condensing two hours of discussion into one sentence: they ultimately identified the problem of the students of their generation as a sort of mental illness, and, like Trexler, they would only recover their poise when they accepted their illness as health—and got on with their work."[30] And get on they did. The group changed its name to The Second Tree From the Corner Seminar and published a list of "essential institutional problems in serving the human needs of its members and of society," which would make worthy reading by any of today's progressive college educators.[31] One student said the seminar was "the best thing that ever happened to me at Carleton." [32] In 1987, Greenleaf wrote, "That was over 15 years ago, and I still hear the occasional reverberation from that meeting. Such is the influence of thinking that sees things whole and of language that tells us what one sees that is powerful and beautiful."[33]

In 1969 Bob wrote E. B. White to tell him about The Second Tree From The Corner group at Carleton. White responded with a short note that read, in full:

Dear Mr. Greenleaf,

I was glad to hear about the group called TSTFTC. I hope something good comes from it.

Knowing youth, though, I am quite prepared to have it suddenly changed to mean: To Stifle Trade From The Caribbean.

I'm glad the young are restless. But I sometimes feel that they are missing something—a feeling of appreciation and wellbeing that I remember well. I think the young are a bit too sure that nothing is any good.

Sincerely,
E. B. White[34]

In 1984 Greenleaf wanted White to read his essay *My Debt To E. B. White,* but White was already blind in one eye and could no longer read. So Bob recorded it on an audio cassette and sent it along with a note. White wrote back, in part:

> I'll be eighty-five in July, am in my second childhood, and it's very doubtful that I am seeing life whole at this juncture—if indeed I ever did. Like a child I seem to concentrate on the fragments and ignore the larger picture My triumph these days is a successful attempt to tie my shoe laces.
>
> Thank you again for your extravagant remarks. I would settle for being half the man you make me out to be.[35]

Bob's grandson Michael had a different kind of response when he heard the audiotape of Bob speaking his essay. Michael wrote his grandfather to explain why he enjoyed it. Michael said he even got "choked up" listening to it, "mostly because it is a very rare thing to hear Grandpa Greenleaf string so many words together at one time for one duration!"

After their wedding, the Greenleafs attended the Unitarian church of John Haynes Holmes, the minister who married them, and they became friends with the Holmes family. The Reverend Holmes was a different kind of mentor than White, an iconoclastic activist whose community involvement must have reminded Bob of a larger scale version of Rev. John Benson's Social Gospel ministry at Montrose Methodist in Terre Haute. He was one of the founders of the National Association for the Advancement of Colored People (NAACP) and the American Civil Liberties Union (ACLU); a key figure in the political drama that rid New York City of its corrupt mayor, Jimmy Walker; and an early supporter of Margaret Sanger's controversial birth control efforts. Like Eugene Debs, Holmes was against The Great War and, also like Debs, he paid a price for his political stance. In its paper *The Register,* Holmes's own American Unitarian Association denounced his pacifist stand as treason; former U.S. President William Howard Taft accused him of using freedom of speech to mask sedition; and his worship services were regularly visited by Secret Service men. At least he survived the war without being tossed into jail, and his church grew through the controversy.

In the year of Bob and Esther's wedding, the Community Church had more than 1,800 members of 34 nationalities from six continents, and Holmes wrote in his newsletter that "we have rich and poor, high and low, black and white, ignorant and educated, Jew and Gentile, orthodox and agnostic, theist, atheist and humanist, Republican, Democrat, Socialist and Communist. All of which means that we are representative of New York City! . . . It is in this sense that we are a public and not a private institution—a community church, in the true meaning of the phrase.'"[36] Clearly, Holmes cared more about getting things done than about theological or political labels, and that way of action in the world was one that Bob had admired all his life. Greenleaf's personal instinct, however, was to pursue a course of gradualism to accomplish change rather than follow Holmes's strategy of taking absolute positions.[37]

Bob and Esther were always seeking new people and experiences. It was an interesting time to be looking. The stock market crash had completed the destruction of an optimistic myth of steady progress in America's religious and social history. Beginning in the last two decades of the nineteenth century, the rosy view of the intelligentsia was that society—and humankind—was getting better and better every day in every way, with education, science, and technology leading the way. Man was perfectible, perhaps not to flawlessness, but to the point where good will could create true community. Furthermore, entire societies could be reformed. This theologically liberal—and essentially Protestant—view was behind the Social Gospel Bob witnessed in his youth, a major driver of the reform movements at the turn of the century and the Progressive Era itself. World War I ended that fantasy for many, but Robert Greenleaf's generation came of age between the wars and, in spite of their Roaring Twenties college days, held on to a remnant of their parents' hopeful assumptions.[39]

"The great stock market crash was a very traumatic experience on the heels of the euphoric boom years of the 1920's," he later recalled. "There came out at that time a rash of utopian ideas of how to return to these euphoric boom years, and I remember two of them: Technocracy and the Townsend Plan, but there were many others."[40] Bob's practical side, his suspicion of once-and-for-all answers, made him wary of such schemes.

Then, in 1931, he went to a meeting where he met Eugene R. Bowen. Mr. Bowen, a former farm machinery executive whose career had been ruined by the Great Crash, was now in charge of the Cooperative League of the U.S.A., headquartered in New York. Here was an idealistic man promoting a scheme that had a history: an economy with a large proportion of consumer and producer cooperatives.

Bob was not totally unfamiliar with cooperatives. One of the philosophical fathers of the movement was Robert Owen, the wealthy Scotsman who, in 1824, took over the Harmonist movement at New Harmony, Indiana, and tried to create an ideal society. Owen was a true revolutionary who despised private property, but through the years the idea of a cooperative society had matured and yielded the Roachdale Society of Equitable Pioneers in England, the National Grange (a farmer's coop), and experiments in the Scandinavian countries.

In 1932, Bob and Esther decided to try cooperative living for themselves. (Newcomb Greenleaf has suggested that Esther probably enjoyed living in a community more than her private husband.) They moved to an apartment in the Consumer Cooperative Services complex, located in the Chelsea neighborhood on West 21st Street.[41] There they were befriended by a woman whom Bob would later name as one of his most important servant mentors.[42] Her name was Mary Ellicott Arnold, and she would further initiate the Greenleafs into the ideas and culture of the Cooperative Movement.

Mary Arnold had been instrumental in organizing the cooperative where the Greenleafs lived. It included a cafeteria, library, lecture hall, apartments, and even a credit union.[43] She was also General Manager of New York's Consumers' Cooperative Services and board member and treasurer of the Cooperative League of America. By the time Bob and Esther met her, Arnold and her lifelong companion Mabel Reed had already lived a life of adventure, serving as Indian agents in the Klamath region of California from 1908 to 1909, and engaging in cooperative activities ever since.[44]

A few years after the Greenleafs moved out of the Manhattan cooperative, Mary and Mabel left New York for Nova Scotia, helped start cooperative projects in housing and education at Reserve Mines, Cape Breton, and became involved with the founders of the Antigonish Cooperative Movement.[45] Three years later, they traveled south again and began working with the lobster fishermen of Maine, then did cooperative work in Arizona, Pennsylvania, Puerto Rico, and Bolivia, all the while writing pamphlets, study guides, and books. Bob kept in touch with Mary through the years.

Bob and Esther developed a deep friendship with Eugene Bowen, who suggested they visit Europe to see successful cooperative movements first-hand. It sounded like a worthy adventure. For three years the Greenleafs saved their money until, in 1934, they could sail off to Europe for a nine-week learning trip and delayed honeymoon. They went to study their passions—Cooperative Societies and modern architecture—but also found time to sightsee. They rode trains through Germany, where the shadow of Nazism was already darkening the country. The Germans still had their beer halls though, and in one of them Esther drank alcohol for one of the few times in her life. (She had signed a Lincoln Society temperance pledge card in 1911.) Bob bought a Bavarian hat, but as he watched Germany's growing belligerence after they returned to America, refused to wear it. The Greenleafs also visited Holland and were able to spend many happy hours hiking the cities and countryside.[46]

In Denmark they learned of the work of Nikolaj Frederik Severin (N. F. S.) Grundtvig (1783–1872), a man whom Greenleaf would later use as an example of a servant-leader. Grundtvig's life and work showed young Bob that an abiding and nurturing spirit could be nourished on a national scale.

If ever a country and people needed spirit, it was Denmark in the mid-nineteenth century. Danish peasants had been liberated from serfdom in 1788, but the Napoleonic Wars from 1807–1814 and Denmark's separation from Norway after a four-hundred-year union had devastated, isolated, and demoralized the little country. Danish farmers and peasants were described as "unprogressive; sullen and suspicious; averse from experiment; incapable of associated enterprise."[47] Yet, in these people, Grundtvig found hope for the salvation of the country. "O, what high souls, Here in lowliness dwell!" he wrote in one song.[48]

N. F. S. Grundtvig was the son of a Lutheran minister. His early, rationalistic education was mostly dull, but three events awakened him spiritually. On April 2, 1801, he witnessed the bombardment of Copenhagen; a year later his cousin fired him with ideas of German Romanticism and, about the same time, he struggled to suppress passions when he fell in love with a married woman. "Life to him became a battlefield where the powers of good and evil are forever in conflict, and where everything depends upon the choice of sides made by each human soul."[49] He discovered this same world-view in Scandinavian mythology, and in 1808 began writing books, plays, and poems that presented his people's ancient stories with a touch of Romanticism. He became famous as a poet and scholar.

After the peace of 1814, when everything lay "torpid, poverty-stricken and hopeless," Grundtvig strangely found new hope. It was based on his conviction that he and all of Denmark were spared by the grace of God. His Christian principles told him that all could recognize their kinship with fellow humans, and this made him "radically demo-cratic to the very core."[50] He began writing songs with populist lyrics.

> And be we poor and lowly
> Yet are we sons of kings
> And higher than the eagle
> Hope may spread out its wings.[51]

He wrote poems for all his countrymen, not just the esthetically liter-ate. "By his poetry he would sing a higher life into them. He had come to regard poetry not as an art, but as a life-giving power in every human soul, and a mighty influence in promoting the common life of an awak-ened people . . . he created through his poetry a new Denmark."[52] Still, he wondered how he could harness the volcanic potential of common people for sustained change. He had lost hope of working through the church for such an undertaking. Grundtvig had been ordained as a Lutheran clergy-man in 1822 but immediately ran into conflict with ecclesiastical authori-ties. A number of laypeople—farmers, artisans and cottagers—had been holding religious gatherings in homes, because they believed the Gospel was no longer being preached in churches. Religious officials went so far as to sue the rebel leaders for trying to exercise religious freedom, even though their outside services were "conducted in an Orthodox Lutheran spirit."[53] Grundtvig found himself on the side of the outsiders and was forced to resign his ecclesiastical office.

Then he visited England. In contrast to listless Denmark, England was bustling. Grundtvig "asked himself why it was that everything in Denmark was quiet and lifeless, whilst England was pulsating with vigorous life, the air resounding with hammer blows, with the whistling of engines, and with the din of traffic and other noises by which modern civilisation proclaims itself in a city like London."[54] Where did the English get their spirit?

He found two answers. First, the religious and personal liberties en-joyed by the English proved that "where the spirit of the Lord is, there is liberty."[55] Second, he noticed the "wholesome habit the British had of looking upon real life as the final test, in contrast to the Danish and German tendency to let theory and preconceived ideas dominate their thought and action."[56]

When the Danish king was forced to begin granting modest political and religious freedoms, Grundtvig began promoting the idea of free Folk High Schools for all young adults. The curriculum would consist of "The living word in the mother tongue"—Danish poems, songs, mythology and history, all taught without textbooks. Young adults would spend intensive residencies at the schools and, borrowing from the English philosophy, would apply their knowledge in real life as the final test of learning.[57] Knowledge was not the most important outcome, however; spirit was. "Spirit is power," said Grundtvig, and his Folk High Schools also became known as "schools of spirit."[58] Grundtvig first proposed the schools in 1838, when he was fifty-six years old.

Robert Greenleaf admired Grundtvig's emphasis on spirit, practical learning, and the use of poetry. He also noticed that, while Grundtvig inspired the Folk High School movement, he allowed others to carry the ball. "He addressed himself to the masses rather than to the cultured," wrote Greenleaf. "The 'cultured' at that time thought him to be a confused visionary and contemptuously turned their backs on him. But the peasants heard him, and their natural leaders responded to his call to start the Folk High Schools—with their own resources."[59] By the end of the century, the farmers had taken over the government of Denmark, thirty-five percent of the members of the lower house of parliament had been trained in Folk Schools, and other graduates were modernizing Danish culture and agriculture. By 1934, the year the Greenleafs visited, Denmark had established old-age pensions, socialized medicine, unemployment and accident insurance, and an eight-hour workday. Folk High Schools had empowered citizens to start cooperatives so they could control production and distribution without recourse to outside capital. Ninety-seven percent of all dairies were run by cooperatives, and the Folk School movement had gone international.[60]

When Bob and Esther returned, they both wrote articles for *Consumer's Cooperation*, a national magazine for cooperative leaders, and Bob was ghostwriter for a Cooperative League pamphlet titled *Sweden: Land of Economic Opportunity*.[61]

By the age of thirty, Bob Greenleaf had already embraced four ideas that would be at the core of his later servant writings. His father was the model for the idea that *servanthood*—the desire to "make things better in my little corner of the world"—was the most important component of leadership. E. B. White's writings taught him the importance of *seeing things whole*. The AT&T culture and Nikolaj Grundtvig's schools showed *it was possible to nurture spirit*, even in large organizations and societies. Finally, his bias about education was confirmed—*deep learning should be practical and experiential*, a lifelong adventure.

As he entered his fourth decade of life, Robert Greenleaf was riding high. Already he could say, "I have had a satisfactory measure of success in business, even without discounting the times, and I have a substantial opportunity for progress in salary and achievement before me."[62] He was in a staff position, in which he could follow his old professor's advice to change things for the better from inside a large institution.[63] He was married to a sparkling woman and stimulated daily by Big Ideas.

Further adventure—and tragedy—were just around the corner.

A Passion for Learning

So my search shall bear fruit—not in final accomplishments on which I shall rest—but in ever widening horizons. My satisfaction shall derive from the contemplation of these horizons and in the satisfactions that accrue from expanding my powers to explore them. Life then is growth; when growth stops there is atrophy. The object of the quest is the capacity to grow, the strength to bear the burden of the search and the capacity to live nobly—if not heroically—in the situations that develop.[1]

ROBERT GREENLEAF

They called it The Great Depression, but there was nothing great about it, at least not for most stockholders. Owners of AT&T stock, however, were the exception. There was no reason for them to expect that the company would continue paying pre-Depression dividends of $9.00 per share. In 1932, net earnings were only $5.96; in 1933, $5.38; 1934 figures were again $5.96; and in 1935, per share earnings totaled only $7.11.[2] AT&T had laid off 20% of its work force. At its most desperate time, Western Electric had laid off 80% of its employees.[3] Still, like clockwork, shareholders got their $9.00 per share checks from AT&T.

Company President Gifford, who had replaced Theodore Vail at the helm, argued that the company had a moral obligation to pay the high dividend and would make up the difference from surplus until the last penny was exhausted. He had another reason, though, which he explained to the Federal Commerce Commission in 1936. A lower dividend would have lowered the price of stock, which would have had a domino effect, lowering workers' wages and, finally, threatening the overall financial security of the company.[4] Whatever the mixed motives, including "The Spirit of Service," the fact is that the $9.00 dividend held, and it caused AT&T stock to be seen as one of the safest investments in the country. Every cent paid from surplus during those years was replaced many times over through enthusiastic purchases of company stock in the years following the Depression.[5] In the long run, doing the right thing was also a profitable decision.

Bob Greenleaf was secure in his own job at the communications giant, even though he was at the lowest level on the District Staff. He explained his responsibilities this way. "At that time, the corporate staff's organization chart looked exactly like the organizational chart of an operating company, and for every function in an operating company there was somebody on the [corporate] staff who was thinking about, and looking at, that function. My staff group was thinking about the personnel function in the Plant Department. There was a similar [corporate] staff for Traffic, Commercial and Accounting."[6] In other words, Bob was a roving researcher, evaluator, teacher, and troubleshooter, visiting various Bell Companies' manufacturing plants around the country to identify sources of personnel troubles, developing criteria to assess potential new hires, evaluating those who were worthy of promotion, and setting up procedures for training supervisors.

One of his first assignments was to research and write a paper on the number of college graduates being hired by AT&T. This task led to a more general assignment to look into the then haphazard AT&T employment practices. Even though little hiring was being done during the Depression, the company knew things would pick up and wanted to be ready with tools to evaluate potential employees. Bob was not satisfied that any existing assessments could match aptitudes and potential with job requirements. A corporate executive insisted that he investigate phrenology, the ancient art of reading character by studying the shape of the head and its bumps. During that period, phrenology had adopted pseudo-scientific language that made it more palatable to modern thinking, and this had won it several devotees among AT&T executives.

Phrenology looks for external manifestations of internal character, personality traits, and aptitudes. Esther knew a little about the field. In 1924, her uncle Arthur Newcomb and his wife, Katherine, had written a two-volume illustrated book on the subject, in which he used photos of the heads of Esther and her two siblings, among others, as illustrations of certain types. The caption for Esther read, "Young woman of fine texture. Almost pure plane type of profile. Natural talent for music, literature and art, with refinement, gentleness, sympathy and affection."[7]

In the 1930's, interest in phrenology was renewed, so Bob was able to take an evening course in the subject from Merton Holmes, author of the 1899 book, *Descriptive Mentality From the Head, Face, and Hand.*[8] In the book's preface, Holmes says that "each mental faculty has a direct influence upon one or more parts of the face, hand and body," so he assessed the whole body in his readings, including lines in the palms.[9] Greenleaf recalled that he was impressed with the man but not the system.

> Merton was gifted at this. Each evening we had a clinic session with someone who was brought in by a member of the class. Half a dozen times I took somebody with me to see what he had to say about them. The old man was absolutely on target every time! He read them like a book. But I couldn't take his system and make anything out of it, and I don't believe anyone else in the class could.[10]

Bob was under pressure to keep trying to see if it could be adapted for the company's purposes. He saw no way to duplicate or adequately evaluate Holmes' intuitive techniques. This stalemate began to change when he met the mustachioed and goateed Johnson O'Connor.

In 1922 O'Connor had developed an aptitude test for his employer— General Electric— that was so successful he left the company and established a center for aptitude evaluations that eventually became the Johnson O'Connor Research Foundation. Along the way, he also started the Human Engineering Laboratory. When Bob met him, O'Connor's operations were based at the Stevens Institute of Technology in Hoboken, New Jersey. O'Connor believed every person was given a combination of innate—what we might call "hard-wired"—potentials in areas such as figures and symbols, color perception, inductive and analytical reasoning, idea flow, numerical aptitude, spatial or "structural" visualization, musical aptitude, manual dexterity, and memory.[11] His research showed that women scored as high as or higher than men on all categories except spatial visualization, so he held no prejudice against hiring women for any position for which they were qualified.

In O'Connor, Bob found a bright, quirky, fellow seeker who shared some of his attitudes. O'Connor believed in a liberal education for all young people but thought that living two years in a great city and taking advantage of all its cultural opportunities would provide a better education than many four-year colleges. He insisted that people "get the facts," to continue a process of lifelong learning that would maximize their capacities, but he also advised them to "forget the facts" in order to broaden personal awareness and experience the fullness of life. Like Bob, he was a born teacher who cared deeply about words. In fact, O'Connor would find much of his future fame through work on developing vocabularies. Furthermore, O'Connor's wife, like Bob's, was creative; she was an architect.[12]

When Greenleaf heard about O'Connor, he crossed the river to New Jersey and took a course with him. He realized that O'Connor's validated tests could prove or disprove some of the claims of phrenology, so they planned a little informal research experiment. Two people trained in phrenology would make judgments about the capacities of students and then compare their estimates to actual test scores. The experiment was never completed.

> About that time, the president of Stevens Institute heard about this, and he got Johnson O'Connor and I in and knocked our heads together. He said, 'Now look, you fellows are getting set up to prove that something is *so*, that everybody believes is *not so*. Maybe it ought to be done, but I don't want it done here!' So, that was the end of the experiment.[13]

Bob's varied duties gave him a reason to broaden his learning far beyond phrenology. He followed the latest thinking in higher education, psychology, industrial and social psychology, labor relations, and political and legal trends. They all affected personnel matters at AT&T. After five years of traveling, listening and sensing, Bob identified a common theme in the successful AT&T and Bell operating units: leadership.

> The traditional attitude of a boss rarely gets the highest type of per-formance out of any group . . . As I go about the country among our organizations and attempt to trace the source of the vitality in one unit or account for the sluggishness in another, it always traces back to the presence or lack of dynamic leadership. I have seen organiza-tions which were on the verge of violent eruption, because of ill feeling, incompetence, and lack of organization, literally transformed as if electrified into units of unusual cooperativeness and productive-ness by the insertion of a capable leader into that organization.[14]

Greenleaf observed the best practices of those he considered top lead-ers and described them in terms one would normally associate with a sup-portive coach or a great teacher. "I know well the great impetus of a word of encouragement, a constructive criticism, or a redefining of objectives when I seemed to have lost my way," he wrote in a 1934 letter to his old college president.[15] He noticed that the best leaders and supervisors oper-ated outside the traditional command-control model.

> You see, we are evolving a new concept of administration in indus-try. Experiments in our manufacturing plants have borne out the fact that under optimum conditions employees have insisted that they were receiving no supervision when, as a matter of fact, they were receiving much more attention than that usually given. The master and servant relationship is going. We say now that no one should be made a supervisor to whom the workmen do not go for guidance and counsel before any designation of supervisory status is made. In a conference, it is not always possible to spot the boss. If he is wise, he knows how to drive hard with a light hand. His organization will work with zeal and inspiration and never be conscious of his direction.[16]

Such leaders were to be cherished, but one never knew where they would emerge. In spite of his exposure to O'Connor's work, Greenleaf was skeptical that tests alone could predict success. In 1935, he wrote about this uncertainty in the context of admission policies for universities but drew on his assessment experience in industry. "In the past few years I have given considerable attention to this question of appraising aptitudes, interests and achievements, and I am not happy with the prospect that we shall ever be able to do a precise job of saying who should enter and who should not."[17] Still, he knew his kind of leadership when he saw it.

> Leadership is our most important attribute. Insofar as I have any influence in organizations of any kind, I shall trust it like radium, to be sought zealously and nurtured and extended (if possible), for nothing but chaos is ahead unless some of us emerge to mould a more cohesive society and yet let man remain free in spirit.[18]

By 1935, Greenleaf was already making the argument that great leaders worked through others and that worker empowerment was good business. Speaking before a gathering of industry professionals, he said, "The advanced thinkers at supervisory levels are beginning to see the possibilities in the idea that an industry that sets the development of the potentialities of its people as one of its primary aims is ensuring the accomplishment of the end and aim of the industry."[19] In that same speech, he offered an idea that presaged by twenty-five years Douglas McGregor's Theory X and Theory Y views of workers and management. The old-fashioned controlling boss described by Greenleaf corresponds to McGregor's Theory X. The Theory Y approach honors workers' capacities.[20]

> The old hard-boiled boss is rapidly becoming a thing of the past. This negative sort of supervision had as its criterion the discovery of *weaknesses and limitations* in people, a sort of pessimistic philosophy, for limitations are mighty easy to discover, and when in search of them, many fine qualities may be obscured . . . A search for the *capabilities and possibilities* in people is gradually supplanting the search for their limitations. It is a more optimistic philosophy. But the basis for such a change in philosophy is far from sentimental, for it is the wise supervisor who realizes that the grist for his mill is contained in the possibilities in people and not in their limitations.[21]

Bob Greenleaf was not the first to voice such sentiments. We have no evidence that he read Mary Parker Follett, for example, but it would be a surprise if he had not, because her work was widely known and studied before World War II. Follett was a social worker, political scientist, and theorist who applied her insights to management. She argued for equal participation by workers in problem solving and leadership. Rosabeth Moss Kanter summarized Follett's leadership views: "Follett proposed that a leader is one who sees the whole situation, organizes the experience of the group, offers a vision of the future, and trains followers to be leaders."[22]

Follett's voice was part of a growing reaction against the division of labor that had been popularized by Frederick Winslow Taylor's notion of Scientific Management (1911). Taylor showed how time studies, routing schemes, and planning *by management* (not workers) were tools in the "scientific" approach to maximizing production and minimizing costs. By giving workers highly specialized tasks and rewarding them according to the quality and quantity of their accomplishments, Taylor believed workers and corporations would both prosper.[23] According to some critics, the only things left out of this formula were the needs, capacities, and growth potentials of workers. Industrialists called this area "the human relations problem" but, unlike Follett, or even the great AT&T builder Theodore Vail, Taylor and most of his contemporaries saw worker dissatisfaction as a pesky side issue to be handled, not something that went to the heart of the meaning of corporate enterprise. Still, in spite of Follett's writings and the building reaction to Taylor, Greenleaf's ideas did not represent mainstream thinking in 1935.

―――――――

Just how deeply Bob was thinking about diverse disciplines—and especially education— became evident in a remarkable exchange of letters between him and Dr. Donald Cowling, President of Carleton College, Bob's *alma mater*. Shortly after he went to New York, Bob ran into Cowling ("Prexy") at an alumni gathering. For the next ten years, they met once or twice a year in New York over a bottle of wine, which Bob likely did not share, because he was a teetotaler. It was fun for the president of a conservative, church-related college, though. "Once when Prexy was quite mellow," recalled Bob, "he remarked slyly, 'You know, I can't do this in Northfield.'" They were unlikely friends. "He was a staunch conservative while I was a mild New Dealer," said Greenleaf. "He was absolutely dedicated to Carleton and I, being something of a maverick who didn't fit the established ways of colleges, was sharply critical of all collegiate education."[24]

In May 1934, Bob wrote a letter that opened various educational issues for discussion, the first in a series of wide-ranging correspondences about the ultimate aim and administration of higher education. What prompted the letter was his need to explain why he was withholding financial support from his *alma mater*, a decision that "has not been pleasing to me."[25] What Bob was seeing in the "real world" led him to believe that colleges and universities, including Carleton, were missing the mark.

> From this point of vantage I have watched the whole panorama of the collapse of our industrial order which had promised opportunity to so many, and the fruitless struggle for recovery has passed in intimate review. During this period I have followed closely the general educational field through various courses in the graduate schools, extensive reading, and the many contacts which New York offers. In all of my contacts with the field of education I sense grim tragedy. While the fabric of our economic order is being shattered before our eyes, the schools, to whom we should logically turn for some direction, seem almost unaware that a new society is in the making.[26]

Greenleaf went on to quote Van Wyck Brooks in *America's Coming-of-Age*: "The typical university graduate has been consistently educated in twin values which are incompatible. The theoretical atmosphere in which he has lived is one that bears no relation to society, and the practical atmosphere in which he has lived bears no relation to ideals." He then quoted a report by Henry Pratt Fairchild titled "Retrospect and Prospect," which came out of a 1932 conference on The Obligation of Universities to the Social Order that Cowling himself had attended.

If Dr. Cowling was willing to take the risk, Bob was prepared to assist Carleton with Dr. Fairchild's challenge to overhaul the entire college into an institution that effected "an immediate and practical translation into terms of direct social guidance and participation." Bob went on to say, "Little in your program, as I know it, meets this challenge in any substantial way." What Bob had in mind was something that more closely resembled the cooperative schools and societies that had so fired his imagination in recent months.

It was an audacious—some might say cheeky—letter for a thirty-year-old who had barely graduated from Cowling's school. Years later, Bob admitted that with age he became "less critical of the performance of educators and more critical of their pretensions. But in those days, I was more critical of their performance."[27] Still, the issues were vital to him and, to his credit, he volunteered to work with Carleton in pursuing them by making an analysis of "all phases of the college program and point[ing] out those parts which are not in line with the socialized philosophy of education as I see it," and by outlining "a practical program of student participation in cooperative enterprise on the campus which would be interwoven with the more theoretical curriculum so as to achieve substantially Dr Elliot's idea of a 'serviceable fellowship' between theory and practice."[28]

Dr. Cowling's response came six months later. "Personally," he wrote, "I feel quite convinced that what this country—and the world—needs is more education of the type that Carleton and similar colleges represent—discipline in abstract thinking and a philosophy of life which will lead those so trained to devote their powers to the public good. We certainly do not need a greater emphasis on vocational or technical education. . . ." He defended admission standards for students and claimed that, while he had been forced to address physical needs on campus, "my chief interest has never been in the material side of the college." Without any hint of irony, he accepted Bob's offer to study ways in which Carleton did not conform to Bob's personal philosophy of education and to make recommendations for change.[29]

Bob wrote a follow-up letter in which he admitted he was thoughtless to not recognize all that Dr. Cowling had already done for Carleton. He went on, however, to articulate his general dissatisfaction with a higher education system that robbed both students and faculty of meaningful glory.

> Here was genius, wisdom, experience, and inspiration; here was youth, vision, and energy; here was a world crying for understanding and patient leadership; here was an opportunity—for four years society was willing to work and save so that its great teachers might be free to create a selected environment within which the more precious attributes of civilization might flourish more profusely. And what did we do with that opportunity? We so entangled it with a maze of irrelevant institutional impediments that none but the hardiest of pedants could emerge from it with any sustaining sense of satisfaction. This is a harsh statement, but anything less forceful would conceal my real feelings and would be insincere.[30]

Bob frankly admitted that he and Dr. Cowling might simply disagree. Bob's ultimate authority for his comments was his own experience at Rose Polytechnic Institute, Indiana State Normal School, and Carleton—as a student, not an administrator. Still, he believed Carleton was "failing to meet the needs of youth of these times," except for a handful who were predisposed to a scholarly life. As for Bob's offer to conduct a study and offer recommendations, "I feel that it would be futile for me to submit specific plans of action until an understanding on more fundamental considerations can be reached," especially if Carleton was not willing to pursue the risk of experimentation.[31]

In this exchange, Bob spoke for every bright student (of any grade-point average) who had been dispirited by university specializations, cloistered mind-sets, and arbitrary administrative policies. He was young enough to still be warmed by the fires of idealism, old enough to give some thought and form to possible solutions. Dr. Cowling spoke for the traditional view of a liberal arts education which, in spite of its flaws, challenged the best to become better by exposure to grand ideas and ideals. He also wrote as a genuinely humble, but beleaguered and often misunderstood, scholar and college president who willingly poured out his life's energy for the survival of Carleton during the worst financial crisis in the school's history. Dr. Cowling knew that, without a college, there could be no experimentation. Greenleaf believed that there was no reason to have a college unless it ventured forth in fresh ways to serve the needs of students.

Dr. Cowling passed Bob's letters around to several of his deans for comment. The Dean of the College reminded his president that "In order to graduate, Mr. Greenleaf had to be given credit for four hours in Mechanical Drawing from the Rose Polytechnic Institute with a grade of 'D plus.' I should not say from my study of his record that his judgment could be completely relied upon due to the fact that his education was not completely taken in a liberal arts institution."[32] It was a response which, in its own way, supported some of Bob's arguments about the narrow mindset of many college administrators. Feedback from the head of the Department of Psychology and Education was more thoughtful, but noted that "Mr. Greenleaf's argument seems to contain a latent confusion with regard to the essential function of a college such as ours."[33]

On his next trip to New York, Dr. Cowling had lunch with Bob and Dr. Fairchild (whom both had quoted in defense of their positions) and a lovely dinner with Bob and Esther. Two weeks later, Bob sent Dr. Cowling a twenty-two page, single-spaced letter, his *magnum opus* on the subject of higher education until he wrote a book about it over forty years later. In it, Bob expanded on some of the problems he saw with traditional liberal arts schools and offered suggestions for improvement. He was both accommodating and frank in his comments. "At the risk of impertinence," he wrote, "I have assumed that full and enduring understanding could be achieved only if the discussion were freed from all diplomatic obscurantism."[34] Bob's summary (included in the Notes for this chapter) does not capture the power of some of his writing. [35] A few excerpts on selected topics:

On the role of teachers:

> I should very much place the teacher in the position of guide, counselor and friend and define the teaching-learning process as one of exploration and discovery by the students with the advice and counsel of the teacher.
>
> I have seen in this business [AT&T] a quality of teaching that has not been matched in my experience with formal schools. And it has been done with administration. . . . You select a college which is rent with internal dissention, whose teachers have atrophied mentally and spiritually, and which has lost its purpose and morals, and let me send in as educational administrator a former superior of mine who is not a high school graduate. Give him a year, and if you do not swear that a miracle has been performed, then I will undertake the proverbial hat-eating act with pleasure.

On college admissions policies and the importance of a diverse student body:

> Certainly if one of the objectives of the college is the nurturing of leadership, the door must be wide open, for it is so evenly dispersed throughout all types of people that the restriction of your acceptance standards to a particular type will admit only a negligible percentage of such people.
>
> One of the great fallacies in our present concepts of education is the idea that we must all keep in step with the deadly routine from six to twenty-two, whereupon we are hastily stamped 'educated' and

> shoved on to make way for the next group on the treadmill. The
> presence of a substantial percentage of older people would leaven
> and mature the whole group and would closely link it with the
> world of practical affairs, the influence of which is altogether too
> slight in the colleges.

On preserving ineffective colleges and universities:

> At times I lose my reverence for institutional permanence. What
> spineless people our progeny will become if we leave to them, en-
> dowed in perpetuity, all of the cultural facilities they will need. Far
> better that many of our institutions should vanish than that our
> children and grandchildren should be spared the necessity for antici-
> pating some of their own needs and building their own institutions
> to supply them.

On teaching the whole person through theory and experience:

> You raised the point, in our discussion, that comparatively little use
> was made of many of the cultural advantages of the college program
> such as music. It occurs to me that this is an inevitable result of
> departmentalization. . . . Thus (music) becomes separated from the
> cultural whole and becomes not something to experience and enjoy
> informally, but rather something to study and struggle with on a
> formal classroom basis.
>
>   Is it not possible that one might assemble a faculty of scholars,
> perhaps excellent teachers in their chosen fields, and yet not have one
> truly educated man among them; that is, one whose experience in the
> arts had given him a sense of the only enduring verities our civilization
> has produced—poetry, music and art? . . . Thus every member of your
> staff should be constantly alert to cement bonds of experience to related
> fields and the arts. In other words, almost everyone on the faculty
> should feel a deep responsibility to educate the whole man. Not all of
> them should dwell on Olympian heights of scholarly achievement. . . .
> I should coin the term 'balanced faculty' as the objective.

Greenleaf made three suggestions for immediate action. First, introduce four new courses into the Economics Department: Current Economic

Problems, Politics, History and Development of Cooperation, and Techniques of Cooperative Enterprise. Second, establish a College Extension Department "which would serve to ally the college and the Southern Minnesota Community in the work of extending the benefits of the civilizing influences in the community." As a model, he referred to Grundtvig's "poetical-historical" concept of education for the masses of people. "Now you may say that the community at large in which you are located is not your concern," wrote Greenleaf. "If you stand by this opinion, then I say that you are denying a sphere of influence to the college which, in time, may be of far greater importance than the formal work of the college on the campus. . . . If you do not accept this challenge, who will?" Bob's third recommendation was that "a faculty should be assembled half of whose members had had their predominate experience before coming to your faculty in other fields than teaching." He decried the convention that "an advanced degree is necessary for membership on a college faculty" and expanded on a position that, even today, would be controversial, and would likely cause accreditation papers to be pulled from schools that tried it:

> In fact, even the high schools are clamoring now for masters degrees. No milder term than 'disgusting spectacle' conveys my regard for the whole business. Everybody with whom I discuss this question agrees with me that the accomplished scholar is apt to be a poor teacher, and that the genius is certain to be a poor teacher . . . Teaching ability is an art and I would grant no relationship to scholastic distinction, scientific achievement, or even the writing of great books. I would recommend a faculty first of great teachers, about half of whom have had vital experience in other fields than teaching. And I would beware of formal labels, for teaching is a sensitive indefinable art. Teaching ability is not so unusual among intelligent people by and large, but among a highly selected group of scholars, it may be exceedingly rare.

For the next several years the conversations continued. During one dinner, Dr. Cowling, exasperated, turned to Bob and said, "Well, didn't you get *anything* out of your years spent at Carleton?" Bob's impertinent reply: "Yes, I got something very valuable to me; I learned how to make a little bit of work look like a whole lot."[36]

Dr. Cowling never committed Carleton to any of the experiments Bob suggested. "Prexy was the model of the responsible man," wrote Greenleaf. "He felt the obligation to do his best. But he kept putting me off because these were the Depression years and the college was broke. Any innovative effort would cost money, so we always left it there." The discussions—but not the friendship—ended sadly for both of them.

> Then one visit he appeared with a broad smile. He had just received a gift of a half million dollars. Now he could do something; what should he do? We spent an evening at it but the conclusion was— nothing! He would do the conventional thing and endow a chair. He was sixty, and he had spent too many years enmeshed in a monolithic educational ideology. He had let go too long the full examination of the assumptions he operated by. He must settle, he conceded, for what he had; he must continue to run his college as colleges were conventionally run, much as the thought of advancing the growing edge excited him. It was a sad evening, which both of us acknowledged.[37]

Bob continued to admire Dr. Cowling, who always listened to his ideas, engaged them seriously and responded with his honest differences. When Prexy died, Bob wrote a tribute to him for Carleton alumni, which he later included in the book *Servant Leadership*.[38] Prexy was conservative and conventional, but Bob judged him a great person, one who led through serving.

During the first year of Bob's correspondence with Dr. Cowling (1934–1935), he continued his wide-ranging travels for AT&T, luxuriating in the excellent train service available at the time. In 1928, he had paid five dollars for a quick flight over Cleveland in a noisy Ford Trimotor, but he did not travel by air again until 1962, not because of a fear of flying but a fear of the frantic.[39] "If I went to the West Coast, which I did quite frequently," he explained, "I had that one day and two nights between Chicago and the coast when there would be no telephones, no visitors, no nothing. You could have your meal in your room so you really didn't have to talk to anybody. And boy, I used that retreat time! Of course, there are people who get jittery when they hit a slack time. I doubt whether they are as effective or creative, but they don't like that open time."[40] Even after airline service was well established he insisted on taking trains for his AT&T work. "I found trains a good place for meditation," he later recalled. "Meditation early became one of my regular occupations. . . . I like my solitude." [41] Train travel also gave him more control over his own schedule. "They couldn't say, 'Bob, we need you in Los Angeles tomorrow,'" recalled his daughter Madeline. "He didn't want anyone messing with his life like that."[42]

In 1935, Greenleaf saw an example of the importance of corporate foresight reminiscent of Vail's statesmanship. The National Labor Relations Act (The Wagner Act) was passed in 1935. The legislation took labor disputes out of the courts and put them under the National Labor Relations Board, which was given sweeping powers to judge unfair labor practices. It also gave workers the right to unionize, a frightening prospect for large employers. Because a similar law passed in 1933—the National Industrial Recovery Act (NIRA)—had been declared unconstitutional just before passage of the Wagner Act, a group of fifty top corporate lawyers met in New York and decided unanimously it was likely The Wagner Act would also be voided by the Supreme Court. They would go back and advise their companies to disregard it. Although Bob was just a "kid on the sidelines" watching the action, he vividly remembered what happened next.

> When that recommendation was brought back by our lawyer, he was challenged by my boss at the time, who was way down in the middle of the hierarchy. In fact, he wasn't an executive at all. He was a guy like my father, with just a fifth-grade education. He came up in the company the hard way, starting as a cable splicer. His grammar was not impeccable, but he was a very good thinker and a powerful debater. He said, "Look at it this way; this is clearly social policy. It was enacted once and turned down, and this one may be turned down too, but this will keep coming back until it is confirmed. It is clearly going to be the law of the land. And we'd better make our peace with it and not contest it."
>
> Well, there was a real rowdy brawl about that, but this boss of mine was a persistent guy and he ultimately prevailed. Of course, two years later the Supreme Court affirmed The Wagner Act unanimously, and the steel and automobile companies that had

disregarded it went through a really rough time. . . . I am mortally certain that if AT&T had defied the law, we probably would have been broken up then, one way or another. We were more vulnerable than those other companies.[43]

Something more personal was on Bob's mind in 1935, though: Esther was pregnant. They packed up their Manhattan apartment and moved in with Esther's parents, who owned a small dairy farm at Mount Kisco, an old Quaker community north in Westchester County. By happy accident, the Woods—a fine old Quaker family—were their next-door neighbors and would have a profound influence on their lives in the near future.

They named their baby Elizabeth, but she was stillborn. The devastating loss affected Bob deeply but did not drown him in despair as it did Esther. He would have done anything to help her feel better but knew that each person's grief must follow its own path. Bob bought Esther a baby grand piano because, among her many gifts, she was a musician, and he hoped that music could soothe the pain.[44] While she stayed home and played the piano, Bob continued his work and travels.

There was occasion for joy two years later, when they were once again living in Manhattan. On April 15, 1937, Bob rushed Esther to the hospital when she went into labor with her second full-term pregnancy. The contractions were coming fast and furious. Nurses put her on a gurney and, while running to the delivery room, shouted, "Don't you let that baby come too soon!" They were afraid she might deliver in the hallway.[45] On that day, in the delivery room, Newcomb Greenleaf was born, a live, squealing, healthy boy. The parents were overjoyed. Soon after carrying Newcomb through the red door of their Manhattan apartment, they decided their growing family needed more living space and, besides, Esther could use some help with the baby. So they moved back to Mount Kisco to continue their adventure together and start a new one with the Society of Friends.

CHAPTER 10

Openings and Convincement: The Quaker Way

There is urgent need in the world for a new religious movement, one that has the force and vigor that 17th century Friends had in their day.[1]

ROBERT GREENLEAF

D uring their first stay in Mount Kisco, the Greenleafs had planted roots within the local Quaker community. Their neighbor, Levi Hollingsworth Wood, was a lawyer who worked for peace, civil rights, and education for blacks and Quakers. Like John Haynes Holmes, he was one of the grand activists of the Reformist Era, a founding member of the American Civil Liberties Union, the American Friends Service Committee, and the National Urban League.[2] When Bob first met him, Wood lived with his second wife, Martha, and his maiden sister, Carolena. Bob and Esther were especially taken with Carolena, whom Bob called "an extraordinary person." Through her influence, they joined the Mt. Kisco Quaker Meeting (Quakers call their congregations "Meetings") and became active in the larger Religious Society of Friends community.

A book could be written on the influence of Quaker thought and practice on Robert Greenleaf's corporate work and servant writings. The
Quakers had been organizational pioneers for three hundred years. They
evolved the art of consensus decision-making, designed meetings for full
participation by every member, and replaced professional clerics with lay
leadership. From their earliest days, Quakers had seen themselves as
"seekers," even though they did not originate the term. They found God
in silence, not creeds, believed in plain-spoken speech, honesty in business dealings, and personal integrity. Friends looked to the "Light within"
each human as a source of authority—and mystery. All these connections
to Bob's psyche were heightened when he looked into the life of Quaker
founder George Fox. "The traditions of Friends, mainly as framed in the
work of the first generation, hold for me the great promise," wrote Greenleaf.[3] To better understand Robert Greenleaf's mature philosophy and
practices regarding religion, spirituality, and organizations, one must look
back at that first generation of Quakers.

The Quakers emerged from the religious travails of seventeenth-
century England, when politics and theology were intimately related.
Even religious scholars need a scorecard to understand the complicated
doctrines that were swirling through the country when George Fox (born
in 1624) came of age in Drayton-in-the-Clay, Leicestershire.

> The unpure Familists, who pretend to be godified like God; the illu-
> minated Anabaptists; the Independents with their excess of liberty;
> the Sabbatarians, who are for keeping the old Jewish Sabbath; the
> Anti-Sabbatarians, who say every day is a sabbath to a Christian; the
> Traskites, who would observe many Jewish ceremonies; the Millenar-
> ies, who believe in the reign of Christ and His saints on earth for a
> thousand years; the Etheringtonians, with a hodge-podge of many
> heresies; and an atheistical sect, who affirm that men's souls sleep
> with their bodies until the Day of Judgment.[4]

Then there was George Fox, the son of a weaver, a young man who,
like Bob Greenleaf, was a serious, plain-spoken person blessed with an
upright father. He apprenticed to a shoemaker and also worked as a wool
dealer. (William Penn wrote that Fox was especially well suited for his
work with sheep "both for its innocency and solitude."[5]) In Fox, Greenleaf
found another person who craved time alone.

Just before he turned nineteen, Fox was horrified when several friends asked him to join them for beer. They professed to follow Christ but Fox believed their behavior betrayed them as selfish, pleasure-seeking hypocrites.[6] So this intense boy, confused and often disgusted with the rigid, competing claims of ministers and mystics, priests and prelates, and the inconsistencies of those who practiced a shallow Christianity, walked away from home to search for truth and true religion. He broke relations with the church, opened himself to whatever revelations might come, and became a dedicated *seeker*. For four years, Fox spoke with all manner of people looking for final answers, but got conflicting reports. Some ministers told him to relax, smoke a little tobacco, and take pills for his low spirits.[7] Nathaniel Stephens was one cleric who was impressed with the young man but broke with him because Fox preferred to take his Bible to the orchards on the Sabbath rather than attend church.[8] And so it went.

Along the way, Fox began having little revelations, which he called "openings," to higher truths. Then, in a crucible-like moment in 1637, he had his major revelation.

> When all my hopes in them and in all men was gone, so that I had nothing outwardly to help me, nor could tell what to do, then, O then I heard a voice which said, 'There is one, even Christ Jesus, that can speak to thy condition,' and when I heard it, my heart did leap for joy. . . . and I saw professors, priests and people were whole and at ease in that condition which was my misery, and they loved that which I would have been rid of. But the Lord did stay my desires upon Himself, from whom my help came and my care was cast upon Him alone.[9]

So it was that George Fox became a prophet and reformer with a key message: "every man is enlightened by the Divine Light of Christ."[10] This was not an abstract doctrine for Fox but something which he knew "experimentally." Fox preached that direct revelation is available to all true seekers, Christian and non-Christian, without benefit of "steeple houses," priests or rituals, and is presented to us through the "Inward Light" or the "Seed of Light." That idea did not set well with many good followers of Christ. In 1672, Fox visited America and traveled to the Carolinas where he met a doctor who thought the Divine Light might exist, but certainly not in Indians. Fox acted to prove his point, not for himself but for the occasion it would provide "for the opening of many things to the people concerning the Light and Spirit of God."

> I called an Indian to us, and asked him whether, when he lied, or did wrong to anyone, there was not something in him that reproved him for it. He said there was such a thing in him, that did so reprove him; and he was ashamed when he had done wrong, or spoken wrong. So we shamed the doctor before the Governor and the people. . . . [11]

At least the local authorities did not throw Fox into jail, as the English were wont to do throughout his ministry. Fox and his followers did not help matters by some of the ways they behaved and spread their message. They often attended churches, waited quietly until the services ended, then stood up and testified to their revealed Truth, which frequently conflicted with the theology of the priests or ministers. Mob scenes were not unusual. Early Friends would not take an oath to man or king, tip their hats, wear fancy clothes or speak fancy language, drink alcohol, swear, celebrate holidays, go to theaters or sports games, wear wigs or jewelry, or support war—all practices the authorities considered suspicious.[12] Fox was hauled before courts and magistrates sixty times, imprisoned eight times for a total of about six years, and suffered terrible, unspeakable privations.[13] Other Friends endured arrest, torture, persecution, and even martyrdom.

In one account, the term "Quaker" was first used by Justice Gervase Bennett in 1650 to describe Friends who literally shook, or quaked, with emotion in their meetings.[14] Another version has it that Fox told the judge *he* should "tremble at the word of the Lord," and the jurist responded by cynically calling Fox a "Quaker."[15] The phrase "Society of Friends" came into general usage around 1665, during the great organizing period of the movement. Well before George Fox began his public ministry, a loosely-knit group of people with similar interests had popped up in England and Holland. In England they were called "Seekers." These people found no satisfactory pattern of worship, so they gathered to wait in silence, prayer, and openness for power from on high to lead them forward. The Puritan revolutionary Oliver Cromwell called Seekers "the best sect next to a Finder, and such shall every faithful, humble seeker be at the end."[16] Many Seekers (those who did not become Ranters, members of another sect) joined the Quakers but liked their old name, so Quakers also became known as Seekers, even though the two movements were not identical. Today the group is known as the Religious Society of Friends.

The Methodists of Bob Greenleaf's youth would have agreed that God could directly touch humans outside church structures, but they were not so radical in their individualism, retaining clergy and the rites of baptism and communion from their Episcopal roots. When Greenleaf proclaimed in *The Servant as Leader* that "everything begins with the individual," he was stating a secular version of a very old thought in Protestant history. Individuals do not sustain movements, however; organizations do. In fact, Greenleaf claimed that organizations were "how you get things done." He was enormously interested in how the Quakers reflected their scripture-based but anti-clerical ideas in the Society of Friends organization. After all, clerics are the leaders of faith communities. What do you do after you kick them out?

You make everyone a leader. Each Friend deserves to be a leader, because God is equally available to each as the Light within. Like the Seekers, early Quakers sat in silence at their Meetings, with no singing or prearranged rituals that could get in the way of His Spirit. This form of Friends worship has persisted to modern times. "Anyone, old or young, man or woman, learned or unlearned may, by the touch of the Lord's Spirit, be bidden to speak," wrote historian Elizabeth Braithwaite Emmott. "Without this call, none should venture to break the silence, but anyone who refuses to obey such a call is hindering God's purpose in that meeting."[17] Naturally, certain people arose as elders and ministers, but they were not ordained as ministers by any Meeting. Their role was simply "recorded" in the minutes.

That process worked well for spiritual matters, but what about organizational and business decisions? In those early years, a version of *Roberts Rules of Order* was not available to dictate the form of the meeting. Even if it had been, the Quakers would not have used it, because a vote would have silenced contributions from Friends who were acting in response to the Inner Light. To put it another way, *Roberts* is simply not as radically democratic as the Gospel, at least as Fox understood it. So, through hundreds of years, the Religious Society of Friends developed a way of handling decisions based on consensus rather than votes. "I have been in a few meetings where people got mad and called each other names," said Greenleaf, "But they never voted. That seems very solid in the tradition."[18]

Consensus is not unanimity. It is a position everyone can accept, even if it is not what was originally wanted or proposed. Underneath the consensus is an even larger issue, at least for Quakers: the will of God. "In all our meetings for church affairs we need to listen together to the Holy Spirit" says the *Quaker Faith & Practice* of the Britain Yearly Meeting. "We do not seek consensus; we are seeking the will of God. The unity of the meeting lies more in the unity of the search than in the decision which is reached. We must not be distressed if our listening involves waiting, perhaps in confusion, until we feel clear what it is God wants done."[19]

In the Quaker practice of consensus, Greenleaf found a proven way of making decisions that honored all voices and used some of his favorite strategies: silence, listening, and a reliance on *spirit* as expressed through individual insight. He also learned about the critical role of the chair—called the Clerk by Quakers—who makes consensus work. A Clerk is a situational leader, no better or worse than anyone else. He or she is a *primus inter pares*—a first among equals—not a final arbiter. Greenleaf observed Clerks closely, then tried out the role himself and developed an understanding of what it requires.

> First, there seems to be a critical quality of faith, a firm belief by the clerk that consensus is achievable no matter how deep the divisions seem to be. Any manifestation of anxiety by the clerk, either by manner or facial expression, no matter how subtle, practically assures that the meeting will get hung up. Then there is the art of stating and restating a possible basis for consensus, inventing and reinventing both ideas and language. Proceeding toward consensus on a controversial matter is slow, sometimes requiring adjournment for several sessions. It is true gradualism; it can take a lot of time and patience, especially by the Clerk. But the end result is worth it.[20]

Bob immediately saw applications for consensus decision making at AT&T. From his earliest days as a Quaker until the day he retired, he used the consensus approach until it became part of his natural strategy. He did not feel a need to write an internal memo explaining what he was doing, to become a consensus evangelist, or even to inform his colleagues they were involved in a consensus process—unless they asked. He just did it.

> In any meeting on a contentious issue, whether I was in the chair or not, I often emerged as the consensus finder by manifesting faith in the process and searching for the unifying ideas and language. . . . I sometimes either initiated, or was asked to serve on, a task force of senior managers who had the assignment to find an answer to a critical question. Consensus was important because a task force report with a minority opinion attached was not of much value. . . . I am grateful to the Quakers for giving me the opportunity to gain confidence and skill in the process before I took it into the sometimes highly charged business environment.[21]

Besides the fine art of consensus, Greenleaf learned a deeper meaning of persuasion from the Quakers—specifically, from one remarkable American Friend named John Woolman (1720–1772), whom Greenleaf cited in *The Servant as Leader* as a vivid example of a servant-leader. John Woolman's *Journal*—a spiritual autobiography—is a classic in American literature. In it, he tells how, in 1743, his employer sold a slave to a Quaker Friend and asked Woolman to write out a bill of sale. Woolman did so but was "so afflicted in my mind, that I said before my master and the Friend that I believed slave-keeping to be a practice inconsistent with the Christian religion. This, in some degree, abated my uneasiness; yet as often as I reflected seriously upon it I thought I should have been clearer if I had desired to be excused from it, as a thing against my conscience; for such it was."[22] One must use the imagination to understand the casual acceptance of slavery's contradictions in Woolman's time by otherwise good and ethical people.

> In 1743 scarcely a man in Christendom—a white man, that is—saw the injustice of slavery. There had been a few lonely voices—mostly Quaker—crying in the wilderness, but no general recognition that holding property in human flesh was un-Christian. Indeed, many Friends—those who could afford to—held slaves without compunction.[23]

Quakers were widely respected for their honesty in business dealings, humility, and simplicity, so their example as slaveholders was a powerful negative model. If any bothered to think about it, they might say, "Even the Friends hold slaves, so it must be proper."

After his sensitivities were awakened to the evils of slavery ("a dark gloominess hanging over the land"), Woolman was recorded as a Friends minister and began three decades of travel up and down the Colonies, persuading Friends to free their slaves and provide for them a new life.[24] He made his living as a tailor, although he also had experience as a surveyor, baker, merchant, scrivener, and planter. After one of his first journeys, he reaffirmed a key learning: "We were taught by renewed experience to labor for an inward stillness; at no time to seek for words, but to live in the spirit of truth, and utter that to the people which truth opened in us."[25] Be still; access inner wisdom; speak only when you have something to say. It is a good description of the way Robert Greenleaf approached life in his later years after absorbing the wisdom of Quakers.

But it was Woolman's technique for persuasion that most interested Greenleaf.

> The approach was not to censure the slaveholders in a way that drew their animosity. Rather the burden of his approach was to raise questions: What does the owning of slaves do to you as a moral person? What kind of an institution are you binding over to your children? Person-by-person, inch-by-inch, by persistently returning, revisiting, and pressing his gentle argument over a period of thirty years, he helped to eliminate the scourge of slavery from the Religious Society of Friends, the first religious group in America formally to denounce and forbid slavery among its members.[26]

Woolman's Socratic approach was strengthened by his congruent behavior. Even though writing wills and bills of sale for slaves was profitable work, more than once he refused to write wills for men who held slaves or planned of disposing of them by selling them. It was common at the time for Friends to feed and lodge itinerant ministers for free, but Woolman remembered the words from Exodus 23, 8: "Thou shalt not receive any gift; for a gift blindeth the wise, and perverteth the words of the righteous." Woolman wrote in his journal that "Receiving a gift, considered as a gift, brings the receiver under obligations to the benefactor and has a natural tendency to draw the obliged into a party with the giver."[27] (It was an insight Bob Greenleaf would pass along to nonprofit foundations in his later years.) Woolman did not wish to collude with slaveholders in any way that indicated he might approve of their behavior, but he sometimes felt a duty to reciprocate.

> The way in which I did it was thus: when I expected soon to leave a Friend's house where I had entertainment, if I believed that I should not keep clear from the gain of oppression without leaving money, I spoke to one of the heads of the family privately, and desired them to accept of those pieces of silver, and give them to such of their Negroes as they believed would make the best use of them; and at other times I gave them to the Negroes myself, as the way looked clearest to me. . . . few (Friend slaveholders), if any, manifested any resentment at the offer.[28]

Woolman's technique of asking questions, reinforced by his personal ethos and behavior, was a powerful tool in leading slaveholders to their own conclusions about the institution of slavery. Woolman did not believe he *personally* persuaded; he saw himself as a channel for others to become convinced *in their own hearts*, and for their own reasons. His approach was an extension of Quaker tradition; those who joined the Religious Society of Friends did so by *"convincement,"* a word that means one becomes convinced of the truth of the Quaker way through inward reflection and mature commitment. Still, Woolman always ran the risk of being seen as judgmental, which would have hindered his work. He was saved from that trap through his consistent acceptance of slaveholders as persons of worth and honor. "What is most essential to remark is how, hating the evil and loving the slave, he never ceased to embrace the evildoer, the slaveowner, in his love," said historian Frederick Tolles.[29] This was how George Greenleaf treated his political enemies in Terre Haute, and what Bob Greenleaf meant when he wrote, "The servant as leader always empathizes, always accepts the person but sometimes refuses to accept some of the person's effort or performance as good enough."[30]

Greenleaf cast a critical eye on the Quakers' ability to create an organization that could sustain Fox's original vision and wondered if the Friends' difficulty in doing so was not the result of a blind spot in the vision itself. Prudence had dictated some internal organization for early Quakers, mostly based on geography. Local gatherings held in homes were called Preparative Meetings. These participants joined together in increasingly larger numbers for Monthly, Quarterly, and Annual Meetings, where business was conducted. Through the years, Quakers quarreled over various theological issues, resulting in four branches of the movement by the early twentieth century. They became a diverse denomination but, as Greenleaf the institutional watcher saw it, not a coherent one.

> The Eucharist holds the Catholics together but the Quakers don't have [a unifying element] so they range even further in their diversity. But as an institution, they were born of an anti-clerical revolt. When Luther postulated his revolution he made a big point of the priesthood of all believers, but he didn't really work out what this meant in practice. . . . The Quakers had a priesthood of all believers all right but they also had no leadership (after the first generation) so they've never really made much of a mark with it. . . . I think the problem still remains—how do you have a priesthood and still have a priesthood of all believers?[31]

Bob had an answer:

> The first task of the growing edge church is to learn what neither Luther nor Fox knew: how to build a society of equals in which there is strong lay leadership in a trustee board with a chairman functioning as *primus inter pares*, and with the pastor functioning as *primus inter pares* for the many who do the work of the church. Having accomplished this, the second task is to make of the church a powerful force to build leadership strength in those persons who have the opportunity to lead in other institutions, and give them constant support.[32]

Greenleaf's ideas about how Quaker processes could apply to other faith traditions, and his ability to use them effectively at AT&T, shows how he was able to integrate religious-based learnings without insisting on rigid doctrine. At AT&T, he simply acted for persuasion and consensus as he understood it, made time for reflection so the "Light within" could provide inspiration in the moment, and felt no need to be a Friends missionary. His example would be witness to his beliefs. This approach is markedly different from the approaches of people who believe effectiveness depends upon publicity, personal recognition, and accept-ance of the latest "system." It is also different from the approaches of those who believe witness to faith means witness to a particular *doctrine* of religious belief.

By continually testing theory—and theology—in the real world, Bob was also applying the philosophy of education he espoused to Dr. Cowling: learning is transformative—to the learner and others—when it is experiential. This was an operating assumption throughout Bob's life, from the algebra classes he taught in Cleveland, to his training and development activities at AT&T and his later consultancies with schools, businesses, and foundations.

Bob's Quaker contacts would soon enable him to meet a new circle of impressive leaders, including Eleanor Roosevelt. First, however, there was an urgent family matter to attend to: the birth of another child. In 1939, Esther paid a third visit to the hospital's maternity ward. This time the delivery went well, and Providence gave them a daughter, whom they named Anne. Esther fed Anne, dreamed her daughter's dreams, and established that mystical bond which it is only given to mothers to know.

All was not well with the infant, however. She soon contracted an infection all too common in hospital nurseries of that time, one for which there was no treatment in those pre-antibiotic days.[33] Doctors told the Greenleafs they would have their daughter no longer than a week.

While she still could, Esther cuddled, cooed, and held Anne Greenleaf. Bob brought his twin-lens reflex camera into the hospital, rolled Anne's crib into the light streaming through a large window and parked it next to a warm, old-fashioned radiator. A vase of congratulatory flowers sat on the windowsill, slowly wilting. Bob frantically took one snapshot after another of his daughter, seeking to preserve some piece of her short gift of life. One can only guess how he felt when the pictures slowly emerged in his home darkroom developer tray, illuminated by an eerie red safe light.

Loving their daughter was not enough to save her. As predicted, Anne was gone within a week and only the pictures remained. Once again, Bob and Esther were crushed by the death of a child, but Esther was devastated. After the funeral, she went home to take care of Newcomb and face her raw grief. Bob returned to his demanding work at AT&T, where he could at least stay busy and productive.

Bob, in fact, had a new project to occupy him. In early 1939, a seventy-two-year-old man named John Lovejoy Elliot took a train from New York to Philadelphia to meet with Clarence Picket, Executive Secretary of the Friends Service Committee. Elliot was active in a movement called the New York Society for Ethical Culture. Years earlier, he had started the Hudson Guild Neighborhood House, helped people on New York's West Side organize to help themselves, established the League of Mothers' Club among the settlements, and founded the School for Printers' Apprentices. In 1938, Elliot negotiated with the Nazis to secure the release of two leaders of the Vienna Ethical Society from prison, and now he was back home to start the Good Neighbor Committee, which would help European refugees resettle in America with language instruction, work training, and economic assistance.[34]

Elliot asked Mr. Pickett, "Is there a live Quaker in New York who would work with me on this Committee? I know plenty of dead Quakers who are alive in the flesh, but I don't want any of them." Pickett told him about a young AT&T man named Robert Greenleaf who was "bound to be a little more alive than some of those old Quakers."[35]

Soon thereafter, John L. Elliot appeared at Greenleaf's AT&T office and introduced himself. He had come to 195 Broadway to ask Bob to be an incorporator and first treasurer of the Good Neighbor Committee. John was the President, Eleanor Roosevelt was the Chairman, and Clarence Pickett had told him that "the Quaker should be treasurer because people trusted Quakers more than other people." Bob gulped and said, "Sure." [36]

Bob traveled up to Hyde Park to meet the First Lady, then served on the committee with her and John Elliot through the life of the project. Years later, he reflected on the experience. "This was a very interesting occupation for a short number of years. This [Committee] didn't perform very long; ultimately all the refugees made whatever adjustments they were going to be able to make. But in the course of it, I got very well acquainted with John Elliot and his history, and what had led him to be the kind of 'cause man' that he was—the starter of useful work. This left a very deep impression on me."[37]

Bob only knew Elliot for several years—he died in 1941—but they shared an impulse to be a *seeker* in the present, rather than an unthinking follower of past tradition and revelation. In 1926, Elliot had written, "Profound as the respect and reverence of any man must be for the religions of the past, I cannot stand in awe before them. But I am filled with the sense of wonder and awe in the presence of the spiritual nature as it manifests itself in the daily lives of men and women."[38]

The exposure to Elliot got Bob and Esther interested in the Ethical Culture movement, which was founded in 1876 by Felix Adler. It defines itself as not a secular humanist, but an *ethical* humanist, movement. From the beginning, Ethical Culture stressed "deed over creed." The proof of one's efficacy was in behavior, not theology. Adler wrote that "the creed is a formula, something that can be recited, a profession of faith, and experience shows only too clearly that the profession may be on the lips or even in the mind and yet remain without effect in practice. Deed then, not creed, [means] the effect on actual conduct to be the test of any philosophy of life." Years later, Bob would incorporate a similar pragmatic standard in his "best test" of a servant-leader, a test that was graded by outcomes, not motives, right theology, or personal theories. [39]

Adler admitted to a motivating religious impulse in founding the Ethical Movement but claimed no exclusive revelation. Like Buddhism, the Movement was not theistic. God was to be found in perfect divine life that undergirded all existence, not a divine being. For Adler, "the essential life of the universe is perfect and therefore divine. The two words perfect and divine are synonymous."[40] It was not a mainstream Christian religion, but then Bob and Esther were never very traditional in their religious choices, and for some years they attended both the Ethical Culture Movement and Quaker Meetings.

Esther became pregnant again in June 1940. In August, Bob began a personal journal that he called "the record of a search for a more effective life—a life that is continually useful in some constructive contribution to the common good, a life of richer experience with my family, my friends, my community, my business associates, the trades people, the man who cuts my lawn for me, and with my inner self. This, I expect to be the record of a search without end."[41] In the first entry, Bob was reflective in a way that was more joyful than in many of his later entries. Perhaps he was anticipating the birth of his child or simply feeling the youthful juice of being alive.

> Spend all you have for loveliness. Buy it and never count the cost for one white, surging hour of peace. Count many a year of strife well lost, and for a breath of ecstasy give all you have been or could be.

> The rewards of living a full life may be measured in joyous moments rather than in days or years. These are the treasures that return to mind in the quiet hours of the declining years: the moments nobly lived, challenges met, the truth spoken, the slur turned aside, the tumult quelled, the helping hand extended, the simple expression of gratitude, the burden borne—these all. Meeting life and feeling the response of living—taking responsibility, prudently if possible, but taking it and leaving it joyfully once taken. Setting one's courses on a star and steering toward it, minding not the reefs that waylay.[42]

After the death of two children in hospitals, Esther was wary of the standard medical care of the day. Besides, she grew up in a family where it was normal to explore alternative medical treatments. She decided she wanted her next child born at home, where there were no hospital nursery infections, and found an obstetrician in Manhattan who would accommodate her wishes. So the Greenleafs packed once again and moved back to New York City. Elizabeth (Lisa) was born at home, 1435 Lexington Avenue, New York City, on March 28, 1941. She survived, and thrived, to become a brilliant artist like her mother.

With two children, it was time for the Greenleaf family to look for a home of their own. In late summer, 1941, they found it—for $7,000—at 27 Woodcrest Avenue in Short Hills, New Jersey, a suburb on the Lackawanna Railroad line. The timing was right and Bob knew it, because he expected a war. Sure enough, after Pearl Harbor, housing became tight and they would have had a rough time finding a house.[43]

> The two-story home was a wonderful place to raise children and get away from the jangling busyness of the city. It had four bedrooms, two baths, a large kitchen and pantry, dining room, living room with fireplace and a gracious front porch, all situated on one acre of land. It needed a lot of work, with the first order of business replacing the coal furnace.[44]

By moving to Short Hills, Bob had made an unusual choice, one which the self-proclaimed "insider/outside" later explained to Newcomb. "He said they deliberately moved to New Jersey because all the AT&T top brass executives lived up in Westchester. If he had lived in Westchester, he would have been expected to join that country club crowd, even at his level in the company. He definitely did not want to do that. 'Country club' was a swear word in our family. Yet, Short Hills became a country club town later on, after their move there. It was hard on us growing up in a family that regarded country clubs as terrible, terrible institutions in a town where the social life was centered on country clubs."[45]

Bob, Esther, and the children—including one to come—would live in the Short Hills home for twenty-eight years. There they would plant a magnificent organic garden in the back yard. Bob would put on his bib overalls and frolic with the children of visitors. Esther would continue her artwork, and Bob would eventually join her in artistic creation, expanding his earlier views on what was "proper" in art. By the time of their next move, Bob would be on the verge of his most important triumph. But that was all in the future. First, there was a war to endure.

CHAPTER 11

Quaker at War

Simply practice being aware. Look, and be still. Feel, and be still.
Listen, and be still. Give the practice of awareness time, time when
you are alone.[1]

ROBERT GREENLEAF

Pearl Harbor ruptured the last vestige of American isolationism. Now
the European war was also America's war, and companies of every size
were mobilized to produce more, faster, and better. AT&T was one such
company, and Robert K. Greenleaf was in the thick of things.

Corporations were urged to take advantage of every available human
talent in support of the war effort. In 1941 Bob was moved from the
AT&T's Plant Operations section—with oversight of personnel around the
country—directly to the Personnel Department. One of the first things he
noticed, even before Pearl Harbor, was the absence of black people in non-
menial jobs. He thought that situation should change. The Personnel staff
in Manhattan was relatively small, with about thirty female clerks. Bob interviewed every one of them, told them he intended to hire a black
woman and asked how they felt about it. Years later he recalled, "They all
said 'fine' except one who said, 'Well, when she comes, I go!' and by golly

she did. But anyway, we hired the first non-menial black in the (AT&T) system, and it worked out pretty well. The other girls took her in socially, and when I retired, she was still there—still in a clerical job, but it was a non-menial job."[2]

When America entered the war, it was clear that AT&T would need to work closely with the government to win the conflict. In fact, the United States formally declared AT&T's communications network and the Western Electric production facilities as military resources. Bob was a Quaker by "convincement" so he did not fully share the pacifist leanings of cradle Friends. Still, he pondered the ancient ethical dilemma of using force in the service of a greater good.

> What about love for one's fellow man? What about the use of force? Can one use force which may mean doing violence to somebody, and do it in the spirit of love for fellow man in the broad sense?
>
> These are indeed perplexing questions and those in authority are not of much help; eminent men so contradict one another that the layman is confused rather than benefited by their counsel.
>
> For my own part there is an acute inner conflict. Personally I am averse to force—that is, I don't want to get my own hands in it. Yet I believe that an orderly world must impose some restraints and that these are morally right and exercised in the spirit of love for fellow man. I see no essential difference between the power exercised by the policeman and that exercised by an army. Yet I personally want no part of either but feel them to be necessary. That poses a neat moral question; have I any right to live under the protection of someone who takes risks and does the dirty jobs that I can't bring myself to do?[3]

As it turned out, Bob did everything he could in his position. After passing rigorous security clearances, he and his boss were listed as Consultants to the Board of War Communications with the right to look at classified documents, the only people in the Personnel Department with secret clearance.

There was plenty of work, because the government saw AT&T's network and Western Electric's manufacturing facilities as giant security problems, wide open to sabotage and espionage. It fell to Bob and his boss to do the legwork to investigate and certify key people around the country, decide which employees were so valuable they should be exempt from the draft, try to meet the almost impossible security demands imposed by wartime civilian and military planners, and negotiate with people in the highest levels of government. Because of his boss's abrasive personality, many of the negotiations eventually landed on Bob's desk. "I had some lousy bosses along the way and one of them was during the war," he later recalled.

> I was home taking a few days of vacation during the summer and I got a call from this boss saying that he had been down to Washington and started some negotiations with one of the government agencies and couldn't go back to finish it. He would send out the papers if I would go back down (to Washington) and pick up the negotiations. I said, "Sure."
>
> So I went down and walked into the chilliest ice box I've ever been in. Boy! This was really frigid! We slugged away all day, trying to negotiate whatever it was we had to work out, and I kept wondering, "Now, what the hell is wrong here anyway?" At the end of the day I invited these fellows to go out with me. I plied them with a few drinks then I finally said, "Now, what the hell goes on here? This is the chilliest thing I've ever been in." Well, they said, "If you want to know, we'll tell you! That fat man (my boss) came down here and really pushed us around and called us a couple of snotty little bureaucrats. Finally we said to him: Look, you get out of here. If we count ten and you are not gone we will call security and have you thrown out."
>
> I didn't know anything about this. My boss had sent me down to feed the wolves because he had literally been thrown out![4]

Bob did not run into the office of AT&T president Eugene McNeely and tell him about the incident. In fact, McNeely was unaware of it until well after the war. Nor did he speak unkindly about his boss around the office. He did his job, bided his time, voiced his opinions directly to bosses when they were solicited, and tried to operate with integrity in his own sphere of operation.

During this period his informal influence grew within the company, especially with President McNeely. Bob was able to help him get things done precisely because he was *not* "empowered" to do so. It makes an interesting story because it shows how Bob applied his Quaker learnings about persuasion within a hierarchical, bureaucratic organization, and did so *without* the formal authority so important to many managers. Here's how it worked.

Bob recognized that McNeely was in a position to coerce and manipulate, but not persuade, employees. He held too much power to persuade, because others would wonder about his hidden agenda. "Have you ever tried to persuade someone whom you were sneaking up on?" asked Bob.[5] So, Bob did the persuading.

> Every once in a while I would find myself listening to McNeely talking about a nettling organizational problem, someplace where the outfit was really snafu, and he wouldn't know how to get at it. If, after listening, I felt I understood what he was talking about, I might say, 'Gene, would you like for me to get into that to see if I can straighten it out?' And he would say, 'Please do.' Now, he would never *ask* me to do that because if he asked me, I would be empowered. In other words, I would be seen as his agent; but if I volunteered on my own, then I was on my own. I would have to rely on persuasion.[6]

"Persuasion" meant something different to Bob than it does to many modern thinkers on the topic. We know that John Woolman was his model for a master persuader, and that Bob learned the process in Quaker meetings and applied it in the workplace. Here is Greenleaf's own definition of persuasion:

> Persuasion involves arriving at a feeling of rightness about a belief or action through one's own intuitive sense. One takes an intuitive step, from the closest approximation to certainty that can be reached by conscious logic (which is sometimes not very close) to the state in which one can say with conviction, "This is where I stand!" The act of persuasion, thus defined, would help order the logic and favor the intuitive step. But the person being persuaded must take that intuitive step alone, untrammeled by coercive or manipulative stratagems of any kind. Persuasion, on a critical issue, is a difficult, time-consuming process. It demands one of the most exacting of human skills.[7]

Word eventually got around that Bob might be acting at President McNeely's behest, and for awhile it spoiled his ability to persuade. In other employee's eyes, Bob was now empowered by the president with what was, to Bob's thinking, the most limiting kind of power.

> I think if top managers could realize the tremendous liability of holding this power, and how it really disqualifies them to persuade, they would know they can't be accepted as a persuader. A persuader can't have an axe to grind. This is part of the problem of our structures. We've never thought through what to do with persuasion when you set up a hierarchical structure, and yet many don't know any other way to organize [their structures].[8]

The war dragged on, and everyone was expected to do his or her patriotic duty. At their Short Hills home, the Greenleafs had a large victory garden (encouraged by Uncle Sam so commercially-produced food could go to the fighting forces), but Bob wanted to do more. He decided he could make a small contribution to the war effort by becoming a beekeeper in his spare time. Sugar was scarce and, besides, some strange attraction drew him to bees. As usual, he read all the books on the subject he could find, then outfitted his yard with hives and the proper apiculture accoutrements, bought enough head coverings, gloves, and body insulation to dress a knight in armor, wrapped strong rubber bands around his pant cuffs and long-sleeved shirt cuffs, and waddled forth to his destiny with bees.

Greek mythology tells us that, in return for the honey that sustained him, the infant Zeus gave bees their sting, to be used only for defense. Because they abused this power, Zeus sentenced bees to death whenever they used their stingers.[9] Zeus and Bob Greenleaf murdered a lot of bees that way. He was stung repeatedly and never developed immunity to the venom's effect, as the books said he should. "I was not a natural beekeeper," he wrote. "They didn't like me, and I didn't like them. It was a bad deal."[10] Newcomb vividly remembers those days. "We were always fascinated with photographs in *Life* magazine of some guy with bees crawling over him, because that was not our experience with bees. You got close to the hive and they were after you."[11] One day a hive began to swarm and went after the neighbors—and succeeded. One hapless woman stood on her back porch and cried while she combed bees out of her hair. It seemed like a good time for Bob to give up his three-year-old bee business. The war would have to be won without the honey output from the Greenleaf hives.

Fifteen years later, though, an amazing thing happened, an odd gift of stinging-insect grace.

> I was eating a picnic lunch out of doors, and the yellowjackets were out in force, being their natural annoying selves. . . . My rational estimate of yellowjackets would be definitely lower than bees, and bees and I didn't get along. To my surprise, this day I felt no annoyance at the yellowjackets, and I found my hand going out for them to crawl on if they wanted to—and some of them did. Later I found that this urge extended to all stinging insects, including bees . . . Now I find that something has been added to the interest I originally had in bees: I have an *affection* for them and their kind.
>
> These natural gifts, these dispositions to hold attitudes that give largeness of self, come unannounced. They have a newness and a freshness about them, and sometimes they go when they are most wanted. One cannot ask for them because until they have been given, one really doesn't know what they are.[12]

A further point of this story is Bob's *openness* to novel experience. Others with a similar history of bees and stinging insects might have discounted the strange impulse to allow yellowjackets to climb on their bare flesh. Bob did not; he paid attention and took the risk.

Paying attention—cultivating heightened awareness—was a major theme of Bob's life and work, one that receives little emphasis from contemporary admirers of his writings. Bob liked the Freudian image of consciousness as an iceberg. Nine-tenths of what we know lies "below the waterline," in the realm of the subconscious. For those rich resources to be useful, we need to bring them "above the waterline," into conscious awareness. Heightened awareness is not the same as intuition but is important for the intuitive leap. Sometimes this awareness is a life-or-death matter. Pilots of small planes, for example, are trained to always be aware of emergency landing sites in case the engine unexpectedly fails.

One day during the war, Bob used his "above-the-waterline" consciousness to save a man's life on the subway.

> The doors had closed on his arm as he was about to enter [the subway car], and he could not get loose. The conductor failed to notice as the train took off, dragging the man down the platform to certain death if the train was not stopped before he reached the end of the platform. . . .
>
> I became aware of the emergency by the commotion at the end of the car. A crowd converged on the door, clawing at it and shouting, 'Stop the train!' 'Open the doors!' An emergency cord hung overhead. No one pulled it. A similar cord was in the opposite end of the car. No one near it was going for it either. Two or three precious seconds went by before I realized that it was up to me; so I ran for the cord at the opposite end, bowling over a few people as I went. And I made it just in time.[13]

Bob wondered why he was the only regular subway rider who knew where the emergency cord was located, so he conducted his own research on the matter. For the next few months, he described the subway incident to various acquaintances—all daily subway riders—and asked what they would do. "Pull the emergency cord!" they answered. "All right," Bob said, "There are three subway systems in New York, and the cord is in a different place on each system. This is the Independent line. Where is the cord? You have about five seconds to act: one, two, three, four, five." He tried the test on about fifty people, then gave up. No one could answer.[14]

Bob concluded that "very few people accept that this is a dangerous world—morally, physically, intellectually—and hence [they] do not choose to be aware of where they are, who they are, what kind of world they live in, or what [the world's] traps and hazards are." [15] The responsible person, the person of heightened awareness, accepts the dangers but is not paralyzed by them. He or she prepares for emergencies by predetermining how to respond in emergencies.

> Awareness is a combination of a constant conscious scanning of the environment and the concurrent searching question, "What would I do if I were in the action spots within my view?" The scanning is done partly by reading and listening to language. But it is also direct and elemental looking, listening, smelling, feeling, and constant questioning: "What is going on here?"

Above-the-waterline thinking is important for more than emergencies, however. It is the essence of life—and leadership.

> The trap that sometimes brings failure to otherwise successful people is to substitute routine for awareness. Awareness is a constant reaching out and responding to everything in the environment: the people, the sunset, the sounds of the street, the smell of flowers, the clackity-clack of the subway wheels. It is not tiring or boring. In fact, it is quite the opposite: it is the essence of life. Be able to withdraw into the silence, but do not turn off the current to the antenna so that you miss the signal that will bring you back in a flash.[16]

Bob's views on awareness were not abstract or idealistic. One is again reminded of the training given pilots. Most people know an avid private pilot they would call a "flying nut." This person seizes any excuse to mosey out to a little airport, hop into a small thirty-seven-year-old machine that weighs less than a car—and sometimes even costs less—"kick the tires and light the fires" and soar into blue sky. Even in clear weather (VFR in pilot lingo), pilots must constantly scan instruments, watch for outside traffic, work the radio, check course headings, observe checkpoints, notice possible emergency landing sites, manage fuel, listen for funny engine noises, comfort passengers, and simply fly the plane. It does not sound like much fun given the high stakes of failure, but they are addicted. Not many pilots are poets, but most are laconically articulate when it comes to flying. If you ask them why they pursue such an expensive and time-consuming pastime, they usually pause for a moment, get a faraway look in their eyes, and say something like, "Well, I feel pretty alive up there; I come back refreshed. I do have to focus to fly the plane, but I enjoy doing that as well as I can because I don't want to 'buy the farm.'" For pure pilots, heightened awareness is an end in itself and a matter of life and death, just as it was for Bob Greenleaf and that man on the subway train and, according to Bob, just as it is for each of us every day.

When he reflected on the narrative of his own life, Bob always referred to a pivotal idea he embraced when he was about forty years old. He claimed it came from a magazine article titled "The Uses of Old People," written by Hoosier radio commentator Elmer Davis.

> The gist of the article was that there are useful and necessary things
> to be done that are best done by old people, partly because old peo-
> ple have greater perspective of experience, but mostly because the
> things that need to be done do not fit into a career or they are too
> risky for young or mid-career people. He advised that younger peo-
> ple should look forward to old age as presenting an opportunity to
> be prepared for, rather than as a time to be put out to pasture when
> one wears out. It was a persuasive argument and, again, my doors of
> perception were open a bit wider than usual and that message came
> through loud and clear: begin now to prepare for what can best be
> done in old age.[17]

Greenleaf went on to describe how, after having his insight to prepare
for old age, he eschewed trivial pursuits like golf and bridge (which he
never engaged in anyway) and spent the years between forty and sixty in
preparation for his later years, *even though he did not know what he was
preparing for*. There is no doubt that Bob had been "preparing for old age"
since he was a young man, turning his avid curiosity and lust for learning
towards thinkers and doers and Big Ideas. In this case, however, he got
the timeline wrong, confusing an article by Elmer Davis with one by
Catherine Drinker Bowen.[18] No matter. The idea of preparing for old age,
when it came, simply crystallized something he was already doing—
preparing for later years by pursuing vivid learning and vivacious people. There is no doubt he did so to "be useful," to make a contribution
inside and outside AT&T's womb, but he also had a practical reason. He
was already thinking about an early retirement. Bob did not know what
he would do then, but he wanted the freedom and credentials to do it
well and make a difference. His response to Bowen's article was another
example of heightened awareness; he was open to the fleeting idea of
preparing for old age, was willing to take it seriously and, ultimately, prepared to change his life because of it.

In between having babies and creating a stable home life, Esther continued her artwork. She had long since moved beyond the representational
period she entered for Bob's sake and had begun painting and exhibiting
more abstract pieces. Bob, who was now an enthusiastic partner in her
modernist efforts, hung six of her paintings in his New York office: three of

her representational works and three abstracts. It was unusual to have so many paintings in an AT&T office and most visitors commented on them, which gave Bob a chance to expound on matters artistic.

> They would look around and say, "Well, these representational pictures, I think I know what they mean, but I don't know what these others mean." The answer I evolved was, "Well, these representational pictures of objects are music with words, and the abstracts are music without words. After all, instrumental music is abstract; it's just a concoction of sound and rhythm and it doesn't have any meaning. You either like it or you don't and that's all there is to it. This is the same way. It's a concoction of color and form that has no meaning. It's just the way she felt, and color and form interested her more than being a camera and recording something."[19]

Bob was not only proud of Esther's work; he was enjoying his own explorations into painting, pottery, and jewelry making, all under her tutelage. He set up a workshop in the basement where he began making heirloom furniture, using his hands to create something tangible. He was growing in every way.

So was his family. Madeline Greenleaf was born in New Jersey's Orange Memorial Hospital on January 30, 1943. She completed the Greenleaf family, but Bob's education as a father was just beginning, at the precise time his professional competence was reaching new heights.

12

Researcher and Teacher

I believe we are entering a period in which the institutional struggle to survive will usher in the "age of the development of human potential" . . . and the frontier for the second half of the twentieth century will be creative achievement with the thinking, feeling, acting, and growing of people.[1]

ROBERT K. GREENLEAF, C.1955.

War may be Hell, but the increased knowledge it generates spills out of Hades and into all of peacetime society. World War II saw an explosion of knowledge that went far beyond radar, military tactics, and more efficient ways to blow fragile human flesh into smithereens. While the guns were blazing, men and women had to be recruited, evaluated and trained—quickly and efficiently; they had to be managed, transformed into spies in enemy cultures, killers on the battlefield, and healers in the hospitals; they had to be *led*. Bob Greenleaf was destined to embrace some of that hard-won wartime knowledge about how to select the right people for available jobs and use it to change the history of personnel assessments in American business.

It all started one morning in October 1943, when the war was in its most furious hours. At an executive staff meeting of the super-secret Office of Strategic Services (OSS), Colonel G. Edward Buxton, who was filling in during the absence of legendary Director William "Wild Bill" Donovan, heard a suggestion from psychologist James A. Hamilton that the OSS should establish a psychological assessment unit modeled after Britain's War Office Selection Board (WOSB). [2] Its main purpose would be to weed out those military and civilian recruits who could not stand the stress of working behind enemy lines while they gathered intelligence, sabotaged facilities, organized resistance, and operated in the never-never land of independent action under overall military direction. The assessment unit needed to do more than eliminate people with obvious defects, however. It also had to spot individuals who combined specific skills with the capacity to improvise creative solutions on the spot, unusual people who could work alone or with a team and embrace a commitment to die for each mission if necessary. No existing tests could measure such things, but the need was great. "We simply must have men who can shoulder responsibility and use initiative with common sense," wrote one field commander. "We have had at least eight men, who for various quirks in their make-up have had to be pulled from the field. One was definitely a psychiatric case."[3] Another wire from the field was more pithy: Send us "a few first-rate men rather than a boatload of mediocrities."[4]

Buxton and Donovan approved the idea of an assessment unit. Colonel Henson L. Robinson saw to organizational details, while Harvard's Dr. Harry Murray quickly gathered a group of brilliant and sometimes-quirky scholars, researchers, practitioners, trainers, and intelligence experts at "The Farm," a country estate forty miles outside Washington in Fairfax, Virginia, which came to be known as "Station S" or "S School." The core group included such men as Dr. (later First Lieutenant) John W. Gardner, Ph.D. and, eventually, the brilliant social psychologist Kurt Lewin as project consultants. Dr. Murray, who had already made significant contributions to surgery, biochemistry, biology, physiology, and psychology, was a perfect leader for this group. He was described as "a unique combination of thinking machine, dreamer, two-fisted drinker, and scientist whose inner driving force suggests a band of Scotch Presbyterians raising from their knees to do the will of God."[5] Their mandate: figure out how to evaluate, select, and prepare civilians and military recruits to be effective spies, saboteurs, organizers, and even killers, not just in Germany and Japan but in Africa, Asia, South America—anywhere their services would be needed.

In December, the unit evaluated its first batch of recruits using *organismic*—or Gestalt—principles, explained in the book. "Some standard procedures, elementalistic in design, were included in our program," they wrote in their report, "because the best of these instruments is especially efficient in picking out disqualifying defects of function and so in eliminating men who are definitely inferior. Organismic methods, on the other hand, are to be recommended in addition whenever it is necessary to discriminate unusual talent, to measure ability in the range running from low average to high superior."[6] In other words, the unit sought to evaluate the whole person, using what they called "multiform" instruments in order to make "sufficiently reliable predictions" of suitability.[7] Their arsenal included written tests, interviews, problem-solving challenges, and contrived situations that allowed them to make judgments on capacity for leadership, teamwork, psychological health, and physical endurance. OSS staffers took note of *every* behavior by recruits: where they sat, what they ate, how they spoke, which bunks they slept in, what they talked about in informal moments, how they responded when challenged by OSS people who masqueraded as lowly staffers at Station S. The psychiatrists even got them drunk to see if they could hold their liquor without letting go of secrets.[8] Every person was assigned a fitness category after a thorough review of test results and personal impressions by all trainers. By the end of the war, 5,391 recruits had been assessed by the OSS in one-day or three-day periods. Successful recruits were then sent on for further training before being placed in the field.

Validation studies covering the first eight months of 1944 showed an impressive success rate for graduates—including a large number of young women—operating in the European Theater of Operations. "The percentage of unsatisfactory cases was found to be 0 (zero) in four of the six branches, whereas in one of the two remaining branches this figure was 6 percent, and in the other 14 percent."[9]

In 1946 Bob Greenleaf read an article in *Fortune* magazine, titled "A Good Man Is Hard To Find," that described the OSS assessment work.[10] The book *Assessment of Men*, describing the work of the OSS unit, was published in 1948; in May of the following year, an article titled "An Executive

Development Program" in *Personnel Journal* described an assessment program developed by The Mead Corporation that drew heavily on the methodology of the OSS unit.[11] But even before those publications, Greenleaf saw the relevance of formal assessment in a business like AT&T, which—like the OSS—also needed to predict the suitability of individuals for employment and promotion. This possibility was recognized by the OSS's own staff, who wrote in 1948, "It would not take much ingenuity to modify some of the techniques and to invent others of the same type to meet the requirements of other institutions."[12]

Bob realized the importance of timing, however. He knew that the new AT&T president—a slick, hard-driving, abrasive, but financially savvy man—would likely not approve such an effort, so he put the *Fortune* article in a file and bided his time.[13] In the next few years, he dropped hints here and there that the company might look into an assessment program some day but wrote no memos, mounted no visible promotional campaign, and twisted no arms. He was patient, as patient as George Greenleaf had been thirty-five years earlier standing quietly in front of a broken steam engine until he had gathered enough information—and intuition—to do something useful.

In 1951, the time was right. After only a few years in office, AT&T president Leroy Wilson died of leukemia and was replaced by Cleo Craig, one of Bob's old bosses. Craig was a somewhat introverted intellectual, a diplomat who personally despised company politics, a whiz with numbers, and a leader who was not afraid to give subordinates wide latitude in how they did their jobs. More importantly for Bob's assessment project, Craig understood the importance of research.[14]

Still, Bob began slowly, in a stealth mode. During the next few years, he invited prominent psychologists and researchers to make presentations to key managers and executives so that they could learn what he already knew: although there was plenty of research about the developmental cycles of children, there was almost none about adults. It was as if people quit growing intellectually, emotionally, and spiritually the moment they reached the age of twenty-one. Only recently had psychologists like Carl Rogers and Abraham Maslow been focusing on human potential rather than psychopathologies, and no research had yet focused on the capacities and adult development cycles of managers.[15] It was probably during this period that Bob had a conversation with Newcomb that revealed his personal strategy on this and so many other efforts. "Over the years I am sure that my father tried many times to pass on to me some of what he had learned," recalled Newcomb.

> While I generally paid little attention, one lesson was so surprising that it did stick in my mind. "Suppose that you had a really good idea for your organization. How would you go about trying to get it accepted?" It must have seemed a strange question to me, and I don't recall how I responded. "This is how I have learned to do it," said Bob. "First, decide who are the key people in getting the idea adopted. Then begin to tell them the idea, but only suggestively and a bit at a time. Let them come to the idea themselves, so that they think that it is their own idea." "But how will they know that it really was your idea?" I asked. "They will never know," he answered, as if that were the core of the beauty of the stratagem.[16]

It would be several years before a full-blown assessment effort, along the lines of the OSS model, could be mounted. In the meantime, Bob became involved in multiple overlapping projects, each of which moved the giant bureaucracy toward a more precise—and often innovative—process of executive selection and development.

To understand how he arrived at the place where top executives and the Board granted him nearly universal trust in these efforts, one must look at a presentation for which he became famous within AT&T and its hundreds of operating companies. It was called by various names through the years: "What Is A Manager?" "Executive Ability" or, in its printed version, "Management Ability." Bob gave the talk to managers at all levels within the company. In the Acknowledgment section of a version printed by Pacific Telephone, the original author is listed as anonymous, but the Division Plant Manager goes on to say, "There is no doubt that [the author's] wisdom and delivery are evident between the lines, giving credit to his effort."[17] Most people who had been around the company awhile knew the author was Robert Greenleaf, and a drawing of a green leaf on the pamphlet cover was a sure giveaway.

The gist of the talk was a succinct definition of *operational* (not theoretical) management ability—also called "executive ability" in overheads that survive of his in-person presentations. Here it is: *"Management ability is the ability to state a goal and reach it, through the efforts of other people, and satisfy those whose judgment must be respected, under conditions of stress."*[18] Greenleaf expands on each phrase of the definition and then notes that bosses have the problem of deciding who is "developable" as a manager. "Will I bet my chips on this person or will I bet them somewhere else? I haven't enough chips to bet on everybody. . . but I still have to make this decision." To give guidance on that decision, Greenleaf outlines further considerations, starting with the "Basic 'Good' Man." (When Greenleaf developed this talk, every manager *was* a man.) His bullet-point summary gives a fair idea of the content, but it omits the richness of the written explanations— and of Greenleaf's style of writing, which is far more folksy than in his later essays. It is, in fact, reminiscent of the writings of Norman Vincent Peale, Napoleon Hill, or the best authors of American success literature— conversational, with a liberal sprinkling of apt stories.

Greenleaf covers the basic points one would expect in a short treatise on management abilities: integrity, effective intelligence, enthusiasm, attitude, skills, money sense, time management, and communication. But he also works in "Greenleafian" themes that one would likely not find anywhere else, even in today's management textbooks. A few examples:

> The older senior manager has the notion that he can accelerate the development of a young understudy if he can take him aside and say: "Look, Bud, I've learned it the hard way. This is how you do it. This is the essence of the Art of Management."
>
> Apparently this can't be done. Although a philosopher would probably be horrified at this definition, wisdom might be defined as the ability to face a practical situation and, without enough data, swing on it and make a decision that holds up with time. It is something which apparently cannot be passed from one man to another. Everybody has to learn out of his own experience. If I, as the young understudy, happen to look up to the fellow I happen to be working for and have a great deal of respect for, and if he undertakes to pass on his wisdom to me, I might just be so gullible as to try to incorporate it in my way of working. And the chances are, if I do, I have taken on a limitation. Wisdom is not acquired in this way . . .
>
> The idea that growth is an arithmetical process, that a man is something like a straight-sided bucket (not a very good bucket) in which it takes the same amount of water for every inch you raise the water, and that growth—human growth—is a matter of adding

for each increment of growth an equal amount of knowledge and experience, apparently isn't the case. As a man progresses in a business hierarchy, each level introduces a wider and wider scope of operation. He must learn as he goes along to compress the amount of information it takes for him to operate with respect to any situation . . .

In any situation does your "basic good man" automatically ask, "What's cooking here—what's going on—what's eating this fellow?" rather than to swing on it first and then ask the questions? This is a fairly critical requirement. If you had someone on whom you were going to bet all of your chips—a fellow that you really wanted to go all out to develop—and if you had a chance to rub Aladdin's lamp and bestow one trait on your basic good man—one rub, one wish—this is the one you should give him. Other things being equal, the man who gets this feeling first, will go the furthest. . . . He sees people as ends as well as means . . .

Am I clear about my faith? This can be taken in any way—as a religious belief or as a philosophical belief—but people who take risks believe in something. You don't venture without something, some feeling of certainty about what you're venturing into. In other words, faith is certainly about something about which you haven't got the evidence to be certain. To take a risk you have a belief that it's worth taking—and that's faith.[19]

The *Management Ability* pamphlet was used for years after Bob retired from the company. In 1970, one executive wrote Bob, "I often smile when a young manger says, in commenting on the booklet, 'These thoughts are really new and great.' A wish today would be for a sequel, yet I also feel that this need can be served by rereading and striving to do better in carrying out the principles outlined in the original. You did leave many of us a code to live by."[20]

The *Management Ability* talk and publication, plus Bob's years of research and work in evaluating and developing managers, made him the logical choice to spearhead an innovative program that developed executives through exposure to the humanities—the Bell Humanities Program. It ran full-bore from 1953 to 1958 and continued in shortened forms until 1970.

The AT&T humanities program to develop executives had its roots in the 1920's, when Chester I. Barnard, whom Greenleaf called "a genius," was vice president of the Bell Telephone Company of Pennsylvania and arranged for promising young executives to take courses in the humanities at the University of Pennsylvania.[21] By 1952, one of those young men, Wilfred Gillen, had risen in the ranks to run the Bell System operating company in Pennsylvania. He persuaded AT&T president Craig to revive the program. Bob Greenleaf was given the assignment of making it work.

The first effort began in the fall of 1953, when twenty middle managers, along with their families, settled in at the University of Pennsylvania for a *ten-month* course designed by the university, paid for by AT&T, and offered under the umbrella of U. Penn's Center for Humanistic Studies.[22] The curriculum included courses in logic, music, art, American civilization, architecture, and city planning—even a course on *Ulysses*.[23] By 1960, one hundred thirty-four managers had participated in this program. In 1956, Dartmouth and Williams colleges began shorter, eight-week humanities programs for AT&T executives, and similar programs were developed at Northwestern and Swarthmore. Through 1964, nine hundred forty-three middle managers were exposed to the Bell Humanities Program.[24] Every university offering the short courses developed a slightly different curriculum, but most included units on philosophy, American history, law, art, music and literature, economic thought, and social history.

One wonders why a corporation would go to such expense for so few people, with such uncertain results. Greenleaf provided the answer in a historical background to the humanities program. Beginning with the Great Depression and extending through the austerity of World War II, hiring and organizational development was restricted. By the postwar years, top leadership was aging and retiring. The need for well-trained new blood was crucial, because AT&T and its operating units numbered over two hundred-fifty companies.[25] Furthermore, the world was different. "Looking back," said John Markle II, "we see that our predecessors were concerned mainly with production, sales, finance, and technological advancement."

> Today, in addition to these matters, we feel the effect of the increasing influence of social, political, and economic changes which have taken place; and a business now has to consider itself in relation to the community, to the nation, and to the world—as well as its position within its industry. The Institute was not set up to help along the cause of the humanities or liberal arts, however deserving, nor was it aimed at making dilettantes out of businessmen.

The program was treated like any other business decision; that is, a particular approach was applied to a current problem in management development because it was felt that the money would be wisely spent and, in due time, would pay off. [26]

As Greenleaf discovered, there were precious few ways to fairly determine the long-term impact of such a program, and Mr. Greenleaf was a demon for evaluations. Faculty did their own assessments and Bob sponsored several company efforts along those lines. He never expected immediate business results from the investment. "The only objective for manager education which seemed dependable for the future," he wrote, "was that of inculcating a research and experimental attitude toward work and a sustaining interest in personal growth."[27] In 1957, he hired Douglas Williams Associates to evaluate that year's Northwestern University one-semester course, taught to nineteen executives. The report showed that participants "overwhelmingly liked [the experience], considered it worthwhile, and felt it to be of value to self *and* the Company." Participants reported more tolerance of other peoples' views; they were more likely to take more risks, consider complexity, and factor in broader issues when making decisions, and "five of the nineteen explicitly stated that they looked more now into the background of a person to seek a decision's effect on thought and behavior—*the whys*. . . Virtually every man left Northwestern with a heightened awareness of and interest in 'social, political, and economic' problems and concerns." Most participants had their awareness heightened so much they were critical of the company's policies during the then-current recession. The faculty was equally enthusiastic: "They find it a stimulating experience to work with our men, and they believe that it has helped them do a better job with their regular teaching."[28]

Even though he gave full credit to each participating university for designing the humanities courses, Bob was deeply involved in discussions with deans and faculty members, helping shape the curriculum, offering contacts for outside speakers—like Peter Drucker—and often serving alongside the speakers as a visiting lecturer. The most impressive teacher he met during this period was Dartmouth's John Finch, who spent the summer with tough, experienced executives digging into Shakespeare's history plays. Bob told the story of a "sensational" class he observed with the master teacher.

In Richard II the young Prince Hal had a rousting companion, the buffoon character Falstaff. When Hal becomes king, this fellow is no longer a suitable companion for a king, so Hal cuts him out cold; this is real brutal. In this particular class session there were fifteen level-five people, all of whom were somebody's candidate for a general officer, so they were a real hot gang. Among them was a big six-foot, 4-inch ex-Marine captain from World War II, a wonderful guy but just hard as nails.

Professor Finch said, "Now you fellows aren't king yet, but you might be. Have any of you ever had a Falstaff you had to cut for the same reason as Hal?" Fourteen guys in a row said, no, they never really had that experience. When he got to the ex-Marine, the big guy leaned out on the table, gave these guys a cold look and, in his best "Marine captain language," biting every word, said, "You sons of bitches! Every goddamn one of you has had your Falstaff! You ditched him for the same reason that Hal did, and I know it!" He started with man number one and, pointed to each of the fourteen guys in a row. They all sheepishly admitted that, well, now that they thought about it, they'd done that.

Nobody who was there would ever forget that moment if they lived to be a hundred. It took a master teacher to bring that off, and I am sure that he knew who was man number fifteen when he asked the question, and that this would probably be what would happen."[29]

Greenleaf believed in the value of exposure to the humanities. He and Esther had always done it on their own, attending concerts, lectures, and poetry readings from their earliest days together in Greenwich village. In the case of the Bell Humanities Program, he was leery of the way the program was initiated. Douglas Williams was there and later reflected on the humanities effort and another program that was dumped in Bob's lap at around the same time, an effort to turn installers and repairmen into salespeople who promoted new equipment for residential users.

Each of these ideas had been the creation of one highly placed officer [AT&T President Craig], thinking that his "creation" would be advantageous to the Bell System. To be successful in the Bell System, new changes had to be *hammered* throughout the top ranks so there would be general support before the change was put into effect. The fact that this had not been done meant these two innovations were doomed. . . As Bob would, he gave it his best shot, knowing the odds.[30]

Bob was also concerned about the way participants for the humanities program were chosen. None of the top people who picked candidates for the program used the same criteria. "Often they would not select a likely candidate because he was too valuable in his current job," recalled Douglas Williams. "They might pick a person who already had a liberal arts degree because he would be 'at home' in this course (just the opposite of what was intended). Or a man would be selected who had performed well in a risky venture, or was perhaps tired from the grind he had been on for a year—as an award to 'get away from it all.'" [31]

Sure enough, when Frederick R. Kappel replaced President Craig in 1956, it was the beginning of the end for the Bell Humanities Program. In 1958, a high-level committee recommended that support be withdrawn for the programs at Pennsylvania, Swarthmore, Dartmouth, and Williams. They would be partially replaced by a new Management Objectives Program (MOP) with a tighter focus on business issues. The MOP curriculum, started at Dartmouth, was designed by AT&T staff under Greenleaf's direction, but it still incorporated elements of the humanities. Three courses emerged for the eight-week session: "(1) The Language and Literature of Decision (taught by a professor of English); (2) Analytical Thinking (taught by a professor of philosophy); and (3) Leadership and Goal Setting (taught by a representative of [AT&T—usually Bob Greenleaf.])"[32] MOP continued at Dartmouth for ten years.

Simultaneously with all this activity, AT&T ran a four-week course for department heads at Asbury Park, New Jersey, called the Bell System Executive Conference. Begun in 1953, the Executive Conference had three goals: to broaden thinking and outlook, to increase present effectiveness, and to stimulate interest in further self-development.[33] In the course of studying economics, international problems, social developments, and a score of other issues, participants were treated to frequent lectures by some of Bob Greenleaf's buddies: historians, sociologists, psychologists, ethicists, and theologians among them.

The Executive Conferences were not cheap. From November, 1953 through June, 1955 alone, the total cost, including conferees' salaries, was $1,387,500, and this was just one of several management development programs underway during the same period.[34] Outside speakers included Peter Drucker and other management consultants; Edwin Nourse, former Chairman of the Council of Economic Advisers; professors from MIT and the Harvard School of Business; one or two super salesmen, merchandisers and accountants; and Dr. Edwin Aubrey, Professor of Religious Thought at the University of Pennsylvania.[35]

In reading through reports of various top executive committee meetings about the direction of executive education and the traditional and non-traditional courses AT&T offered throughout the 1950s, one is struck by the fact that Robert K. Greenleaf is usually listed as the secretary or simply as a representative. He almost never chaired the high-profile committees, even though he would have been the logical choice to head many of them. "As any who have had the assignment can testify, the post of *ex officio* secretary to such a prestigious group as the committee of Presidents can be a very influential one," he wrote in the final report on the Bell Humanities Program.[36] This was his favorite way of getting things done: staying under the radar, exerting quiet influence, and positioning himself as a listener who could assist in probing, clarifying, and building consensus.

In the midst of his duties for the humanities program, Bob had not forgotten about his dream of a comprehensive assessment project. When he judged that enough support would be in place, he went to President Craig and proposed a small, contained project to assess just one group of beginning managers, all recent college graduates. In order to see how accurate the assessments were, the company would conduct longitudinal studies (that is, research would be repeated at intervals) and track the careers of assessed managers. Craig approved the project.

Bob believed the current methods of assessing and orienting new hires was a mess. Bell Labs, Western Electric manufacturing facilities, Long Lines (which provided long distance service), and the scores of regional Bell companies all used different methods of assessment and orientation, so there really was no consistent method.[37] Of particular concern to Bob was the practice of making beginning managers spend their first months— in one company, the first two years—on rotating assignments in every area of the business. The idea behind this was that "experience is the best teacher" and that new employees should get an overall picture before getting on with their individual jobs. Bob thought this was a waste of time and money, but there was no data to support or refute his position, and there was plenty of emotional attachment to the old way just because things had always been done that way. He knew that if he began by suggesting elimination of companies' long-held programs, his assessment idea would never be approved. Best to sneak up on it.

In 1956, Bob hired his most important ally in the assessment effort: Dr. Douglas W. Bray, a Yale-trained psychologist who had worked with the Aviation Psychology Program in the Army Air Force during the last year-and-a-half of the war and since then had built a distinguished career as a researcher. Like Bob, Douglas Bray had also been impressed by the book *Assessment of Men*, shared Bob's concern with actual behavior rather than theories about behavior, and held the belief that the whole person should be evaluated with a battery of tests.[38] Bob turned Bray loose to design the first assessment program, hire staff, and conduct follow-up longitudinal studies, while Bob managed ongoing support from the AT&T president and board. Finally, ten years after Bob conceived the idea of a comprehensive assessment effort, the program was underway!

In the summer of 1956, Dr. Bray's staff administered a week-long battery of assessment procedures to the first group of seventy-four beginning managers from Michigan Bell Telephone. Like the OSS, AT&T's staff discussed each person individually to make final judgments, considering results from written and oral tests, specialized tasks, personal observations, and interviews. Bray then followed up with his longitudinal Management Progress Studies, a task that eventually took twenty-five years of his remarkably productive career and made him a legend in the field of assessments.[39]

When Bray's first annual follow-up report came in, Bob was vindicated. New hires found it devastating to wait for months—or even years—before getting on with their careers. With hard data in hand, he was able to change that ineffective practice in many operating companies. More importantly, he and Douglas Bray had invented the idea of corporate assessment centers. Within two years, other AT&T operating companies were begging for similar programs. Top executives who would never have approved the initiative now bragged about it. In its first four years of operation, the program assessed four hundred twenty-two beginning managers from various AT&T companies. Within a decade, the idea had spread to other corporations, and thousands of assessment centers were operating all over the world. Bob later called his support of assessment work "one of my greatest contributions" to AT&T.[40]

Bray dedicated his book *Formative Years in Business* to Robert Greenleaf and always had fond memories of his association with the supervisor who supported him as he changed corporate history. "His style was to listen and encourage good ideas rather than discourage bad ones. He was not a rigid, patterned kind of guy but was relaxed and open. Bob never said, 'Do it my way.' If you were in the ballpark, he simply encouraged you. I never had a problem with him. He never questioned that what I was doing wasn't right."[41]

The Management Progress Study ended with the breakup of AT&T in 1984, but it still stands as one of the most impressive research projects in the history of American business. Among its many contributions was its emphasis on the whole person, an exploration of human capacities rather than liabilities, and emerging "life themes" of adults.[42]

Before he ever heard of the assessment work of the OSS, Bob was well-prepared to understand its significance. Even though he often said, "I am not a scholar," by the end of the war he had developed into a crackling good researcher, with personal knowledge accumulated from hundreds of studies. Bob knew there was nothing mystical about research. It was simply an organized way to get close to the truth of a matter—not the full truth, because that was seldom possible when it came to personnel issues—but the pieces of truth one could reasonably observe, measure, and manage.

In the course of his travels during the 1930's, Bob occasionally visited the Western Electric Hawthorne Works, a manufacturing plant in Cicero near Chicago, and heard about some unusual research going on there. The results of the famous "Hawthorne Studies" were destined to transform management and usher in a new era of human relations in business. Bob Greenleaf was in the middle of it all; he knew the key players and used their findings in his ongoing work at the company. The Hawthorne results eventually validated Bob Greenleaf's personal views about management-worker relations, but the findings gave him more than personal satisfaction. They also offered a proven set of principles about effective listening.

The Hawthorne Studies began in 1924 with a simple experiment based on a reasonable hypothesis: that worker productivity varied according to the level of illumination in the work area. If substantiated, this hypothesis would have validated Frederick Taylor's Scientific Management idea that managers could twiddle with the external environment and, like automatons, workers would move production up or down in response to changes. It would also have been a boon to General Electric, which sponsored the original study with the hope of selling more light bulbs to manufacturers. But a funny thing happened on the way to tabulating results. Productivity went *up* every time the light levels went up, went down, or changed in any way. In fact, researchers had to dim illumination to the level of moonlight before it affected output negatively. Other factors must have been affecting worker behavior, but what were they?[43]

In 1926, Hawthorne executives and outside investigators were joined by Harvard Business School professor Elton Mayo, an Australian with training in psychology, philosophy, and worker relations. In a study of fourteen men in the "bank wiring room," Mayo's team discovered that group norms among workers were more important than external variables. Researchers then tested other variables on a group of female workers who assembled electrical relays and discovered that an increased number of five-minute rest periods did help production ("Gee, that's the berries!" said one worker), but that fatigue and workday length had negligible effects. The researchers' overall conclusion would shake the corporate world and make Frederick Taylor's assumptions about worker motivation obsolete. Their report said, "The mental attitude of the operator toward the supervisor and working and home conditions is probably the biggest single factor governing the employee's efficiency."[44] Or, as another contemporary writer put it: "The ability and willingness of the supervisor to listen rather than to shout orders; to know and understand each worker in his group; to be genuinely interested but not domineering; these are some of the aspects of good supervision that turned out to be vastly more important than hours or rest periods or method of payment in improving the mental attitudes of the employees and thereby increasing their productivity as well as their satisfaction."[45] Participants in the studies felt valued because they had been listened to, and they knew that their opinions mattered. They had more control over their situations and less conflict with management. They developed internal motivations for performance that were more important than external conditions.[46]

The Hawthorne studies caused an earthquake in management circles. Imagine a screen upon which traditional assumptions about workers had been projected since the beginning of the industrial revolution: individual people were expendable and replaceable like gears in a machine; the main role of managers was to crack the whip and keep up quotas; human alienation and loss of community were inevitable at work and, in fact, had nothing to do with one's work; bosses were there to boss and workers were there to perform or be fired, regardless of the human cost. The Hawthorne studies ripped down that screen of projected assumptions, revealing the soft human flesh and diamond-hard human spirits that it had masked. The "Human Relations School of Management" was born, and its new gospel was supported by solid research which showed that attention to group and individual human factors increased productivity and profits.[47]

Once the Hawthorne team realized the importance of clean communications vertically (up and down the hierarchy) and laterally (between workers), and the power of simply allowing workers to express themselves, they created a position never before seen in an American corporation: the counselor. The counselor was not a therapist, nor was he or she a go-between who solved problems by shuttling messages between workers and supervisors. In fact, counselors had no formal authority at all, for three reasons. First, employees at every level "might not feel free to discuss their problems. . . They would tend to communicate to [the counselor] only those aspects of their situation which would place them in a favorable light . . . In the second place . . . vesting authority in the counselor would tend to weaken the supervisor-employee relationship because it would inevitably take from the supervisor some of his responsibilities in dealing with his people." Finally, the counselor was primarily oriented toward the human problems of the organization and should not usurp the prerogatives of the supervisor, who was responsible for other areas besides human resources.[48]

Counselors acted a lot like Bob Greenleaf when he volunteered to look into some matter for the AT&T president. Their power came from the fact that they had no traditional power, no axe to grind, no overt or covert mission to accomplish beyond improving each person's experience at work. They also acted like the Quaker Clerks who sought to understand each person's point of view through listening and restating positions.

What did counselors actually do, then? How could any company justify their salaries? Theirs was a specific function of "adequate diagnosis and understanding of the actual human situations—both individual and group—within the factory."[49] In other words, counselors found out what was on people's minds, asked questions, listened deeply, and explored possible courses of action that could be taken *by the person being counseled.*

As present-day therapists know, a role like that requires good training and clear ground rules, but the Hawthorne people learned that the counseling role need not be restricted to professionals with advanced degrees. Counselors were recruited from men and women who had a sincere interest in people and their problems and were able to make that interest evident. They modeled the kind of behavior they wished others to express toward them. Counselors (also called "interviewers" by the company) guaranteed absolute confidentiality and were taught to assiduously refrain from making any value judgments about what they were told. "The interviewee must feel free to say anything he wishes to the interviewer, and this process is not encouraged if the interviewer registers approval or disapproval." The counselor "sees to it that his own sentiments are not acted upon by those of the speaker" because "the counselor's sole object is to lead the employee to a clear understanding of her problem such that she herself comes to realize what action to take and then assumes responsibility for taking it."[50]

Bob Greenleaf was already aware of the power of listening. He had been teaching some of these same skills and attitudes to managers in Bell System facilities around the country. "True listening builds strength in other people," he wrote years later in his famous essay.[51] For him, listening was about *doing* (learning listening skills) and *being*—bringing one's full presence to the encounter. Fritz Roethlisberger, one of the primary Hawthorne researchers, held a similar view.

> [While listening] there is awareness of the growth problems of individuals and the rhythm of growth—ascents, plateaus, declines. There needs to be awareness of what is not being said as well as what is being said. Awareness of feeling-tone is very important. Undercurrents of feeling need to be sensed. Someone may have a feeling of urgency about a problem or an idea, and he may not be expressing it except by subtle signs. These must be seen and understood.

> Openness to communication is the tendency to view everything heard or seen (or sensed in any way) with unqualified wonder and interest. Later, for purposes of analysis or action, one may form a value judgment about what he or she saw and heard. But the initial attitude and response would always be: "This is interesting. I wonder what the meaning is—what is being said to me?" [52]

Roethlisberger was the man who inspired Bob in 1939 to design his first formal listening course for AT&T. Through the years, he taught it hundreds of times.

As airy as the Hawthorne counseling program may sound to hard-nosed business people, it was successful for over twenty years. Five employee counselors were on the Hawthorne staff in 1936. The number peaked at fifty-five in 1948 and went back down to eight in 1955. When new management took charge, he program was discontinued.[53]

Greenleaf had his own insights about the Hawthorne studies, based on his personal experience with key players. Besides Dr. Mayo and his colleagues, Bob credited four Western Electric executives with the passion and vision to pursue the research: works manager Clarence Stoll, his assistant C. L. Rice, Rice's superintendent David Levinger, and superintendent G. A. Pennock, all "unusual men in the human side of enterprise." When the last of these four retired, the counseling program began its fatal decline, but Greenleaf believed that it was successful in its heyday because it was congenial to the culture already established by these four remarkable people and that "its justification was philosophical rather than statistical." In fact, when other manufacturing plants attempted to introduce a counseling program, "it usually was rejected, sooner or later—not because it was either a right or a wrong thing to do, but simply because it was not congenial with the whole culture . . . Compatibility of method and culture is as important as understanding organic compatibility of human tissue."[54]

It is an irony of history that, among researchers, the "Hawthorne effect" has come to mean a phenomenon that *skews* scientific results. If a study shows better employee attitudes or higher productivity after a change, that could simply be because management cared enough to make *any* change and ask about it, or encouraged different behaviors through the act of observing behaviors. This criticism has substance if behavior changes are not lasting (or supported by the culture), but it is questionable if research is based on the same assumptions that were disproved by the first Hawthorne illumination studies, especially the idea that external changes are more important motivators than personal or group interactions. "We take data from which all human meaning has been deleted," wrote Elton Mayo colleague F. J. Roethlisberger, "and then are surprised to find that we reach conclusions which have no human significance."[55] Rather than learning the big lessons from Hawthorne, too many repeat the original mistakes. "The results were not screwy [in the original Hawthorne studies], but the experimenters were!" [56]

For years, AT&T had invested millions to understand public attitudes toward the phone giant. A statistical research division within the company handled design, methodology, and number crunching. After the war, interest grew concerning the attitudes of AT&T employees, and that research was assigned to Bob Greenleaf in the Personnel Department. In February of 1948, Bob made a speech before school administrators, titled "Human Relations Research in the Bell System," in which he summarized some of the ongoing work for which he was responsible. (Today those same studies would likely fall under the banner of "human resources.")

Greenleaf's humanistic approach to work and his recognition of corporate obligations to stockowners came through in his overview of personnel research. Like Theodore Vail, he believed that nurturing growth in people was the smartest thing a corporation could do for employees and for profit.

> In terms of time spent, one's job is a major factor in life. Whether that life provides challenge, interest, satisfaction, personal security and social status depends in large measure upon whether the job and the job environment provide these things . . . The Best Possible Force of Productive Employees, one that has the maximum opportunity to fulfill the expectations of people—*as individuals*—is our central objective. [Italics added]
>
> We view human relations research as the whole process of discovering and getting integrated into the business the useable knowledge about people and the conditions under which they grow and develop and do their best work. . . . At the same time, this obligation

> of management must be considered along with the other obligations to the owner and to the customer. These obligations dictate that we have work to do.[57]

Some of the studies on which Greenleaf reported were quite large; others were so informal as to not be considered legitimate research. A cooperative labor-management study interviewed three–hundred fifty management people, the president of AT&T, one–hundred fifty union officers, and one thousand non-management people. Other projects looked at criteria for employment, selection of supervisors, emerging employee attitudes, and the relationship of supervisors to those being supervised.[58]

The latter study, of supervisors and the supervised, was conducted by AT&T district superintendents who were given training in methodology and evaluation. One of Greenleaf's favorite strategies was to involve company employees who were close to the action, rather than farm the research out to professionals. Ever the realist, he knew that if results were to lead to action, "it usually requires of those who are asked to accept it that they change some well-established personal point of view or habit. Experience indicates that people do not readily change a well-established habit or attitude simply because they know about a better way and concur that it is superior."[59] This insight is the reason he wanted to make managers part of the research team. "We believe that the way to accelerate the discovery, acceptance and use of the best human relations principles is to involve as many management people as possible in research, to apply a good learning principle—participation in discovery—as an important means of moving toward the central objective."[60] Participation, an approach too often ignored in corporate studies, is validated by Michael Q. Patton, one of the contemporary legends in research evaluation.

> In essence, research and my own experience indicate that intended users are more likely to use evaluations if they understand and feel ownership of the evaluation process and findings; they are more likely to understand and feel ownership if they've been actively involved; and by actively involving primary intended users, the evaluator is training users in use, preparing the groundwork for use, and reinforcing the intended utility of the evaluation every step along the way.[61]

Bob liked to assign two-person teams to behavioral research tasks—trusted employees who had some basic knowledge of research but were not too elevated in the hierarchy. "If a study team is well chosen, a curious development takes place. The team attacks the problem with more than twice the determination and zest than either member would have separately."[62] He insisted on sound methodology; after all, Bob had learned from the masters. The team had to agree on the criteria for a study, establish benchmarks for each of the criteria, and develop a study design for getting and analyzing quantitative and qualitative data. Both team members participated in gathering data, largely through interviews, but Greenleaf believed that "the valuable contribution of the team comes out of the 'huddle' after the interview. This is where the biases are canceled out and deeper insights and convictions are developed."[63] Team members were forced to agree on the data and what it meant, which required skills of rational analysis, collaboration, and intuition. "Ultimately, [a team member] would acquire a feeling of certainty about [the] assessment. Then [one] could be said to 'know'," said Greenleaf.[64]

Bob believed the team approach was good for the company and good for development of participating individuals.

> Study teams will reach conclusions and make recommendations that persons in high positions of authority would hesitate to reach and make! The study team members can do this partly because they do not have formal authority—no one will be coerced by their recommendations—and partly because they have been commissioned and have been freed to develop the insight out of which firm conviction is born. Therefore, they speak with the kind of authority that only wisdom bestows.
>
> A study team does its best communicating [to management] orally. Something of the members' conviction and firsthand insight gets into the general stream of management knowledge.[65]

Bob also used research assignments as a way to nurture, mentor, and challenge up-and-coming employees. More than once he put roadblocks in the way of team members, just to see how they responded.

Since moving to New York in 1929, Greenleaf had also learned about the scientific applications of research and development from the people at

Bell Laboratories. He jumped at any chance to go visit the facility at 463 West Street in Manhattan and, after 1941, at their modernistic building in Murray Hill, New Jersey. He loved to look at the gadgets and spend time with some of the best scientific minds in the world. Even though he never wrote about those conversations, he would have had the opportunity to speak with people like John Bardeen, Walter Brattain, and William Shockley, the team that invented the first transistor in December 1947. Other Bell Labs employees gave the world the first sound motion picture, the first electrically operated digital computer, long-distance television transmission, the fax machine, the laser, cellular telephone technology, communications satellites and, of course, the touch-tone phone.[66] The people at Bell Labs both plumbed the realities of the physical world, just to understand nature (pure research), and invented new technologies to apply their findings in practical ways (technology).[67] That mixture was not so different from the methods of the Management Progress Study, which conducted basic research into adult lifecycles and drew conclusions for application of that new knowledge in the corporate structure, and in programs that fostered the growth and applications of individual human skills.

Bob's favorite room at the Bell Laboratories' Murray Hill location was the anechoic chamber, an enclosure that was absolutely silent. The avant-garde musician John Cage once sat in a similar chamber. When he emerged, he complained that the room was not totally quiet as advertised; he still heard noises in there. Engineers asked him to describe the sounds and then gave Cage an explanation. "The low sound you heard was blood flowing through your arteries. The high sound was your nervous system in operation." Bob Greenleaf, the lifelong meditator, the introvert who had to act in public roles every day, reveled in the chamber's total silence. He would sit on a chair on the suspended wire-mesh floor, surrounded by foam baffles that allowed no audio reflections, and stay until they kicked him out, lost in the richness of the void.[68]

Meetings With Remarkable People

I have a philosophy. I call it the hole-in-the-hedge philosophy. There isn't much to it. You don't bother much about goals, plans, accomplishments. When you see a hole in the hedge, and the grass looks greener on the other side, you go through. If you don't like it over there, you can come back. You can even be fickle about it and go back and forth while you make up your mind. As a matter of fact, you don't worry much about making up your mind. Something usually happens to make it up for you.

It isn't a philosophy that is likely to make you rich or famous or even do much good in the world. I don't recommend it to the ambitious or the overly serious. But you have a lot of fun. Also get into some trouble.[1]

ROBERT K. GREENLEAF, 1954

In midlife, a wondrous gift often comes to those who have made themselves eligible through curiosity, learning, and openness to the bitter—and sweet—juices of life. A more complete solar system begins to take shape in the evolving psyche. The young sun of self-centered ambition and petty ego transforms into a more mature, life-giving source of solid values. Old planets of abiding interests find their proper orbits; fresh knowledge and spirit give shape to emerging bodies; a passing comet of insight may be captured and made a permanent part of the structure. This is still a time of dynamism, of *seeking*, but the shape of the search becomes clearer. The mind works faster and makes richer, deeper connections; heightened powers of discrimination filter out trivial knowledge. It is the time of the beginning of wisdom.

Robert Kiefner Greenleaf had such a time in the years between 1946 and 1964. The once-budding astronomer sought to populate his internal solar system not with dead planets, but with the luminosity of astonishing men, women, and ideas. He found them everywhere, and many of them, including the ideas, sought *him* out.

Shortly after the war, AT&T aided Bob's emerging inner cosmology by putting him in charge of executive development for the entire system. This responsibility was an addition to his duties overseeing all personnel research. He was a confidant to the company's president and various board members. Douglas Williams knew Bob well during this period.

> One of his most important responsibilities was that of an informal consultant/adviser to rising stars destined to become associate company presidents or stellar vice presidents at the top of AT&T. They wanted these strongly developing officials to be helped in their rise by working with Greenleaf. After they got to the top, many of these men continued to consult with Bob. Intuitively, Bob was a good listener, [which was] of enormous significance in this role of his.[2]

Formally, Bob was an assistant vice president at the fifth level, but that did not mean much to him. He had created every one of his operational titles since his early days in New York. He was once offered a promotion to vice president but turned it down. According to his daughter Madeline, "He said they'd make him do things he didn't want to do." Besides, said Newcomb, "There was a certain level in the phone company at that time where they all played golf together; they all belonged to a certain small collection of country clubs."[3] Bob was neither a golfer nor a country clubber. What was important to him was to be in a position that gave him the latitude to scurry through any interesting hole in the hedge. By the end of the war, he was free to work with every stratum in his far-flung organization, to initiate projects, coach, mentor, persuade, teach, scheme, and fulfill Professor Helming's advice to change his company from within. He was also free to choose interesting assignments outside the company, which gave him the opportunity to meet top thought-leaders and work with interesting organizations.

Bob's *informal* titles did have meaning to him because they were chosen by others. He was variously known within the company as "The Conscience of the Bell System" and "The Abe Lincoln of AT&T."[4] An incident that happened in 1958 shows why Bob was held in such high esteem and also demonstrates his willingness to show his sword when it came to spending the company's money responsibly. Bob recalled the event in detail:

> The public relations people were taken in by a couple of hucksters who were selling an economic education program and set up a conference to let these fellows tell their story. This was a big meeting of about twenty-five people—three presidents of companies, assorted vice presidents of this and that, and a couple of vice presidents of AT&T, including my big boss and his subordinate who was my immediate boss. I think I was the only executive in there who wasn't an officer. These fellows were given a couple of hours in the morning to make their presentation.
>
> They weren't very far into it until it didn't smell right to me. So I went out to a phone and called my office and got one of my fellows. I told him what was going on, who these fellows were and what they were selling, and I said, "Put everybody on it. I will call you back at noon and I want to know what you found out about this." So I went back and listened to the rest of it. They were very smooth, slick salesmen. They did a good job, and we adjourned at noon.
>
> I called the office during lunch and got a report on these guys. It was absolutely damning. This was a very sleazy outfit; they had a bad reputation. I had no idea how they ever got this far. So we reconvened after lunch and it was evident from the initial conversation that they had made a sale.
>
> Well, in this conference was a fellow who I had hired when I was in Ohio, a great, long-time friend. Big man, shock of white hair, a very impressive guy, good voice and all. He apparently had eaten

too much at lunch. When we reconvened, he sat down back in a corner and went to sleep while the discussion continued. When they were about at the point of concluding that we would buy this I passed a note down to my boss and said, "Hang on to your hat. I'm gonna shoot this thing down!"

So I took a deep breath and first said, "Before you make up your mind I want to tell you what I did this morning," and told them about the work that our gang had done. I am sure the combined resources of the CIA and the FBI couldn't have done a better job than my gang did in a couple of hours. They had absolutely damning reports on these two fellows and their wares, and I gave it to them with both barrels. I said. "Now this bothers me. I am really the 'low man on the totem pole' in this meeting. Why the hell was it up to me to do this? If this much assembled brass could be taken in by a couple of slick hucksters like this it really shakes my faith in the future of the business. I think I will sell my stock," and I sat down. There was a stunned moment of silence and they all started to talk at once, and some of them were shouting. Oh, it really was a donnybrook.

My friend Jack woke up when the party got noisy, rolled his eyes and took in the situation: this was Greenleaf against the field. He pulled his chair up to the table and in his strong stentorian voice, started to pitch on my side when somebody promptly challenged him. "Jack, what the hell goes on here? You've been asleep back there. You don't even know what this fight is all about!" Jack, who was a man of great poise, leaned back and with laughter in his voice and tapping on the table, said, "I know I've been asleep (long pause still tapping), I know I don't know what this fight is all about (another long pause, still tapping), but one thing I do know, I know which side I am on!" And there was a roar of laughter. The fellow chairing the meeting said, "Well I can see we are not going to settle this at this meeting," adjourned the meeting and the topic never came up again.

You can imagine I didn't earn any great credits from my public relations friends for that![5]

The informal title in which Bob most delighted was given by president Cleo Craig, who once introduced him as AT&T's "kept revolutionary." Perhaps Bob liked this impish comment because it acknowledged the role he secretly chose for himself when he joined the company in 1926. Craig blew his cover, but also blessed him for his unusual corporate efforts. Around the time Craig made the comment Bob wrote, "I stay put, keep poking around at holes, spend remarkably little time doing what other people want done. [I have become] a sort of professional at this hole-in-the-hedge business. Hole-in-the-hedge men must be patient, must live a long time, and ultimately come to be viewed as slightly peculiar."[6]

Douglas Williams described what it was like to spend time with Robert Greenleaf during this period.

> He had an ever-present, chuckling sense of humor. He was one of the most enjoyable men to be with I have ever met. I keenly remember that talking with Bob in his office at 195 Broadway was a stimulating, gratifying experience. He would pull out the lower drawer of his desk put a foot on it, lean back, put his hands behind his head and look at the ceiling. He was a person with whom you could engage in participatory thinking. I always felt the better after partnering with him.[7]

Bob always remembered the motto of one of his early, impressive bosses: "If it ain't fun, it won't get done!" and noticed that it was natural for that same able supervisor to lead so that other people grew. "It wasn't something that he was trying to do because somebody told him he ought to. That's the way he wanted to be; life was more fun that way. . . . I think that's a test. If it's grim, it's probably not going to work very well." [8]

After the war, Bob realized that "henceforth the military establishment would be a much larger factor in our peacetime society than it had ever been before. Since I had no military experience I concluded that I should cultivate relationships with the military people."[9] He worked on small projects with the Army and Navy but forged his closest relationship with the Air Force. He was given security clearance and a formal appointment: Consultant to the Secretary of the Air Staff. In that role, he gave talks to high-level officers in the Pentagon and was a regular lecturer for several years at the Air War College at Montgomery Field.

In one presentation on "Listening—A Basic Executive Skill," presented to the Third Air Staff Management Development Conference, Greenleaf showed his mastery as a teacher. He began by asking questions and responding to the answers, using the key technique he would be teaching that day—the skill of mirroring a statement, something he had learned from the Hawthorne counselors and psychologist Carl Rogers. For example:

General Eckert: "I wonder after listening to the other comments if we might not break this down into two categories: the listening that has to do with getting the job done—in other words, for decision purposes—and the other kind of listening, to get the most out of people. . . . The extent to which one should listen for this [latter] purpose, I don't know."

Mr. Greenleaf: "In other words, you have one level of listening which might be called 'information getting,' to get the points which other people have to contribute to the problem at hand. Then, you have another level of listening, where you are trying to understand what makes this fellow do what he is doing."

General Eckert: "And to stimulate him to get things done."
Mr. Greenleaf: "Yes."

During the session, Bob waited for the right question that would allow him to go into his prepared slides. It came soon enough: "How do you get from listening to results?" Greenleaf then presented bite-sized, bullet-point content and, after the break, asked for responses. Finally, he engaged the group in an experiential exercise based on the case study of a manager who got dramatically different results from a foreman by altering his approach to listening by using the mirroring technique.

Pedagogically, Bob was brilliant. He started with the learners' own experiences; modeled what he taught; combined content, experiential learning, and reflection; took care to relate his lessons to the military situation; and refused to indicate in any way that he had a final answer to fit all situations. "Now, in presenting this kind of an idea, I am not making any judgment at all about when it is appropriate to listen in this manner and when it isn't," he said in his summation. "It all depends on what your goals are at the moment, what the other pressures for your time are, how you would weigh the time that it would take against what you could do with that time doing something else. All I am suggesting to you is that if, in the course of your executive work, you find yourself in a position where you want to spend some time to understand the attitudes of other people, where you want to spend some time to influence the attitudes of other people, here is a skill by which it can be done."[10]

The session was also an example of Bob's approach to persuasion. Preaching and moralizing to this group of powerful men would have been counterproductive. It was more effective to let them make the intuitive leap and decide for themselves the rightness of his position.

Greenleaf enjoyed his years working with military leaders and, in a way, was comforted by the people he met.

> I found the military mind was not materially different from the managerial mind in industry. I found social relationships within the officer ranks of the Air Force to be more democratic than in the managerial hierarchies I was familiar with. The upper echelons of the Air Force are staffed with exceedingly able people—and I did not find them to be "trigger happy" people, not as disposed to be belligerent as some comparable people I knew in industry. It was reassuring.[11]

Through the years, Bob had read the work of Kurt Lewin, the German-Jewish refugee scholar who brought his family to America in 1933. Lewin started his academic career studying medicine but shifted to psychology, philosophy, and mathematics at the University of Berlin and became passionately committed to doing social science.[12] Lewin brought rigor to experimental research on topics most thought were beyond the reach of legitimate scientific inquiry at the time: needs, hopes, fears, aspirations, personal will, anger, leadership styles, group dynamics, and the social climate of groups and minority groups. These were exactly the issues that engaged Greenleaf. "[Lewin] demonstrated that such work could meet the accepted standards of scientific research by using operational definitions of variables, control groups and experimental groups, outcome measures, etc.," wrote Lewin's daughter. "He developed a mathematical approach to psychology that he called *topological psychology*. He also wrote about his philosophy of science for psychology, which he called *field theory*."[13] Many of Lewin's ideas gave context to discoveries made in the Hawthorne studies, especially his key insight that behavior can be understood as the function of interaction between the person and his or her environment, expressed in his famous formula: $B = f(P,E)$.[14]

Lewin was known as a practical theorist ("There is nothing so practical as a good theory," he wrote in 1943), but he was also a philosopher of science, a transcendent teacher, and a shrewd, perceptive observer of human nature who could clear his mind of preconceptions and be open to the here and now. During the war he pioneered "action research" which involved asking those being studied—in his most famous case, housewives—to change things in some way and then studying the effects. Like Greenleaf, he loved to have fun along the way and was "commonly described as being enthusiastic, encouraging, lively, innovative, congenial. . . . Rather than being a grand system builder or a charismatic patriarch, Lewin comes across more as an osmotic stimulant, or a catalyst of new thought."[15] One can see why Bob was attracted to this scholar, even though they had never met.

In 1945, Lewin founded and led a research center at MIT for the study of a new discipline he called group dynamics. The following year, he participated in a Connecticut workshop on minority relations and discovered the importance of feedback in group process—that is, the power of relationships between individuals in the "here and now" of group experience rather than the "there and then" of intellectual discussions. It was the world's first "T-Group"—or Training Group, a relatively unstructured group that harnesses the power of shared experience to further adult learning and transform behaviors.[16]

Lewin decided that he wanted to explore this new phenomenon; he had the idea that extended interpersonal interactions with a group could help remove forces that commonly restrain new ideas, allowing individuals to explore alternatives to their habitual behaviors and modes of thought. People could then *change* and, eventually, change society. He looked for a site where participants could live together in a "cultural island" for three weeks and do this work. He found it at Bethel, Maine, and made preparations for a conference there in 1947. The event took place, but Lewin could not attend. He died in February 1947.[17]

At the urging of his friend Dr. Carl Hoverland, a psychologist at Yale, Robert Greenleaf did make it to the Bethel conference. Disregarding instructions to leave families at home, he packed up the whole Greenleaf tribe and took them along. So it was that Bob was present at the legendary founding meeting of the National Training Labs (NTL, now the NTL Institute). It was a singular event, packed with intensity.

Those who experience a traditional T-Group for the first time find it unlike any other group experience. There is no agenda, no problem to be solved. Participants are not encouraged to exchange opinions and intellectual ideas or to discuss issues, nor is the trainer a traditional group leader. Everyone sits in silence until someone finally speaks, often out of anxiety or a need to impose structure, seek safety, or establish commonality. Feelings about self, power, and authority emerge. Interpersonal relationships and intrapersonal dynamics become the *content* of group interactions. It can be an exhilarating—and, for some, frightening— experience.[18]

In Bob's small group at Bethel, he met Kenneth Harold, a young instructor at Columbia Teacher's College. They became fast friends and decided to lead their own T-Group when they got back to New York. Bob convinced the New York Adult Education Society to sponsor a group the following winter, and he always remembered the experience.

> It was a very odd and interesting assortment of people. It contained a couple of psychiatrists, a couple of lawyers and a little bit of everything . . . In the second meeting, one of our psychiatrists had seen one too many patients that day. He walked in the door talking wild and sat down at the table . . . This was one of the most interesting meetings I ever experienced. We devoted our three hours to putting this fellow back together and we succeeded. It was quite an undertaking, because I got everybody else into the act without saying so. For years afterwards, when I would meet one of these people on the street, they would say, "Do you remember that night we put this fellow together?" And I would say, "I sure do. I remember it vividly to this day."[19]

Not long after the Bethel conference, T-Groups—which also came to be called "sensitivity groups"—took off like one of the military's Atlas intercontinental ballistic missiles.

> From the mid-1950s through the early 1970s, T-Groups spread at an alarming rate. One might identify the activity as the growth of a specific social movement. There was a philosophy related to achievement of a democratic society and holding to values of respect and dignity for the individual. There were heroes such as Lewin, Maslow, Rogers, McGregor, who somehow were tied in to the movement. There was Bethel, the Mecca of the movement. There were converts

> all over. For example, some of the corporate presidents who partici-
> pated in one of NTL's President's Labs wanted the government to
> establish a Manhattan Project for T-Groups. There was a [body of]
> literature, and there were units like NTL all over the world.[20]

That is what happened, but not necessarily what would have happened had Lewin survived to direct the Bethel conference. "I have often
wondered where we would be today if Lewin had lived," wrote Greenleaf, "because he was a rigorous experimental psychologist. His students
turned out to be cultists and the 'sensitivity' movement emerged from the
session I attended. . . . I think that would have been anathema for Lewin
from all I know of him."[21] After the eight evening meetings he conducted
with Ken Harold, Bob quickly disassociated himself from the larger movement. "I decided this was enough of this for me. I would not have anything more to do with it. But I also learned something."[22]

Greenleaf's strategy was to always learn something from his experiences. When he heard about new ideas like T-groups, he tried them out in
the real world, reflected on lessons learned from the experience, then
modified the theory and tested it again. This experiential learning cycle
was both scientific and humanistic. The key to it, and the element so often
missing in traditional learning and teaching, was *reflection*, which opens
the door to intuitive insight. Even when teaching arithmetic and algebra
to working men in Cleveland, Greenleaf made space for both cognitive
thinking and reflection, and the idea of a servant-leader would eventually
come from Bob's own reflection on a lifetime of experience.

A few years before the Bethel conference, Bob attended a series of
seminars led by Alfred Korzybski (1879–1950) and developed greater
subtelety in his use of language and his cognitive map of the world. Korzybski founded the discipline of General Semantics. His 1933 book *Science and Sanity: An Introduction to non-Aristotelian Systems and General
Semantics* remains influential to this day.[23] Korzybski's experiences as a
Russian soldier in World War I—he was wounded three times—caused
him to reflect on the causes of human violence and the differences between humans and animals. He decided that because of the flexible
capacity of the human nervous system and our facility with language, we
could "time-bind" experience across generations, but this same genius
caused us to make the error of believing that language represented the

full reality of a situation. We needed more consciousness and precision in how we used language.

Korzybski formulated several famous rules that summarized his key insights.

- "The map is not the territory." That is, the map of reality we create with language is not reality itself. Most people learn this truth through the childhood phrase "Sticks and stones can break my bones, but words will never hurt me," but as adults we act as if words really were sticks and stones. Korzybski would say that this simple misidentification has led to countless wars.

- "The map does not cover all of the territory." Our words and descriptions of what is true cannot possibly capture the full richness of infinitely varied "reality."

- "The map is self-reflexive." The map itself—our language—becomes part of reality.[24] One way out of the *insanity* of identifying language with reality is by training ourselves to use qualifiers. Do not describe the way something "is," but explain how it relates to the whole. In writing, use quotes and dashes to indicate specific sources and general implications.

There is much more to Korzybski's thought but, to paraphrase sales guru Zig Ziglar, we need to be trained away from our "stinkin' thinkin'" about language.

Greenleaf did not connect with Korzybski personally ("He was not my style of fellow," Bob said) but believed he benefited from the encounter. "I think there's probably a residue from my having made a foray into that field, but it is not very clear what it is. I have a feeling that we don't do *anything* that doesn't leave a permanent residue, but we don't always know what that is."[25] After his exposure to Korzybski, Greenleaf did often use qualifying phrases in his writing. Several of his favorites were, "From my worm's eye view" and "From my small corner of the world." Similar comments—and their accompanying attitudes—were also integral to the approach to persuasion he learned from John Woolman. They were embedded in his comments to Air Force generals and business colleagues. And Korzybski's ideas certainly gave support to the non-directive style of language that emerged from Bob's natural humility.

·····

When Bob and Esther joined the Quakers' Yearly Meeting at Mt. Kisco in 1935, Bob became quite active in Friends affairs. In 1937, he was a delegate to the Society of Friends World Conference where he heard a presentation by Dr. Elton Trueblood, a prominent Quaker scholar, author, teacher, and theologian. At first, Bob was not especially impressed with Trueblood, and he would soon become disillusioned with the Friends. After the World Conference, he took the lead in promoting a Friend's Center in New York, and he "Got in the middle of a fight between 'old and weighty Friends' in the two local meetings. Dirty, name-calling, no evidence of Light—inner, outer or any other kind. No place for a hole-in-the-hedge man."[26] His daughter Anne's death in 1939 caused him to further question the Quaker connection. "We lost two children—numbers one and three—inner resources not adequate, no help from Friends," he wrote in a private journal. "More trouble in the Society."[27]

After moving to Short Hills in 1941, the Greenleafs severed most connections with the Friends, tried the Unitarians again and dropped them, then became free agents for eight years with no ongoing church affiliation. The lure of the Quakers was strong, however, and Bob and Esther found their way back. They formally joined the Summit, New Jersey Friends in 1951. Three years later, Bob wrote in a private note, "[I] still have reservations although I am now Chairman of Ministry and Counsel. Speak very seldom in meeting, give all the Friends machinery above the local meeting a wide berth. Have a long way to go before I will feel 'right' about any formal religious affiliation. Hole-in-the-hedge philosophy isn't working here."[28]

Bob's renewed interest in the Friends came, in part, from four small books by Dr. Trueblood, which he discovered in 1950. Unlike Trueblood's 1937 World Conference address, these writings "meant a great deal" to him.[29] One of the books, *The Predicament of Modern Man*, published in 1944, was praised by Reinhold Niebuhr and Norman Vincent Peale and was reprinted in a condensed version by *Reader's Digest*.[30] In one chapter of this slim, readable volume, Trueblood analyzed the creed of a "power culture" in which leadership had lost sight of human equality.[31] In the book's most memorable line, Trueblood called ours a "cut-flower civilization." "Beautiful as cut flowers may be," he wrote, "and much as we may use our ingenuity to keep them looking fresh for a while, they will eventually die, and they die because they are severed from their sustaining roots. We are trying to maintain the dignity of the individual apart from the deep faith that every man is made in God's image and is therefore precious in God's eyes."[32] Trueblood also wrote about the "insufficiency of individual religion," which may have put off the Bob Greenleaf who admired the Friends' individualistic approach to revelation, but attracted the Bob Greenleaf who believed that organizations were "how you get things done."

Bob wrote to Trueblood, who suggested that he look into the Laymen's Movement, an organization formed in 1941 to encourage people to integrate their personal spiritual values into their daily life and work. Some of the early members were Norman Vincent Peale, J. C. Penney, John D. Rockefeller, and Dwight D. Eisenhower.[33] Bob became involved in the Movement and found it "my most congenial affiliation. Holes plentiful, manna for a hole-in-the-hedge man. Feel I am making some progress."[34] In 1951, Bob finally met Elton Trueblood in New York at an annual meeting of the Laymen's Movement. After the meeting in the city, Bob accompanied Dr. Trueblood to a retreat house in Rye, New York that had recently been given to the Movement. This place would come to be called the Wainwright House and would figure prominently in Bob and Esther's life for the next few years as the meeting place for world-class doers and thinkers.

Greenleaf was destined to help Rev. Trueblood create a powerful movement of his own that would bring small group experiences to local churches. About the same time that the Bethel conference was inventing T-Groups for the secular world, Elton Trueblood was rediscovering the power of small groups in the religious community. As chaplain at Stanford, he invited interested parties to attend lunchtime discussion groups, and the idea of small groups spread to every living unit on campus. Across the country, similar religious-based gatherings, sometimes called "cell groups," were happening on campuses like the University of Michigan at Ann Arbor. The Inter-seminary Movement was exploring group possibilities, and the Iona Fellowship—based on the model of St. Columba-was picking up steam. Trueblood knew this was nothing new. Even the Third Order of St. Francis was designed for "meeting the needs of those who were involved in common life."[35]

In 1947, Dr. Trueblood moved his family to Earlham College, a Quaker school in Richmond, Indiana, where he wrote a best-selling book called *Alternative to Futility* that argued for a cross-denominational fellowship dedicated to renewal of church and society. Members of the fellowship would engage in commitment, witness, fellowship, vocation, and discipline, all within existing church structures.[36] "In the new order there are no clergymen and no laymen, but all are engaged in the same divine vocations," wrote Trueblood, "which means putting the claims of the Kingdom of God first, no matter what profession one may follow. *The formula is that vocation has priority over profession.*"[37] Trueblood thought discipline was the key ingredient too often missing in Protestant groups. Two of the five elements of discipline he proposed were solitude and silence.[38] These were sweet thoughts to Robert Greenleaf, who loved his time alone.

Small laymen groups began popping up here and there, but Trueblood had no name for them until 1949 when he read the words in Matthew 11: 29: "Take my yoke upon you, and learn of me . . ." It was a luminous moment. "Within a minute or so, as an entire complex of thinking came together. . . . Suddenly, we had a name for our hitherto nameless fellowship."[39] The name was Yokefellow, and Yokefellow groups began to flourish in churches throughout the country, all without much central organization. In 1952, at the urging of Edward Gallahue, an Indianapolis executive who founded the American States Insurance Company, Trueblood acknowledged the need for a cabinet to provide business counsel, spiritual support, and financial backing to the Yokefellow Movement. Meanwhile, the Lilly Endowment in Indianapolis stood ready to support the group's evolution. Trueblood was a personal friend of Eli Lilly, grandson of the pharmaceutical company founder, and also acquainted with the Endowment's first Director, Harold Durling, who attended the original lay conferences at Earlham College.[40] Bob Greenleaf liked the idea of Yokefellow. "The idea of the yoke, with its emphasis upon the ministry in common life, appealed to [Greenleaf] as both fresh and valid," wrote Trueblood in his autobiography.[41]

On a clear, lovely day in 1952, Elton Trueblood, Earlham College President Thomas E. Jones, and Robert Greenleaf gathered on Bob's front porch in Short Hills, New Jersey. There was no prepared agenda, just an eagerness in all parties to listen to each other.

> Mr. Greenleaf's contention that summer day was that new situations
> require new institutional developments. The parish congregation,
> valuable as it has been in the Christian Cause, frequently does
> almost nothing to implement the idea of the priesthood of every
> believer . . . Participation is often limited to such a marginal opera-
> tion as that of ushering! New vitality, we agreed, will not come until
> there is a radical change in expectations . . .
>
> Mr. Greenleaf's vision of what is needed bears some
> resemblance to the monastic dream of the Middle Ages. Just as the
> monasteries were once centers of renewal, affecting entire areas of
> Christendom, so in our time there must be institutions for the train-
> ing of men and woman who can be involved in the ministry of com-
> mon life. . . . Those centers should not, Mr. Greenleaf explained, be
> identical with theological seminaries, which exist to train the profes-
> sionally religious, nor with centers devoted to social service, how-
> ever valuable and necessary they are.
>
> What developed, largely because of Robert Greenleaf's imagina-
> tion, were two new operating units, the Yokefellow Institute and the
> Earlham Institute for Executive Growth. Neither of these would
> probably ever have come into existence apart from the dialogue at
> Short Hills.[42]

From that humble beginning, centers of Yokefellow work opened in
various parts of the country. The movement had its first national conference in 1954, branched out into ministries in prisons and other settings,
and gradually embraced the whole world with Yokefellow International.
Trueblood had the "redemptive fellowship" not bound by denomina-
tional labels that he had proposed in *The Predicament of Modern Man*.

Bob's second idea, the Earlham Institute for Executive Growth, was a
more modest effort but one that allowed him to help Earlham do what he
believed Carleton College should have done nineteen years earlier—reach
out to the local community. In 1954, Bob had further conversations with
Jones and learned that he "wanted to do something for business and industry as a way of saying thanks for their financial support of . . . Earlham."[43]
Greenleaf proposed a series of weekend meetings that would include case
problem discussions; skills training in "talking with people" (in other
words, listening); discussions with guest speakers; intensive exposure to

principles of economics, human relations, management policies, and functions; and, finally, individual analysis of each participant's job and performance, including a detailed study of an actual problem on the job.[44]

Robert Huff, the Institute's first director, wrote Bob to prepare him for the initial meeting and described some of the Richmond businessmen who would attend. "For the most part they are fine men with a genuine concern for employees and a strong community pride. They do tend toward self satisfaction and smugness." Huff expressed hope that the Institute could develop programs that "might administer to their personal needs as top managers and owners which would reflect in better human relations, happier, less strained lives, and a better community. Such conferences on a community basis, rather than industry or wide geographic basis, might be able to produce great returns and might set the pattern for other colleges and communities."[45] In the next two years, Greenleaf, at his own expense, rode trains with names like The Indianapolis Limited and The Spirit of St. Louis to Richmond to speak with the Earlham faculty and attend each of the Institute's first sessions with local businessmen.[46] He returned frequently as guest speaker.

The Institute for Executive Growth carried on for nearly fifty years, graduating over eight thousand management people from their Executive Training and other programs. It kept the core of Bob's vision, which James Beier (then Assistant Director and later Director of the Institute) summarized in an article for Earlham's alumni magazine. "Mr. Greenleaf's concept for executive training was based on the fact that no matter how much an executive knew about a particular business function such as production, sales, finances, etc., he had to get the thing done through people. And how well he could accomplish this goal would largely determine his success or failure as an effective leader and executive."[47] Today we might use the notion of "emotional intelligence" to describe one's capacity to get things done through other people, but Greenleaf clearly believed executive leadership required more than human sensitivity. It also demanded hard data, an understanding of principles, listening skills, self examination, and discipline.

———

Bob and Esther got involved with Wainwright House activities soon after Bob discovered the conference center. Wainwright was only thirty miles from downtown Manhattan. Its peaceful grounds, glorious Main house (an exact replica of the chateau de Raincheval in France) and "nonsectarian holistic educational" programs soon attracted the likes of Aldous Huxley, Joseph Campbell, and United Nations Secretary General Dag Hammarskold, who hosted conferences there on conflict resolution.[48] The Greenleafs helped plan various programs and retreats. The one with the most lasting history was a course called Receptive Listening.

Years before, drawing from the lessons he learned from the Hawthorne studies, Bob had developed a three-day course in listening for AT&T managers called "Talking With People." It was something for which he became famous inside and outside the company. One day an assistant dean of the medical school at Cornell heard about the course and came to Bob with his problem. The school had recently done a study of its graduated doctors and learned that patients did not consider them good listeners. This was more than a communications problem; it was also a medical problem, because patients were the most important source of information in determining a proper diagnosis and course of treatment.

"So," said the assistant dean, "we did what we thought was the most logical thing. We went to the head of the Department of Psychiatry and asked him to put together a course on listening for fourth-year medical students. As it turned out, if we'd gone out on the street and tapped somebody on the shoulder to come in and do this, we couldn't have made a worse mistake. We put up a fellow who never listened to anybody himself!" The savvy students quickly realized that their teacher did not know how to listen, rebelled, and caused the course to be cancelled in mid-semester. It was a disaster.

"Now we hear you are teaching managers to listen," said his visitor. "How in the world are you doing it?" Bob's most important bit of advice, besides finding a new teacher, was to change the name of the course from Listening To Patients to Talking With Patients because people did not generally think they needed training in listening but loved to hear themselves talk. "We don't talk about listening in our course," Bob told his visitor. "We teach it, but we don't *talk* about it." Bob gave the man AT&T's manual for the course and never heard from him again. He always remembered that incident however, and reported on it in various writings.[49]

Near the end of Bob's career with AT&T, President Eugene McNeely called him and said, "I've always heard about your listening course. This interests me. I'm not a very good listener. How can I get into one of your courses?"

> I didn't tell him that I agreed he was right; he wasn't a very good
> listener! So I said, "Well, it would be a little difficult to put you in a
> course, but if you really want to know what this is all about and are
> willing to take a few hours, come down to my office, and I will teach
> it to you." So, by golly, he did.
>
> We had about six two-hour sessions. I didn't teach him the
> course we taught to others. I taught it the way he ought to get it. I
> really gave him the business and was awfully rough on him. He was
> mad and hot at times, but it did little good. We didn't make a good
> listener out of him. He was too old for that and had been the way he
> was for too long."[50]

For his Wainwright House course Greenleaf took the lead in creating
a two-hundred-page Leadership Manual. It included readings from authors like Carl Rogers, Eric Fromm, and Rudolph Steiner on everything
from non-directive counseling to Quaker worship, Zen philosophy, guilt,
and the Brothers Grimm. There are sample letters to participants, meditations, a self-administered analysis of personal goals, and instructions for
engaging in an "experiment in depth" based on Jung's four psychological
types. It was a typically eclectic effort from Robert Greenleaf. For three
years, he and Esther led the course, which in its original version was presented over three weekends spaced a month apart.

   The Receptive Listening Leadership Manual can be read as an echo of
Bob's own spiritual journey to that point. It's all there: the exploration of
wisdom from various faith traditions, an attempt to understand the nature of love and the depths of the psyche, a celebration of silence and reflection, poems and prose and prayers that seep into the soul. Those who
volunteered to lead Wainwright House's Receptive Listening course were
likely to be a dedicated band of seekers—they could handle a course with
"listening" in the title—but there was still misdirection in the name of the
course; this was really an experiment in spiritual evolution and individual
maturity.

   Some of the best pieces in the manual were written by Bob, and they
have to do with group leadership. His introductory essay is called "Some
Rough Notes on Growth Through Groups." Even that title is significant. It
is not called "How To Lead A Group" or "Principles, Goals, and Objectives of Group Formation and Performance." Anything along those lines

would indicate that the writer had The Answer on how to do group leadership and would imply that the role of the group leader was to be one of teacher rather than peer, authority rather than fellow pilgrim. The phrase "Rough Notes" refers to a work in progress. The course is ultimately about growth rather than listening skills. "Growth is best seen as conscious striving but not to a predetermined end," Greenleaf wrote. [51] It is the language of a hole-in-the-hedge person, always looking for openings, always leaving openings.

Still, Greenleaf did offer solid principles for group leadership. First, he did not believe in leaderless groups, although he thought a *laissez-faire* style of leadership like that used in T-Groups might be appropriate at times. Here is how he described the need for a leader in a group *dedicated to personal exploration*. (He would not say this leadership style was appropriate for all groups in all settings.)

> One might well say, "Undertake the journey only with a guide!" But where are the guides? For all practical purposes, there are no guides. There are those who seem to have the gift of guidance—for some people. But the chances of any one person finding the right guide for him is rather remote. One alternative is the small group of ten or twelve dedicated seekers with one of their peers as a leader. And there *must* be a leader—*i.e.*, someone with a little "lead" on the group, someone with reasonable objectivity about the group, someone the group respects. The leader might (and should) be changed once in a while. But there must always be a leader—someone competent to *be* a leader and who accepts the responsibility of a leader . . . What the leader *is* in a group is a result of interactions.
>
> The principal qualification is *awareness*. A leader of a growth group must be sensitive to where he is currently directing the group on the scale bounded by comfortable accommodation on one extreme and harassment on the other; and must recognize the danger signals of these extreme states. But there are no rules.
>
> The leader must have an idea about possible goals but not a fixed goal. The leader is growing with the group. The goals, both immediate and long range, emerge as the search proceeds. They are not "thought up" by anybody. They come as a spontaneous gift because somebody, preferably the leader, is consistently examining the discussion and asking himself "where are we and whither are we

> tending?" . . . Some general statement such as, "The group is the
> place where we will seek to become more effective loving persons"
> should suffice for a statement of purpose.[52]

Greenleaf warned against the ego traps of leading a growth group. Pre-planning may work if one has a submissive group. "Thinking" may work as a strategy "if a person has great erudition and the group members are of inferior intellectual achievement and accept the virtual student role." Both of these strategies satisfy the ego needs of the leader but not necessarily the growth needs of the group. Although the Wainwright Manual contains detailed pre-planning and several heady intellectual articles, these are *inputs*, not outputs.

> A leader must recognize that, once a group achieves some character,
> the members will initiate most of the new points of view . . . The
> members of the group must support one another in times of doubt
> and difficulty and love the person who rebels or rejects, who will not
> "let go" to withdraw and who cannot bring himself to give . . . All
> must be loved."[53]

There is much more: leaders should bite their tongue and allow group members to arrive at their own conclusions, not as a strategy but because leaders will likely learn something new in the process, and group members will own the new insights; an effective group of this type requires discipline in preparation and commitment to attendance; all group members are there to give, not "to get"; the endless cycle of withdrawal and return must be respected; followership is as important as leadership.

One of the most interesting contributions to the Receptive Listening course came from Esther—the "creative periods" for each session, using ink blots, finger painting, clay modeling, creative writing, collage, and cray-pas. These were not mere craft projects, but activities that elicited feelings rather than ideas. "We know we are getting close to a rapprochement between the conscious mind and the deep psyche through creative art activity," says the manual.[54] Following the same Zen-like approach to leadership described in the rest of the manual, the leader is asked *not* to give—or ask the group to give—"interpretations" of creative expressions, nor should participants be instructed to create consciously coded symbols. They should simply have fun and let things flow. The leader may then say something like, "Well, what does this little figure say to you? It looks like something or other, doesn't it?" Esther (with Bob) wrote, "I have come to the point of wondering whether any of the work is accidental. Is it not all dictated by an infinitely clever, infinitely fast super-mind from within?"

Esther was ahead of her time. The recent discipline of expressive arts therapy takes a similar view of confronting artistic products, according to one of the more influential books in the field.

> No sooner does a client divulge a piece of material—a memory, idea or feeling—than the overly zealous therapist moves in to process and perhaps over process, often seeking interpretations of the material that can limit, rather than enhance, one's understanding of it. In viewing therapy as an *artistic* process, we find that *the process itself* (not the process-*ing*) offers by far the most significant therapeutic value. We simply open the door to images and then engage them and learn what they have to teach us.[55]

In Esther's creative arts projects, images spoke from the depths, just as intuition spoke from the depths during the periods of silence and withdrawal that Bob built into the course. Both approaches tapped into the same awe-filled Source, using different modalities. This convergence is evidence of the profound influence Esther was having on Bob's work and thinking.

After three years, Bob and Esther turned the course over to others, and it continued in one form or another for decades. To this day, there is a Greenleaf Room at Wainwright House.

The Greenleafs went on to adapt the listening program to their local Friends Meeting, calling it Spiritual Growth, and holding meetings in their home on Sunday evenings. "This was then taken by members of our group to other Meetings, but after several years it died out," Bob recalled. "The Quakers seemed not to have it in them to sustain something like we started. And my way of working at that time [was to] start things, get them well established, and then move on."[56]

One day in 1956, Bob got a call from Thomas J. Watson, Jr., son of the legendary Thomas J. Watson, Sr. who had turned the moribund

Computing-Tabulating-Recording Company into the powerhouse known as IBM. One month before his death, Thomas Watson Sr. had given his eldest son the reins of the company, and the forty-two-year-old heir was faced with a vexing problem. His father—Greenleaf called him "old TJ"— had hated organizational charts, saying everyone worked for *him*. About two hundred salesmen took him literally and often called from a prospect's office to close the sale. Bob noted that "Old TJ loved it because it confirmed his no-organization theory. The fact that the rest of the organization was constantly scheming to get the job done without involving him apparently never reached him." Factory managers had their own organizational charts but never dared admit it to the old man.[57] Young Thomas Watson knew the no-organization-chart idea had been stretched too far, but he did not want to lose whatever it was about IBM that had made it so unique and profitable. "So," said Bob, "he picked his most respected officer, who was nearing retirement, and gave him the task of figuring out what to do—and then retire. He had to talk to somebody who wasn't in IBM, and he couldn't talk to consultants because he didn't trust them. They would want to come in and organize it for him, according to their formula."[58]

Bob and three other prominent executives were asked to meet for an evening every two weeks throughout the winter and brainstorm the reorganization options. "It was a fascinating winter," wrote Bob. "One of the fragments that stays with me was that this was a problem with everybody in management, who conceded that the old man was a genius but was cracked on this point. In a way it made for great *esprit* because they had to make it work."[59] So it was that Robert Greenleaf helped reorganize IBM.

At Wainwright House, Bob met a dazzling array of people, many of them famous. Bill Wilson ("Bill W."), co-founder of Alcoholics Anonymous, lived nearby and attended conferences there. He and Greenleaf became good friends and Bob did some writing for AA publications.

AA was Robert Greenleaf's kind of grass-roots group, organizationally and theologically. According to AA historian "Mitchell K.," John D. Rockefeller, Jr. saved the group from grandiosity in 1938 when he declined the opportunity to give the fledgling organization $50,000 in seed money. "I am afraid money will spoil this thing," he said. Instead, Rockefeller put $5,000 into an account at Riverside Church that Bill W. and co-founder "Dr. Bob" drew upon for their basic necessities of life.[60]

The experience with Rockefeller led Bill W. and Dr. Bob to formalize an organizational blueprint called "The Twelve Traditions." They include: financing solely by member donations, open membership, autonomy of each local group, non-professional management, no political or sectarian activities, no ownership of property, and a guarantee of personal anonymity. "[Anonymity] reminds us that we are to place principles before personalities; that we are actually to practice a genuine humility," says the Alcoholics Anonymous "Big Book."[61] It continues, "Each A.A. group needs the least possible organization . . . Rotating leadership is the best . . . All such representatives [including trustees] are to be guided in the spirit of service, for true leaders in A.A. are but trusted and experienced servants of the whole."[62]

Theologically, AA emerged from Christian sources, especially the Oxford Movement, but has no doctrinal requirement. The group simply affirms the existence of a power greater than oneself, a theology much like that espoused by the Ethical Culture Movement, so familiar to Bob and Esther.

Bob was impressed with the work of AA. "Although I have never been [a member of AA], I have had occasion to feel that I missed something—the fellowship—by not being one," he wrote.[63] Bob would later describe AA as an *ad hoc* church.[63]

Rev. Harry Emerson Fosdick was a supporter of AA—his church was the repository of Rockefeller's $5,000—and also an occasional lunch mate to his friend Robert Greenleaf. In Protestant circles, Fosdick was—and still is—known as one of the century's great speakers. He reached millions through his books, radio addresses, and his pastorate of the influential Riverside Church from 1929 to 1946. Like Norman Vincent Peale, Fosdick stressed a practical brand of Christianity but also once wrote, "I would rather live in a world where my life is surrounded by mystery than live in a world so small that my mind could comprehend it." Fosdick became a valued member of Bob's circle of friends.

One evening Bob went to a dinner at the Wainwright House and sat to the left of a woman who was a sparkling conversationalist. In the middle of dinner she turned to him, pointed at his lower abdomen and said, "You know, you haven't thought about this for a long time." "What?" he asked. "The cecum, in your colon. It doesn't bother you. It's a symptom that you're aware of, but I believe I'd have it checked out if I were you." Bob was amazed. In his early twenties, he was treated for pain in that very area, but it disappeared after he married and he had not thought about it for nearly twenty-five years.[64] The woman's name was Eileen Garrett, and she was a famous trance medium. Bob and Esther became acquainted with her and the other most-famous trance medium in the country at that time, Arthur Ford. Both Greenleafs developed an interest in parapsychology.

"These two were extraordinary 'sensitives,'" said Bob, "I spent enough time with them to know that they knew what was on my mind, but I was never convinced that they knew more than that. Both were fascinating people and well worth knowing quite apart from their special gifts."[65] Still, Bob developed a theory that in the early stages of humankind, all had the gift of universal, wordless communication. As humans developed their intellect and began to manage the environment, these powers became a liability because of too much communication from too many sources. "As a matter of natural selection and survival, the people who had less of it got along better," he told his friend Gerald Heard. "I have a feeling that we are just holding this in a kind of threshold now, that somehow if you can learn to live with this communication, you could turn the natural selection process around."[66]

In one of Greenleaf's many conversations with psychiatrist Karl Menninger, Bob told him of his contact with trance mediums. Karl asked Bob to arrange for a reading sometime when he was in New York. "Of course," he said. "I would not want her to know who I was, though," said Menninger. "No way!" replied Bob. "She would know who you were and would tell you your name. Besides, if I tried to pass you off as somebody else, she would know I had lied to her." Dr. Menninger, who was a well-known author of the 1930 best-seller *The Human Mind* and other books, preferred that the public not learn that he had had contact with a psychic, so the meeting was never arranged.[67]

Bob and Esther's minds were expanded in other ways through an important friendship with Sir Laurens van der Post. Van der Post, born in South Africa, was one of the twentieth century's most extraordinary seekers: an author, farmer, Japanese prisoner of war, humanitarian, consultant to heads of state, anti-apartheid activist, film-maker, philosopher, chronicler of the Kalahari Bushmen, and much more. He was also Carl Jung's close friend. In 1958, Jungian analyst Martha Jaeger wrote to Sir Laurens describing a recurring dream she had about a praying mantis. Van der Post regarded it as strange that he had received this letter from an unknown woman, because the word "jaeger" means "hunter" in German, and at the time he was having difficulty writing a book called *Heart of the Hunter*, which was yet another volume about the Kalahari bushmen, for whom the praying mantis was a god.[68] At the time she wrote the letter, Martha Jaeger was Robert Greenleaf's therapist in a journey of dream therapy.

Like Greenleaf, van der Post was interested in looking for grand patterns in the human experience. He believed that poets, prophets, artists, thinkers, mystics, and seers all had something to teach about the heroic, inner mythic journeys. Part of his personal journey was to probe the human spirit and make the unconscious articulate.[69] Bob never wrote about the influence Sir Laurens had on his thinking, but Newcomb Greenleaf recalls hearing van der Post's name often from Bob and Esther. In Sir Laurens, Bob found another towering intellect who eagerly sought holes in the hedge, cultivated profound awareness, and felt a responsibility to leave the world a little better than he found it.

Writer Margaret Wheatley may not have known of this connection when she quoted Sir Laurens at the 1999 International Conference on Servant Leadership, but Greenleaf would have approved of her choice of his words.

> Laurens van der Post, the Great South African writer, photographer, philosopher, said that things had gotten so serious in the world that he really feared for us. Someone asked him, "Well, what would you recommend, Sir   Laurens? What would you recommend that we do?" He said, "I would declare a year of silence."[70]

In 1956, the psychiatrist Will Menninger, Karl's brother, sought out Greenleaf for advice on how to raise money from businesses for the famous Menninger Clinic he had co-founded in 1919 with his father, C. F., and brother in Topeka, Kansas. Bob suggested that they establish a seminar on industrial psychology to spark interest and arranged for the Menningers to make a presentation at a Chicago conference (at which Bob presided) of the American Management Association. This conference put the Menninger Clinic on the national radar screen in the business community. Meanwhile, Dr. Will Menninger and Dr. Harry Levinson conducted a study of mental health problems in industry and designed a series of week-long seminars for executives and physicians under their new Menninger Division of Industrial Mental Health. The first seminar was held in 1956, and Robert Greenleaf was invited to make a presentation. According to The Menninger Clinic, "This was the first specialized function at a psychiatric institution and eventually provided evidence that psychiatry could be effectively applied in industry."[71] It was also one more idea Robert Greenleaf helped bring to fruition.

Through the years, Bob visited the Menningers several times in Topeka and made some lasting memories.[72]

> I owe much to my work with the Menningers . . . I had the chance to take a close look at their foundation as an institution, and it is a very unusual one.
>
> One day as I was walking across the campus with Karl I mentioned that the place had a great spirit and I wondered how it got that way. He stopped and looked at me intently. "Do you really want know?" he asked. "Sure," I said, "tell me all." "It's not one of these damned doctors," he replied, firmly. "It's our business manager, Les Roach. Everybody knows he is the guy, but you will have to ask him how he does it."
>
> So I asked Les. And he told me, "All I do is, wherever I spot some tension or trouble I go and talk to all of the people involved, whether they are doctors or janitors. I just listen to what they want to talk about. Most everybody wants to talk if somebody will listen. And usually they get around to talking about the problem. I don't ask questions or offer advice. I will give a straight answer if they ask a question; otherwise I just listen until the problem goes away. Sometimes it takes a long time." This is how an able, unpretentious man did his important work.[73]

Years later, Bob would have called Les a servant-leader.

"One of the byproducts of my involvement [with the Menningers] was getting to know psychiatrists as a special breed," wrote Bob, "and they are different." Karl Menninger told him psychiatry was a "dangerous profession." In fact, when Bob first became involved with the program he learned that several residents at the Menninger School of Psychiatry committed suicide each year.[74]

One day during an intermission of a conference that I was auditing and Karl was chairing I was standing talking with Karl in front of a large photographic portrait of Sigmund Freud. I asked, "Where would we be today if this fellow had been pastor or priest or rabbi? The insights he received could as easily have come out of pastoral counseling as medical consultations." Karl was quiet for several seconds and said, "I have never thought about that, but I am sure we would be in a quite different place." I have wondered how we would be doing, better or worse? If better, how can we get from here to there, prudently?[75]

Dr. William Wolf was another doctor who had a deep influence on Bob and Esther during the 1950s. "Uncle Bill," as they called him, held both an M.D. and a doctorate in chemistry. He wrote the first medical textbook on endocrinology, called *Endocrinology in Modern Practice*, and was interested in other subjects—like biorhythms—that were considered on the fringe of medical practice in his time.[76] When Wolf became interested in psychiatry he traveled to Vienna to be analyzed by Freud; eventually he developed his own approach to psychotherapy.

One evening Bob visited Uncle Bill in New York and complained of stomach pains. For ten years, he had been under treatment for an ulcer, eating crackers and milk before bedtime and taking pills for the pain. "I didn't know you had an ulcer," said Uncle Bill, who then spent a good deal of time asking questions and listening carefully to the answers in the way doctors of his generation were taught to do diagnosis. He put Bob on the table and gently massaged a point on his spine. "Did anything happen then?" he asked. "Yes," replied Bob. "It stopped hurting." "You don't have an ulcer. This is where a bundle of nerves leaves the spinal column for your stomach. You have one of those trick backs that tightens up once in a while and when muscles squeeze those nerves your stomach hurts. When your stomach hurts, all you have to do is to gently massage these muscles and relax them. It will quit hurting."

Amazed, Bob asked how Wolf knew such a thing, when other doctors had missed it. Uncle Bill told the story of how, when he was a young doctor, the New York Medical Society asked him and another doctor to enroll in a chiropractic college diploma mill in order to testify against the operation and shut it down. They were successful in their case, but ironically, in the course of reading the lessons, Wolf learned things that had been quite useful in his medical practice. "If you had gone to a good chiropractor he would have found the trouble right away," said Uncle Bill, "because that is all he knows. He probably would not have told you how to fix it yourself, but he would have found it. You made the mistake of going to a medical doctor who treated it as a complicated medical problem." Bob called it an interesting lesson in how the world moves along.[77]

Uncle Bill gave the occasional lecture series on health, meditation, and the further reaches of human capacities. In notes he took from one series, Greenleaf jotted down some quite Eastern ideas about non-attachment.

> What do we mean by non-attachment? Do I have the pleasure, or does it have me? [With non-attachment] there is nothing to protect and defend; one must eliminate defenses by not needing them . . . Basis of interaction would be to express and clarify the common denominators—what is true to life and incontrovertible (breath, eat, live, drink, realize oneness) . . . One avoids labeling; be non-attached to labels. Meditation should be of the type that makes you free— eventually unattached . . . Once we judge we have erected a wall against understanding . . . The fulfillment of a desire is its death.[78]

The notes go on for pages. Between the aphorisms and instructions for meditations are references to Jung, Gurdjieff, Marcus Aurelius, Aldous Huxley, Hindu masters, and others. Uncle Bill was a brilliant man.

During the 1950s, two people entered Bob's life who would have a profound influence on his evolving views of religion and spirituality: Rabbi Abraham Joshua Heschel and Gerald Heard. Bob first met Rabbi Heschel in 1955 in his office at the Jewish Theological Seminary. Heschel was Professor of Ethics and Mysticism (a title Greenleaf adored) and already an acclaimed author.[79] Greenleaf asked Rabbi Heschel to speak to young executives attending the Bell Humanities Program the following summer at Dartmouth. Heschel accepted, and he and his family became friends with the Greenleafs. In some ways, it was an unlikely friendship.

Abraham Joshua Heschel (1907–1972) was descended from the early leaders of Hasidism, an eighteenth-century pietistic movement.[80] According to his biographers, Heschel was an intellectual prodigy. "By age thirteen, Heschel had mastered the texts qualifying him to become a practicing rabbi: the relevant sections of Talmud and all four parts of the *Shulhan Arukh*, the code of Jewish law pertaining to every aspect of social, personal, and ritual life," but his parents made him wait until age sixteen for the ordination.[81] His first essay was published when he was fifteen; he became a poet and an accomplished scholar. Heschel escaped the holocaust by accepting a teaching position with the Hebrew Union College in Cincinnati, a move aided by his friend Martin Buber.

Greenleaf wrote about his bond with Rabbi Heschel, with whom he shared little in personal background or scholarship.

> We did meet at the level of social concern: he with his political activism and I with my efforts to reconstruct within the system . . . But the firmer bond, and one of profound meaning to me, was the shared belief that the highest level of religious experience is awareness of oneness with the mystery—as he would say, the feeling of awe and wonder and amazement . . . What kept our friendship close was a common need, a shared feeling of not being supported in this sense of the mystical by the religious sentiment of our times."[82]

Heschel's work speaks to the reality underlying religion, something he found to be concrete and poetic. The same primal, wordless awe Robert Greenleaf experienced atop Mt. Wilson in 1919 is echoed in many of the Rabbi's writings: "Thus there arose, as though spontaneously, a mother tongue, a direct expression of feeling, a mode of speech without ceremony or artifice, a language that speaks itself without taking devious paths, a tongue that has maternal intimacy and warmth. In this language, you say 'beauty' and mean 'spirituality'; you say 'kindness' and mean 'holiness.'"[83] Somewhere along the way, wrote Bob, "the study of religious awe, not philosophy, became Heschel's priority. . . . [to] analyze and arouse piety and teach secularized readers the ways of attachment to God through prayer, study and action . . . [This] radical amazement [became] an emotion of reverence before the very miracle of daily existence [and] reintegrated him into the Jewish way of life" during a period when Heschel was undergoing his own spiritual crisis.[84]

Like Greenleaf, Heschel decried the descent of religion into lifeless symbols. "It has become a truism that religion is largely an affair of symbols," he wrote. "Translated into simpler terms this view regards religion as a fiction, useful to society or to man's personal well-being."[85]

Heschel also shared Greenleaf's concern with what Greenleaf called *awareness* and Heschel called *consciousness*. "This seems to be the malady of man," wrote Heschel, "*His normal consciousness is a state of oblivion*, a state of suspended sensitivity. As a result, we see only camouflage and concealment. We do not understand what we do; we do not see what we face. Is there a meaning beyond all conventional meanings?. . . The awareness of transcendent meaning comes with the sense of the ineffable."[86]

In the Old Testament prophets, Heschel found an example of courageous humans who were willing to encounter the mystery directly and do something about it. First in his doctoral dissertation on prophetic consciousness and later in his book *The Prophets*, Heschel used the methodological tool of reflection to "analyze the components of prophetic inspiration (God's presence within human awareness) and to develop a taxonomy describing this process."[87] Just as Greenleaf nurtured intuitive insight for practical business problems, Heschel learned to cultivate insight for his academic work. "Insight is a breakthrough, requiring much intellectual dismantling and dislocation," wrote Heschel. "It begins with a mental interim, with the cultivation of a feeling for the unfamiliar, unparalleled, incredible . . . Insight is the beginning of perceptions to come rather than the extension of perceptions gone by. Conventional seeing, operating as it does with patterns and coherences, is a way of seeing the present in the past tense. Insight is an attempt to think in the present."[88]

Even though Heschel came from a rich Jewish tradition and Greenleaf from a Protestant background, Heschel's emphasis on a direct encounter with ultimate mystery—which he would call God—was not so different from Greenleaf's attention to conscious withdrawal that invites mystery to become available as *awareness*, which then allows creative insight to emerge.[89] In the end, both the Rabbi and the businessman were not interested in analyzing or even understanding the mystery *per se*, but in the human response to it—here, now, in one's particular historic situation.

Bob wrote about Rabbi Heschel as a model of a servant-leader.[90] Shortly before his death, Heschel was asked if he had any advice for young people.

> I would say: Let them remember that there is a meaning beyond
> absurdity. Let them be sure that every little deed counts, that every
> word has power, and that we can—every one—do our share to re-
> deem the world in spite of all absurdities and all frustrations and all
> disappointments. And above all, remember that the meaning of life
> is to build a life as if it were a work of art.[91]

In the course of their lives, Bob and Esther made hundreds of friends—not mere acquaintances, but true friends. Bob stayed in touch as often as possible. It was part of his discipline. When he traveled, he carried an address book so he could mail off numerous letters and notes. When an article of interest crossed his desk at work or at home, he would often copy it and send it to friends who might be interested, accompanied by a personal note written on a 3 × 5 card paper-clipped to the document. Bob became famous for those small cards, many of which he mailed separately in envelopes, and hundreds of people who knew him still cherish their short, scrawling messages from a friend who cared enough to keep *spirit* alive between them. In fact, Bob's famous salutation was, "In the spirit."

Building a rich network of friends was as much a part of Bob's "preparation for old age" as was his reading and exposure to new ideas. He kept a traditional filing system where he deposited everything from articles on Emerson to correspondence to obscure reading lists, but he was not a pack-rat. Things he saved were either useful or had the potential to be useful. In a 1985 interview, after reviewing Bob's ventures into disciplines as varied as semantics, T-Groups and listening, Joseph Distefano asked him, "Were you conscious at the time of these elements being linked together and giving you some unity that you might eventually write about?" Bob's answer:

No, not really. I've got a pretty good filing system in my head, and I mostly just filed them away as important ideas. At the time, I had no notion that I would ever set out to be a synthesizer . . . I never had a master plan that said, "Here is where I'm going to wind up and these are the things I will do to get there." All I got from Elmer Davis was just "prepare yourself," and I just prepared myself the way you would keep your muscles in tone. You never know what you will use your muscles for, but you keep working on them so that they will be there when you need them, and that's really what I did."[92]

14

Crisis of Questions

No matter what you do, this darkness and this cloud is between you and your God and because of it you can neither see Him clearly with your reason in the light of understanding, nor can you feel Him with your affection in the sweetness of love. Be prepared, therefore, to remain in this darkness as long as must be, crying evermore for Him whom you love. For if you are ever to feel Him or to see Him, it will necessarily be within this cloud and within this darkness. And if you will work with great effort as I bid you, I trust in His mercy that you will achieve it.[1]

MEISTER ECKHART

When conceits are silent and all words stand still, the world speaks. We must burn the clichés to clear the air for hearing. Conceptual clichés are counterfeit; preconceived notions are misfits. Knowledge involves love, care for the things we seek to know, longing, being-drawn-to, being overwhelmed.[2]

ABRAHAM JOSHUA HESCHEL

By the late 1950s, Bob Greenleaf was getting restless. He was successful, secure, and admired in his job at AT&T, in his endeavors with outside companies and universities, and in the work he and Esther pursued with the Quakers. He was still deep into an era of seeking—meeting unusual people of accomplishment, reading mind-expanding books, preparing for an end that he could not quite yet fathom. Time was passing, though; he was in his fifties. Bob had a crisis of questions: What was his personal greatness? Did he have the courage to claim it? How could he best design the remainder of his life to make his contribution to individuals, organizations, and society? Should he stay at AT&T until age sixty-five or take an early retirement? Several shadows of his psyche still held him back, but what were they, and what could he do about them? Precisely at this moment in his life, when he was open to answers and new questions, the right people, ideas, and experiences appeared to nurture the unfolding path of his life.

In 1957, Bob and Esther attended the Friends Conference on Religion and Psychology organized around the theme of "The Roots and Fruits of Hostility." Bob presented a session on "Meeting Hostility in Others" and Esther conducted a workshop on painting.[3] Jungian analyst Dr. Martha Jaeger presented a session on meditation. Jaeger, who was therapist to Anais Nin when the writer had a breakdown in 1942, was well known at the conference, having made her first presentation on "Training in Pastoral Psychology" in 1943 and through the years conducting workshops with titles like "Functions of Symbols," "Neurosis as a Means of Self-Discovery," and the "I Ching."[4] At some point, Martha Jaeger said to Esther, "Why don't you try painting what you feel rather than what you see or imagine?"[5] That question started Esther on a new era of abstract painting.

Two years later, Dr. Jaeger would also be a key figure in Bob's life, but first he would work with a remarkable person he met at the next year's Friends conference at Haverford College—Dr. Ira Progoff.[6] With his plastic-rimmed glasses framing a somewhat round face and penetrating eyes, and a half-smile that could break into a wide grin or shift subtly into utter seriousness, Progoff was one of those people who really was as wise as he looked.

When he was very young, the Brooklyn-born Ira Progoff watched his grandfather, an Orthodox rabbi, rise from a prostrate position before the Ark and tell him, "You are the one who will do great things."[7] Progoff had no idea what those things would be until he discovered Swedenborg, Lao Tsu, Whitman, Martin Buber, Jan Christiaan Smuts, and dozens of other luminaries, completed his Ph.D. on the social meaning of Carl Jung's psychology, and then studied for two years with Jung in Zurich, where he also met the Zen master D. T. Suzuki.[8] At the time Greenleaf met him, Progoff was Director of the Institute for Research in Depth Psychology at the graduate school of Drew University in New Jersey and had written, among other books, *The Death and Rebirth of Psychology* (1956), the first publication in what would be a classic trilogy on depth psychology. He was not yet famous for his Intensive Journal system that would give thousands of ordinary people a tool to connect with their emotional and spiritual depths, but he was already recommending journals for his patients. Furthermore, he believed that psychotherapy should be for gifted and ordinary people as well as the emotionally crippled.[9] "An awareness of man's spiritual nature has gradually replaced the materialism upon which psychology was based in its analytical period," he wrote. "Its special knowledge is directed toward enlarging the capacities of life in modern times, thus making it psychologically possible for a revitalization to take place in the arts, in religion, and in all the fields of creative endeavor."[10]

At the 1958 Friends Conference on Religion and Psychology, Dr. Progoff was the key speaker. His topic was *The Cloud of Unknowing*, the mystical classic by the fourteenth-century monk Meister Eckhart. Progoff's translation and commentary of the work had been published the previous year, making it widely available for the first time. Progoff specifically remembered Bob from that conference. "Robert Greenleaf, one of the participants, an executive with AT&T, turned his life around after that meeting. He went on to early retirement and opened up the most creative time of his life."[11]

To protect confidentiality, Progoff did not mention that Greenleaf was also one of his "dream therapy" clients during the year following the conference. He urged Bob to begin keeping a journal—Bob's journal efforts had been spotty for the last fifteen years—coached him on how to remember dreams, consider their symbolism, and engage in waking conversations with dream figures—a technique he called "twilight imaging," adapted from Jung's "active imagination" approach.[12]

Bob bought an illuminated pen so he could record dreams without waking Esther. Some nights he wrote snatches from three or four dreams. Then, every week, he brought his nighttime dramas to the good doctor for discussion and reflection. Perhaps Bob's dreams could give him insight into what to do next in his life and how to do it. Dr. Progoff certainly thought that could be the case. He believed that certain dreams (but not all) carried the seed-nature of a person, and through working with them on a consistent basis, recording and enlarging upon them, one could generate a flow of new thoughts, ideas, insights, intuitions, awarenesses, and guidance regarding which areas of one's life needed examination.[13]

Bob worked with Progoff for nearly a year, switched to Martha Jaeger for another year of dream analysis, and continued to record occasional dreams through 1962. His journal from this period contains descriptions of dreams, comments about their possible meanings, waking "twilight imaging" conversations with dream figures, and traditional journal entries. It makes for fascinating reading.[14]

Analyzing the meaning of dreams—those of oneself or others—is tricky because dreams have so many layers and are intensely personal to the dreamer's situation. Even though Jung taught that certain universal, primordial archetypes emerged in dreams, he never believed in the value of a rigid "catalogue of meanings." Nor did Progoff. He sought to "evaluate" clients' dreams, not interpret them[15] The best we can do today, decades after Greenleaf scratched out his dreams in darkness, is look at common themes and Bob's own notes on interpretations.

On the surface, some of his dream scenes express his developing ideas about education, awareness, and management.

> 9 Nov. - I am sitting in a faculty meeting with some of my [Dartmouth] colleagues, but there are others including some women. P.R. makes quite a speech in favor of examinations: "How would we know anything about the economy if we had no kilowatt measure?" I rebut saying, "But a kilowatt measures something that *is*. When a teacher instructs a class he has no idea what the full effect is qualitatively, so how can he measure something when he doesn't *know* what *is*?" (nodding of heads) I say, "I have no objection to examinations if you don't grade them."
>
> Sun 15 July - We are having a large party at our house and I am standing with a group of people on the lawn (including some neighbors). I am making a speech about how our experience stands in the way of our perception.
>
> 22 May - I am talking to a colleague of [?] here in Denver. He shows me a peculiar plastic spike about a foot high and three inches cross section - slightly tapered and truncated at the top to have a

> sharp point. It is sitting on the ground. He is telling me about one of his subordinates who has not been doing his work properly and says that he intends to impale him on the spike as punishment. I remonstrate that that is no way to discipline a subordinate.

These perorations were the exception. Most entries were—well—more dream-like, but communications was a recurring theme. In a surprising number of dreams Bob spoke tenderly to animals—an owl, dogs, rabbits, cats, birds, squirrels—and listened as they whispered back. (The only dream animals he harmed were rats.) In several dreams, he found himself invited to participate in radio panels where many could hear his message.

Bob has healing abilities in several dreams:

> 10 Nov. – (1.) I am in a group that is studying spiritual healing. I get the sense that I have some of this power - feel the tingle in the ends of my fingers - see radiation.
> (2.) I am with a group that is gathered to take a bus. This bus is going where people make a serious business of spiritual healing. I am debating whether I (a.) am qualified, and (b.) ought to go along. Others are in on the discussion.
>
> Tues 11 Dec - I have developed a therapeutic device for healing people. It consists of a row of little music box movements mounted on a long board. I select the appropriate tune for the individual and his ailment.

One group of dreams concerns Bob's relationship with his anima, which is the "inner face" of the female psyche. "The anima is an archetypal form, expressing the fact that a man has a minority of female genes, and that is something that does not disappear in him," said Jung. "It is constantly present, and it works as a female in a man."[16] A woman must confront the animus, which holds male traits in her unconscious. Full maturity requires addressing the hidden power of the opposite gender. "If the personality is to be well adjusted and harmoniously balanced, the feminine side of a man's personality and the masculine side of a woman's personality must be allowed to express themselves in consciousness and behavior. If a man exhibits only masculine traits, his feminine traits remain unconscious and therefore these traits remain undeveloped and primitive. This gives the unconscious a quality of weakness and impressionability. That is why the most virile-appearing and virile-acting man is often weak and submissive inside. A woman who exhibits excessive femininity in her external life would have the unconscious qualities of stubbornness or willfulness, qualities that are often present in man's outer behavior."[17]

> 1 Mar – I'm buying a new camera. It's quite a process of examination and testing, but I finally make up my mind. Then a young woman invites me to dinner and I go along. [Greenleaf's comments on the dream follow.] I am going to get a new view of the feminine; [establish] rapport with anima. My own camera, my own lens, my own image is about to evolve.

In one dream both the anima and a "shadow" appears. As Jung defines them, shadows of the psyche are repressed material, the things we do not want to remember or confront. They cannot be eliminated, but their negative power can be transformed into positive strength if we bring them to consciousness and accept them as part of the whole self.

> Tues 28 May - I am at a party with some questionable characters. Can't recall any except the host, who invites me to stay the night. He gets my watch away from me as we go in the bedroom. Then Esther and the police appear. They take him, and Esther sternly takes me in tow. [Greenleaf's marginal notes] . . . Man is shadow who wants to control my time or take me away from time schedules - may be true? Esther is anima; must put my energies with anima. Policeman is the arbiter in a reality situation. Must get my shadow back; [I] have a terrific moral code. Esther and the cop are playing tricks on the shadow; duty driven down underneath . . .

Bob's unpredictable mother appears. In one dream, he and Esther walk toward a railroad track and watch Burchie Greenleaf walk down a track to the right. Burchie's track slopes down into water and she keeps walking until she is submerged. They have to rescue her.

Perhaps his most vivid shadow, however, one that he was forced to confront a number of times during dream therapy, was his bad temper.

In 1960, he had a dream about a squirrel that dug its claws into his arm and would not let go. The image haunted him. In his journal the next day he wrote, "I still have the problem of my deep violence—or is it that? Gerald Heard says it is frustration. Perhaps there is a creative drive that is blocked. I wonder what it could be?" So, he "cleared the screen"—entered into a restful, open state—and had an imaginative conversation with the squirrel, who spoke of violence and yet another shadow—Bob's desire for comfort and security.

> So I talked with the squirrel. And he said that the part of me that doesn't trust myself is my capacity for great things. The untrusted part is my concern with possessions, thinking about possessions, protecting the future in terms of possessions. The capacity for greatness doesn't trust this in me, [and] apparently will not materialize until this aspect of me is in check or transmuted.[18]

By this time, Bob had been working for several years on a book he called *The Ethic of Strength* and had also been writing a short paper, titled "A New Religious Mission," in which he speculated on the emergence of a religion that "probably will not be exclusively Christian and which, while ultimately conservative (because it will work to assure the future), will have the initial impact of being disturbing and unsettling to older, conservative people."[19] In his conversation with the dream squirrel, Greenleaf wondered if his interest in an emerging religion was part of his capacity for greatness. The answer: perhaps, but that was not the point.

> Write. Write for all seekers but have powerful people in mind—politics, business, labor, education—worldwide. Be universal. When you really engage with this talk, the violent feelings will disappear.
>
> Don't worry about money, you will have more than enough. Don't ask for any. You will have the time.
>
> I don't want to give you anymore now. Your family suffered from your frustration reactions, but this has been a developing experience for them. When you get your great work underway, love and gentleness will flow. You don't have to worry about it.
>
> I will talk to you when you need me but come when you want.

Two years later, one of Bob's dreams showed how he could harness the power of his anima to address the shadow of violence.

> 7 March 1962 - I have a cauldron of a peculiar sort . . . about three feet in diameter. It is mounted out of doors. I am going to demonstrate it to some people - a teen-aged girl among them. The water is boiling, and I drop a live frog in. The girl is horrified as he jumps out and scrambles to a nearby pool. Later I look in the pool and he is as a man. I'm not sure whether I use my stick to help him get to shore, but I have some fear of him.
>
> Then I am on my way to a meeting (after some intervening episodes that are not clear) and am walking across a campus—like a lawn—with a man and his young daughter. There is some building going on. Then I notice the frog, except I think he is a man, going along another walk toward the meeting place. And I have a feeling of fear.
>
> 5:30PM Same Day – [twilight imaging] conversation with the young girl. "Tell me, young girl, what was your feeling when you saw me boil the frog?"
>
> "It was one of horror. It was a hideous, revolting act."
>
> "What was the meaning of it, as you saw it?"
>
> "It was your violent self in action."
>
> "Is there nothing I can do about it?"
>
> "Yes", she said, "Talk to me and know that I am a gentle young girl. Talk to me often. Then I can come in and make a creative transformation myself, naturally, instead of your gentleness being a matter of control. You will still have your masculine assertiveness and initiative, but you will be naturally gentle."
>
> "The man-frog walking to the meeting I was going to—what did he symbolize?"
>
> "That meant, simply, that the consequences of your violent feelings are always with you to plague you, even when you are in your public role. But this can be changed, even at your own age."

Readers of Greenleaf's writings, and even those who knew him well during his lifetime, may wonder about this shadow of violence. There is no account of him aggressively harming anyone—especially his family— but there is no doubt he could have a bad temper. By all accounts, Bob followed his father's advice to "keep sweet" with Esther in spite of their occasional disagreements, but the next chapter shows how his children experienced another side of Bob during their childhood and teenage years.

To his lasting credit, Bob was honest about his shadows, and had the courage to confront them directly through dream work, reading, reflection, and changes in behavior. Therein lies the plot of Bob's mythic epic— a recognition of the dragons living in his depths, a struggle where he confronts them, fights the good fight, and *makes friends with them* so he can use their power to emerge into greater consciousness. In his reflections on one dream in which he joins two other men to pursue an "altruistic idea," Greenleaf wrote, "I have taken my shadow along. I accept him."

In spite of his hole-in-the-hedge philosophy, Greenleaf's dreams exposed his anxiety about leaving the security of AT&T. Responsibility to his family was part of his concern. The message of the dreams: Get over it.

> Sat. 13 April - I doze off and see a dirty wash basin with a couple of uncooked eggs (out of the shell) floating in dirty water. [His notes follow.] Egg = new seed, new phase. We can't get free from all anxiety and guilt if we want to progress - must face reality. I'm afraid of conflict and anxiety; have a strong-arm method with self and others.

One dream was especially prescient, anticipating the future role of his work.

> 4 July 1962 (Hanover) – I'm at a meeting with [Harvard Business School] professor (with whom I had dinner last night). It is some sort of supernatural society. I have the ability to soar, which I do. I have darts of gold which I throw as I soar. There is a problem of leadership in the group below, and I use my darts to bring people together into an appropriate relationship.

Reading the dreams as a whole, one can see a progression, a determination to leap into the next era of life. "There have always been reactionary forces in the world, forces that would sterilize the life process, that would inhibit growth," he wrote in a journal entry. "One would not want a world without them. It would be a pretty dull place. Growth is meaningful only when the opportunity is won against the opposition of reactionary forces. Growth is the measure of the man against the opportunity." And Bob *was* growing, emotionally, professionally, and, especially, spiritually.

> 2 Sep. - I'm looking out a NY apartment window at [the] skyline at night. The tall buildings all have illuminated stained glass windows. I have my arms outstretched and am proclaiming "God, God, God!" with great fervor. I have a feeling of ecstasy.

A circle, a triangle, and a cross are drawn at the top of one journal page. Written below are notes on how to focus on the three symbols, and this prayer "to sharpen perception."

1. Lord give me the strength to do your work.
2. Free me from my deeper violence.
3. Clear my mind to hear thy voice.
4. Clear my speech to convey thy word.
5. Give me the sense to serve where you want me to serve.
6. Help me to keep in contact with thee under stress.
7. Help me to hear and speak thy word under stress.
8. Make me a loving, feeling, warm person.
9. Help me to be gentle and constructive.
10. Give me the strength to withstand evil.

Simultaneously with his dream therapy and journal-keeping, Bob entered more far-ranging zones of consciousness through his friendship with Gerald Heard. When he met Gerald at Wainwright House, he encountered a legend. Some say that if history had any justice, Heard would be a legend to this day. Gerald was an intellectual Irishman who grew up in England, a close friend of Aldous Huxley, a man who enjoyed a reputation in the 1930s as a "prodigiously energetic polymath, writer, broadcaster and man of ideas."[20] In *Down There on a Visit*, Christopher Isherwood modeled the character of Augustus Par after Heard. He also called him "witty, playful, flattering, talkative as a magpie, well-informed as an encyclopaedia, and, at the same time, life-weary, meditative, deeply concerned and in earnest . . . If you couldn't get hold of Bernard Shaw, perhaps he was the next best thing . . . the most fascinating person I've ever met . . . "[21] Heard wrote thirty-eight books on topics that included natural theology, the evolution of human consciousness, flying saucers, novels, science fiction, prayers, and meditations.[22] He had a photographic memory and knew, or had known, everyone from W. H. Auden to H. G. Wells to the Swami Prabhavananda, but Greenleaf found him to be "a lonely man."[23]

Perhaps part of the isolation came from the fact that Heard was a homosexual in a time especially intolerant of sexual deviation. When he and his partner Michael began visiting the Greenleaf home, Esther asked Bob who Michael was. Bob told her he was "Gerald's secretary." Esther accepted that and forevermore believed it. For all her adventures in art and creativity, Esther was quite reticent to talk about sexual matters.

In Gerald, Bob found another hole-in-the-hedge man who, according to Huxley, operated "between the pigeonholes." His childhood had been terribly painful, beginning with a broken spine, a crushed vertebra, an incident at age twelve where he was run over by a horse and buggy, a bad fall that led to a broken shoulder, and more injuries during his young adulthood. "I wasn't permitted to settle down," he told Bob in 1958. "When I had finished my terribly inefficient education, I came out into the world realizing I must educate myself . . . Always, there were two consuming things [for me]: the great problem of human suffering and the problem of whether there is any meaning in life. Those two things were necessary to fend off this terrible melancholy so that one wouldn't commit suicide."[24]

When it came to religious matters, Heard sought that which was both beneath and beyond the great faith traditions. He called it the Eternal Gospel, which was "on the one hand, that essential sense of obligation and intuitional moral knowledge which has emerged and become defined as the common denominator and working factor in all the great religions. On the other hand, it is that element owing to which those religions are great and enduring."[25]

This position reinforced Ira Progoff's view of religion. After his World War II experiences, Progoff began to wonder what would have happened if Hitler had succeeded in destroying all the recorded wisdom of mankind. "Suppose all the Bibles of the world were burned, the Old and the New Testaments, the Tao Teh Ching, the Upanishads, the Koran, and all the others. If that happened, what would befall mankind?"[26] He decided humanity would renew the eternal spiritual truths with fresh wisdom, all expressing contact with the Unity of Life. "The great source is there to be contacted where 'deep calleth unto deep,' but each civilization and period in history has to find its own way of reaching it . . . It is a work that each person has to do alone, but it is helpful to know that many of us are working alone together."[27]

Gerald Heard was making his own contributions to eternal wisdom, and his influence on Bob Greenleaf was profound. He encouraged Bob's reading and thinking about broad theological issues, the future of humanity, and the formal study of meditation.[28] They chatted about everything from Jung to organizational theory to witch doctors in South Africa and Catholic liturgy, but the most important area of new experience Bob encountered through Heard was exposure to the hallucinogenic drug LSD.

Lysergic acid diethylamide was first formulated in 1938 by Dr. Albert Hoffman of the Sandoz Chemical Works in Basel, Switzerland, but its mind-bending effects were not discovered until 1943, when the doctor accidentally ingested a minute quantity and had the world's first LSD trip.[29] By the late 1940s, the drug had made its way to America, where it was authorized for experimental use. Psychiatrists were naturally interested. Not a small number first tried the substance on themselves, with the idea that if a therapist could experience something approximating a psychotic state, he or she could have greater empathy with patients. Then they began studying LSD's effect on patients to see if it could alleviate depression, schizophrenia, alcoholism, cancer pain, sexual dysfunction, or simple neuroses and, for good measure, enhance creativity.[30]

By the mid-1950s, mind-altering drugs were emerging into public consciousness. In 1954, Aldous Huxley published *The Doors of Perception*, in which he disclosed his experiences with mescaline and his belief that hallucinogenic drugs "bypassed . . . the reducing valve of the brain and nervous system" which protected us from being overwhelmed by the "Mind at Large."[31] William Blake once said it more elegantly: "If the doors of perception were cleansed every thing would appear to man as it is, infinite."

Huxley had an answer for the reductionists who claimed that mystical and religious states were merely a function of chemistry.

> Knowing as he does (or at least as he can know, if he so desires) what are the chemical conditions of transcendental experience, the aspiring mystic should turn for technical help to the specialists—in pharmacology, in biochemistry, in physiology and neurology, in

> psychology and psychiatry, and parapsychology. And on their part, of course, the specialists (if any of them aspire to be genuine men of science and complete human beings) should turn, out of their respective pigeonholes, to the artist, the sibyl, the visionary, the mystic—all those, in a word, who have had experience of the Other World and who know, in their different ways, what to do with that experience.[32]

Robert Greenleaf read Huxley's book and was fascinated. From then until the end of his days, he often used Huxley's phrase to describe times in his life when "my doors of perception were opened a bit wider than usual," like that afternoon when an innocent remark from Professor Helming became a roadmap for a career. Bob's interest was piqued even more when Gerald Heard introduced him to Huxley and a small group of intellectuals who were experimenting with LSD, including Alan Watts, Anais Nin, Keith Ditman, Betty Eisner, and Dr. Sidney Cohen, a psychiatrist at UCLA who took LSD a number of times and was to become one of the best-known researchers on the drug's effects.[33]

In 1958, when the substance was still legal, Gerald Heard, Dr. Sidney Cohen, and a third person (with the initials JB) met Bob at Heard's home in California and initiated him into the fantastic realms of LSD. Bob wrote up that experience, the first of several over the next few years.

> I had three sessions with Gerald in which I took the drug and he sat as what he called my invigilator. I am not quite sure what that word means, but that was the word he used. The physical senses all became very sharp; colors became iridescent . . . I listened to music under the influence of this and I've never had any other musical experience even roughly comparable to this . . . a fairy land of widened perception.
>
> After I had come down in the evening, I called Esther to report my experience and told her that for the first time, I realized what she saw in color that I had never seen . . . That was a permanent learning. From that point on I had that heightened perception of color that I didn't have before the LSD experience.[34]

Bob was open with his family about the LSD experiences. He had no choice. During and after the trips the children saw a more open, vulnerable, and joyful father. Newcomb was already living away from home and "thought it was strange," but his two sisters kept him informed about the drug's effects. "He was such a trip!" recalled Madeline. "He was relaxed, unpressured, unconcerned, he was floating, and he wasn't a floaty guy. We were once in a rental house in New Hampshire with a big, long back yard, and a field behind it of black-eyed Susans. He sat out for hours looking at the black-eyed Susans. Finally it got dark and cold. He came in and Esther put a blanket around him. He sat, just ecstatic, just ecstatic, and it was wonderful to see him."[35]

Madeline's older sister Lisa appreciated the effects of the drug on her father. "It brought him into deeper harmony with the complexities of his nature. He became much easier to live with, more grounded and centered in his own self. I really think it allowed his still calm and creativity to find its place. I believe the LSD opened up Bob's doors so that he began to function much more effectively, in so many ways."[36]

LSD may have been legal under supervision of a doctor, but even before the days of Timothy Leary, it had a stigma attached to it. "We were told, 'Never, ever, under pain of death, tell anyone about this,'" recalled Madeline, "because, of course, he worked for AT&T and we lived in a community where we went to school with the kids of presidents of AT&T. Not that I didn't tell other people about it, but I never told him that I told anyone!"[37] Bob also had LSD sessions with "Uncle Bill" Wolf and others but never took the drug after it was declared illegal.[38]

"This was an adventure, a mind-stretching adventure," said Bob nearly thirty years later. "I regret that we are not a mature enough society to permit this drug to be used that way. I don't question declaring it illegal because the way it developed, and the way it was being used—particularly in the youth culture—was very destructive. I am just glad that I had the experience while it was still legal because it meant a great deal to me."[39]

Bob never took marijuana or any other drug because he did not see that they had the same "developmental possibilities" as LSD. "To what extent my total perception of everything was influenced, I have no sure sense of that," he said later, "but I have the feeling that it had a rather total effect, that I was more aware of everything, although the evidence is not as striking as it is in the case of color where the contrast between my color perception before taking LSD and after was quite striking."[40]

Huxley and Heard also believed that awareness was the drug's great gift, *if used appropriately*, by the conscious choice of reasonably healthy people, and in the presence of a guide. In his final hours, Aldous Huxley took the drug in order to be "more conscious."[41] Dave Kahn, the business-man who made possible Edgar Cayce's astonishing career as a psychic and was close to both Gerald Heard and Aldous Huxley, also wanted to use LSD to be more aware and pain-free on his deathbed, but by then the drug was illegal and he was denied the opportunity.[42] Dr. Sidney Cohen continued his work and, in 1960, published a classic paper on its effects.[43] Ironically, some of his later research was cited by lawmakers to ban the substance.

After several years of personal introspection in the midst of profes-sional action, Robert Greenleaf was moving closer to claiming his per-sonal greatness. His *life* was his greatest teaching—to himself and others—but his writing would be the way he made a difference and moved his "little corner of the world" to every corner of the world. It was time to get on with it, but he still faced the challenge of integrating his learning into his family relationships.

CHAPTER 15

Husband and Father

In the end, nothing really counts but love and friendship. [1]
ROBERT K. GREENLEAF

When Bob came home from work every day he immediately went up-
stairs, changed out of his drab Manhattan business suit, and either headed
for the basement workshop or, in the summertime, the huge organic garden behind the house. The garden was a thing of beauty, with a large as-
paragus patch, rows of tomato plants, and every imaginable kind of fruit,
vegetable, and salad green. These were all "live foods," not the "dead
foods" warned against by Gaylord Hauser, inventor of Vege-Sal, food ad-
visor to stars like Greta Garbo and Gloria Swanson, and nutritional guru
to Esther Greenleaf. Esther was picky about what went into her family's
bodies, and she wanted as many locally-grown, organic "live foods" as
possible on her table.

From his books and radio programs, Esther knew of Gaylord
Hauser's cautions against coffee, chocolate, and processed foods like
white flour and refined sugar. He much preferred wheat germ, molasses,
and nearly-raw beef liver. Esther was also a disciple of several other early
nutritionists, like Adelle Davis and Carleton Fredericks. On the New York

radio station WOR, Fredericks had the audacity to recommend vitamins for various illnesses, advice that earned him a criminal conviction for unlawful practice of medicine.[2] True to her Hargrave family's homeopathic roots, Esther persisted in decrying evil foods—especially sugar—and patrolled her family's sugar consumption with vigilance. Newcomb vividly remembered the times W.H. Wright, one of Bob's friends and colleagues from Ohio, came to visit.

> He would always bring a large Whitman's sampler box. My mother would say to him, "Please don't bring that! This is really *not* what we need." And he would say, "Don't be silly! Of course I will!" So he just kept bringing them and they kept asking him not to, or at least my mother did. One day he said, "Really Esther, I do believe you think chocolate is a sin," and the name stuck. For a long time, the word for chocolate in our house was "sin." The religious and the nutritional were very closely linked.[3]

Alcohol was another one of those sins, and the Greenleafs neither drank nor served it when friends from their country-club community came to dinner. They did keep a bottle of whiskey on the top shelf of the cupboard in the back hall to "take care of snakes," and in later life, Bob took an occasional sip of wine when his adult children brought it home, but that was the extent of the drinking. Madeline thought that, for Bob, alcohol represented loss of control.[4]

Esther shared Bob's penchant for *seeking*. Her outgoing social skills were a balance to Bob's more introverted style. She was willing to join in her husband's adventures, and he was quite delighted to join in hers, as daughter Madeline well remembered.

> When they read about someone or read someone's work that influenced them, they pursued them; they were willing to go find them. Esther once heard that Adelle Davis was giving talks nearby so they went, introduced themselves, and became good friends with her.[5]

Bob and Esther were, quite simply, a powerful team. Both read voraciously, but because so much of Bob's reading was work-related, Esther gradually become his advance intellectual scout in areas ranging from theology to biology to thrillers.[6] She would plow through the entire output of an author and then suggest the books Bob should read. He, in turn, stretched canvases for Esther's paintings, built her a kiln, and let her coach him on creating jewelry ("for my three women") and, yes, even painting abstract art, which he no longer considered "a bad joke." Esther had an expansive, civilizing influence on Bob, evolving his narrow Midwestern sensibilities into more discerning and catholic appreciations. Theirs was a lifelong love story. Letters they exchanged during Bob's frequent travels always began with "Dearest," and ended with "Love" or "All my love."

When the children were young, Bob and Esther teamed up to make memorable kid-magic. Newcomb, Lisa, and Madeline all received their own personalized wooden jigsaw puzzles. Esther painted the pictures; Bob cut them out and put them together. In 1951, Madeline's puzzle was a painting of her in a Halloween outfit surrounded by all her favorite dolls and toys. Bob also made special furniture for each child. Esther painted the pieces and used them in wonderful decorating schemes for each room.[7]

In 1946, Bob and Esther honored their children by privately publishing a little book called *Poems, Stories, Drawings by Elizabeth, Madeline and Newcomb Greenleaf*. The writing is delightful, and the drawings are reproduced in color. The book ends with "Three New Year's Resolutions for 1946: Newcomb: Drink ALL my orange juice! Elizabeth: No hitting; no pinching! Madeline: No more calling peoples pickle-puss!"[8]

Once when the children were little they asked their daddy what he did when he went away to work. He said, "I twirl around in a chair." On the rare occasions when they visited his large office, usually at Christmastime, he allowed them to hop on his swivel chair and spin round and round, gleefully squealing "Oh! Oh! Oh!" Bob let them go and laughed along with them.[9]

Bob's parents did not celebrate Christmas in a big way, or any other holiday for that matter. Fatherhood gave him an excuse to not only indulge his own children with Christmas joy but experience it himself for the first time. He and Esther were lavish, almost outrageous in overdecorating the big Christmas tree, stringing lights around the house, buying (or making) and wrapping far too many gifts, and filling the stockings to overflowing, each stocking gift individually wrapped in high style. Bob adored the experience so much he branched out to Valentine's Day. Esther and the girls were treated to elaborate breakfasts every February 14, savored beneath hearts strung across the ceiling. They received gifts of enameled jewelry designed and made just for them by Daddy—or "Bobby," as Esther always called him.

Like so many multiply gifted people, Bob could be curious and playful. Kites were his favorite purchases from Army surplus stores. He bought the giant models, two dozen at a time if he could find them, which the Army had used to carry small transmitters aloft. He frequently took them on trips and even launched one of those beauties over the sparkling waters of the Gulf of Mexico. One of his favorite kite flying spots was the back field of his in-laws' farm in Ringoes, New Jersey. While the girls dressed in antique clothes and played at tea with Grandma Ethel Hargrave, Bob sat alone in a lawn chair with the wind whistling through his hair and flew a giant kite for glorious, uninterrupted hours.[10] When the wind was not blowing, he sometimes joined his father-in-law William Hargrave on the porch to play duets of Stephen Foster melodies on cheap plastic recorders, with Bob taking the harmony line. Bob played instruments—and sang his rumbling bass—by ear, using an innate musicality that brought him great joy throughout his life.

During moments of elation at home, Bob sometimes let his emotions out by dancing in the kitchen. His moves combined those you would see at a Hoosier hillbilly hoedown and a clog dance. The rubber soles on his size-thirteen leather shoes made black marks on the linoleum floor as he swung his arms and tapped out the rhythm—chuck-a, chuck-a, chuck-a—performing with abandon in front of his delighted wife and children.[11]

Bob tolerated dogs but loved cats. He found a congenial soulfulness in those creatures who, like him, combined playfulness and reserve, cunningness and transparency, all while accessing extraordinary sense perceptions. Tuffy, the Greenleaf cat, played a game with Bob for hours. Tuffy sat on the stool by the kitchen table and Bob threw a soft treat at him. Usually it hit him on the nose (Bob's aim was good). The cat jumped down, ate the treat, then hopped back up, ready for the next shot. One year Madeline and her husband took Petunia, their Siamese cat, to Bob and Esther's home for the Christmas holidays. Bob and Petunia worked out a new game in the back hallway. Bob held open a paper bag; Petunia ran into the bag; Bob closed the bag and slid it to the other end of the hall-way. Petunia fought her way out, Bob held the bag open again, Petunia dashed back in and they repeated the sequence, over and over and over. "That was the playful Bob who was always there," said Madeline, "but whom we didn't always see."[12]

Bob allowed himself to experience a playful childhood for the first time in other ways, and Newcomb shared in some of these rich moments.

> During the years after 1945 the surplus shops of lower Manhattan were full of marvelous electrical, optical, and mechanical devices from the second world war, elegantly finished with burnished brass, now being sold for a song. Week after week Bob would come home with a new treasure. Together we would disassemble these beauties, with the goal either of reassembling them in working order or sal-vaging prize parts from their innards."[13]

Bob's basement workshop nurtured connections with his Indiana craftsman roots. He was an excellent plumber, electrician, and carpenter. He could cut, weld, buff, and build, and he fashioned his heirloom furni-ture with meticulous precision. "I loved being with him in the shop," re-membered Newcomb.

> It was a magical center of my boyhood, both because of what it con-tained and because of the extraordinary mastery which Bob displayed over the many crafts he practiced there. Whatever need arose, he had the right tool (from Bunsen burner to jigsaw to oscilloscope), the right part (stowed systematically away in an immense warren of drawers and boxes), and the skill to do the job well.[14]

Bob's interest in mechanical, electrical, metal, and wood crafts was natural, given his exposure to George Greenleaf's mastery of machines and the fact that he spent his childhood in an age when the Erector Set was introduced and became the most popular toy in America.[15] One sus-pects more was at work here, though. His workshop gave him not only solitude but one more sphere of *control*. Personal control of situations did not seem to be an issue at the 195 Broadway AT&T headquarters building, but it sometimes was at 27 Woodcrest Avenue in Short Hills, New Jersey.

Newcomb saw his father as "very traditional" at home, in the way "traditional" was defined by Bob's generation. "The man was the boss at home," said Newcomb. This tradition meant that Bob was "not always an easy person at home," even with Esther.[16] In the early fifties, Bob opposed Esther selling her paintings. That was not something a wife did, especially the wife of an AT&T executive. It was inconsistent with a "traditional" family structure. Anyone who grew up in Bob's generation, or even his children's generation, can verify that this attitude was the norm in America's hearths and homes at the time.

For all his childlike capacity, Bob as a young father could be stonily distant. "Bob was a man of great silences," said Lisa. "Sometimes, it was a 'suck the life out of the room' kind of silence. If he really did not want much going on because he needed the space, he just made you give him the space without saying so."[17] Bob seldom talked about work at home. At the dinner table, he usually ate quietly while others shared their day. Occasionally Esther asked, "What do you think about that, Bobby?" He usually made an appropriate response to indicate he had been listening and went back to eating. After dinner, he often disappeared into his basement workshop.

Newcomb, the oldest child, may have got the worst of the silences, which, combined with Bob's temper, sometimes terrified the young son. On the other hand, Bob's anger could sometimes be downright funny, as Newcomb discovered while working with his father in the basement workshop. "If he hit his thumb with a hammer, he got very angry and he wanted to swear, but he felt that he couldn't swear in front of me. So, I had to leave the room and shut the door. Then he would swear a blue streak. I would hear him stop swearing, go back in, and we would resume our work."[18]

Other times, Bob's temper wasn't so funny. It could flare up if the children were late coming out of the Friends Meeting House, late to the table, or in response to any number of trivial events. According to Newcomb, Bob was aware of his temper—even afraid of it—and struggled to control it, but he was even more afraid of Esther losing *her* temper. That would cut too close to the quick, triggering the memory of Bob's own out-of-control mother. "I was brought up in a home of wrangles and jangles; I've tried to forget about it," Bob once wrote in a journal.[19]

Through it all, Bob and Esther "kept sweet" with each other. It was a genuine, loving sweetness, not a shallow, saccharine version. Even Newcomb saw it.

I never once heard them raise their voices to each other. My mother once told me a story. She said, "One time Bob was angry at me. When I started to get angry at him he immediately stopped. He said, 'Now you can't get angry because *I'm* angry. And if you get angry then we'll have a big fight and that will be terrible.' He said, 'You can get angry as long as I'm not angry but if I'm angry then you're not.'" This was presented as great wisdom. He was particularly afraid of fights within the family. In a way, I think he was more afraid of her anger than she was of his. She didn't get angry that much.[20]

Bob yearned for a peaceful home life and sometimes tried to achieve it by controlling the people who lived with him. Alas, it did not work. He and Esther raised three strong, smart children, and beginning in their teenage years, each, in his or her own way, stood up to him.

Madeline worked out a signal with Esther. When Madeline was about to cry, she would grab her throat, and Esther would jump in and try to defuse the situation before Bob sent her to her room, but often it was too late. "I was the only one who got sent repeatedly to my room after dinner because I egged him on," remembered Madeline. "I'd always go in tears, but I'd do it again, and I'd do it again. And then if I said I was sorry, he would say, [here she lowers her voice] 'If you were sorry, you wouldn't have done it'" [laughs].[21] Sometimes Bob and Madeline would not speak for days or even weeks. In spite of her tears, Madeline's two older siblings believe that she was least affected by Bob's attitude during her childhood. Madeline attended Earlham College and eventually went on to become one of the most admired employees of *Time* magazine.

Around the age of fourteen, Lisa took her own stand. Bob was self-controlled physically—that is, he never threatened to strike any of the children—but he certainly had the power to affect them emotionally when his own control of the family was threatened. Lisa felt that Esther's interventions got in the way of her opportunity to simply thrash things out with Bob and clear the air. Without those healthy confrontations, Bob sometimes came across to Lisa as distant and arrogant.

There were also moments when a father's blessing was given. Lisa took ballroom dancing lessons at the Racquet Club in Short Hills and became a fabulous dancer, winning prizes while literally having a ball. When she was fifteen she came home after a dancing triumph and told

Newcomb all about it. He said, "Did you know they don't allow Jews at the Racquet Club?"

She was stunned.

"That's right," he said. "They can't even walk in the door."

Lisa's heart broke, because their next door neighbors were Jewish, and the father, Max, was like a surrogate father to her. That evening at the dinner table she announced, "They do not allow Jews at the Racquet Club and I will never go there again!"

Bob's eyes widened. "You mean to say you will never go back, that you would give up your dancing?"

"That's right—never!"

"Then I will personally take you dancing in New York!" he beamed.

Years later she remembered the moment. "Bob had high standards and was hard to please, but I hit the jackpot that day. This time I did it right!"[22]

Lisa was destined to make her name as a gifted artist and, in later life, a therapist.

One could speculate that the source of Bob's temper (which he called violence) was residual anger from the behavior of an erratic mother, or his frustration at being a hole-in-the-hedge man in an age of hedged-in men who preferred security over seeking, and it leaked out at home because it could not be expressed openly at work. The truth is, no one knows for sure. If he speculated about the source of this shadow, he did not record it in his notes and journals. His concern with the issue was two-fold: (1) *consciously* accepting that a shadow of violence existed, and (2) understanding its effect on his psyche, especially in its ability to interfere with his ability to make his contributions to the world.

Esther was the protector in this family psychodrama, the buffer between Bob's darker side and his children. "Not that we needed that much protection," said Newcomb. "It was just that occasionally he would get angry and he had rather rigid ideas about a lot of things."[23]

Because of time spent with his own father, Bob had a strong sense of what a man should do for and with his son. Bob had no personal interest in sports, but Newcomb did, so Bob took his son to baseball games and played catch with him in the backyard. Newcomb was a New York Giants fan and remembers games at Ebbets Field when the Dodgers' Jackie Robinson drove Giants pitchers crazy by his astounding moves off first base.

On the trip to Terre Haute for Burchie Greenleaf's funeral, Bob looked up a famous local resident, one Mordecai Peter Centennial Brown— "Three Finger Brown"—the Chicago Cubs player who pitched the decisive shutout game in the 1907 World Series and won two out of every three games pitched in his long career. Brown asked Newcomb what he wanted to be. "I want to be a baseball player," said the youngster. The future Hall of Famer responded, "Well that's good, but what if you can't be a baseball player, then what do you want to be?" "Well, then I want to be a radio announcer for baseball," came the reply. Brown massaged the three fingers on his right hand that had given so many pitches their weird, unhittable spins and tried again. "What if you can't be that?" "Oh," said Newcomb, "then I guess I'll just have to be an umpire." Brown bristled at the suggestion. "Oh no!" he said, "Don't be an *umpire!*"[24]

Bob wanted to expose Newcomb to his work. He frequently took him along to his downtown office and on business trips. They went to Montreal and Chicago; they visited a steel mill in Bethlehem, Pennsylvania, and various other factories and Bell System plants. "He passed along to me numerous stories and aphorisms about the working life," wrote Newcomb. "He had in mind the model of his father, who had involved Bob both in his mechanical work and his political career." Alas, it did not work. "I was defining myself in opposition to him, particularly over the issue of education. I embraced education for its own sake and went on to a career in mathematics, taking pride for many years in the 'purity' and lack of application of my research."[25]

Curiously, during his teenage years, Newcomb began calling his parents "Bob and Esther," and his sisters eventually followed suit. Later in life, Madeline went back to referring to them as "mum and pop." Newcomb already lived away from home by the time Bob started his dream work and other transformative experiences of the period from 1958–1962, but he recognized that "[Bob] was a very different person later on."[26] Newcomb married early, had two children in quick order, and enjoyed a brilliant academic career, culminating in a Ph.D. in mathematics at the age of twenty-four and a teaching career at several schools, including Columbia University.

In spite of exposure to Bob's shadows, none of the children believed they had a terrible childhood. Later in life, they recognized the poignancy of a man who, like so many males of his generation, was caught in the double-bind of loving his family deeply and being unable to express those emotions openly. Lisa Greenleaf saw the pattern clearly.

> He knew he didn't give us much emotionally—he knew that. And, he did so many very considerate, thoughtful things. They were often very potent things, like making things for us, and handing me all the English poets in these beautiful little books. I was a teenager at the time and didn't even know I needed to read them, but I took them to my room and began reading—Keats and Shelley and Byron, Wordsworth and so on—just at the time in my life when they were perfect!
>
> I always wanted a harpsichord. Bob actually went to a harpsichord place and priced them, at which point he said, "Oh, I don't think so!" He considered buying a kit but realized there was no way he was going to put that thing together. But he *did* consider it. At any rate, I started getting depressed in my teenage years. Sometimes I'd walk through the room and say, "I am very depressed." One time I did this and Bob looked at me and he said, "Let's talk harpsichords." I said, "Huh?" He said, "What about a harpsichord? What would it mean to you to have a harpsichord?" I felt my spirits just rise. I said, "That would be great." And we talked a little bit and he said, "You know, you weren't really all that depressed. See, just the mention of a harpsichord brought you right out of it." He said, "You see, real depression, real deep depression, wouldn't have been affected by the mention of a harpsichord. Just so you understand."
>
> At that moment, he was there. He knew depression. And he knew that there were some depressions that were just circumstantial; a cheerful thought or a desired object would bring you right out of it. He was showing me that by letting me discover how I felt. If he had said, "You know, this probably isn't real depression," it probably wouldn't have affected me at all, just made me feel worse. Yet what he did was bring me right up out of it and show me where I was.[27]

Lisa sensed in her father a quality that author Parker Palmer also recognized in him: a "sadness that comes when one is too experienced to expect miracles." [28] Lisa saw it as depression.

He was a man who, I know, battled depression. Absolutely. I don't really like that phrase, "clinical depression" when applied to Bob because, from my own experience—and I am enough like him to know what his insides were like somewhat—he had a deep call to the depths. He was living a life in the business world. The two don't go very well together, so his *being* got caught between the business world and a call to the depths—which to me is what depression is, it's a call to the depths . . . Depression doesn't mean there's something wrong with you. I believe that depression means there's something right with you.[29]

Later in life Bob was asked if he was the model of a servant for his own children. "Not in the way my own father was [to me]," he replied. "My kids didn't know anything about my work and never saw me in action the way I saw my father. I never was one to carry my job home, but if I had, that would have been all we'd have talked about."[30] He loved his family but had difficulty expressing that love directly, and his work took him away from them for weeks at a time. Even as he tried to balance responsibilities to family and work, he had a growing sense that he belonged to the larger world, that some great work was luring him forward beyond AT&T.

CHAPTER 16

Breakout From AT&T

As I see it, leadership that devotes itself wholly to operating successfully in the here and now—essential as this is—will not measure up to its total responsibility. Leadership is equally called on to build vitality for the long pull . . . A business must generate vitality under all the circumstances that confront it—not only in times of crisis, but just as much under conditions of success . . . [1]

ROBERT K. GREENLEAF, 1960 Ghostwritten speech for
AT&T President FRED KAPPEL

Beginning with his Jungian dream work in the late fifties, Greenleaf began thinking seriously about taking early retirement from AT&T. By 1964, his first year of eligibility, all the children would have left home, and he and Esther would be free to travel while he taught, consulted, and wrote. Bob had been a teacher for AT&T employees from his earliest days with the company, and since 1950 had been a visiting lecturer at schools like Dartmouth, MIT, and Harvard Business School. He had consulted on a formal or informal basis with companies like IBM and had built a solid writing portfolio, even though many of his pieces were ghost-writing or were published anonymously for Alcoholics Anonymous, the Laymen's Movement, the Cooperative Movement, and Quaker newsletters.

As far back as his high school years, Bob Greenleaf had been a superb writer. His identification with the common working man urged a simplicity of expression, while his broad reading and deep reflection lent depth to ideas. Bob's bosses at AT&T recognized this ability early in the game. His *Management Ability* pamphlet and uncountable internal memos usually went beyond mere reporting; they addressed pressing business issues and embodied a concern for human growth in managers and subordinates, along with practical suggestions about what steps the company should take to secure its long-range future.[2] Given all this talent, it was natural that top executives—especially AT&T presidents—would ask him to write their speeches.

Bob was as good a ghostwriter as he was at everything else he was asked to do. This ability was fortunate, because he found a paucity of ideas in the "top people" for whom he wrote.

> In all the time I did this I never had anybody ask me to write a speech and say, "These are the ideas I want to use." All they told me was the occasion and the conditions of the talk. I had to produce the ideas; they didn't have them . . .
>
> I have a theory, and this is strictly a "curbstone theory," that long years of managerial work really destroys creativity and that people who get into top spots like this just don't have ideas.[3]
>
> The people I grew up with in the grassroots of the business in Ohio were not like that. They were real people, very persuasive, very effective people; no ghostwritten speeches.[4]

No job is more anonymous—and thankless—than that of a ghostwriter. Why would Bob consent to do it? First, his preference was to operate behind the scenes More importantly, however, it was a way for him to live out his long-term mission to influence and change his company from within.

> Ghostwriting is, in a way, a reprehensible activity. In other words, you build reputations for people who don't deserve them. But I really don't see any other way to operate. I did a lot of ghostwriting, and I found it a terribly influential spot to be in.[5]

White House ghostwriters would agree, especially the best ones like Peggy Noonan, who wrote some of President Reagan's finest speeches.[6] Greenleaf was able to use others as a mouthpiece for his ideas about how a business could achieve greatness.

His speeches followed classic form, right out of any good textbook: establish rapport with the audience, preview the ideas, make at least three key points and support each with statistics or stories, visualize possible results, call your listeners to action, and summarize. It's no different than the familiar advice: "Tell 'em what you're going to tell 'em. Tell 'em. Tell 'em what you told 'em." Greenleaf added plenty of stories that were *motivated by the content*, had the speaker freely admit he did not know all the answers, and provided lines that flat-out inspired the audience.

As for content, every ghostwritten speech was different, but most contained common elements:

(1) *Frank attention to economic realities.* Every business must make a satisfactory profit, protect its assets, develop new products, and strengthen its position in industry and the economy.

(2) *Concern with relationships,* "that is, the rights and duties that exist between the business and the people whose lives it affects." Does the business conform to legal and ethical standards, maintain good shareholder relations, and satisfy the wants of customers? Does it maintain good relations with competitors to improve the industry? Does it earn the respect of communities in which it operates and influence favorably the climate in which *all* businesses operate? "Are the people in the business growing in terms of morale, attitude, ability, initiative, self-reliance and creativity? Is the business contributing as it should to the welfare of its people . . . to do for themselves in such matters as economic security, health, safety, family stability and community responsibility?"[7]

(3) *Concern with improving management.* A company should continually improve its knowledge of and control over its business, nurture future top management, and contribute to the body of management research.

(4) *Overarching themes.* Set goals beyond the immediate, safe ones. Delegate responsibility, expecting that some will fail, and make each person responsible for both successes and failures. Encourage lifelong learning; offer extensive training but expect each employee to be responsible for his or her own personal growth and development. Practice foresight as an ethical responsibility.[8]

Greenleaf used dozens of pithy stories to illustrate his points. When insurance executives asked President Cleo Craig to give a speech describing how the Bell System forecast coming trends, Greenleaf supplied a ready story for the speaker.

> Apropos of how to look ahead scientifically, let me remind you of the eminent astronomer who paid a visit to Mt. Palomar Observatory. He peered long and intently through the big telescope. Finally he said, with the air of a man who has discovered one of the secrets of the universe, "It's going to rain." An assistant who was standing by said, "Is that so, Professor? How can you tell?" The great astronomer replied, "My feet hurt."
>
> Now, just as he tried to take all the important facts into account, so do we in the telephone business. We look to see where people's feet are taking them.[9]

Greenleaf, who was a reader of Emerson, often used short, vivid language to make points.

"If a man puts a fence around what he wants to know, the inevitable result is that what he does know will serve him less and less."[10]

"Be courageous in separating those who cannot meet the standard. In the end this is better for all concerned . . . we all know that management takes backbone."[11]

"If you can get the idea of quality into people's blood and people's bones, they are alert and receptive to a goal that is beyond their reach."[12]

"Every business needs something to strive for, something to become, something to achieve, goals to reach. What kind of a business should it be? What should be its role in the industry or the economy? What position is it striving to attain?"[13]

Writers know that one learns how to write by writing. After honing his craft writing for others, Greenleaf finally hit a point where he wanted to write for himself. He had recognized that impulse in his earliest journal entries and, several times, jotted down notes that he expected to be part of a "spiritual autobiography." Most importantly, he knew he now had something to say.

A year after he began his dream work, Bob began writing his first book, which he called *The Ethic of Strength*. It took six years to complete.[14] In the preface, Greenleaf says the book "was the fruit of many discussions over the past ten years with individuals and groups of persons interested in their own growth and development" and was augmented by lectures he gave at MIT and Harvard Business School through 1965.[15] The audience was young people who, Greenleaf assumed, "wanted to excel, to assume some important responsibility and carry it with distinction . . . I assumed further that they were especially concerned about their ability to be right and just and honorable in all of their dealings."[16]

In the manuscript, Greenleaf argues that one needs *strength* to make ethical decisions. He defines *strength* as "the ability to see enough choices of aims, to choose the *right* aim, and to pursue that aim responsibly over a long period of time."[17] It sounds traditional enough, but the fact that Greenleaf always italicizes the word *strength* is a tip-off that his meaning is anything but traditional.

> *Strength* . . . isn't like muscle, to be developed by exercise and flexing. It does not come as the direct result of conscious striving. It is not the end product of a series of logical steps. It does not emerge spontaneously as the result of embracing a belief. Nor is it the product of "good works," useful and desirable as these are. And it is not likely to come from the routine practice of religious observance, granted that this, too, may have its virtues.[18]

Much of the rest of the book is an attempt to lure readers beyond knowledge and analytical systems toward the role of a *seeker* who is open to new knowledge, able to live in joyful awareness of the moment and committed to growth, all in the context of radical responsibility. And what is the source of this capacity? *Entheos*, a sixteenth century word from the roots *en*, "possessed of," and *theos*, or "spirit." Greenleaf wrote that "*Entheos* is the essence, the power actuating the person who is inspired [by spirit] . . . I choose the word *entheos* with this connotation because to be strong in the times we live in—to choose the right aim and to pursue that aim responsibly over a long period of time—one must have inspiration backed by power." Greenleaf's contention is that anyone who makes decisions should, as an *ethical* imperative, develop this kind of seeking, openness, and *strength*.[19]

The last, one-page chapter of the book recounts a dream Greenleaf recorded in his journal on March 2, 1957.

> Along the way I had a dream.
>
> I am riding on a bicycle through a beautiful level woods in which there is a labyrinth of paths. In my left hand I carry a map of these paths. I am riding rapidly and buoyantly following my map.
>
> The map blows out of my hand. As I come to a stop, I look back and see my map flutter to the ground. It is picked up by an old man who stands there holding it for me. I walk back to get my map.
>
> When I arrive at the old men, he hands me, not my map, but a small round tray of earth in which are growing fresh grass and seedlings.[20]

Bob did not explain the dream. It does not take much imagination, however, to see the value the dream places on organic processes over sterile procedures. The dream's wisdom figure offers a potent symbol that suggests a predetermined course through the labyrinth of possible paths will not work. When making important decisions at work or at home, says Greenleaf, we need to cultivate *strength*, nurtured by *entheos*, to choose the right aim and to pursue it responsibly over a long time. This approach is not simply "another way" of making decisions. It is an ethical requirement for making *any* decisions.

Bob's journal shows that he was alternately excited and discouraged about the book. It remained unpublished during his lifetime, and he left no clues as to the reason. When it was discovered in the Greenleaf archives at Andover Newton Theological School in 1992, even his son was surprised to hear of its existence, although letters show that some of his contemporaries were aware of the project. To this day, *The Ethic of Strength* remains fresh and useful.

Meanwhile, Bob was working on other writings, perfecting the form that would become the most natural for his message—the essay. In 1962, he published a small pamphlet called "Education and Maturity," a reproduction of a talk he gave at Barnard College in 1960.[21] "The most important lesson I have learned about maturity is that the emergence, the full development, of what is uniquely *me* should be an important concern throughout my life," he wrote.[22]

> This I learned the hard way. There was a long "wilderness" period in which I sought resources outside of myself. I looked for an "answer"

> to the normal frustrations of life (*frustration* used in the sense of the blocking of motives to which one cannot make a constructive response). Good years went by. No answers came. It took a long time for me to discover that the only *real* answer to frustration is to concern myself with the drawing forth of what is uniquely me.[23]
>
> This is the central idea of maturity: to keep your private lamp lighted as you venture forth on your own to meet with triumph or disaster or *just plain routine*.[24]

Greenleaf goes on to outline four requirements for living into maturity. First, if one accepts responsibility, one must expect commensurate stress. "I see no exceptions: no completely whole persons, nor any chance of it. You must not look forward to any idealized achievement, no perfect or enduring adjustment to your life work."[25] Second, one most hold fast to the essential inner person while participating in legitimate, external conformity. Third, find personal significance outside the complications of status, property, and "achievement." Finally, engage in processes of growth, drawing on the power of *entheos* to track the "changing patterns and depths of one's interests."[25] "The ultimate test of *entheos*, however, is an intuitive feeling of oneness, of wholeness, of rightness; but not necessarily comfort or ease."[26]

Bob and Esther continued their practice of attending lectures and conferences, making friends with people who interested them and had something to teach. For years, Bob's interest in poetry had drawn him to Robert Frost, and more than once he attended Frost's readings and engaged in dialogue with the master American poet.

When Frost died in 1963, Bob wrote an "engagement" with his poem *Directive*.[27] Bob's take on the poem, which he never claimed was the only "right" interpretation of it, echoes his struggle to face the losses that would be associated with giving up old patterns should he retire early, to find new solid ground, and to embrace emerging spiritual understandings. One line from the poem jumped out at him: "If you'll let a guide direct you who only has at heart your getting lost."

> This is a big *if*; who wants that kind of guide? Don't we ask for a guide who is certain of his destination, and then only after we are certain that it is a destination we want to go to?

> The tradition built around the ministry of Jesus of Nazareth, the one in which I grew up and which has the greatest symbolic meaning to me now, seems especially emphatic on this point. Jesus seemed only to have at heart our getting lost; he was mostly concerned with what must be taken away rather than with what would be gained. We find clues to what must be lost in such sayings as "unless you turn and become like children you will never enter the kingdom of heaven," and "it is easier for a camel to go through the eye of a needle than for a rich man to enter the kingdom . . ."[28]
>
> To be on with the journey one must have an attitude toward loss and being lost, a view of oneself in which powerful symbols like [quoting from the poem] *burned, dissolved, broken off*—however painful their impact is seen to be—do not appear as senseless or destructive. Rather the losses they suggest are seen as opening the way for new creative acts, for the receiving of priceless gifts. Loss, *every* loss the mind of man can conceive of, creates a vacuum into which will come (if allowed) something new and fresh and beautiful, something unforeseen—and the greatest of these is *love*.[29]

Bob was as reflective in his personal letters as he was in his essays. The year before he wrote the commentary on *Directive*, he and Esther visited an old friend who had recently been diagnosed with a very serious illness. That night Bob went home and wrote a letter to "B" in which he offered "not advice, but just some reflections stimulated by our discussion." Bob's letters to friends and colleagues were always gracious, always curious about the recipient's situation, but also full of thoughtful insights about ideas that were important to him and Esther at the time. They were gifts from the heart, often compassionate, always stimulating. The one to "B" is worth quoting at length.

Greenleaf congratulates "B" on accepting his physical situation as an opportunity. "I just hope that when the opportunity shall be mine I can do as well," he wrote. The letter continued:

> The longer I live the more convinced I become that sanctification is the purpose of all existence on this earth. This is our opportunity to become saints as much as we can. Every loss, *every one*, can be converted into gain within this frame of reference. *Everything*: work,

family, friendship, loss and suffering, achievement and reward, is a means to this end—or can become so.

Out of sainthood comes our best knowledge of what is right, of what we should do. One does not do right in order to become a saint. Rather one becomes a saint in order to know what is right, what one should do, and to gain the courage and strength to do it.

This is the time, it seems to me, to turn to the development of an inward religion. You have made your contribution, and a good one, to outward religion. Don't reject that. Simply move on to the next stage: the acceptance of the idea that you have all of the strength, all of the resources within you as you sit by your beautiful window and look out upon the quiet serenity of the countryside. Make this quiet and serenity yours. Lose yourself in it and listen. Don't ask for anything; don't expect anything—but listen. Learn to take long periods of silence with the mind clear of everything but an awareness of the quiet and the serenity . . . Keep in mind that line from John Milton's *Sonnet On His Blindness*: 'They also serve who only stand and wait.'

This is the key word: *wait*. Wait upon the inward voice. Hold in your mind the attitude of awe and wonder before the great ineffable mystery of creation of which we are all a part; but lay aside all theological notions, all rational ideas from outward religions, even the familiar concepts and names . . . You may find that the inward guidance will suggest views of this opportunity that you would not otherwise think of . . . This is your great chance to find a new level of awareness about these things."[30]

In addition to his duties with AT&T, Bob managed to invest another lifetime of activity with outside organizations. From 1950 to 1957, he was a member of the faculty for the Graduate School of Credit and Financial Management at Dartmouth College and an occasional lecturer at the School of Industrial Management at MIT and Harvard Business School. He was a trustee of the Russell Sage and Yokefellow Foundations and upheld membership in various professional organizations like the Society for the Advancement of Management and the American Management Association. Meanwhile, he continued his formal and informal work with the Quakers.

Esther stayed busy too. Besides raising the children and entertaining, she continued her artwork, attended conferences, hosted study groups with Bob, and read voraciously. The Greenleafs were good friends with Peter and Doris Drucker, who lived nearby in Montclair, New Jersey. Bob considered Esther to be Drucker's intellectual equal and always remembered how she would "nail him when Peter took off on a fanciful idea once in a while." One time, Esther lectured Peter soundly on the evils of Coca Cola, a substance she consigned to hell right next to chocolate.[31] Esther also stayed involved in volunteer efforts. Through a Quaker venture in New York City, she taught pottery to inmates at the women's prison in the Greenwich Village area. One afternoon a week, she made her way through the guards and bars to turn pots with thieves, prostitutes, and murderers. She found some of them to be "very remarkable people."[32]

In the fall of 1962, Bob took a leave of absence from AT&T to serve as visiting lecturer at the School of Industrial Management at MIT (renamed the Sloan School of Management in 1964) and Harvard Business School. According to author Warren Bennis, who was a young MIT professor at the time, Douglas McGregor had asked Bob to the MIT campus. It was an unusual move, because the renowned MIT program, which was established with the goal of educating the "ideal manager," did not usually invite practitioners as visiting professors.[33] By 1962, McGregor's 1960 book *The Human Side of Enterprise* was the talk of managers everywhere. In it, he presented two contrasting theories of human motivation: Theory X assumes workers are lazy and must be motivated by threats and authoritative management. Theory Y assumes workers are creative, eager to work, and wish to participate in decision making. Needless to say, Greenleaf was a Theory Y man. Partly as a result of McGregor's work, a movement was brewing, which would culminate in the creation of the discipline of organizational development a few years later.

Author Peter Vaill, one of the pioneers in the organizational development movement, was a doctoral student at Harvard Business School when Greenleaf taught there. He recalls that during this period, Bob was also in consultation with principal Hawthorne researchers Fritz Roethlisberger and William Dickson about an effort to convince American businesses to adopt the idea of internal counselors (also called listeners or facilitators) along the lines of the Hawthorne model. The idea never really caught on, in spite of the 1966 book by Roethlisberger and Dickson, *Counseling in an Organization: A Sequel to the Hawthorne Researches.*[34]

One of the classes Bob taught at MIT was "Intuition in Strategy and Decision Making." It was oversubscribed, and Bob had to teach two sections. "This was not so much because the study of intuition was popular as it was the desire of many of those highly trained analytical minds to heckle the fellow who had the temerity to offer such a course in that bastion of conscious rationality," he wrote the editor of *Business Week* twelve years later. "But we had a great time and some of my students confessed an enlarged view of their human potential as a result of the effort."[35]

At a lunch in June of 1962, George Baker, the Harvard Business School Dean, asked Bob if he would share his reflections after his academic year at the school. The following summer, Bob wrote the Dean and expressed deep gratitude for the experience ("I found my own creative wheels spinning in new and significant ways . . .") and wished that other strategically-placed business people could have a similar opportunity. Then he shared several ideas sparked by his time as a professor. "These are not recommendations, or even suggestions," he wrote, "because I do not have a full enough understanding of what is possible or the priority of needs to urge anything."[36] Surprisingly, the first comment had to do with architecture.

> I have some sensitivity to architecture. I devote a little time to following architectural trends, and I try to understand what is going on. I am impressed that on the Business School campus there is no contemporary or experimental architecture, although there are some new buildings. One may look across the river and see some, but not on your side. This concerns me because, aside from architects and designers, business men are more involved in contemporary design than any other group . . . One way to prepare critical taste in such matters is to have some of it around when students are organizing their values in many ways. It is something to consider when another building or remodeling opportunity comes along.

Bob had noticed the Harvard students' "obsessive preoccupation" with job searches near the end of their time at the school. His idea was "a voluntary seminar in the first term of the first year with the aim of discovering how to prepare the student to deal with his job-finding in a way that favors a good choice in terms of reward, satisfaction, and using his life well."

His third idea was an experimental program for the top twenty-five or so students in the MBA program, chosen for their "scholarship, character, personality, and public conscience." Following their first year, they would spend fifteen months in "three intensive six-week seminar type programs on the campus before, between, and after two five-month internships attached to a top statesman—a person of great personal stature in government (governor, senator, cabinet officer) and a similar man at the head of a large or medium-sized business." Greenleaf wrote, "I am not concerned with what [this top group] will do for themselves, or even for their employers; they will do very well. But I am concerned about the broad social obligations which men like these should have because of their great talents; and I wonder what the chance is that they will recognize and meet these obligations." It was an idea that used old-fashioned apprenticeships to develop natural talents—in this case, those of the gifted elite. The value of this approach would have been obvious to every laborer and craftsman back in Terre Haute, Indiana who learned his own trade in exactly the same way.

Bob did more than teach during his year at Harvard and MIT. He also managed to attend a National Training Laboratories conference for middle managers, work with the National Council of Churches in drafting a proposal on Executive Development for Church Leadership, and draft a proposal with Professor Joseph Fletcher for a Center for Applied Ethics. During the Christmas break, he and Esther traveled to England, Holland, Belgium, France, and Spain under a fellowship from the Ford Foundation, visiting schools of management in business and government.[37] He was spreading his wings, making global connections, learning with the eagerness of a one-year-old, and reaching conclusions with the experience and wisdom of the fifty-eight-year-old man he was.

In Europe, Bob found some version of the organizational principle of *primus inter pares* ("first among equals," as opposed to a top-down pyramidal structure) implemented at Philips, Royal Dutch Shell, and Unilever.[38] While in England, Bob visited the Administrative Staff College in Henley. He was not impressed with its operation but did solidify contacts that would lead to five trips to India in the next decade. He also found that university programs for management education in England tended to be moribund, while the best companies were lively and innovative, the exact opposite of the situation in the U.S.

In his report on the experience, Bob admitted that he had had little time to adequately understand the complexities of the university, governmental, and corporate organizations he visited but believed that his findings would "be the central focus of my personal effort for the next few years."[39] Those efforts would focus on ways to identify and nurture those young people who would bring character, purpose, and excellence to public and private domains.

> There must be at least a thousand among the hundreds of thousands graduating from college each year who are of the potential stature of Washington, Jefferson, Hamilton, Madison, the Adamses. Where are they twenty-five years later when they are at the peak of their powers and should be available for the critical and difficult roles in business, government, education, philanthropy? . . . Some would argue that we are amply provided for, but the almost frenzied search for men for the top posts, everywhere I turn, would deny this . . . If our goal is simply to survive in a mediocre world, we are doing all right because we are getting along; we are even making "progress." But who wants this as a goal? I don't! If greatness is not the goal, the game is not worth the candle . . . [40]

He goes on to suggest a plan to identify, nurture, and follow up with exceptional young people. It is a scheme much like the one he proposed to Dean Baker at Harvard, writ large, but with a caution.

> Actions taken in implementing this point of view are loaded with all of the risks of developing an elite. The risks are real and they are great, but they must be taken . . . Excellence is excellence and not everyone can achieve it. Those who can achieve excellence need not only the opportunity to develop it, they need encouragement or there won't be enough excellence around to make the kind of society we all want to live in.
>
> The American dream was conceived and launched by exceptional men. It can only maintain its greatness through the leadership of such men. When they do not emerge, we are living on capital, and this cannot go on indefinitely if the major institutions that set the pace do not maintain the vitality that only great men can produce. There is

> an equalitarian strain in our American culture that denies this, and it
> serves to produce a healthy tension so long as it does not predomi-
> nate. But if it becomes the dominant influence for long enough to
> make mediocrity acceptable generally in high places as a perma-
> nent policy, the American dream does not have much of a future.[41]

Bob practiced what he preached. At every opportunity, he encouraged outstanding young people to claim their gifts and all young adults to dedicate their lives to distinction. When possible, he personally participated in their development. During the year at Harvard and M.I.T., he met a second-year student with whom he was impressed. Bob arranged for him to spend a year studying and working with a west coast business. Every four to six weeks the student returned to Cambridge to spend a weekend with Bob, report on his findings, and be challenged to do more. The young man was paid a good salary and, through Bob's influence, was able to count it toward his doctorate.

Another outstanding student Greenleaf met that year was Joseph J. Distefano, a mathematician working on his M.B.A. at Harvard.[42] The following year Les Rollins, Assistant Dean of Harvard Business School, arranged for Joe and another student to travel to New York every two weeks to work with Greenleaf. Years later, at the opening session of a group led by Greenleaf in Brown County, Indiana, Distefano told a group what it was like to have Robert K. Greenleaf as a mentor, both during that eight-month mentoring period and afterwards.

> I explained how I had met Bob, noted the frequent and enriching
> interactions I had had with him, and then said that I was there
> because I was a masochist. That *did* require some explanation, even
> with the wide assortment of idiosyncratic people who were there.
> I elaborated by noting that every time I had seen Bob, we would talk
> about a number of ideas; I would ask him two or three questions; he
> would neatly turn them around on me with Rogerian skill, and I
> would go away traumatized by the prospects of wrestling with them,
> knowing full well that our next conversation would inevitably start
> by his "innocently" asking what I had thought about the questions
> in the interim. Then I would go back to see him, and the cycle would
> be repeated all over again.

"If that isn't masochism," I exclaimed, "I don't know what is!" After appropriate chuckles and some nods reflecting similar experiences, others related their stories.

The next morning Joe sat next to Bob and Esther at breakfast. Bob silently slipped the tag from a Salada tea bag into Joe's jacket. It read, "THE PEARL CAUSED THE OYSTER GREAT PAIN."[43]

Early in 1964, Bob took a three-month leave of absence from AT&T so he and Esther could travel to India on a project for the Ford Foundation. It was the first of numerous journeys he would make to that country in the next seven years, investing a total of over one year there. As the decade of the sixties unfolded, he would make a lasting contribution to management research and development in India, one that is evident to this day.[44] During that first trip though, his most important move was the definite decision to take early retirement from AT&T at the earliest option, on his sixtieth birthday in July 1964. He seemed to have made the informal decision to do so five years earlier when he began to slowly dismantle his staff and find advantageous placements for them elsewhere. "I had a staff of twenty," he wrote later, "and when I left, there was just one assistant, with whom I shared a secretary. I have wondered why nobody asked why I did that."[45] From India, he wrote the office in New York to announce his intentions.

When his letter arrived at 195 Broadway, nearly everyone was stunned. Bob was close to the AT&T president and board members. He was allowed to mount innovative projects, affect the culture of the company in positive ways, and work with outside organizations. The man had been allowed to define his own job for over thirty years! In short, Bob Greenleaf "had it all," including widespread admiration. "Aren't you happy here?" asked AT&T president Fred Kappel. Bob told him he was ready to work on his own time, with people he chose, outside a bureaucracy. "This I don't understand," said Kappel. I have never known anyone, in this business or anywhere else, who throughout his whole career has done only what he wanted to do. Where will you ever find anyone else to pay you to do this?" Greenleaf's feeble reply was, "I want to try."[46]

In fact, Bob was ready to live into the future for which he had been preparing. The teaching and consulting activities of the last few years had stimulated his juices. The situation at AT&T was not likely to become any more congenial to a "conceptualizer" like Bob. The managers, the "opera-tionalizers," had been promoted to the top spots. After the breakup of AT&T in 1984, he was able to be more open about his feelings on this changing climate.

> I think the great problem with AT&T was that they were so enam-ored with managing that they refused to even think about the fact that there was important work to be done that was best done by people who were not managers, and the personnel function was one of them. We had a string of lousy personnel vice presidents . . . who could run a unit in the field, they had good judgment, they were decent people . . . but when you put them in a spot where they had to supply the ideas, they just didn't have any, just didn't even know what an idea was.[47]

As an example of how controlling bureaucracies tended to deaden managers' creativity, Greenleaf once told the story of a person who was promoted to president of a Bell Company just after the war. This outfit had been poorly run, and its employees were dispirited. The first thing the new president did was visit the territory. "He went into an office that had just been totally repainted," remembered Greenleaf, "and on the wall at the entrance was a tattered, faded old war poster that had obviously been taken down when the wall was painted and then put back up. 'What's that terrible thing doing on the wall there?' he asked. 'Well,' said the office manager, 'the order came out to put it up and no order ever came to take it down.'"[48]

Bob also believed most boards were populated by nuts-and-bolts managers, rather than big-picture thinkers. One day the Chairman of the Board invited him in to talk over a problem. After listening, Bob sug-gested that the solution might become more evident if the speaker devel-oped a better understanding of how the problem came about. The man who was ultimately responsible for the performance of the largest busi-ness organization in the history of the world responded, "I don't want to understand the damn thing. I just want to know what to do about it!"[49] For thirty-eight years Bob had been able to work comfortably within the bounds of such thinking, and even try to change it where he could. In fact, during his last five years with the company, president Kappel told him privately that his real job was to train his bosses.[50] Still, he was now ready to invest time with those who *did* wish to understand the problems and do the right things about them.

Bob agreed to stay through September so he could teach one of the scheduled Dartmouth sessions and tidy up some loose ends. On one of those final days, an old friend approached him. His friend, the president of an AT&T subsidiary, was nearing the mandatory retirement age of sixty-five. "I would like to spend my retirement years in a constructive and interesting way like you are going to do," he explained. "Can you advise me?" Bob's response was not what his friend wanted to hear, but it is something every working person *should* hear if he or she wishes to make solid contributions after retirement.

> It was a tough question, but I had to face it. As gently as I could I told him there was no way for him to do what I was going to do. I had spent nearly twenty years preparing for old age. I had used some vacations for teaching assignments (which were also fun for the family because they took us to interesting places). I had exposed myself to unique learning opportunities like Kurt Lewin's group development and Alfred Korzybski's general semantics. I had taken a year's leave for a joint lectureship at Harvard Business School and MIT's Sloan School of Management. I had, in the course of my work at AT&T, developed a wide acquaintanceship with university faculty people.
>
> I knew of only one person who had retired from an affiliated company presidency and moved to a radically different role, and that was Chester I. Barnard. My friend had been a conscientious top executive and had not developed the public reputation that Barnard had. Neither could he have the opportunities I had because, as a top chief executive, he had not had the latitude that I had had in my special kind of staff work which I had consciously cultivated—both my role in the company and my eye on my old age . . . I did not tell him that he had waited too long to think about it. He died soon after retiring, probably because of an empty life.[51]

Bob always expressed gratitude for his time at AT&T—for the learning, the income that allowed him to provide for his family, and the opportunity to live out that vision Professor Helming accidentally sparked in 1926, but he knew the company would not try to replace him, and he was right.

During the years after his retirement, Bob wrote numerous reflections on his time at the communications giant but seldom mentioned the impact he might have had on others. For those kinds of judgments, one must look to others, like William Sharwell.

Mr. Sharwell worked closely with Bob from 1955 to 1960. His experiences were typical of those of hundreds of people who worked directly with Bob during his thirty-eight years at the company. [52]

> He was a legend within AT&T . . . He had a tremendous influence on me in his quiet way of managing things. He'd talk over a task with the core staff which had five or six guys like me from various disciplines—some psychologists, a few sociologists, I was a businessman—then someone would be assigned to it. You just went ahead and did the best you knew how; there were no protocols. You'd see him around all the time, and he would talk with you. If things were going the way he thought they should, that was the end of it. Give people a job to do and let them do it. But you did have to be accountable. There was no question about that!
>
> He came across as sort of a country bumpkin from Indiana but you've got to watch out for those guys because he was anything but! He "blundered" his way to genius.
>
> AT&T had the second mainframe computer—the Social Security people had the first—which we used to process management attitude surveys. Of course, you would get a lot of numbers, and we spent a lot of time after the surveys trying to figure out why people felt as they did, and this meant interview studies. So, we did a lot of interview studies.
>
> I got a very liberal education. Greenleaf had a great habit of bringing in authorities in the field he was interested in to simply spend a day informally with his staff. I'm talking about guys like Rabbi Joshua Heschel, psychologist Erik Erickson, a famous statistician, and many others. I mean, you sit with Eric Erickson for a day and you learn stuff! And Heschel was a genius. We read all his books, and he contributed a lot to us.

On a morning before one of those day-long seminars, Bob arranged to meet Eric Erickson for breakfast and walk with him to the 195 Broadway building. Dr. Erickson seemed very nervous, not anxious to get to the conference. He finally admitted that he did not understand business or the jobs of business executives, and did not think he had anything to say them. Bob calmed his fears and the day was a smashing success.[53]

Sharwell was able to experience first-hand Bob's playfulness at home and strategic prowess at work.

> One day, a few years after I worked for him, Bob said, "Why don't you come over, and we'll have a picnic." So I took the family over to his place in New Jersey. We had two kids then, about three and five years old. Greenleaf was dressed like a farmer—shorts flapping around his knees, shirt hanging out. The principal object of the day was Bob giving the kids rides in a wheelbarrow.
>
> Greenleaf was a man who wanted to try things. During the period I worked with him, Billy Graham ran his first TV crusade in Madison Square Garden. One day Greenleaf said to me, "We ought to go up some night and see what that's all about." So, somehow he got some tickets—which were the hardest tickets in town to get— and we went up to see Billy Graham. It was a very interesting evening. But he would try things like that.
>
> We did some crazy things at work too. For example, there was an annual lecture at Columbia Business School, and the General Electric Company sponsored it. It consisted of three lectures, two weeks apart, and then the incorporation of the lectures into a book. There had been three or four of these, and Greenleaf, of course, knew everybody. He knew the guy who was responsible at GE for managing the lectures. So they were talking one day, and the guy said he thought they were going to discontinue the lectures. They couldn't find any CEO that had anything to say and Greenleaf said, "You invite our guy, and I guarantee he'll have something to say." [Ed. note: In a 1986 interview, Greenleaf credited Sharwell with the idea of inviting the AT&T president to present the lectures.]
>
> Bob and I wrote his speeches, but it was a hell of a fight because we had a CEO who was smart and strong-minded. He didn't want to say some of the things we wanted to say. My vice president and I argued this a couple of times. He said, "You are going to get fired if you talk to the CEO like that." I said, "Well, OK, I get fired, so what?" But we got this CEO feeling comfortable with the manuscript, he spoke it well, and the book was published.

> It was very funny; the public relations department was not inter-
> ested in this originally. We could not get them to touch it. Then the
> lectures were such a hit that they suddenly became interested. We
> were afraid they'd get the manuscript and change it before publica-
> tion. Greenleaf had an answer to that. He had a friend who had just
> retired as a foreign editor of the old *Herald Tribune*, a guy named Joe
> Barnes. He called up Joe Barnes and said, "I've got a consulting job
> for you. I want you to be the editor of a book." Barnes said, "I'm
> editing *Berlin Diary*," which was a hot book at that time. "You won't
> have to work too hard on this," said Bob. Well, that closed off the
> public relations department. They couldn't compete with Joe Barnes.
> That was Greenleaf. He always talked about looking for the hole in
> the hedge.

At the release party for the book, AT&T president Frederick Kappel,
who had given the ghost-written speeches, presented Bob with an auto-
graphed copy. Bob thanked him and then, with a twinkle, asked Fred if he
would like Bob to autograph a copy for *him*.[54]

William Sharwell was eventually promoted to head up New York
Telephone during a period of outrageously bad service. At times, Wall
Street telephones had no dial tone. Sharwell, a man who, by his own ad-
mission, did not know how to hook up a telephone, "spent a couple a bil-
lion dollars" and fixed the problem. Ironically, after building up the Bell
System for so many years, he was asked to pull it apart as the Operations
Divestiture Officer during the time of the AT&T breakup. His affection for
Bob Greenleaf lasted into old age.

> Greenleaf had more influence on my life than any other man. My
> father died when I was very young—five years old—so I never had a
> father. It wasn't that Greenleaf was a father but that he was a friend;
> he was there, and he helped me and told me when I was wrong. He
> also helped me when I was right, and he caused me to think about
> things I never would have though about. He was truly a mentor.

PART
III

Leader: 1964–1990

THE FORCES FOR GOOD AND EVIL IN THE WORLD OPERATE through the thoughts, attitudes, and actions of individual beings. Societies, movements, institutions are but the collection or focus of such individual initiatives. What happens to our values, and therefore to the quality of our civilization in the future, will result from the conception, born of inspiration, of individuals. Perhaps only one individual will receive it. The very essence of leadership, therefore, derives from openness to inspiration, to insight, that either produces the nobler ethic or guides one's choice among alternatives.[1]

Robert K. Greenleaf

New Skin for New Wine

*The best strategy of developing the Center's program at this time seems
to be one of responding to opportunities rather than an organized,
idealistically-oriented program. Our major aim of helping the colleges
build for more responsible participation in society is going to be a
most difficult one to follow. The colleges, at this point, are more
concerned with survival in short-range terms than with an influence
that would be as difficult as the one we are urging—even their own
survival might depend on it in the long run. Consequently my own
personal efforts will be to exploit available opportunities rather than
a bald frontal kind of program. By this process the Center may never
be credited with a major contribution, but its influence might
nonetheless be greater.*

ROBERT K. GREENLEAF
President's Report, Center for Applied Studies, Inc.
November 29, 1968

With Bob's early retirement he entered into a new phase of leadership.
While his learning would continue until the day he died, he was now
ready to apply to the wider world all his preparation, all the accumulated

insight and wisdom, all the lessons from his failures and triumphs. If a better society required good and able people to step out, he was ready. Otherwise, of what use was all that preparation, all that *seeking*?

Robert Greenleaf was now an official consultant. Once word got out that he was available, organizations lined up for his services, but many wanted to hire him as an employee rather than a consultant. Three universities, including Dartmouth, offered professorships, one with no explicit teaching requirements. "There were other offers of long-term foundation consultancies," he wrote. "A prestigious management consulting firm invited me to join them; a large foundation asked me to be their executive. I turned down all of these offers because I made a firm resolve when I retired from AT&T that I would not go on anyone's payroll. I had had thirty-eight years of bureaucratic participation, some of it onerous, and I wanted no more of that . . . I decided that henceforth I would work at my own pace at only the things I wanted to do and only with people I enjoyed working with."[1]

It may have been harder to turn down offers from four major publishers to write a book. In that decision, Bob trusted his intuition. "I did not *feel* a book coming on," he recalled years later. "That would come, if it came, in its own right rhythm."[2]

Bob wanted an umbrella organization to give legal and financial structure to his work and board members who could advise and support his activities. While he believed that every important effort started with the individual, he also believed that organizations were the way to get things done in America's modern, complicated society. So he dusted off the proposal he and Joseph Fletcher worked on during Bob's year of teaching at Harvard and MIT and, on September 10, 1964, held the first meeting of incorporators for the Center for Applied Ethics at 50 Federal Street, Room 1000, Boston, Massachusetts.[3]

The legal Statement of Purposes said the Center would promote, research, publish, educate, and consult in "the broad range of ethical concerns in the fields of law, business, government, education, medicine, religion, and other areas of professional practice . . ." That part reads like a boilerplate paragraph, but the statement goes on with a twist: "and to develop inward resources, by reference to perspectives provided by great theologies and ethical systems, which will enable decision makers in professional disciplines to be governed by individual moral and religious insights in exercising their reasoning-intuitive processes."[4] This legal document manages to mention, in one sentence, reasoning, intuition, morality, religion, universal and individual codes, external research, internal resources, decision-making, and professional disciplines.

In a "covering note" that first proposed the Center, Greenleaf wrote, "[The Center] is proposed because too much of the current concern with ethical conduct is with code and law, too little with ethical man striving to do his creative best."[5] That same document set the tone for the Center's relationship to religion.

> The personal frames of reference of those sponsoring the Center differ somewhat in detail and emphasis, but for themselves they agree to regard ethics as religiously sanctioned. They believe that the primary source of new depths of ethical insight is man's ultimate concern. Most of them own their religious roots to be in the Judeo-Christian tradition, although they find helpful guides in other religious traditions and philosophical systems. However, they respect the man who looks for better performance, ethically, better than what the law or code requires, even if he does not acknowledge a religious concern . . .
>
> [The Center] will not be a new religion or another Church, but it will be concerned with religion, values, and ultimate purpose as the source of man's best creative acts in the world of affairs.[6]

In his work at AT&T, and in his later writings, Greenleaf frequently mentioned two important questions that individuals and organizations asked far too infrequently: "What are you trying to do?" and "Whom do you serve?" You cannot do everything, and you cannot serve everyone. One must choose the focus and do what is reasonable and possible with available resources. The first question, "What are you trying to do?" was covered by the memorandum proposing the Center. A statement approved by the Center's board in 1967 clarified the second question, "Whom do you serve?"

> [The Center] will not aim to serve those who lack competence for whom training is needed, or the poorly adjusted personalities for whom therapy is needed, because other facilities to give them help are available. The Center aims to serve able people who carry responsible professional roles.

> The Center will also hope to reach directly students of under-
> graduate, graduate and professional schools . . . who have a special
> interest in strengthening their ethical roots.

Greenleaf always understood that focusing on strong people could bring charges of elitism; it was something he mentioned in his letter to Harvard's Dean Baker in 1963. He believed, however, that able leaders were present in every strata of society, and their potential leadership was not merely a function of their position, education, income, ethnicity, or religion. That was a lesson he had learned from Terre Haute's working folks, from AT&T's tough linemen and from the experience of Danish Folk Schools. If a person, young or old, was not judged to be a person of promise, he or she could *become* one through his or her own learning and reflection, taking advantage of every available person and resource, however meager. After personally training thousands of people at AT&T, Bob did not believe any program or system could turn around those who were smugly satisfied and unwilling to step out as leaders. All one could do was offer the opportunity to grow, and nurturance for those who had already decided to make a difference with their lives.

Consultant Greenleaf's first new contract was with Ohio University in Athens, where he was able to experiment with a model of undergraduate education he had been developing since his long correspondence with Carleton's president Cowling in 1934. OU was headed by Dr. Vernon Alden, who had been hired away from Harvard Business School in 1961. At age thirty-eight, he was the youngest president in OU's history. Alden had worked with Lyndon Johnson to prepare the War on Poverty legislation and chaired the committee that developed the U.S. Job Corps. He was a heavy hitter, one of the brightest young men in America; he was also an imaginative risk-taker.

When Harvard Business School's Assistant Dean J. Leslie (Les) Rollins retired, Alden lured him out to Southern Ohio—without portfolio or salary—to begin working on a scheme. "We wanted to create a program at a large state university that would be much more like the experience that a bright young student would have in a small private college," Dr. Alden recalled years later.[7] In other words, they wanted their Athens on the Ohio to be more like a Harvard on the Charles. Rollins was one of the founders of Greenleaf's Center for Applied Ethics, and Alden knew Bob from his lectures on corporate ethics through the years at Harvard.

Vern and Marion Alden frequently entertained Bob in their home during those years, reveling in conversation that ranged over wide areas but often landed back on the themes of undergraduate education and leadership.[8] When Bob became available as a consultant, Dr. Alden asked him to help Les develop a program that would identify and nurture students from every discipline with exceptional potential.[9] Through their combined contacts, OU secured funding from the Mead and Mellon foundations so no money would be diverted from the university's normal budget.

Bob and Les went to work. With the able assistance of Frank Zammataro from admissions, they pored over the transcripts and applications of more than a thousand incoming freshmen. They interviewed nearly a hundred and chose around twenty-five to be part of what became known as the Ohio Fellows Program. The program had an unusual design for its time. Ohio Fellows could choose their courses. During the summers, they were placed in internship positions with top decision-makers—often presidents or directors of organizations—in business, government, and nonprofit settings. They were sent around the world to meet photographers and governors and engineers. Whatever their passion, their goals should not be limited![10] Finally, Ohio Fellows were encouraged to have formal and informal discussion groups and were treated to a succession of lectures from mind-boggling speakers, many of whom were secured through Bob and Les's contacts: Secretary of State Dean Rusk, Secretary of Defense Robert McNamara, columnist Ann Landers, anthropologist Margaret Mead, Ford executive Lee Iacocca, Senator Ted Kennedy, Cleveland Mayor Stokes, historian Arnold Toynbee, religious historian Houston Smith, even U.S. Presidents Eisenhower and Johnson. The lectures were open to all, but Ohio Fellows were able to spend time with the speakers in small groups.

Greenleaf frequently presented his essays to Fellows discussion groups. At a reunion in 2002, former Ohio Fellows from around the country converged to remember and celebrate their days in Athens. They spoke of Les Rollins' consistent, tough, but loving challenges to excel. They recalled Bob Greenleaf's brilliant writings, his penetrating questions and deep silences, and that *look* which seemed to communicate, simultaneously, a statement and a question: "I accept you," and "Are you realizing your greatness?" One woman said that Bob Greenleaf planted a seed that changed her life, enabling it to grow into a life of service. A man remembered how a speech given by a visiting lecturer—Jack Sheen of Corning Glass, later a member of the Federal Reserve Board—and exposure to Rollins and Greenleaf moved him to forget the law profession and work with small banks. The core of that OU graduate's current message to clients was, "The reputation for unbending professional and personal integrity is not an intangible asset. It is a measurable cash value asset."[11]

In April 1967, Greenleaf gave a rousing—and absolutely unsentimental—talk to freshmen who had applied for appointment as Ohio Fellows their sophomore year.

> Regardless of what your chosen vocation may be, and it can be any legitimate calling your talents justify, do you see your life, be it long or short, as having a total impact that leaves the large society—neighborhood, city, state, nation, world—a little better than if you had not lived in it? It is important that many of you make this choice now because plenty of people, by design or by accident, will leave it worse.
>
> An Indian woman in Bombay told me of an interesting incident with a traffic policeman who had flagged her down and lectured her for crowding pedestrians at an intersection, an easy thing to do in an Indian city because there are so many people. When my friend protested that she had the right of way, the officer spoke to her sternly: "Madame," he said, "it is not a question of law or rights. You are an educated, intelligent person. These are poor ignorant people. You have the obligation to look out for them."
>
> We all do have the *obligation*, because we are educated and intelligent, to care for the less fortunate. It is not simply a matter of charity; everybody should be charitable. Obligation is a consequence of privilege . . . [12]

Greenleaf quoted E.B. White, Robert Frost, G. K. Chesterton, Saul Bellow, Emerson, a document on system analysis, and even a medical doctor who wrote a book on how to take people with medical training (that is, M.D. degrees) and turn them into *doctors*. Sixty-three-year-old Greenleaf advised nineteen-year-old kids on ways to nurture creativity and intuition, and on the importance of developing tough, behaviorally defined outcomes. He allowed that, "The hippie movement, for all its nightmarish qualities, might be a part of the searching of the younger generation for a new ethic, and we of the staid middle class should bestir ourselves to try to understand it in these terms." By contrast, Greenleaf referred to a recent television documentary about hippies, which took the shallow position that, "Terrible temptations are being held out to our groping youth. How can we protect them, and ourselves?" If students were to take responsibility for their own self-development, they had better begin by accepting the world as it is—busy, stressful, imperfect, paradoxical—and go from there.

> What can you do with these three years so that you may move from a self-image of a responsible person (which I urge you to adopt now) to a life style of greatness (which can be a reasonable goal at the end of three years)?
>
> You are attending a good university. Some day it may become a great one. I think it will be. But the paths to institutional greatness are many. Any person in the close constituencies of the university, any one person with his own efforts can make it great—if he is persuasive and can lead.[13]

A core of faculty members volunteered to help with the Ohio Fellows Program, but most were suspicious that it was subversive, which, of course, it was—subversive to the normal way of doing things in universities. Perhaps that is a strategic reason why, in spite of the program's innovative design and news value, the school kept internal and external publicity to a minimum. Dr. Alden explained an even more important reason for operating "under the radar," just like Greenleaf did so frequently at AT&T: "We felt it might distort the program if it were publicized too much."[14]

A young administrator named Kenneth Blanchard was one of those who understood the Ohio Fellows program and was an eager supporter. Ken came to OU in 1966 after a frustrating job search. At least five schools had declined to invite him for on-campus interviews after positive initial contacts. Even though he had a Ph.D. and was destined to become one of the most respected business thinkers and authors in the last two decades of the twentieth century, an official from Dartmouth told Ken that several references reported he had no academic interests and was not especially intelligent! Greenleaf's friend Joe Distefano alerted him to the experiment at OU; Ken wrote Vern Alden, and Alden referred him to the School of Business Administration, which promptly hired him.

Ken Blanchard took an immediate interest in the goings-on of Rollins, Greenleaf, and the Ohio Fellows Program, and he and his wife Margie reveled in the visiting speakers. During his first year at the university, Ken joined Greenleaf and the Ohio Fellows for a weekend and was "enthralled with his thinking. In fact, when I got a chance to teach, I tried to put his servant-leadership concepts into practice."[15] Blanchard later recalled that the weekend was "really the only the time I spent time with [Bob]. He was a very gentle, caring man, a very insightful man. He really challenged you in his gentle way. In retrospect, I would love to go back and sit in on more. . . . Margie and I were twenty-seven years old and were trying to figure out who we were, and at the time I had no anticipation that I was going to be a teacher. The faculty all said I couldn't write; I needed to be an administrator, you know . . ."[16]

Like Greenleaf, Ken Blanchard was a rebel in his own quiet way. When he began giving students final exam questions on the first day of class, faculty members asked him what he was up to. "My servant-leadership response was: 'not only am I going to give them the final exam during the first day of class, but what do you think I'm going to do all semester? I'm going to teach them the answers! You better believe it, so when they get to the final exam, they'll get A's!' To me, life is all about getting A's, not about following the normal grade distribution curve."[17]

When Blanchard heard that Paul Hersey, chairman of OU's Management Department, was a fabulous teacher, he asked Hersey if he could audit his class in organizational behavior and leadership. Hersey said, "Nobody audits my class. If you want to take it for credit, you can," and walked away. So, Blanchard enrolled in the course like any student (the school finally decided it would only charge him $55 tuition), wrote the class papers, and became friends with the professor. The next year, Hersey walked into Blanchard's office and said, "Ken, I've been teaching for ten years, and I think I am better than anybody, but I can't write. I'm a nervous wreck. I'd like to write a textbook, and I'd like to find somebody to write one with me. Would you be willing to do that?" Ken said, "Well, we ought to be a great combination; you can't write and I'm not supposed to. Let's do it!"[18]

From that conversation Ken Blanchard, Paul Hersey, and Dewey E. Johnson went on to write the classic textbook *Management of Organizational*

Behavior and to develop concepts that were embodied in Situational Leadership®. Greenleaf had a powerful, if indirect, effect on the latter work because he invited his old friend and co-founder of the Center for Applied Ethics, Joseph Fletcher, to OU for a lecture. In 1966 Fletcher, an Episcopal priest, had written the book *Situation Ethics: The New Morality* in which he outlined three approaches to making moral decisions: legalistic, antinomian (lawless or unprincipled approach), and situational.[19] Fletcher urged a situational approach based on what love requires in each situation. "Only love is a constant," he wrote, "everything else is a variable."[20]

"Joe Fletcher really had more of an impact on me because of the situational ethics," says Blanchard. "I was grappling with my own spirituality, and he was kind of a rebel saying nothing was fixed."[21] Spirituality was the vehicle for Greenleaf's influence to return to Ken Blanchard's life in the early 1990s, when he began reflecting on Jesus as the ultimate servant-leader. Today, his FaithWalk Leadership organization helps people live their faith in the workplace and follow the servant-leadership model of Jesus.[22] Meanwhile, Blanchard's 1982 book *The One Minute Manager* has sold more than ten million copies—and counting.

Greenleaf was as much a mentor to the school's president as he was to its students. When non-academic employees staged a strike in 1968 (Athens is in a pro-union part of the state), Ohio's Attorney General told Dr. Alden that state law made it illegal to recognize the union and provide for check off dues. Alden heard of threats to dynamite the heating plant and decided to let the students out for an early spring break. "During that period of time, Bob worked very closely with me," said Alden. "He was a kind of counselor and father figure. Because I was so busy, up to my ears dealing with the strike, he wrote several memoranda that we used in dealing with the press or dealing with the public at-large. And at the end of the strike, he wrote a philosophical paper describing the medieval roots of the university, saying we were very vulnerable to a union, which is really part of the contemporary corporate era. Business is much more capable of handling that kind of threat than is the university. So, that paper is what I used in addressing the university community when the strike was over."[23]

Vern Alden's administration survived the strike. During his time at Ohio University, enrollment and faculty doubled in size. He oversaw a significant expansion of campus infrastructure, an increase in research activities, a broadening of academic programs, and growth of the university's role in regional development and international programs. Today, you can visit the Vern Alden Library on campus, look up his impressive record, and read his book *Essays on Leadership,* which includes many of the ideas he got from Bob Greenleaf.

In October 1964, Bob and Esther returned to India, where Bob was destined to make a significant contribution to that country's management research and development efforts. Douglas Ensminger of the Ford Foundation had asked him to look into ways of revitalizing the Administrative Staff College (ASC) in Hyderabad. ASC was a training school for top administrators based on a military war college model begun by Sir Noel Hall after the war and set up at Henley on the Thames. It was not a very creative model but was simple to understand and easy to export to various countries in the British Commonwealth. By the 1960s, the ASC operation at Hyderabad, which was housed in one of the nizam's (ruler's) old palaces, was "doing little to contribute to India's urgent needs for top administrators."[24] Bob was not surprised. He had asked some of his friends in Europe about Sir Noel Hall and concluded that even though the idea of the Staff College was glamorous for its time, the man behind it was a slick "huckster."[25]

During that first trip to India when Bob decided to take an early retirement from AT&T, he met the Minister of Heavy Industry, a "remarkable" Madras lawyer named Combatore Subramamiam, who asked him to solve an especially heavy problem. Even though India had iron ore and coal near their new steel mills, it was cheaper to ship all raw materials to Japan for processing into bars and sheets than to do the work in-country, even with India's pittance wages. Rather than prove how smart he was by giving a quick answer, Greenleaf suggested a two-year project to study the problem thoroughly, using an international team of consultants with experience in such issues. Subramamiam agreed, the Ford Foundation provided the funding, and the Staff College gave permission to house the three-person team on their campus as an independent venture.

Bob spent half of that first trip traveling and getting a feel for the country and its industries, following his instinct to "seek first to understand" through research, personal contact and, finally, reflection. In the course of his journeys, he learned a lesson about the effects of recent Indian history.

Minister Subramamiam told me of his desperate need for a few key executives immediately. I said I was about to take off on a three-week visit to major industries and that I would look around, which I proceeded to do. When I returned from my junket I had six names of people who were carrying important roles in Indian industries whom I thought could do more. I wrote each up on a kind of résumé sheet and took them to the Minister. His eyes bugged out and he asked, in a startled way, where I got these. "I told you I would look around," I said, "and these are a few people I saw."

He was dumbfounded, and I was struck by the deprivation as a consequence of 300 years of colonial rule in which an exceedingly able and fine man like Subramamiam would be so deficient in such an elementary aspect of high executive positions: the continuous search for able people. It had not occurred to Subramamiam, able man that he was, that if you are leading an important institution and you need an exceptional person for a key job, you should bestir yourself to go out and look around, either in your institution or elsewhere. You don't just sit there and hope that person will by some miracle appear.

By the time Bob and Esther returned to India, Nehru had died, Subrainamiam had moved on to another role, and the new Minister of Heavy Industry had no interest in the project. To make matters worse, one of the consultants arrived in India and decided he would rather write a book. All was in jeopardy. "Fortunately, I had reflected extensively about what could be done with the Staff College," Greenleaf wrote later. "I concluded that they had a problem because they had accepted a foreign (though glamorous) import model [of management training] and that they would only do better when and if they replaced it with a program that was generated out of their own experience."[26] Bob's idea was to "move the consulting project into the Staff College as a consulting company, a business that would develop clients among the widest possible range of Indian institutions, and use it as a resource of knowledge that would guide the development of future programs to serve Indian institutions."[27]

The Staff College principal, R. L. Gepta, was agreeable, but the strongest supporter of the idea was the exceptionally strong chair of the

Staff College's board, Dr. C. D. Deshmukh, who was also the top administrator at the University of Delhi. The only problem was the Staff College
faculty. "They were in an uproar about it and half of them departed immediately because they could see that this institution was working in the
direction of an earthy, practical resource for India and away from the prestigious showpiece that they thought they had."[28] A strong board chair
saved the day, however, just like J. P. Morgan had done in the early years
of AT&T.

The consulting enterprise flourished. After the Ford Foundation
money ran out, it continued as a self-sustaining non-profit organization
and was able to provide financial support for the Staff College. It continues to this day, consulting with sugar mills, refineries, energy companies,
and indigenous and international financial organizations like the World
Bank. Faculty members stay in touch with current trends by working on
research through consulting contracts, then share their fresh knowledge in
the classroom.[29]

Eleven years after Greenleaf's final trip to India, the president of an
American university asked him about the advisability of starting a business that could funnel money back to his school. He told the story of the
Administrative Staff College. "I didn't start a business to make money for
the [Administrative Staff] College," he wrote. "I would have been happy
if the consulting company had been the idea resource that helped the College find a new way of serving India that made it a useful institution for
those times. And I suspect that you wouldn't do much for [your school] if
all you did was start a business that would earn some money."[30]

Through five trips to India over six years, voracious reading, and
wide exposure to Indian society, Greenleaf developed contrarian views
about Gandhi, the future of India, and America's hubris as expressed
through foreign aid. On the latter, he wrote, "It seemed to me presumptu-
ous that the more favored nations, because they have the surplus cash to
finance an exchange, would be willing to teach the Indians our Western
ideas but we had little or no interest in learning what they might teach
us—different things, but perhaps of greater significance to us than what
we have to share might do for the Indians."[31] When he presented this
view to the Ford Foundation staff during his final visit in 1970, he drew a
blank. "There was no interest whatever in using Ford Foundation resources for learning what the Indians could teach us to our benefit."[32]
When Bob returned to America, he wrote a memo to Ford Foundation

headquarters summarizing the same conclusions he presented to their staff in New Dehli. The result: "My memo was not acknowledged, and I have not heard from the Ford Foundation since."[33]

Greenleaf had an unusual take on Gandhi and his strategy of change. Gandhi had the vision of India as a village-centered handicraft society which, in fact, was what it had always been. "[Gandhi's] place in history may be that of the greatest leader of the masses of people the world has ever known," wrote Greenleaf, "But there is a question that the consequence of his work was the best that a person of his genius could have done for the world, or even for India." [34] Greenleaf considered Gandhi's non-violent tactics essentially coercive, especially when judged by the model of Quaker activist John Woolman, who persuaded his fellow Friends to give up their slaves. "Massive nonviolent withholding of cooperation and a fast-unto-death by the leader are destructive," wrote Greenleaf. "They are useful to stop something or destroy something, but little of importance can be built with them. (Nehru judged those tactics correctly.)"[35] Gandhi eventually gained compliance, but not lasting change of the kind he wished. Nehru, an urbane, classical socialist, had no intention of following Gandhi's ideas; he wished to lead the new country toward Western industrialization.

Many with whom Greenleaf spoke believed the country was not yet ready for independence. Maybe not, Bob decided, because he noticed that the ruling elite tended to take on the "worst of the arrogance of their recently displaced colonial masters. Since population growth had offset most of the gains in food production (that had been stimulated by foreign aid and technology) I wondered whether the life of the masses seemed any different to them from the conditions of colonial times."[36] Then there was the religious violence that led to the creation of Pakistan and Bangladesh, a bloodbath that resulted in an estimated million deaths at the time of independence.

Greenleaf drew a moral from all this.

> As I have reflected on my India experience, which looms substantial in retrospect, plus later thoughts about our own earlier issue of slavery, I have become confirmed in where I stand on tactics for change: I will always prefer persuasion to coercion or manipulation, evolution to revolution, and gradual to precipitous change.

> I am not recommending that mine is the best or only legitimate position. There are conditions of evil in the world that, at this stage of civilization, are likely to be restrained only by force or the threat of force. But, it seems to me, some of us need to hold resolutely to this position, as a sort of leaven in a society in which there is much too much overt violence and subtle or not-so-subtle manipulation or coercion. Gandhi, who was himself nonviolent and advocated nonviolence, does not seem to me to model the role that would provide this leaven in our contemporary American society.
>
> People who consistently follow this persuasive tactic generally do not make waves that are recorded in history. If John Woolman had not left his great journal—a literary classic—and other writings, we would not really know what he thought or how he did his work.
>
> My concern, however, is not primarily for India. India was a stable civilization when Europe was a jungle . . . the Hindu village structure is deeply indigenous and seems likely to survive almost anything that might happen to India. Much can be done by and for India to make life better for all its people. Those in the fortunate position to do something for India should be mindful of the obligation to do it in such a way as to leave the Indians in better condition to do things for themselves. (An admonition that might be given to consultants everywhere, including here at home.)
>
> I am much more concerned about the durability of our own culture, partly because it lacks this stabilizing element (the village structure), partly because it seems so violence-prone, partly because we seem to lack unifying ideas. India doesn't need such ideas as we do because of the strength in their traditional pattern that we lack. But our nation was founded on ideas, and we have not tended adequately to their maintenance—and a village structure is not an option.[37]

Back in America, Bob's consulting jobs grew exponentially. He worked with organizations as varied as the Committee on Structure of the American Institute of Certified Public Accountants (1966), the Harvard Divinity School (1965–71), and the Fondazione Giovanni Agnelli in Turin, Italy (1969–70). He was an Executive in Residence for the School of Business at Fresno State College (1968), and a faculty member of the Salzburg Seminar in American Studies (1968).

During these consulting days, Greenleaf once asked Douglas Williams to join him for an evening meeting with a few top people from a large corporation. "Along at the end of the get-together, when we were relaxing," recalled Williams, "one of them asked Bob, 'What do you do now?' Bob referred to a couple of responsibilities he was involved with but then said, 'Most of the time I just go to the top of the mountain and think big thoughts.' This hard-bitten guy nodded understandingly. That was because he had gotten to know Greenleaf personally over a couple of hours."[38]

By foregoing the retirement rocking chair for a life of consulting, Bob increased his income significantly, according to his daughter Madeline. "I was always a very nosy child and looked at some documents that 'happened' to be lying on his desk at Short Hills. What I remember is that during his last year at AT&T he was making $32,000. But, they were comfortable. Either the first or second year after his retirement, he made $75,000."[39] This, in spite of the fact that letters show Bob frequently asked only for expenses, especially with clients who were old friends—people like the Erteszek family.

Jan and Olga Erteszek were Polish immigrants who realized the American dream through the lingerie business, turning a $10 investment in 1941 into the multimillion-dollar Olga Company. Olga Erteszek was a beautiful, stately, soft-spoken lady. She also happened to be brilliant, and held multiple patents on designs for bras and other lingerie designs. Her husband Jan was a man of faith who wanted to run the company by Christian principles. He believed every person was a trustee of God-given talent and should give back to co-workers and the community. Jan met Greenleaf through the Laymen's Movement in the early 1960s, and he and Olga stayed in touch with Bob through the years, speaking frequently by phone.

The Erteszeks worked to create a different kind of company. They instituted profit sharing before it was popular, reserved no designated parking places for themselves or other executives, took comparatively reasonable personal salaries, and were fond of saying, "Management is a function, not a class." Both believed in hard work, top quality products, personal accountability, and having a moral impact without being evangelists. They were Bob Greenleaf's kind of folks, and were on his short list of recipients who saw first drafts of his essays through the years.

When Bob visited the Olga Company offices in Van Nuys, California, Jan Erteszek's secretary was reminded of her own grandfather. "He was large, raw-boned, and not high on fashion. To look at him, you would think he didn't have a brain in his head, but Mr. E. talked about him all the time and put many of his ideas into practice." More than once, Bob used the Olga Company as a site for student internships. In 1972, Jan asked him to develop a proposal for an Ethics of Leadership Program at Whittier College, where Jan was a trustee.

Jan and Olga Erteszek were typical of people in Bob's constellation of friends and practitioners, people with whom he had serious discussions about experiments in ethical management, risk-takers who operated from an impulse to serve, thoughtful and well-read leaders who got things done. Some of these people and their organizations appear on his resume, but many do not. As an intense listener, he probably felt he learned more from them than he gave.

James W. McSwiney was another one of those special friends. Early in Bob's consulting career Vern Alden introduced him to McSwiney, who was at that time a vice president of the Mead Corporation. Mac, as his friends called him, joined the company at age nineteen and stayed for fifty years. He was named President and CEO in 1968. His colleagues knew him as a larger-than-life leader with a quick mind, a person who chose to focus on solutions rather than place blame, and an executive who worked to nurture the growth of people. "You can't effectively lead unless you help other people," said McSwiney. "Even mediocre people can help you immensely, but only if you provide them with the vehicle . . . If you operate by persistent example it's amazing how other people respond."[40] In Mac's early days at the company, George Mead especially liked him for his candor. "You ask me something and I'll tell you what I think about it," he said.[41]

When Bob met him, Mac was offering a management development program as sophisticated as those Bob had created at AT&T. McSwiney went on to transform board governance at Mead by separating the CEO and chair roles, establish an effective Corporate Responsibility Committee, and prove his foresight by declaring—in 1967—that "the world is going digital" and backing his claim by buying and nurturing a small company that developed inkjet technology and the databases Lexus® and Nexus®.[42] In other words, Mac was a servant-leader before he ever met Bob Greenleaf, and had already taken the next step of applying his philosophy to corporate mission, governance and structures.

Young Robert Greenleaf in Terre Haute, Indiana. *(Greenleaf family)*

Burchie, George, June and Bob Greenleaf. In later life, Bob reflected on this picture: "In front of Father, I was well dressed and looked happy. My sister, in front of her mother, looked sad, was poorly dressed, hair unbrushed—a shocking contrast. I marvel that [June] was a constructive contributor to society and lived such a long life." *(Franklin Trask Library)*

Bob's Aunt Anna and Uncle John Parkhurst. Mr. Parkhurst took an interest in his young nephew, introduced him to astronomy, and convinced him to attend Carleton College. *(Greenleaf family)*

Bob Greenleaf (front row, second from left) is one of the disappointed eclipse observers at Camp Wrigley, near Avalon, Catalina Island. From: "The Expedition from the Yerkes Obervatory for Observing the Total Eclipse of September *10, 1923*, at Camp Wrigley" by Edwin B. Frost. Reprinted from *Popular Astronomy*. Vol. XXXII. No. 4. April, 1924. *(Franklin Trask Library)*

The first AT&T conference to train managers, held in St. Louis during the summer of 1927. Greenleaf, who called it "the most formative experience of my adult life," is the fifth person back on the left. *(Franklin Trask Library)*

Portrait of Esther Hargrave contained in a 1924 book on phrenology. (See Chapter 9) The caption reads: "Young woman of fine texture. Almost pure plane type of profile. Natural talent for literature, music, and art, with refinement, gentleness, sympathy and reflection."

Bob and Esther on one of their many early trips to the hills. *(Greenleaf family)*

The Greenleafs took advantage of all New York had to offer after their marriage in 1931. *(Greenleaf family)*

George Greenleaf, his new grandson Newcomb, and Bob. *(Greenleaf family)*

Bob with his son Newcomb and daughter Elizabeth (Lisa). *(Greenleaf family)*

Bob retained a life long interest in astronomy. Here he instructs Esther on how to use a specially-constructed box to observe a solar eclipse. *(Greenleaf family)*

Bob Greenleaf in his office at AT&T. One of Esther's pictures is on the wall in the background. *(Franklin Trask Library)*

A typical scene of Robert Greenleaf at work at AT&T. *(Greenleaf Center)*

Bob Greenleaf, theologian and author Gerald Heard and Les Rollins at a conference at Harvard Business School. Rollins, former Assistant Dean of Harvard Business School, helped Bob design and implement the Ohio Fellows Program at Ohio University in Athens. *(Franklin Trask Library)*

Summer executive course at Dartmouth, circa 1962. Greenleaf, on right in the front row, invariably had a small smile of pride when these pictures were taken following intense conferences. *(Franklin Trask Library)*

Madeline, Newcomb and Lisa Greenleaf. *(Greenleaf family)*

Bob and "my women" by the ocean. from left: Madeline, Esther, Bob, with Lisa in front. *(Greenleaf family)*

While her husband worked to advance management education in India, Esther visited local women, artists and craftspeople. *(Greenleaf family)*

Esther in the field with her easel and painting supplies. *(Greenleaf family)*

Two paintings by Esther Greenleaf, an abstract and a scene of Newcomb at one of his favorite activities—reading. Bob made the frames for her paintings. *(Greenleaf family)*

Top view of three enameled bowls created by Bob Greenleaf. Bottom right is a wooden jigsaw puzzle painted by Esther, cut out by Bob, and given to their son Newcomb. *(Greenleaf family)*

Esther Greenleaf continued creating her art until the end. Even when she lost her sight she told Bob, "I can still paint in my mind." *(Greenleaf Center)*

Prior to the 1969 commencement ceremonies Greenleaf shakes hands with Mrs. Royal (Dacie) Moses, who received an honorary Master of Arts from Carleton College at the same ceremony where Greenleaf received an honorary Doctor of Humane Letters. Standing behind is John Nason, President of Carleton College and a classmate of Bob's. *(Greenleaf family)*

One of Bob's favorite pastimes was giving wheelbarrow rides to children.

During a 1986 visit, Ann McGee-Cooper presented Bob and Esther with Amish dolls as a symbol of their playfulness together. Bob said he always wanted a teddy bear but was never allowed one. Ann later sent him a small brown bear dressed in vest, tie and top hat, which Bob kept on his bed. *(Ann McGee Cooper)*

Esther and Bob Greenleaf at Crosslands, a Quaker retirement community in Kennett Square, Pennsylvania. George Greenleaf's advice to his son about marriage was, "keep sweet." *(Greenleaf Center)*

Greenleaf's friend and colleague Douglas Williams said, "Bob had an ever-present, chuckling sense of humor. He was one of the most enjoyable men to be with I have ever met." *(Greenleaf Center)*

Bob was an avid amateur musician and photographer throughout his life. *(Greenleaf family)*

The Greenleaf clan with children and Grandchildren. Madeline stands next to Bob on his left. Newcomb is directly behind Esther and Lisa is to the right of Esther. *(Greenleaf family)*

Bob atop a mountain at about the age of thirty. *(Franklin Trask Library)*

Robert Greenleaf on his eightieth birthday. *(Greenleaf family)*

Bob spent most of his time with Mac listening and clarifying issues, not offering solutions. Whether they were meeting in Dayton with Mead's friend Walker Lewis or walking the beach at Mac's house at Sea Island, Georgia, each man learned from the other. "[Mac] needs someone who will listen," said Bob. "My job was providing a focus." [43] In return, Mac was a sounding board for Bob's evolving philosophy of leadership. "I don't think he had had exposure to many people in positions like mine who were as candid as I was with him," recalled Mac, "so he found it rewarding and meaningful, I think, to test some of his ideas and thoughts." Mac read everything Bob wrote and provided extensive feedback. "It wasn't just reading my thoughts, it was analyzing them, commenting on them, and writing," said Bob. "He has probably done as much with what I've written as anybody."[44] William Carr, who wrote a book about McSwiney's time at Mead, speculates that Mac was the model for a fictional character in Greenleaf's 1979 book *The Teacher as Servant*.

> He comes through as a tough, aggressive, high achiever and a successful person. What makes him effective here is that he really has sorted out the issue of power and he is very realistic about what is required to be a servant in this highly organized and very competitive society. Some people are put off by the word *servant*. It connotes soft dogooding to many . . . But here, at the head of this large company, is a fellow as hard as nails who has thought it all through and can communicate what he believes a servant has to be if he is to be a constructive influence.[45]

"I don't know how you capture a person like Bob in a book," Mac said many years later. "He's not someone you read about in history books. For goodness sake, don't write about servant leadership so people can say, 'I'm already doing this because I know it's good.' A lot of people don't do anything except repeat the rhetoric. The trick is to make it happen and [servant leadership] isn't any good unless it comes from the heart."[46]

After the death of Dr. Donald Cowling in 1965, Bob's old "Prexy" at Carleton, Greenleaf sat down and wrote a short memorial about him. John Nason, one of Bob's classmates at Carleton, was now president of the college and asked Bob to expand the piece into a brochure. In 1966, Bob delivered his manuscript: *Donald J. Cowling: Lifestyle of Greatness*. Dr. Nason was generally pleased but concerned about three issues: (1) "At times your approach is a little too personal." (2) "In my judgment you overestimate Prexy's greatness." Nason believed Cowling's autocracy and inflexibility mitigated against greatness. (3) Nason disagreed with Bob's stance of addressing present undergraduates. "Undergraduates are unpredictable and skittish. Sometimes one has to approach them indirectly and downwind."[47] Bob held fast on all points. Education *was* personal to him, and what he had to say about Cowling, for all the personality differences between them, had been filtered through his reflective process. Furthermore, Bob was determined to address current undergraduates. "Students should know that the quality of the institution they now enjoy did not build itself," he wrote in an introduction to the essay, reprinted in the book *Servant Leadership*.[48]

One time Greenleaf asked Nason if Carleton College, in its modern incarnation, would hire a person like Oscar Helming, the teacher who set the course of Bob's career in 1926. After some thought, Dr. Nason said, "No," and this answer saddened Bob. Still, in 1969 Dr. Nason recommended Bob for an honorary doctorate. The news release accompanying the announcement contained several revealing lines about the honoree.

> A self-styled renegade student and at the same time a warm friend and prodigious correspondent with three of Carleton's five presidents, Greenleaf, who has insisted on pursuing his own life style, is constantly surprised that friends wonder why he has been willing to settle for "my little niche in a great corporation where I intend to spend my life chipping away at something that interested me."
>
> Long an advocate of educational innovations, which he calls his "maverick" ideas, Greenleaf has said changes are needed because "adult performance in all fields is pretty mediocre when judged by what it might be" and describes himself as a critic of the pretensions of educators rather than of their performances.[49]

With that wry introduction to the wider world, Robert K. Greenleaf became a Doctor of Humane Letters. You would think the degree might entitle Carleton to expect increased financial support from the "retired industrialist," but one of the school's development officers visited him in Crosslands Retirement Center in 1985 and did not file an encouraging report. "Bob will do what he can but is not considered to be a capital gift prospect," he said in his follow-up memo.[50] The Greenleafs may not have had much extra money lying around, but what the poor prospector could not have known was Bob's history in following his father's example for charitable giving. Loyalty counted for little in his decisions; he was guided by proven, practical results. There was another matter too. When Bob had given to Carleton in the past he asked that his name not be publicized, but they published it anyway. Finally, he wrote a note to the alumni office: "I am not a contributor to the alumni fund because I am resolved not to contribute to anything that publishes lists of donors . . . The college should remove me from the list so I am not an expense to them."[51] President Nason chose Bob on his merits for the honorary doctorate. He knew Greenleaf well enough that he did not expect a *quid pro quo*—an honorary degree for a major contribution—but Bob's attitude must have been surprising to university development officers who expected charitable donations to be the college's reward for recognition.

In the summer of 1968, Greenleaf gave five lectures to the Dartmouth Alumni College on the subject of "Leadership and the Individual."[52] It was a clear, clean, conversational series of speeches which, for the first time, pulled together Bob's most comprehensive thinking about leadership. It remains a good read today, even though some of the references are dated.

"We are in a leadership crisis," Bob said, "because not enough of those who have the opportunity and the obligation to lead have kept themselves contemporary," and because the communications explosion and cultural conditions begged for "an inventiveness and adaptability that leaders heretofore have not had to have."[53] Furthermore, the educational system "is not designed to prepare for leadership."[54] Greenleaf referred to his friend John Gardner's influential 1965 essay "The Antileadership Vaccine," which claimed that colleges turned students into critics and experts rather than vital, inspirited people prepared to assume the tough chores of sustained leadership. Universities, according to Gardner, tended to *discourage* leadership.[55] Bob agreed and also believed that young people were precious because they would be the ones to update the traditional Western values that started with Moses, keeping gems of timeless wisdom but adding fresh moral insights and sanctions. Finally, Greenleaf argued that whatever progress we make must be mediated *first* through individuals and then through institutions. "The only access we have to inspiration, those subtle promptings of intuitive insight from the vast unconscious storehouse of wisdom and experience, is through the mind of an individual."[56] Then he made a statement that sounds like a clarion warning to all of us who live in a wall-to-wall media age.

> I was deeply touched by a quote from a late lecture by Camus. 'Great ideas come into the world as gently as doves. . . . Listen carefully and you will hear the flutter of their wings.' Only the solitary individual in the quietness of his own meditation gets these great ideas intuitively. They don't come in stentorian tones, over the public address system to groups. That only happens *after* an individual has listened carefully to the flutter of their wings. The wings themselves do not flutter into the microphone."[57]

In the other Dartmouth speeches, Greenleaf reworked some of his classic ideas about leadership. The "strategies of a leader," for example, include goal setting—and who could disagree—but also nontraditional strategies like:

- The principle of systematic neglect. An old boss told Greenleaf it was "just as important to know what to neglect as to know what to do."[58]

- Listening. "Listeners learn about people that modify—first the *listener's* attitude, then his behavior toward others, and finally the attitudes and behavior of others."[59]

- Language as a leadership strategy. "Whoever articulates the goal that makes the consensus idea is a *de facto* leader. . . . Some of our best communication, especially to the young, is done obliquely—let it be something they overhear rather than something beamed right at them. Most of us don't like to be lectured to, but we all like to eavesdrop."[60]

- Values. "In just three value choices, we can separate what we want from what we don't want in a leader. We want a leader to be *honest*, *loving*, and *responsible*. . . . As I see it, responsible people build. They do not destroy. They are moved by the heart; compassion stands ahead of justice. The prime test of whether an act is responsible is to ask, How will it affect people? Are lives moved toward nobility?" [61]

- Personal growth. "The leader must be a growing person. Non-growth people are finding it more and more difficult to lead, especially to lead young people."[62]

- Tolerance of imperfection. "Some people, a lot of people, in fact, are disqualified to lead because they cannot work through and with the half-people who are available to work with them."[63]

- Acceptance. "The interest and affection that the leader has for his followers—and it is a mark of true greatness when it is genuine—is clearly something that the followers 'haven't to deserve.'"[64]

Greenleaf concluded his last Dartmouth lecture with this: "Virtue and justice and order are good, but not good enough—not nearly good enough. In the end, nothing really counts but love and friendship."[65]

Greenleaf was offering a *philosophy* of leadership, one based on his lifelong research, experience, and personal reflections. It was not a *theory* of leadership, based on primate studies of territoriality or the influence of one's environment or even the traits of a leader. (Napoleon listed one-hundred fifteen qualities essential for a military leader.)[66] Neither was it based on one's position in an organization, a bullet-point list of tips and techniques that make one a leader, the amount of money a person earns, or the extent to which one is a hero to others. (When asked in 1986 to explain the difference between a hero and a leader, Greenleaf replied, "I don't see any connection.")[67] Bob Greenleaf offered a leadership philosophy of the *"ands;"* a moral leader is one who incarnates doing *and* being, who is plugged in to contemporary issues *and* finds inspiration in the quiet solitude of intuitive insight, who takes responsibility for each decision on its own merits *and* for the impact it will have on others, now and in the future.

Greenleaf did not know it at the time, but his Dartmouth lectures were a warm-up for the most important piece of writing of his life.

18

The Servant Series

Behind what is said in The Servant as Leader is a twofold concern:
first for the individual in society and the tendency to deal with the
massive problems of our times too much in terms of systems, ideologies,
and movements. . . . My second concern is for the individual as a
serving person and the tendency to deny wholeness to oneself by failing
to lead when one can lead, or by not choosing with discrimination
when it is more appropriate to follow.[1]

ROBERT K. GREENLEAF

Late in 1968, while Apollo 8 dashed to and from the moon, Robert Greenleaf was at home reworking his Dartmouth lecture notes. He had an idea, just a phrase really, but it held language that opened a window to everything in which he believed—everything. The phrase was "servant-leader." It had come to him in October while he and Esther were driving through the parched and stunning landscape of Arizona.

The previous year, Bob had consulted with the planning group of Prescott College about the attitudes entering college students bring with them to campus. Largely as a result of his prodding, the college had divided the 1968 freshman class into small seminar groups that met weekly with faculty members for discussions of their evolving perspectives. Greenleaf's view was that, "It is possible that without such an effort, one impact of the academic program might be to accentuate some of the destructive tendencies that are brought to the campus when these students enter."[2] He well knew about those disturbing tendencies because, as the 1960s unrolled, Bob had been in frequent touch with presidents and trustees of major universities like Harvard, MIT, Dartmouth, and Cornell.

The Prescott venture was part of a two-year thrust approved by The Center for Applied Ethics in March of 1967. (The Center changed its name to The Center for Applied Studies the following January.) Bob was to spend much of his time during this period in seminars with up to fifteen undergraduate colleges, working with faculty members to nurture students with the potential to enter public service, helping them to clarify and test their abilities, illuminate the moral implications of public service, and set a lifelong pattern of self-growth.[3] Besides sponsoring Bob's personal activities, the Center had quietly funded summer study programs and other opportunities for students from its earliest years, so this organizational thrust was not new.[4]

"I went out [to Prescott] prepared to do a week of afternoon voluntary seminars," said Bob, "but I found that this upset the faculty for some reason that I do not know. It was not a course, but they were really up in arms about this being done, and exerted an influence on the students that made it virtually impossible for me to carry out the task that I had gone there to do as a volunteer."[5] After the debacle the phrase "servant-leader" popped into Bob's consciousness, and he decided to write an essay with that title.

As with so many other important things in his life, Greenleaf had prepared himself for this moment without knowing the goal of his preparation. In his travels around colleges, he always spoke with students and visited the campus bookstores to see what they were reading on their own. He saw rows and rows of books by the German novelist Hermann Hesse (1877–1962) and decided that "if I wanted to understand the students, I'd better look to see what Hesse was up to."[6] (Newcomb Greenleaf believes Esther may have also influenced Bob's decision to read Hesse since she was his "advance scout" for important books.) Bob read every Hesse book in the order in which it was written, and simultaneously read a biography of the writer so he would know what was going on in the author's life at the time. What he discovered was a gifted but tortured artist who tried to reconcile spirit, nature, and society while suffering from bouts of mental illness, failed marriages, and general turmoil. *Journey to the East* is connected in imagery and content to Hesse's next book, *The Glass Bead Game* (1942), which he—and many reviewers—considered his greatest creative work.

Greenleaf was fascinated by Leo, the main character in *Journey to the East*."

> [*Journey to the East*] is the story of a mythical journey of a band of men who were on a journey to the East, each with his own individual exploration. With the party was their servant Leo, who did their menial chores, got their mules, carried their baggage, all the other personal attentions that they needed. Leo was a man of extraordinary presence who, in addition to his chores, raised the spirit of the group by his own spirit and song. Leo one day disappears and the search falls into disarray. They cannot make it without the servant Leo.
>
> The narrator, one of the party, accounts then for years which he spent searching for Leo. He finally located him and was taken into the Order that had sponsored the search, where he discovered that Leo was actually the leader, the principal person in this Order, a great and noble leader.
>
> From this, I got the idea that the key to the greatness of Leo was the fact that he was first a servant and then a leader, and that's where the term that I have coined for my writing *Servant Leadership* came from.[7]

With students demonstrating on campuses, administrators running for cover, and parents and politicians up in arms, what did Greenleaf think he could accomplish by writing a short essay? It was simply what he could do. Recent consultancies with MIT and Cornell, the Prescott experience, and further contacts with students, faculty, and administrators in the Boston area convinced him that the situation was beyond repair by patchwork. Colleges were in too much turmoil for workshops to do much good. University structure and governance was the larger problem, but neither Bob nor the Center was prepared to tackle such a large-scale issue. The Center could, however, become a "resource for new content," a catalyst for a "new value-oriented influence in the universities," and the way to do that was through the word.[8] The sword did not seem to be working, at home or abroad.

In the resulting essay, *The Servant as Leader*, Greenleaf suggests that a new moral principle may be emerging: "The only authority deserving of one's allegiance is that which is freely and knowingly granted by the led to the leader in response to, and in proportion to, the clearly evident servant stature of the leader. Those who choose to follow this principle will not casually accept the authority of existing institutions. Rather, they will freely respond only to individuals who are chosen as leaders because they are proven and trusted as servants."[9] So *followers choose leaders*—authentic moral leaders—because they have proven their willingness to serve and even risk losing leadership by "venturing out for the common good." But servant-leaders also make choices; they choose to build personal strength, "to opt for leadership as a meaningful lifestyle, toward which an individual may progress by conscious preparation."[10]

Since the ultimate audience of the essay is students, Greenleaf quotes several prominent student leaders, among them Ms. Hillary Rodham, president of the student body at Wellesley College, who turned a few heads with her graduation speech:

> Too long our leaders have viewed politics as the art of the possible, and the challenge now is to practice politics as the art of making what appears to be impossible, possible. If the experiment in human living doesn't work in this country, in this age, it's not going to work anywhere. . . . The goal of it must be human liberation, a liberation enabling each of us to fulfill our capacities so as to be free to create within and around ourselves . . . We are, all of us, exploring a world that none of us understands, and attempting to create within that uncertainty. But there are some things we feel, feeling that a prevailing acquisitive and competitive corporate life, including— tragically—the universities, is not the way of life for us. We're searching for a more immediate, ecstatic, and penetrating mode of living.[11]

Greenleaf applauds the spirit but also notes that society does not owe its citizens a "more immediate, ecstatic, and penetrating mode of living. And those who pursue it too narrowly may lose their way. What we may achieve is likely to be something unasked . . ."[12]

He then confronts the then-prevailing notion that "the system" is the problem. "The better society will come, if it comes, with plenty of evil, stupid, apathetic people around and with an imperfect, ponderous, inertia-charged 'system' as the vehicle for change. . . . The real enemy is fuzzy thinking on the part of good, intelligent, vital people, and their failure to lead. Too many settle for being critics and experts."[13]

Servants may choose not to be leaders, not to "go out ahead and show the way," but like Leo, "The true servant must lead in order to be a complete person!" Leaders are not trained, he asserts, they evolve through their own natural rhythms. One must master the knowledge of a field in which one leads, but "leadership overarches expertise, and it cannot be reduced to a style."[14]

In the essay, Greenleaf touches on most of the major-wisdom ideas he refined in a lifetime packed with learning. A quick summary will suffice.

- The pyramid organizational structure with its dominating leader is no longer adequate. You can blame Jethro for that. (See Exodus: 18) When Jethro decided his son-in-law Moses was wearing himself out, he suggested the management principle of delegation: Place men over groups of tens, fifties, hundreds, and thousands. Moses gets to speak to God, the little people talk to their supervisors. Greenleaf has a wry take on this arrangement. "A close examination of Jethro's principle reveals that it does not assume Moses in the role of servant. Clearly he is the dominating leader, dedicated though he may be to his job, and this arrangement seems designed primarily to assure his survival in that job."[15]

- The leader needs to "have a sense for the unknowable and be able to foresee the unforeseeable" through intuition and reflection. Foresight, in fact, is the central ethic of leadership.[16]

- Everything begins with the initiative of the individual. "The leader has to initiate, push, provide the ideas and the structure, and take the risk of failure along with the chance of success. This is partly what the element of spirit is about; spirit sustains the leader as he or she takes the risk of saying, "'I will go; follow me!' when he or she knows that the path is uncertain, even dangerous."[17]

Most of the highlights of the Dartmouth lectures are covered here: listening, language as a leadership strategy, the art of systematic neglect, personal growth, persuasion, tolerance of imperfection, acceptance of the person. The essay ends with a final appeal to young people, urging them to recognize mediocrity in positions of influence because "That fellow is there because a few years ago someone like me failed to prepare for that job."[18] He urges them to demythologize leadership, to become more open to the meaning of chaos, live closer to the awe of mystery that is beyond "the logic of the spirit," and remember that "not much that is really important can be accomplished with coercive power."[19]

Bob completed the essay in March 1969 and sent several hundred copies out for comments. It had become his habit to solicit feedback from as many people as possible before he committed his words to final print. In the fall, he worked with an editor to revise the manuscript and by March, 1970, had sold three hundred copies and given away another three hundred.[20] Word of the essay spread through Bob's regular—and wide—circle of friends. This piece seemed to take on a life of its own, building an underground network. Students and university faculty and administrators read it, but so did leaders in government, businesses, hospitals, elementary schools, and foundations. Catholic Orders of Sisters were especially enthusiastic.

Clearly, *The Servant as Leader* touched something deep in a vast audience beyond students. When asked about the source of that common spark, Greenleaf suggested that some readers may have had a person in his or her life like Bob's father, a model servant-leader who established a pattern that had lain dormant. "This is not a bandwagon idea; it is not a best-seller kind of thing, but nevertheless, these people do exist and some of them have become very important to me . . . These people now are in all walks of life, and they are to some extent lonely people; but they don't find themselves in environments that reinforce this disposition in their nature . . . I suspect that it's quite common in our society that there are people with high levels of idealism who have had experiences that have shaken their hope that you can live productively with those ideals. Perhaps what I have written has given some people some encouragements, that there are ways to deal with whatever situation one finds oneself in and be more of a servant by trying than by not trying . . ."[21]

As for the Catholic Sisters, Bob guessed that, "they of all people have probably made one of the largest servant commitments with their own lives, and they recognized an articulation of their principles of service that may have been new to them.[22]

More than one Sister took issue with Bob on the source of the servant-leader idea, though. Soon after the essay was published, a Catholic Sister visited Bob for a conversation, one which he recalled vividly fifteen years later. "Where do you find in history the first reference to servant?" she asked. Bob replied, "In the Bible, of course. I've checked the concordance and I found thirteen hundred references to servant." She then asked sharply, "Why then do you attribute what you have written to Hermann Hesse?" He answered, "Because that's where I got the idea of the servant as leader. If I had not read *Journey to the East*, I may never have written anything on this subject." Then, like a good Quaker, he continued, "The Bible did not end revelation. In my belief, revelation is continuous."[23]

A few years later Greenleaf's friend Bob Lynn pushed him on the same point. At the time, Robert Wood Lynn was senior vice president for religion at the Lilly Endowment and a respected theologian with teaching and administrative experience in seminaries.

> I said to Bob, "Surely you didn't arrive at that notion of servant leadership by reading the German novelist. It happened in part because you grew up in a context in which those ideas were alive and at work. The idea would be inexplicable apart from the Christian tradition." He reluctantly agreed that that might be historically correct but that he did not want to limit himself to the Christian tradition.[24]
>
> An idealist to the core, Bob had unlimited confidence in the power of ideals . . . At times I found him simplistic in his confidence in those notions. The ideal of the "servant leader" was one of those large abstractions. It only made sense to me as an abstraction lifted out of the Christian tradition. He and I parted company on this matter . . . I am sure he found me much too "theological," while I thought he had placed his ultimate trust in several thin abstractions that would not finally bear the weight he placed upon them.[25]

Ken Blanchard says something similar; "I know Bob felt that we should be citizens of the world. Countries were arbitrary, and he was concerned about religions separating us, but I think that servant leadership without a spiritual foundation is just another management technique."[26]

Another insight comes from Bill Bottum, an Ann Arbor businessman who was close to Greenleaf in his later years. According to Bill, one day Bob confided that the image of Jesus washing the feet of disciples, as described in John: 13, was one source of the idea of the servant-leader. But Greenleaf told his friend Bill something similar to what he told Bob Lynn; he wanted to speak to people of all persuasions and not have his ideas relegated to the exclusively Christian category.[27]

We can certainly take Greenleaf at his word that Leo gave him the language to crystallize multiple streams of images, ideas, and intuitions, the model of his father, the work of John Woolman, practices of the best leaders and managers at AT&T, and his own inclinations. We can also believe that the Bible played a role in the mix.

For some readers, the source of Bob's catchy phrase was not as much an issue as the word *servant*. Some women and people of color had a problem with this word because of its historical associations to slavery, menial household servitude, sexism, and oppression. As late as 1985, Bob confided that, "I just didn't hear anything from black people. . . . There were a couple of exceptions . . . but to them the word 'servant' is a loaded word."[28] Still, Greenleaf thought that it was worth taking the risk to use *servant*. It might encourage discussions that a milder term would not, and besides, he did not know of a better word to express what he meant.[29] History would prove his instinct correct. Within ten years after his death, black thinkers and authors like Lea Williams, Michele Hunt, Artis Hampshire-Cowan, Bill Guillory, and others would write about servant leadership and relate it to the black experience.

Lou Mobley, a retired IBM executive, was one of the two hundred people who received the first copies of the slender orange essay. He used it for a seminar at Highland Park United Methodist Church in Dallas, where it caught the eye of Jack Lowe, founder of Texas Distributors (TD), a heating and air conditioning firm that had worked with high-powered developer Trammell Crow on some of the biggest construction projects in Dallas, like the Furniture Mart. Jack began ordering more copies and passing them out at work. His repeated orders caught Greenleaf's attention. Bob called up Jack one day and asked, "What are you doing with all those copies of my essay?" It turned out Jack was not only giving them to executives, but to everyone—installers, office workers, people with college and elementary educations. Furthermore, they were all reading it and applying its insights as they met in small groups to redefine TD's mission and structure.

In Jack Lowe, Bob discovered a remarkable person, a natural servant-leader, a businessman who literally *loved* his employee-partners, even when he (and they) could be demanding. Lowe's biographer reported that, "In Jack's eyes, Greenleaf had incorporated religious ideals into a management philosophy, and he loved it. But Greenleaf, content to 'stand in awe of all creation' when it came to religion, hadn't conceived the servant-leader as a part of any particular doctrine, and he seemed mildly surprised that Jack had."[30]

Bob and Esther became good friends of Jack and Harriet Lowe. The Greenleafs were houseguests when Bob came to TD to conduct seminars or just to see what Jack and his company were up to. Bob and Esther were devastated by Jack's death on Thanksgiving Day 1980, and so was all of Dallas. Texans remembered that by the time a court ordered Dallas to desegregate its schools in 1975, Jack Lowe had already formed an Education Task Force to come up with implementation plans. He was so trusted that even the judge in the case let Jack and his diverse group bring him the final plan, provided they could reach consensus. Jack eagerly continued working for the community even when the doctors told him it might kill him, and it did. His heart could not keep up with his frantic pace.

Like James McSwiney, Jack Lowe was a servant-leader before he ever heard of Bob Greenleaf. *The Servant as Leader* essay simply gave language to who he already was, someone recognizable in one of Jack's favorite verses in the tenth chapter of Mark: "Whoever would be great among you must be your servant, and whoever would be first among you must be slave of all."

Jack Lowe's son, Jack Jr., was chosen to lead the company after his father's death. To this day, TD—now TDIndustries—is the longest-running organizational experiment in servant leadership. The company is consistently in the top ten of Fortune 500's list of "The 100 Best Companies to Work For in America." Employee-partners still receive copies of *The Servant as Leader* and discuss it on service runs, in the lunchroom, and in groups. One of Esther's paintings graces the wall of the TDI conference room.

The second—and final—version of *The Servant as Leader* was released in 1973. Greenleaf made revisions that broadened the audience beyond the university community because, clearly, a much wider group was already responding. He removed sections that would have dated it, like "The 1970s," which included the quote from Hillary Rodham. He also deleted several instances of the word love. "The word is overused, has too many connotations and is not precise enough," he explained to Joe Distefano in 1985. "Jack Lowe, Sr. was really mad at me about that; I took a dressing down from him. As long as any of the original versions were around, that's what he bought."[31]

One of the most important additions to the final version was his "best test" for a servant-leader. From his assessment work, Bob had learned that some things that were deemed "impossible" to measure really could be measured. For all his talk about motives, awareness, intuition, and ultimate mystery providing the impulse to serve, the proof of the pudding for this servant-leader was a pragmatic, steely-eyed measurement of outcomes.

> The best test, and difficult to administer, is: do those served grow as persons; do they, while being served, become healthier, wiser, freer, more autonomous, more likely themselves to become servants? And, what is the effect on the least privileged in society; will he benefit, or, at least, will he not be further deprived?[32]

There is a curious addition near the beginning of the essay's final version: a discussion about prophecy. Greenleaf, borrowing from his friend Abraham Heschel's insights on the Old Testament prophets, says, "It is seekers, then, who make prophets, and the initiative of any one of us in searching for and responding to the voice of contemporary prophets may mark the turning point in their growth and service."[33] In that section, Newcomb Greenleaf believes his father was struggling to understand his own role as a prophet. In one letter Bob supported Newcomb's intuition: "If more vocal Old Testament prophets were among us today, I am sure they would rail at our institutions, all of them."[34] By the time this was written Bob had experienced a powerful—and unexpected—response to the 1970 version of the essay. People were already writing and calling, wanting him to be their guru, but that was a role that he would not accept. He would be mentor to a select few but *guru* to none. He saw how the work of Kurt Lewin—and Alfred Korzybski for that matter—suffered when disciples gathered 'round. Furthermore, he was not about to supply people with their answers. That was their job. *Guru* would not do, but *prophet* was acceptable, and if hearers chose their prophets, it was out of his hands. His responsibility was to simply say what he had to say.

In structure and style, the final version is less like a lecture in print and more like prose-poetry. Each section is shorter, more evocative, than the first version, and the whole piece defies an easy bullet-point summary. When asked about this, Greenleaf said, "I have been conscious of the need for brevity. . . . I don't know that I consciously said, 'I will stop here and let the reader supply the rest,' but I did consciously not write for an uninformed audience."[35] Joe Distefano told Greenleaf about an observation from a person who had been influenced by Bob's writing—Father Ray Barnhart, the President of Loyola University.

> [He said] it was a little bit like jumping from the edge of land to the ocean and being surprised, initially, that when you did so you found a rock to land on. When you jumped again there was another rock, and soon he learned to trust that process. When he sees a new essay by you, he simply jumps because he found that, often enough, he got to a place that he valued being when he followed your writing. But he earlier found it disconcerting because it wasn't the delineative, logical-type reasoned series of propositions that led to a place.[36]

Another way of putting it is that *The Servant as Leader* takes the reader on a hole-in-the-hedge journey that parallels Bob's own life experience. "Look! Here is an opening in the hedge, in which he is talking about language. Wait, there are other openings about awareness and foresight and community. But this essay is about leadership, isn't it? What is that paragraph about prophecy doing here? Let's go through that one." Reading it reminds one of Robert Frost's answer to Bob when he asked the great poet about the meaning of his poem *Directive*. "Read it and read it and read it, and it means what it says to you."[37] The essay does have a structure with consistent internal logic, but nothing is spoon-fed. Some readers believe its organization and style are part of its enduring appeal, because it jolts ordinary thought processes, fascinates, and sticks in the craw. Others, like Bob's friend Douglas Williams, believe it suffers from its denseness. "My thinking goes like this," wrote Williams. "Bob's writings should have been gone through by a few successful, hard-boiled managers with plenty of experience on the front lines. Then a top-grade editor who possessed a fine writing style himself, after hearing these tough guys' views, could edit Greenleaf's phrasing so that it would get through to men such as these who were responsible for operating results."[38]

In the spring of 1971, *The Journal of Current Social Issues* was almost entirely devoted to a reprint of the essay under the title: "The Servant-Leader: A New Lifestyle." James Perdue, a university administrator in New York, read the article and was convinced it was the work of a young faculty Turk at a major university. He was surprised to learn the author was a man who was not only not young but was not even an academician and had never worked as a college administrator.[39] Responses to *The Servant as Leader* mounted through the years as people discovered it for the first time, both in its essay version and as the first chapter of the 1977 book *Servant Leadership*. An assemblyman in Sacramento wrote that it helped him understand his journey for a more unitary life; the questions he must search out in his work and his personal life were the same questions. A young doctor named Patch Adams, who thought humor had a role in his mission for health and wholeness, read Bob's essay and found language that described his deepest identity. Patch became one of Bob's correspondents. Nuns and activists and businesspeople—so many seemed to experience a shock of recognition when they first read about the idea of a servant-leader.

In retrospect, the logic of Greenleaf's next few essays is obvious. After addressing the importance of an individual acting as a servant-leader, the next step up the ladder is to consider how institutions may act as servants. In 1972, Bob published *The Institution as Servant*, which looked at organizations in their role as organic, breathing servants to internal and external constituencies. Then he asked himself, "Who is responsible for the overall performance of institutions?" Legally, it was—and still is—trustees, and Bob had direct knowledge of how the best trustees, J. P. Morgan being the most obvious example, did their jobs. In 1974, he published the essay *Trustees As Servants*, which outlined the motivations and roles servant trustees could play and even suggested the possibility of a "trusteed society." The following year, the Center published *Advices To Servants*, a collection of papers and talks Greenleaf had written, mostly in response to challenges that had faced his consulting clients, that integrated the servant-leader idea. In 1977, Paulist Press published the book *Servant Leadership,* which included the previous four publications on the servant theme and additional material. Finally, in 1979 Greenleaf published a novel called *Teacher As Servant: A Parable,* which completed the circle of servant leadership concerns back to undergraduate education.

The second essay, *The Institution As Servant,* did not receive the same rousing response as *The Servant as Leader.* It's one thing to hear inspiring words about individual aspirations and acts of servanthood but quite another to have someone suggest how you should run your business. "People who were intrigued by the first essay were intensely bothered by the second one," said Bob, "particularly people who were chief executives of big things. I recall one very acrimonious session with the head of a large corporation who had been immensely impressed by the first essay and terribly bothered by the second one. He didn't feel I should have written it, and certainly should not have distributed it. It was heresy. You couldn't manage the nation with that kind of idea."[40] Others were less direct but just as upset. Perhaps they were finally beginning to understand that, while Greenleaf was a quiet revolutionary, he was a revolutionary nonetheless, and such people could be pesky.

The Institution As Servant begins with a premise that seems benign enough:

> This is my thesis: caring for persons, the more able and the less able serving each other, is the rock upon which a good society is built. Whereas, until recently, caring was largely person to person, now most of it is mediated through institutions—often large, complex, powerful, impersonal; not always competent; sometimes corrupt. If a better society is to be built, one that is more just and more loving, one that provides greater creative opportunity for its people, then the most open course is to raise both the capacity to serve and the very performance as servant of existing major institutions by new regenerative forces operating within them.[41]

Then Greenleaf starts to sound like the prophet Amos. Institutions, he says, suffer from a lack of trust; governments rely too much on coercion; health and social services work to banish symptoms rather than restore wholeness; too many businesses have an inadequate sense of their wider responsibilities; universities prepare people for narrow professional careers, churches have abandoned their value-shaping roles; organizations of all kinds are led by administrators rather than leaders.[42]

And that's just for openers. Now comes the truly threatening idea: CEOs hold too much power. "To be a lone chief atop a pyramid is abnormal and corrupting. . . When someone is moved atop a pyramid, that person no longer has colleagues, only subordinates."[43] Furthermore, most of these chiefs are unbalanced because they tend to be "operationalizers"—managers promoted to a position that also requires "conceptualizers," or big-picture thinkers. "Whereas conceptualizers generally recognize the need for operators, the reverse is often not the case," wrote Greenleaf.[44]

Bob's solution was to turn the pyramid into a circle. The lone chief then becomes a *primus inter pares*, a "first among equals" in issues of governance. Whenever possible, decisions are made by consensus. Whatever the organizational structure, guardianship by strong trustees and an astute board chair are critical. No one should be powerless in an organization.[45]

Bob had not lost his mind; such a thing was possible. The Religious Society of Friends had operated that way for over three hundred years but, more to the point, Bob had visited three successful international corporations in Europe that used the *primus inter pares* model: Philips, Royal Dutch Shell, and Unilever, although Philips was the only one that actually used the term. Bob suspected that many American organizations that tacked up a pyramid for an organizational chart actually functioned informally with *primus inter pares* decision making, especially at the lower levels.[46] Here and there one can see contemporary—and successful—experiments that prove the model can work, as long as the designated leader is committed to it and has the support of trustees who matter.[47]

The third servant essay, *Trustees As Servants*, published in 1974, attracted widespread attention from the usual quarters, but especially from nonprofit groups. "Trustees (or Directors) are legally and ultimately responsible for the institution and everything that goes on in it," writes Greenleaf. [48] Trustees hold the organization in trust for those who work within it and for the general public. Greenleaf's take on the proper trustee role is a far cry from the behavior of directors who rubber-stamp a CEO's recommendations or serve on a board only for the social cachet the position brings. In fact, he asserts that trustees commonly do not function in a way that builds trust.[49]

For trustees to be trust*worthy*, they must handle power ethically. In one paragraph, Greenleaf summarizes what he means by the ethical use of power and links it back to the "best test" of servant leaders. Greenleaf italicized the entire passage:

> *The role of trustees is to hold what approximates absolute power over the institution, using it operationally only in rare emergencies—ideally never. Trustees delegate the operational use of power to administrators and staffs, but with accountability for its use that is at least as strict as now obtains with the use of property and money. Furthermore, trustees will insist that the outcome be that people in, and affected by, the institution will grow healthier, wiser, freer, more autonomous, and more likely to become servants of society. The only real justification for institutions, beyond a certain efficiency (which, of course, does serve), is that people in them grow to greater stature than if they stood alone. It follows then that people working in institutions will be more productive than they would be as unrelated individuals. The whole is greater than the sum of its parts.* [50]

Greenleaf suggests that rather than reacting to crises, boards should initiate goal setting, information gathering, performance reviews, reorganizations, and behavior that builds trust. To help them in their responsibilities in understanding the dynamics of their organization, boards could hire someone who does research and reports directly to them. Trustees should continue their own learning and remember that *everyone*, including each trustee, needs to be accountable to others.[51] Since the Chair of a board is the positional leader, even in a *primus inter pares* arrangement, Greenleaf made the highly original suggestion that an Institute of Chairing be established.[52] From his long experience with Friends Meetings, he knew that the knowledge, attitudes, and skills required to chair a group that operates by consensus are quite different from those required by *Roberts Rules of Order*, which is cited as the bible for parliamentary procedural questions in the bylaws of most American institutions.

In the years since the publication of those first three essays, one abiding criticism of Greenleaf's thinking has been that it is "too soft." The argument goes something like this: "Greenleaf is an idealist. Does he not understand the realities of ego, power-striving, and, well, proper *order*?

Does he not know how things get done in the real world of organizations? Besides, where do we find these saints he calls 'servant-leaders?' No one I know is that pure!"

Neither was Bob Greenleaf. For all his qualities of servanthood and humility, he had his personal shadows, but they did not happen to include a need to diminish others as persons. He could be tough about doing research the right way, tough about strategy, personal accountability, thorough analysis, integrity, and facing inner and outer realities. As time goes by, fewer people who knew Bob personally will be around to testify to this essential quality, so it is important to get them on record. "Bob was a very tough teacher, who had a lot of idealism but absolutely not an ounce of sentimentality," says Mac Warford, who worked closely with Bob in his later years. "He had a wonderfully compassionate heart, but there was nothing sentimental about it, and I think that's where people have read him superficially."[53]

Dr. Ann McGee-Cooper had a conversation with Bob in which he talked about a number of matters, including the healthy ego. Ann, a gifted author, artist, scholar, entrepreneur, and presenter, was introduced to Bob's writings by Jack Lowe at TDIndustries. She was so profoundly affected that she joined the Greenleaf Center board and based all of her own consulting work on servant-leadership principles. Ann once asked for clarification on a statement Bob made about trustees. "Am I right? The trustee doesn't have the ego need to be the leader; that's not the motive. The motive is to help the right things happen, and so they quietly work behind the scenes helping others to learn the skills." Bob responded:

> I would question the notion that the trustee doesn't have ego needs. Everybody has ego needs. They are satisfied in different ways. I think I understand this because I've got ego needs, but I never wanted to be a manager. [At AT&T] I chose the role of influencing this vast institution with ideas rather than sitting in a position where I had the power to say "yes" or "no" to a lot of things. Managers are people who get their ego needs met out of wielding power in quite concrete ways. I think that the thing that differentiates a trustee from a manager is that the trustee meets ego needs through a much wider vision of leadership. . . . Trustees use power to insist that their visions be listened to.[54]

So Greenleaf was not out to change human nature by eliminating ego needs; he knew better. Rather, he invited people to examine the ways in which their ego needs were met—the moral integrity of their aims. Once that was clear, the means for achieving aims fell into place. Bob saw more hope for people who were at least honest with themselves about their aims, whether noble or diminished, than for those who camouflaged true intentions behind great causes or personal grandiosities of selflessness. The latter could usually be smoked out into the open, because the way they got things done was incongruent with their stated mission. He once wrote the epigram, "Means *determine* the ends," a neat twist on the argument about whether ends justify means or vice versa.

In the same conversation with Ann McGee-Cooper, Bob told her about a man who was probably more representative of the norm than some idealistic management and leadership theorists would like to admit.

> I once knew a Chief Executive of a large company who was kind of sighing and bemoaning the great weight of problems he was carrying. I asked him flatly, "Well, what keeps you at this anyway? Why do you want to do this?" He sat back and thought about it and said, "I only want this job for the opportunity to wield power."[55]

Bob knew it would be unrealistic to expect such a person to change his stripes simply because he read a book about servant leadership, but even this executive could benefit from further reflection about the aims of his use of power.

Another criticism about the servant-leader style is one of time. The world does not always allow time to seek consensus. Moreover, are there not times when the leader simply needs to say, "Do this, and now!" and times when people have to be laid off or fired?

Absolutely, says Greenleaf. But the tough times, the busy times, are handled better when a servant-leader is in charge.

> In any leadership situation problems are apt to arise when swift, decisive action is important. Followers need to accept that when those conditions arise leaders are apt to behave a little differently than they do in more relaxed times. You can't always call a meeting; there may not be time. I suspect that part of the art of servant leadership is to take advantage of the good times to prepare people for the

> tough times. This, after all, is an imperfect society and people do get
> hurt. It is regrettable, but we may not know how to avoid that. And a
> business is not an unlimited bank; it has limited resources. I think it
> is possible to be strong without being tough and that one doesn't
> have to lose her or his gentleness just because some apparent hurtful
> action has to be taken.[56]

Perhaps the best evidence that Bob was a tough—if idealistic—realist
rather than a sentimental idealist was found in his personal demeanor.
"He was a man of sorrow, well acquainted with grief," recalled teacher
and author Parker Palmer.[57] "Along with his vast experience, his deep
knowledge, his wisdom and his hope, Bob possessed what I can only call
an abiding sadness. I want to call it 'sadness as moral virtue.'"[58] Parker
saw the melancholy that arose in Bob when he looked at the "gap between potentiality and reality, between the contents of the human soul
and what's possible in our social relations with one another."

> The tension that comes from living in that gap, a tension about which
> I think most leaders know a lot, is heartbreaking. But it can break the
> heart in a destructive sense, leading to defeat and withdrawal. Or, as
> was clearly the case with Bob Greenleaf, it can break the heart open
> to greater capacity, enlarging it to hold more of both the potentials
> and the realities of human life. I believe that the capacity to stand in
> and walk in that tragic gap open-heartedly with dignity, grace and
> hope is one of the noblest of human virtues. And one on which insti-
> tutional renewal ultimately depends.[59]

Those who have conducted servant leadership workshops are familiar with a common response from some participants: "I believe in this
stuff but, you know, the person who should be listening to this is my boss!
He's the one with the problem." Or, "This will never happen in the system
we have at my workplace." Greenleaf put the responsibility for acting as
a servant-leader squarely on the shoulders of individuals, be they CEOs,
board chairs, janitors, or middle managers. One cannot blame the system
or even those who run the system for one's own choices.

Perhaps a good way of cutting through the rationalizations about
why such a thing is impossible is to consider the metaphor of a hologram.
When recorded on photographic film, a holographic image looks like

static on an unused television channel. Look as you will, you will see no actual image there. But there is magic in this thing. You can cut the film into a hundred pieces, run a laser through any one of them under the proper conditions, and reconstruct the original scene in its entirety. The whole vision is contained in every centimeter. In like manner, Greenleaf believed every individual could create the vision—and reality—of servant leadership in their "own little island, within whatever scope they have, whatever initiative is in their hands. And, they have to be realistic and survive—otherwise they can't serve—so they make some compromises. . . . Whoever you are, if you are leading something, try as much as you can to be a servant."[60]

When Bob worked with Paulist Press to collect his servant essays and other writings into a book, he wanted the title to be *The Servant as Leader*, the same as the lead essay, but the publisher vetoed him and called the book *Servant Leadership: A Journey Into the Nature of Legitimate Power and Greatness*. Bob thought the title *Servant Leadership* was a step backwards from *Servant As Leader*. "I had written *The Servant as Leader*," he told Ann McGee-Cooper, "because you have to come back to what an individual can do. Everybody works under some constraints, and what I'd rather see would be the expansion of the idea that leaders become as much servants as they can, under the realities they operate under, wherever they are and whatever the structure is."[61]

The title of *Servant Leadership* certainly did not hurt sales in the long run. After Paulist Press published it in 1977, the book had an almost unprecedented sales history. Most books enjoy their highest sales in the first several years after publication, but *Servant Leadership* increased in sales each year for more than two decades and never went out of print. Paulist Press published a twenty-fifth anniversary edition in 2002.

The book *Servant Leadership* reproduces Bob's first three essays in the servant series, profiles two servant-leaders, and contains sections on servant leadership applications in business, education, foundations, and churches. It ends with reflections on the servant responsibility in a bureaucratic society, America and world leadership, and Bob's reflection on Frost's poem *Directive*. The book is actually a collection of writing he had done over the previous twenty years, going back to his days of Jungian dream work. Even Bob's close friends had never seen all of these writings.

By the time *Servant Leadership* was released, Bob was in hot pursuit of publication of his next book. It had two working titles: *The Servant as a Person* and *Jefferson House*. Bob sent out the first draft for comments in 1975. By the time the Paulist Press Center published it in 1979, it was called *Teacher as Servant*.[62] It was a novel, the story of undergraduate students who responded to a notice on the campus bulletin board headlined, "DO YOU WANT TO BE A SERVANT?" Those who did respond, and were accepted, moved into Jefferson House, a dormitory housing an experimental community of students. Under the supervision of Housemaster Professor Billings (a volunteer who originated the idea of Jefferson House), students sought to discover the meaning of being servant-leaders in their personal and communal lives. It was a noncredit program but still demanding. Students engaged in study, discussion and reflection, joint activities, internships, and efforts to help make their school a better university.

Bob was excited about *Teacher as Servant*. It fused the idea of servant leadership with experiences like those he helped create for the Ohio Fellows program. It was an opportunity to say what he would do about the lack of programs to nurture leadership on college campuses—a situation that he had observed and criticized since his 1934 exchange of letters with Donald Cowling of Carleton College. Now, with this book, perhaps he could get through to faculty and students.

The ideas in the book were strong, but it was a commercial flop. Bob never seemed to understand why, but reviewers of his draft manuscript did. They were a typical collection of Bob's friends, including the Presidents of Grinnell and Asbury Colleges, foundation directors, teachers, an editor, an executive with the Koinonia Partners in Georgia, a medical doctor in Kansas, and a psychiatrist in Virginia who had recently been getting in touch with her aggression.

The psychiatrist, not surprisingly, criticized Jefferson House residents for not being aggressive enough. The medical doctor said servanthood was not a valid goal; the only worthy goal was commitment to Jesus Christ. Another person wondered how the Jefferson House experience could be turned into a transportable curriculum. The most prescient feedback came, however, from the respondents (almost half of them) who criticized the book as a novel. Bob loaded as much wisdom as possible onto his fictional characters, resulting in characters that were wooden and not believable. "I'm annoyed with the student protagonist because he's such a perfect chap!" said one reviewer. The editor nailed the essential problem:

"Since you are merely using your story to get certain points across, like B. F. Skinner in *Walden Two*, there is a tendency for the story to be dry, speechifying, and high falutin'. Robert Rimmer solves these problems by distracting his audience with sex. Since yours is not a book about sex you don't have this advantage."[63]

In 1987, with the support of AT&T, the Greenleaf Center republished *Teacher as Servant* in paperback, and it has recently been published again as part of the book *The Servant-Leader Within*. It remains an interesting read for its ideas. The book began to be rediscovered—or perhaps discovered for the first time—years after its publication. Twenty-five years after it first appeared, there were at least three incarnations of Jefferson House on campuses around the country, each with a customized version of Greenleaf's original vision.

Bob did not get rich from his publications. After March 1979, all royalties were assigned to the Center for Applied Studies. "I have a bias against the licensing of ideas," he wrote. "I would be happier if there were no copyright laws. In my own case, I would not have copyrighted my own writings if it had been possible to publish them without it."[64]

———

Just after the publication of *The Servant as Leader*, Greenleaf returned to India and was tempted by an offer from his good friend Douglas Ensminger, the on-site Ford Foundation consultant. Ensminger wanted to spend his last two years before retirement working on what he regarded as the country's most critical problem: family planning. "As matters stood there, in 1970," Greenleaf wrote, "nearly all efforts to raise the quality of life in India were being defeated by population gain. This was clearly their most urgent problem." [65] Ensminger knew the strengths of his man Greenleaf. He asked Bob to provide support with "conceptual work" while he served in an action role.

Before making his decision, Bob visited India's Minister of Family Planning, who was not encouraging. "The contraceptive that will work in India has not yet been invented," he stated flatly, but the difficulty of the task was not the reason Bob turned down the offer.[66] On reflection, he decided that Indians needed to work this out for themselves and that it would take a long time. The Minister agreed. Bob did not want to be an instrument of foreign grandiosity in a country he had grown to love. His intuition provided an even deeper reason. "My rational reasons were clear enough, but in my deep gut feeling, it was not work that I wanted to be involved in, important as it was."[67]

In hindsight, one is tempted to ask that fruitless question that historians caution against asking but delight in answering: "What if?" What if Bob Greenleaf had succumbed to this temptation to leave his servant writings just as they were being introduced to the world? After all, he and Douglas Ensminger were a powerful team, and they might have realized some success, gaining lasting fame in Indian history and helping millions of people. What if Bob had not followed his deepest intuition about his personal mission and destiny? No one knows the answer, of course, but we do know that much of what happened after the publication of *The Servant as Leader* would have been different.

———

For the Greenleaf family, the 1970s were years of movement—and moving. In 1969, they moved to Cambridge for a year. In 1970, they moved into a new home they built in Peterborough, New Hampshire. Bob stayed on the go with his consultancies, and when Esther was not traveling with him to India or Italy or some domestic location, she moved ahead with her artwork.

Bob's consultancies included foundations, hospital boards, churches, universities, and the Business Roundtable. He accepted only consultancies where he thought he could be of use, and that was a minority of those proposed to him. He conceded that consultants filled a necessary role by providing technical specialties that organizations could not afford to staff internally but, ironically, he was not convinced the great organizations needed them. "It has been my observation that institutions that I would rate as exceptional (well led) don't use consultants at all," he wrote to one correspondent in 1982.[68] Then again, Greenleaf's idea of a well led company would be one that made room for conceptualizers in their top echelons, people who would bring fresh ideas and function more like internal consultants. He still tried to work with large and small organizations, like Ohio University and TDIndustries, who were open to outside consultants as a way of improving their performance as servants, but he had deep feelings in general about consulting.

> I sense two limitations in all commercial (for money) consulting. (1) People who make a living out of consulting seem inevitably to do a bit of huckstering; *i.e.*, they seem to have to do their work in a way that brings in other work. . . (2) To make a living out of it, consultants don't have much time for either research or reflective thinking. They mostly carry ideas from here to there—but don't originate much.[69]

Greenleaf used his own consulting to not only teach but to learn. In fact, his *first* task was to learn—learn about the client and ask the kinds of questions that would cause them to learn about themselves.

Two interesting consultancies with foundations stand out. One was with the Richardson Foundation, the other with the Lilly Endowment.

From 1964 to 1968, Greenleaf consulted with the Smith Richardson Foundation in Greensboro, North Carolina. After making a fortune from *Vicks VapoRub*, H. Smith Richardson Sr. began to withdraw from daily responsibilities at the Vicks Chemical Company to consider how businesses could stay vital. He initiated organizational and management development programs that could have come right out of Bob's work at AT&T.[70] In 1935, he set up the Smith Richardson Foundation, partly to encourage leadership with a broader focus and longer view.

When Bob first visited the foundation, its programs focused on creativity. He did with them what he did with most clients. He listened carefully, sought to understand their history and vision, and then wrote a paper that started with a philosophical base congruent with the organization's history, moved things along with the suggestion of one or more possible directions for the future, and then gave broad details about how a new program could be implemented. It was one of those memos from Bob that led to the creation of the Center for Creative Leadership (CCL), one of the most respected research and training organizations in the world. CCL may have evolved into its present form without the influence of Robert Greenleaf, but there is no doubt that he was a bumblebee that fertilized its flowering in the conceptual stage.

Bob's long-term relationship with the Lilly Endowment in Indianapolis was one of his most interesting. In 1972, he got a call from his old friend Landrum Bolling, who was now the President of the Endowment. The organization had a problem: The Tax Reform Act of 1969 had mandated that foundations like Lilly Endowment give away at least five percent of its assets each year. The deadline for implementation was near, and the good folks in Indiana needed to decide, in a few months, how to give away millions of dollars to meet IRS requirements. Moreover, to handle the increased institutional demands created by this situation, the staff was growing exponentially, but without much of an organizational philosophy to guide it. (It grew from five to around seventy employees in two years.) Could Bob come and help them out?

The Lilly Endowment was a perfect match for Greenleaf, because the Lilly family's ethos of service and integrity guided the organization and its parent company. One story about "Mr. Eli," grandson of the Civil-War era founder of the pharmaceutical giant, makes the point: After he was elected to the vestry of Christ Church Cathedral, an Episcopal church on Monument Circle in the center of Indianapolis, he was found one day cleaning out a closet and tidying up. "What are you doing in there?" he was asked. "This is what I'm supposed to do," he replied.[71] Mr. Eli was a natural servant-leader, and foundation staff who knew both Mr. Lilly and Mr. Greenleaf saw similarities in these two quiet, unassuming Hoosiers.[72]

One would expect that a consultant who had been asked to help give away millions of dollars would show up with a shopping list of worthy projects. That was not Bob Greenleaf's style. One of the first things he did was talk with the growing staff about the corrosive effects *on the giver* of being in a position to influence charitable decisions. Bob well remembered his first experiences as a representative of the Ford Foundation. He got smarter overnight; people laughed at his jokes and listened intently to what he had to say. They wanted the foundation's money. "This incessant pressure from people who stand as supplicants has a corrupting influence on foundation personnel who are long exposed to it," he wrote, "and this risk presents the same obligation to trustees as would any occupational hazard in any kind of institution."[73]

Bob also believed that no one should work at giving away money for longer than ten years. After that, the grandiosity and temptations to power could become systemic. After reflecting on this advice, more than one top Lilly Endowment executive decided to leave the organization earlier than originally planned.

The Endowment's staff began to read and send out copies of Bob's numerous essays, including one about foundation work that impressed them mightily, *Prudence and Creativity*.[74] Bob wrote that it was not difficult for foundations to be prudent. The trick was to also be creative in order to bring into being "socially useful ideas and procedures that institutions more harried by market pressures are not likely to produce, or to produce as soon. Creativity involves risk, experiment, and perseverance in the face of failure, somewhat the opposite of prudence."[75] Foundation trustees, Greenleaf said, were responsible for seeing that their organizations walked this tightrope between caution and risk-taking. He joined the Lilly Endowment board for a strategic planning meeting—attended by Mr. Eli himself—and out of that and subsequent meetings, the Lilly Endowment overhauled its philosophy of charitable giving, and even revised its logo to reflect the changes.

Jim Morris, who joined the Endowment in 1973 and eventually ran the organization, remembered that "not everyone was comfortable with the guy at first," but Bob became a profound influence in his own life. "Very few of us had come from a conceptual or philosophical background. Bob gave us a conceptual framework for the values that undergirded our work. I used to read his stuff so often that I had it memorized. I had never thought about the word trustee and the role trustees play in holding an institution in trust for all of its constituencies."[76]

Jim Morris was another one of those behind-the-scenes servant-leaders. "I know it sounds corny," he said, "but all I ever wanted to do in my life was be useful." Morris was instrumental in a program of public-private partnerships that helped move Indianapolis from sleepy "Indiano-place" to a vibrant community with mission and thrust. It would take an investigative reporter to uncover his web of positive influences on the city and state, because Jim never wanted the credit, but he did appreciate validation from Bob Greenleaf. He became emotional when he showed a visitor one of Bob's 3x5 notecard messages blessing his community development efforts. Jim Morris eventually left the Endowment to run the Indianapolis Water Company and later became Executive Director of the United Nation's World Food Program.

In 1974, yet another impressive person came into Bob's life through the Lilly Endowment connection. Bob Lynn was a teacher, theologian, dean of a seminary, and on the board of another seminary. He started as a consultant with the Endowment and eventually became a corporate officer in 1976, sponsoring some of the most comprehensive research to date into American religion. By giving small grants for printing Bob's pamphlets and other projects, Lynn was instrumental in keeping Greenleaf's work in circulation—and keeping his Center alive—until The Greenleaf Center emerged as a self-sustaining force. His most important contribution, though, was his influence on Greenleaf's thinking about religious organizations and their potential for transforming society. It was a topic that would dominate Bob Greenleaf's last ten years, a period that was as creative and productive as any in his long life.

CHAPTER 19

Back to Spirit

*Work! Do something! Work to increase the number of religious
leaders who are capable of holding their own against the forces of
destruction, chaos, and indifference.*[1]

ROBERT K. GREENLEAF

In November 1972, during a visit to help out after the birth of Lisa's son
Giles, Esther confided to her daughter that she was not feeling well. She
was soon diagnosed with juvenile diabetes (type 1, insulin-dependent), a
highly unusual disease in an older person, and a shock to a woman who
had devoted so much attention to healing and natural foods. This development got the Greenleafs thinking about how they wanted to invest their
remaining life energies and ensure that they would be able to have
Esther's medical needs seen to. Besides, they were both nearing their sev-
enties, and the New Hampshire winters were not getting any warmer.
They thought about moving to California but decided on Crosslands, a
Quaker retirement center in Kennett Square, Pennsylvania, and moved
there in 1977. Bob once spoke with his friend Malcolm Warford about the
decision. "Bob figured out what the equation was between shoveling to
get through a New Hampshire winter and life expectancy," said Warford,

"and he chose life expectancy, even though he and Esther loved being there in Peterborough."[2]

Their cottage at Crosslands was pleasant and offered a lovely natural setting. Soon after moving in Bob decided to reduce his traveling. He would invite others to visit him, "if I think they are serious" he told one correspondent, but he was beginning to feel the weight of age. Many visitors to Crosslands experienced moments like those remembered by Susan Wisely of the Lilly Endowment.

> Esther would say, "Please sit down—would you like a glass of cold Catawba grape juice?" It was a very welcoming, gracious way of saying, "We know you've had a long plane ride and have been rushing from wherever to get here, and we appreciate it . . ."
>
> I remember just sitting on his porch in a rocking chair, the silences, the way he helped you think without telling you what to do. Even if you said, "I'm interested in how to encourage leadership among youth workers," he would ask questions like, "Who comes to mind as someone who does that well? Who are the heroes and heroines of that enterprise?" And he would give you materials, things that were out of print and he had to Xerox, like an article on the Danish Folk Schools.
>
> So my overall images are of him sitting there on his back porch with a few people, having a conversation punctuated by long silences. If you were uncomfortable with that you clearly weren't going to have a good day.
>
> I've had colleagues who have said they asked a question and expected a brilliant response, but that's not the way Bob worked. He never really did that.[3]

Because he believed in the transformative power of listening and reflection, Greenleaf's style was not much different when he presided over public workshops. A Catholic Sister told a friend that she heard Bob was giving a two-day workshop hundreds of miles from her home in Indiana. Eager to meet one of her heroes, she signed up, hopped into the car and drove to the site. "But I was disappointed," she said. "He sat there and hardly said anything, mostly just asked questions and listened." The friend responded, "So, I guess the workshop was a bust for you." Her eyes brightened and she replied, "Oh no! It changed my life! One of the best things I've ever done for myself."

During his final years at Crosslands, Bob increasingly concerned himself with more universal issues, especially spirituality. (Bob usually preferred the word *spirit* over spirituality, but he did write an essay in 1982 titled *Spirituality as Leadership*.) When *Teacher as Servant* was published in 1979, he still believed universities could be the major leavening force toward a more caring society. Within a few years he gave up that idea. "My efforts to get universities to work on leadership development with students, principally at Ohio University, failed," he wrote Bob Lynn. "As long as new money was pumped in there was a little stirring. But when the money stopped, the effort stopped. It did not take root as an effort the university would commit resources to."[4]

He looked elsewhere for a molding force for a more caring society and discovered seminaries. This idea was a shock to some of his oldest friends, especially seminary faculty and administrators who knew that their beloved institutions could be as hidebound as any on the planet. They wondered where the idea of seminaries came from.

As usual, it came from multiple sources. Through the years, Bob Lynn had spoken frequently with Greenleaf about theology and the structure of religious education. Greenleaf already knew a great deal about religious organizations, having consulted with dozens of church-related groups, from councils of bishops to parish study groups. Then too, he had known some prominent religious leaders and thinkers: Rabbi Abraham Joshua Heschel, theologians Joseph Fletcher and Gerald Heard, religious historian Rufus Jones, ministers Harry Emerson Fosdick and Norman Vincent Peale. In addition, Bob had taught a few sessions at Harvard Divinity School. Still, the evidence is that he had not thought deeply about the potential of seminaries as institutions until his prolonged contacts with Bob Lynn, beginning in 1974.

In March of 1979, Greenleaf was the lead presenter at a Washington, D. C. workshop on "The Bishop as Leader" attended by an equal number of Roman Catholic and Episcopal bishops. They were meeting to discuss ministry from a functional point of view, not from a theological or doctrinal perspective.[5] During one of the breaks in the meeting, Bob left the room to make a phone call. When he came back one of the bishops said, "We were just discussing whether you believed in original sin." Bob had decided not to get into any theological arguments with the group. He shot back, "I don't know whether I do or not. I don't know what it is." Another bishop quipped, "If you would join the church, you'd find out." Bob answered, "I don't want to know that bad."

The exchange made Bob think about how he could better communicate with the bishops in their own language. The next day he said to them, "I've listened to you fellows talk for two days. You've talked a lot about managing and administering, but I haven't heard anything about leading, and that's what you were convened to discuss." They were stunned and asked what he would have them do to lead. That was the question he had been waiting for. "Well, there are probably a lot of things, but one that comes to mind is that part of the problem of our society today is that the churches have not evolved an adequate theology of institutions." They spoke about what that could mean and Bob promised to write a paper on the idea when he got home and send to it them.[6]

It was typical of Greenleaf that a presentation was not ended simply because it was over. He saw each event as the beginning of ongoing dialogue with participants, a way to sharpen his own thinking and challenge theirs; so, he went home and wrote a paper called "Note on the Need for a Theology of Institutions" and sent it out to the good bishops.

The phrase "theology of institutions" is nearly as startling as "servant-leader" because it brings together two ideas that are not normally joined. Theology is "the study of religious faith, practice, and experience, especially the study of God and of God's relation to the world." It is a theory or system, like Thomism, or a "distinctive body of theological opinion." An institution is "a significant practice, relationship, or organization in a society or culture. . . an established organization or corporation."[7] In his paper, Greenleaf does not bother to give his own definition of theology but uses it as a word to point to the ultimate meaning of institutions to individuals and society. He had been doing that kind of theology all his life: prodding AT&T to consider how their actions and policies affected individuals and society, preaching to universities on their responsibility to nurture leaders, writing the line, "The work exists for the person as much as the person exists for the work."

As for the transcendent aspect of theology, that remained a private matter for Bob, not a question of belief in any specific doctrine. Revelation was ongoing, mediated through the quiet universe inside each person, and he remained ever content to stand in awe before the ultimate source of that revelation. In this sense, he was never a traditional theologian, nor did he claim to be. He always maintained that each person should be his or her own theologian.[8]

"Note on the Need for a Theology of Institutions" pulls together themes Bob had written about before, most of it embedded in his own "creed" that begins the paper.[9]

> I believe that caring for persons, the more able and the less able serving each other, is what makes a good society. Most caring was once person-to-person. Now much of it is mediated through institutions that are often impersonal, incompetent, even corrupt. If a better society is to be built, one more just and loving and providing opportunity for people to grow, then the most effective and economical way, while being supportive of the social order, is to raise the performance-as-servant of all institutions by voluntary and regenerative forces initiated within the institutions by committed individuals.[10]

Greenleaf goes on to write that biblical theology is a "theology of persons" and that even "corporations get their legal status from the willingness of the courts to construe them as persons. . . I do not believe that the urgently needed fundamental reconstruction of our vast and pervasive structure of institutions can take place, prudently and effectively, without a strong supporting influence from the churches. And I doubt that churches as they now stand, with only a theology of persons to guide them, can wield the needed influence."[11]

One bishop wrote Bob, "What does occur to me as being very much needed is some work not only on a 'new' theology of institutions but some delving into what the 'old' theology of institutions is or has been."[12] The bishop was onto something. Theology, at least in its traditional sense, must begin somewhere, with a tradition or at least a statement of belief that is useful. "I believe in God" is a beginning, and so is, "I don't believe in your God, but here is what I do believe." Those who have taken seriously Greenleaf's call for established theologians to develop a theology of institutions have found it necessary to work from some tradition.[13] While Greenleaf called for *a* theology of institutions, there will likely be many such theologies if the call is taken seriously, each from its own tradition. In the end, Greenleaf's concern was that places of worship take concrete steps to prepare followers for servant-based action in organizations.

Bob Lynn also put Greenleaf in touch with a universe of outstanding men and women who were doing ministry differently. Two of them were Hoosiers—Phil Amerson and Phil Tom—who related their faith traditions to grass-roots service in local institutions through direct action and trusteeship. Rev. Phil Amerson was a United Methodist minister in Evansville. He and his wife Elaine founded Patchwork Ministries, which asked participants to sign a covenant committing themselves to the support of ministries in the nearby inner city neighborhood. Decision-making was by consensus, and leadership was shared. Phil Tom was the pastor of Westminster Presbyterian, an inner city in Indianapolis. People who attended Westminster were expected to participate in community boards in order to make Indianapolis a more serving community. Along with their doctrinal ministries, both churches were, in effect, training trustees. For years Bob had known Gordon Cosby, founder of the Church of the Savior in Washington, D. C., and had stayed in touch with that remarkable serving institution since its founding. These real-life laboratories proved that it was possible for churches to perform a leavening function in their communities. Churches could train people in the arts of persuasion, *primus inter pares* and consensus decision-making, listening, and the other skills that are necessary to servants.

In 1982, Bob put all these influences together in an essay called *The Servant as Religious Leader*. In that work, he offered more careful definitions of religion and theology. Religion is "any influence or action that rebinds or recovers alienated persons as they build and maintain serving institutions, or that protects normal people from the hazards of alienation and gives purpose and meaning to their lives." Theology is "the rational inquiry into religious questions supported by critical reflection on communal concerns."[14] Few theologians would agree with these definitions, because they make no mention of God, or of the nature of the "purpose and meaning" toward which one strives. Greenleaf insisted that religious leaders should "*strengthen the hands of the strong* by helping them, while they are young, to acquire a vision of themselves as effective servants of society,"[15] and suggested that too many churches "have put too high a priority on preaching and too low a priority on being."[16] Churches and seminaries needed to be about the task of preparing people to lead, by persuasion and prophecy, through their churches and communities.

In the spring of 1982, Greenleaf sent *The Servant as Religious Leader* to a group of United Methodists for advance reading before he met with them about leadership in the church. The group included three bishops, three seminary presidents, assorted lay people, and church bureaucrats. They caucused on the essay before Bob met with them at a Ramada Inn near Crosslands. Bob wrote Jan Erteszek about what happened next.

> They were sorry they came because they were really teed off by what I had written. There were three laywomen in the group who tried to discuss the issues but they were cowed by the church bureaucracy. It was a cold meeting. Finally, near the end, I took on the seminary presidents with this statement: "Back in the Middle Ages there was a preoccupation among theologians about how many angels can dance on the head of a pin . . . My guess is that if our civilization survives for another three hundred years, historians of that period who examine the state of society in the late twentieth century, including what theologians were preoccupied with in our times, will conclude that these preoccupations are just as ridiculous, in view of the condition of society, as we judge those Middle Ages people to have been." The meeting ended on this note and I haven't heard from any of them since."[17]

Greenleaf continued trying to find language to make his point. In 1983, he published three essays, written over three years, under title of *Seminary as Servant*. In it, he completed the logic of his change model and the role of seminaries in it. Seminaries have the opportunity to provide strong leadership to churches, which provide it to individuals and operating institutions. And who controls seminaries? Trustees, of course.[18] Seminaries should be engaged to develop servants and the skills that support effective servanthood in society.

Not many—if any—agreed with Greenleaf about the potential role of seminaries. Bob Lynn, who had the advantage of being a historian, thought Greenleaf was ignoring history.

> I think he saw possibilities at the seminaries that were perhaps romantic and wishful. He thought they could be the carriers of the message of servant leadership, and its embodiment. He's quite correct that they *should be* the embodiment of servant leadership, but I was never able to concur that seminaries would see this as their single work. By tradition, seminaries have been institutions which

> were servants of the church in the sense of doing what churches
> wanted them to do. They couldn't pick and choose their work with
> the freedom that he wanted.[19]

"I thought the odds were totally against it," said Mac Warford.

> Bob was not naive about the ways in which most seminaries were set
> into the same kinds of establishment, conservative pressures as any
> other institution. But, after having gone through all of the other
> available institutions, I think his wisdom was in understanding that
> seminaries, with their marginality, don't even show up on the map of
> institutions in this society. If they could see that, then they had rela-
> tively free space in which to do something not constrained by what
> everybody else was doing. So, in a very realistic way, he thought the
> very fragility of these institutions might possibly be a source of their
> own renewal.[20]

Whatever his thoughts about the theology of institutions, or the philosophy of seminary mission, Greenleaf had one down-home rule for all
practicing ministers. "They should wait until they have something to say
and then ring the bell and tell everybody to come."[21]

Bob was always fascinated to hear stories of how people were imple-
menting his ideas. One day he got a call from a man named Bill Bottum in
Ann Arbor, Michigan who said he just had to meet with him. Bill had
been given some of Greenleaf's essays and, after reading *The Servant as
Leader,* told his secretary, "Find Greenleaf. So many of my other heroes
died before I could meet them."[22] Bill was CEO of Townsend & Bottum
(T&B), an international family of companies that specialized in constructing power generating plants. He was also a fellow *seeker* who, by the time
he called Bob, had spent thirty years reflecting on the Sermon on the
Mount and translating it into language that was accessible and useful for
corporations. Before flying out to Crosslands for a visit, Bill sent Greenleaf
some of his writings.

"I hadn't been there five minutes before Bob said, 'One thing I'd like
to tell you is that I disagree with you about Gandhi. I think he was coercive and we ought to convince people by persuasion.' Then he told me
about John Woolman. We trusted and understood each other. It was like

talking with an old high school classmate."[23] Bill became a missionary for Bob's work, passing out pamphlets to airline pilots, ministers, corporate moguls, and whomever he thought could benefit.

Bill was especially interested in *primus inter pares* as a governing model and asked Bob where he could go to see it in action. "In this country, I'm not sure," said Bob, "but there are several places in Europe." Bill launched into a series of experiments, ranging from eliminating executive parking spaces to establishing training on consensus decision-making through newly-formed councils. Every so often, Bob would call him up and ask, "How's it going? Is that council working out?" That was when Bill realized that not all of Bob's ideas were proven in the field, at least not in detail. Bill was helping to prove them, and they were not always successful!

In 1982, T&B was a juicy target for a hostile takeover, and Bill worried about the effect it could have on his employees. He spoke with Bob about it frequently, trying out creative ideas. Bill could only see one way to protect T&B: eliminate all common stock so there would be nothing for a raider to buy. Bottum transferred common stock to a "trusteed corporation" owned by the Townsend & Bottum Capital Fund, later the T&B Family of Companies. Mr. Bottum then had a company with no stock, no proprietor or partners, and a board of trustees that controlled the Capital Fund.[24] He did not do this to make money; he personally lost money on the deal. He did it to protect the business that nurtured its employees.

"We put the 'promotion of servant leadership' in as one of the bylaws for Townsend & Bottum Capital Fund," said Bill, "but later a bank's lawyers made us take it out, for fear we were going to commit ourselves to treating people humanely, I suppose. About that time I asked Bob if he thought we should have an age limit for trustees to serve on the board and he said, 'Yes, seventy-five.' It's interesting that he was older than seventy-five at that time, so he gave me an answer that would have disqualified his own participation. He saw that as part of the life he was finished living. There were things appropriate to each stage of life."[25]

Bill Bottum eventually served on the Greenleaf Center Board, where he met another one of Bob's memorable friends, Sister Joel Read, President of Alverno College, an all-women's school in Milwaukee. Bob once called Sister Joel "a true servant-leader, even though she is not seen by everybody as that. She did a remarkable job of building that remarkable institution."[26] For four years, from 1969 to 1972, Sister Joel and her colleagues engaged in intense discussion about how they could they assess and develop their young charges once they reached campus. Better assessment would lead to more effective education. They decided they wanted to evaluate "knowledge in action," which meant evaluating people in situations close to the reality in which the knowledge was to be used. Pencil-and-paper tests would not suffice for such an ambitious goal.

In their quest for useful evaluation methods, they discovered AT&T's assessment centers and were able to observe an assessment process. They realized that AT&T used assessments for *identification*; a person was either qualified or disqualified for hiring or promotion as a result of assessment. Alverno could not send unqualified prospects back to high school. What they needed was a *developmental* method of assessment, one that offered not only judgment but opportunities for growth. Along the way, one of the Alverno faculty members discovered Douglas Bray's book *Formative Years in Business* and saw that it was dedicated to Robert K. Greenleaf. When they discovered that this was the same Greenleaf whose essays they had been reading, they traveled to Peterborough and spent many hours in conversation with Bob.

Eventually, with the help of four to five hundred volunteers, Alverno did create a novel assessment method to support "knowledge in action," and many observers credit the school as a pioneer in assessment methods for higher education. "Oh, some would give us credit for that," said Sister Joel. "Others don't even know our name. It's not something you copyright."[27]

Alverno invited Bob to the campus several times. The last time was by video, when he delivered the commencement address to the class of 1984 titled, *Life's Choices and Markers*. In the preface to the printed version he wrote, "What I wanted to convey in twenty minutes . . . is that ideas nurture the human spirit that determines how one comes out of life, and that one chooses, among all the ideas one has access to, which will guide what one does with one's opportunities. And that that choice is crucial."[28]

Bennett J. Sims, Episcopal Bishop of Atlanta, was another person who profited from knowing Robert Greenleaf's writings and the man behind them. He had been a bishop for only two years when a friend from Harvard Divinity gave him Greenleaf's little essay *The Servant as Leader*. The timing was providential, because Dr. Sims was struggling with the deeper meanings of leadership. He got in touch with Bob, who "gave me the direction and the way to lead by inclusion rather than dominance."[29] His first impressions of Greenleaf were lasting ones.

> I'm always impressed with somebody of a luminous intellect. He also grabbed me spiritually, but more intellectually with his understanding of power. He was nobody's patsy, a wonderful kind of paradox; a kind of acerbic strength on the one hand and a gentle loving kindness on the other. I never saw him when he wasn't totally himself. Bob was always authentically Bob—no BS. That spoke to a lot of people; in fact, it challenged me with my BS. I tended to be a little more theatrical.[30]

Power was an ongoing concern with Bishop Sims. His own faith tradition gave him some power, but in the Episcopal Church in America, the bishop's power is circumscribed by many American-style checks and balances. Two-thirds of the signers of the Declaration of Independence and the United States Constitution were Anglican (Episcopalian), including James Madison, George Washington, and Patrick Henry. When the time came to draft the Protestant Episcopal Church's constitution in 1789, its framers were not about to give bishops more power than they gave the U.S. President. Bishop Sims was forced to operate by persuasion, and he saw servant leadership as a restatement of the earliest ethic of the church, one that had been distorted over two millennia.

> Jesus started a movement that was servant-based in Himself; then St. Paul, who did the first and earliest writing in the New Testament, turned it from a movement into an institution. Because it was institutionalized in an imperial context historically, the church became imperialistic, hierarchical, and understood servanthood in terms of dominance rather than participation. We are just moving beyond that; it's taken two thousand years.[31]

The Bishop's views are laid out in detail in his gracefully written book *Servanthood: Leadership for the Third Millennium*.[32] He wished to recover the original truth implicit in the life and ministry of Jesus, to rescue the servanthood of participation from the clutches of the imperialistic church. So he voluntarily gave up his power as a bishop, retired early, and started the

Institute for Servant Leadership in Hendersonville, North Carolina, where he holds classes and conferences.

Greenleaf thought the Institute was a noble idea but "would never fly." "Actually," said the Bishop, "he gave me a combination of encouragement and realism. Encouragement in the sense that he wanted me to do it, but he was realistic in predicting that it would have a very hard go. He had a very strong suspicion of the church as an institution."[33]

Bennett Sims once asked Bob the same question Bob Lynn asked him. "I wrote him and asked, 'How can you advocate servanthood without it having a deeply spiritual base?' He wrote back and said, 'You can't.' So he was very clear about the fact that there is no way to do this apart from a belief structure, that this is the way that God works."[34]

Until his death, Bob remained an interested bystander in the Institute for Servant Leadership. "I talked to him from time to time," recalled Bishop Sims. "He kept pressing me to develop a theology of institutions, and I told him I went way beyond that because I was working on the theology of the most basic institution—the universe. We joked about that. He said, 'That's too much. I'm talking about the practical stuff. You're going off on a tangent.' We had a very congenial relationship."[35]

The 1980s were years of *spirit writing* for Bob. He wrote dozens of papers and short notes on the responsibilities of religious organizations, theology, and the life of the spirit so essential to a servant-leader. He authored five essays on spirituality-related topics, hosted scores of friends at Crosslands, and wrote hundreds of letters in which he wrestled with the ways people of faith and their institutions could inspirit society. He did not show all of these writings to friends. When many of his later manuscripts on religious leadership were published in the book *Seeker and Servant* in 1996, even Bob Lynn was stunned at their quantity and range.

Bob and Esther certainly had had a lifetime of exposure to varieties of religious thought: the Methodism of Bob's childhood, attendance at Unitarian churches and the Ethical Culture Movement, many Sundays at Riverside Church in New York, membership in the Quakers, and exposure to the more cosmic systems of Aldous Huxley and Gerald Heard. Ed Ouelette, Bob's lifelong friend from Carleton, spoke frequently with Bob about the latest trends in theology, so he was not as uninformed as he would have had some believe. Bob and Esther had even looked into Buddhism.

Their son Newcomb, who became a practicing Buddhist, says, "I learned about Buddhism from my parents originally. They were very much into Allan Watts and D. T. Suzuki and others in the 1950s. At the time I thought it was sort of strange; nonetheless it was my first introduction to Buddhism."[36] After Newcomb became a serious student of Buddhism, Bob told Ed Ouelette that he wanted to know more about it. In the summer of 1977, while Newcomb was working as a teacher at the Naropa Institute in Boulder, Colorado, Bob and Esther—ever the learners and adventurers—signed up for the Naropa Summer Institute and had a grand old time. Newcomb went on to write about and conduct workshops on the connections between Buddhism and servant-leadership, of which there are many.

At Crosslands, Bob spent long periods alone in quiet meditation. He considered meditation his most important "work" in his later years. One wonders: During those periods, what did he see that was unseeable, unspeakable, and unwriteable? Did he ever have the privilege, while he was alive, of entering into that mystery, that awe about which he spoke and wrote so often?

20

Twilight

Teach us to order our days rightly,
That we may enter the gate of wisdom.

PSALMS 90: 12
New English Bible

The Crosslands Retirement Center is a lovely place for people of any age to spend time: one hundred eighty-eight acres with clustered cottages and two-story buildings built along a U-shaped ridge. It has all the amenities, including different levels of health care. The Quaker-related institution is as good as any retirement facility and better than many. It is, however, also an institution, and Robert Greenleaf, the life-long institution watcher, had his own judgments about how well this institution was functioning.

Greenleaf wrote an essay—published in *On Becoming a Servant Leader*—in which he outlined his thoughts on retirement communities in general and Crosslands in particular, even though his comments about Crosslands could probably apply to over ninety percent of all such elderly care institutions.

First, he thought segregated retirement communities were a bad idea and would be abandoned some day, and he had held that position before he and Esther moved to Crosslands. On the other hand, Crosslands provided health care when needed, and Esther had diabetes. He had no quarrel with the amenities. "All the services are good, and we feel well cared for. The spirit of the staff is excellent, and our community is financially sound to date and looks good for the future, in sharp contrast to some others that have gone bankrupt."[1] What was missing was more fundamental: a theology for a life-care community.

After eight years living at Crosslands, Greenleaf outlined some of the concrete issues that could frame such a venture.

- Administrators and staff should share in the life of the community but usually do not, even though they are caring and have a good spirit. Greenleaf admits that, "We [the residents] are old and crotchety and often critical . . . So with all of this, we seem much of the time to live in an uneasy truce with them."[2] His suggestion was to have an administrator who lived on site and participated more fully in community life.

- Stop delegating administrative authority to the residents' association. Doing so politicizes the community, and the power often is not well-used, violates the contract under which residents entered the institution, and foments distrust. An able administrator in his or her prime is a better choice to make decisions about resources than "foggy old residents."[3]

Bob and Esther made more than one protest when the residents' association (which was not truly empowered by residents, he claimed) asked for changes, and the administration went along because "that's what the residents wanted."

One day Bob vented his feelings about the human community in which he lived. "What we call community here is synthetic, contrived, far from the real thing. The challenge is to get as close to the real thing as possible, but there will always be a gap."[4] Then again, Bob and Esther were never ones to spend much time chatting about the weather, playing croquet, or using time unproductively. They were not there to *retire* from anything. It was simply the place they lived while they completed their life adventures together, so they were as unusual in this community as they were in any other.

As with other institutions, Greenleaf believed that many of the problems ultimately went back to trustees who, caring as they were, could be harried. "Concern for the quality of life in the community is not a big priority, he wrote. "I am not aware that the philosophy that underlies this operation has been fully articulated."[5]

Bob Lynn saw Bob's contradictions in his position on Crosslands, where he was not personally active in many events or activities of governance. "He was not as intent upon identifying himself on some past tradition as he was creating a place for himself and other seekers within this world. Consequently, he always was willing to be aloof from institutions. I think this was one of the huge ironies of Bob's life that he took institutions so seriously but was consistently removed from the life of any one institution to which he was committed and with which he had to live."[6]

In 1984, Bob suffered a stroke that signaled the beginning of a long period of declining health. Less than two weeks later, the Center for Applied Studies changed its name to The Robert K. Greenleaf Center. Greenleaf did not campaign for the name change but agreed to go along with whatever the Board decided. "He wasn't terribly excited about that," recalled Bob Lynn. "He was so modest and unassuming that he was reluctant to have it changed but it was the only truthful thing to do. There just wasn't any other reality to the Center by that time."[7]

With declining health, Bob became concerned about the future of the Center. In 1985, he laid it out for the Board. "My major concern for the Center is for its future. I may be hanging up my sword any day now, and I would like to feel the work I have done to encourage building greater integrity into our many institutions will be continued and enlarged in new directions."[8]

Ironically, his concern coincided with an uptick in demand for his essays. In 1986, his old company AT&T assigned two bright young people to the full-time duty of developing workshops and publications "as they related to the quality of work life." Fred Myers and Diane Bullard (now Diane Cory) knew that quality of work life was a hot issue of the day and used that umbrella to work in support of the Center. Fred, Diane, and John Braid—their superior at AT&T—arranged for essays to be printed and donated back to the Center and for videotaped interviews with Greenleaf to be recorded. They found office furniture and computer gear for the cause.[9]

Fred Myers became almost like a son to Bob. Fred teased him, engaged in deep discussions, kept him up-to-date on Board decisions, and saw to various needs. Diane Bullard had the privilege of joining Fred in extensive conversations with Bob. Diane remembered Esther as much as she did Bob.

> The link between Bob and Esther was very deep and very gentle and very tender. Whatever they had been through together, in their older age they were clearly reconciled and gentle. Esther had a bigger impact on him than anyone has a clue. [Bob's daughter] Madeline and Fred believed that Esther influenced his thought deeply, whether or not Bob was aware of it. In a way, she was a co-author of those essays. I would give her full credit for influencing and culling his thinking.[10]

Many who knew the Greenleafs would agree with Diane's estimate of Esther's influence. "Esther was a good listener," remembered James McSwiney years later. "She was good at sometimes telling Bob what he heard."[11]

In March 1988, the Center sponsored a symposium on servant leadership in Atlanta. Bob attended a session by speakerphone and took questions from the audience. The gathering brought together people who had known and worked with him in multiple settings, many of them meeting for the first time. One of the hidden agendas for the Board was to determine any possible future for The Greenleaf Center.[12] Response was positive enough that the Board was encouraged.

At the Atlanta Symposium word filtered through the room about "The Forbidden Video." Fred Myers had produced a modest twenty-minute videotape about the life and work of Robert Greenleaf to show at the Symposium. When Bob saw it, he threw a fit and forbade its showing. There was nothing wrong with it technically; it was beautifully done, but Bob said, "None of this is about Bob Greenleaf! It's about servant leadership." This, of course, made everyone in Atlanta more curious. Today, you can buy the tape from The Greenleaf Center in Indianapolis, along with several other videos of Bob talking about various topics. He was not comfortable on camera, and it showed. When Ann McGee-Cooper video-taped him, he warned her, "I think best when I have a pencil in my hand, so what comes out extemporaneously may not be what I would write down someday."[13]

Jim Tatum was installed as Board Chair after the Atlanta conference. Years before Jim, like Bill Bottum, wanted to meet this man whose works had affected him so powerfully. He called the Greenleaf household and said, "We've never met, but I just wanted to call and tell you how deeply I resonate with your writings." Bob responded, "Oh, gee whiz!"[14] The rela-tionship went from there, and Bob eventually hand-picked Jim to chair the Greenleaf Center Board. Several long-time Greenleaf associates called Jim "half John Wayne, half Mark Twain," but he was anything but a coun-try hick from the "Show Me State." An Army veteran who was wounded in Korea, Jim went home to his poor area of southwestern Missouri and started Crowder College. First, he had to lead an effort to persuade the Missouri legislature to pass enabling legislation that would allow junior colleges. Jim is a legend in the educational world, a great believer in the servant nature of junior colleges, a skilled practitioner of consensus and a student of organizations. He also understands the paradoxes of Robert Greenleaf.

> I didn't see him as Joan of Arc or a saint. I admired Bob very deeply, especially his ability to listen to you. . . . When Bob proposed me to chair the Board, I told him, "I don't think all members of the board want to buy into my leadership style." He said, "Well then, fire them. Fire them all!" Here's this nice, soft-spoken guy. [With the Center] he wanted something that was going to be lasting and more vibrant, and a vehicle by which the word could be spread. There was no question that was not getting done. He said, 'Well, here's a pretty tough guy. I believe he can do it.'" [15]

Jim Tatum and a new board did get it done, eventually moving the Center's operations to Indianapolis, and hiring Executive Director Larry Spears, who helped make the Greenleaf Center for Servant Leadership a worldwide force.

Beginning around 1985, at the urging of Bob Lynn, Greenleaf made numerous notes for an autobiography, but his energy—and health—ran out before he could pull it together and before Joseph Distefano, Bob's old friend and personal choice for a biographer, could complete the task. In his most complete introduction to a possible autobiography, Bob called the story of his life "The Autobiography of an Idea,"[16] although he told Joe DiStefano that all his ideas were autobiographical.[17] With a working title that focused on the idea of servant leadership rather than the person of Robert Greenleaf, he was betting that interest in his ideas would supercede curiousity about his life.

> The literal-minded might hold that only a person can write an auto-biography. Let us grant that; but what is a person? Who is the I that wields this pencil? Where does the idea leave off and the flesh and bones begin? I have called this book the autobiography of an idea because that is the way I think about it. But there is a further problem.
>
> If this were an autobiography in the usual sense of an account of happenings, there would be an identifiable bag of flesh and bones that did it. The reader is then entitled to ask, "If this is the autobiography of an idea, then what is the idea whose autobiography this is?"
>
> The idea is what the reader thinks it is at the end. If there were a didactically explainable idea in hand now, an expository essay would suffice. What is offered here is the unfolding of a search—not a search for an answer to something but the disposition to see life, not as a series of discrete events, but as an unending, evolving experience—going somewhere, but who knows where?
>
> Autobiographies are usually written because the author believes that the events of his or her life are worth recording. The story of events of my life would not warrant offering yet another book, but the experience of living this life has had an interesting culmination.[18]

Bob was consoled in his final years by visits from friends, although his energy level did not permit long visits. Teacher and author Parker Palmer was one Quaker friend who spent time with Bob. He got acquainted with Bob and Esther when he was dean at Pendle Hill, a Quaker school in Wallingford, Pennsylvania. Perhaps only fellow Quakers could appreciate the quality of Parker's monthly visits. Parker greeted Bob and sat, and they exchanged a few pleasantries. Then there were long silences. Every now and then one of them would speak. Maybe he would be answered, maybe not. After an hour or so Parker would get up and say,

"I certainly enjoyed this visit, Bob." Bob would respond, "So did I, Parker. Come back when you can." And then Parker would drive back to Pendle Hill.[19]

Esther's diabetes began affecting her sight and ability to get around. Finally, reluctantly, she moved into Crossland's nursing home facility in 1986. Soon thereafter, Bob moved into a smaller studio apartment that was closer to the nursing home. "One of the few times I saw him show pain was soon after Esther had moved into the nursing home facility," remembered Madeline. "He'd go over and pick her up every day and bring her back, and she slept there. It was the only time I ever saw him cry. It broke his heart to not be able to take care of her, but he couldn't pick her up anymore if she fell."[20]

Somehow, Bob managed to write his two last essays during this period, using a new computer word processor supplied by Fred Myers. *Old Age; The Ultimate Test of Spirit* (1987) was "an essay on preparation." He reveals that his most productive years were between the ages of sixty to seventy-five, all because of a long period of learning and preparation for those years.[21] "Spirit," he wrote, "can be said to be the driving force behind the motive to serve. And the ultimate test for spirit in one's old age is, I believe, can one look back at one's active life and achieve serenity from the knowledge that one has, according to one's lights, served? And can one regard one's present state, no matter how limited by age and health, as one of continuing to serve?"[22]

Bob's final essay was *My Life With Father* (1988). It is a profile of George Greenleaf, a statement of gratitude to the man who first exemplified servanthood for his unusual son.

By 1988, complications from diabetes had blinded and crippled Esther and were affecting her memory—but not her will. Esther, "the stable one," refused to eat. She was determined to die on her own terms. Then Bob had a major stroke that left him unable to speak, and Esther decided that Bob still needed her. Maybe she could not get around or see, but she could certainly speak. So, she came back to life as Bob's mouthpiece. Within nine months, Bob had recovered enough speech that he could manage without her and she let go again. During this time, she was incontinent, and Bob cleaned her.

They had talked about the idea of ending their own lives when they were no longer worth living. One day Bob asked Esther, "Do you want us to just both go out now, together?" And she said, "Oh, not now Bobby. I can still paint in my mind." She was blind but was *painting in her head* in the mornings. With that consolation she was fine, but not for long.[23]

Finally, with full consciousness, she again refused to eat in February of 1989. Madeline saw her mother four or five days before the end, when she was still alert. She sat with Esther and held her hand. A woman came in with food and said, "Open your mouth," and then popped in a spoonful of mush. One mouthful was all Esther would take, and she refused to swallow that. The woman offered another spoonful. Esther frowned and clenched her teeth. The woman said, "Apparently, we aren't hungry," and Esther replied, "Apparently we're not." Those were the last words Madeline heard from her mother.

Newcomb stayed with her the last three days of her life. Knowing her wishes, he refused to allow an IV or any other life-sustaining measures. Esther was said to be in a coma, but every time they tried to feed her, she clenched her teeth again. She would not even take water. Her almost superhuman willpower lasted to the end, which came on February 22, 1989. *The New York Times* carried her obituary the next day.[24]

Bob, of course, was devastated. Without Esther, he had no soulmate to simply sit with him every day, no one to call him Bobby, no buffer against the forced congeniality of the residents of Crosslands. All his life he had sought his time alone, but preferred to spend it alone *with Esther*. He was miserable at Crosslands by himself, and the children discussed having him move in with them, but then he had another serious stroke and could not walk, so he stayed put.

This stroke, and subsequent ones, signaled the end, and everyone knew it. Newcomb visited Bob when he could. In August, 1990 Madeline traveled to the Persian Gulf with her husband Greg Jaynes, who was covering the buildup of the Gulf War for *Life* magazine. She returned about a week before Bob died and spoke to him on the phone. He could not talk back, but he listened.

Lisa visited her father every Tuesday for months. She got up at 4:00 a.m., left her young children, and spent five hours (each way) on the train to sit with him for three hours. She remembers it as a profoundly healing time.

> At the end, because of Bob's strokes, his ego was shaved away bit by
> bit. It was really quite excruciating. As he lost the ability to express
> himself, he lost all his shell, and inside was the most tender, delicate
> being. You would say something and he would respond with,
> "OOH!" and tears would spring out of his eyes. I thought, "This is
> who my daddy was all the time! This delicate flower of a person who
> had to protect himself. And, those distances, those brooding airs, that
> arrogance and cocksure facade he sometimes put on, the excessive
> dignity he wore—it all left.

Lisa sat with Bob. She held his hand, cleaned his feet, and massaged his head. When it was time to go, she walked out the door, looked back at her father through the window and blew a kiss. He always smiled and blew a kiss back to her.[25]

Bob died at 2:00 p.m. on Saturday, September 29, 1990. All the major obituaries were accurate, but none, of course, could capture his essence. *The Philadelphia Inquirer* said he was "a management consultant who preached that the human spirit is more important than the bottom line." *The New York Times* said, "Mr. Greenleaf wrote extensively on the topic of servant-leadership, a theme that deals with the reality of power in everyday life—its legitimacy, the ethical restraints upon it, and the beneficial results that can be attained through the appropriate use of power." Bob Lynn told the *Terre Haute Tribune Star*, "He was a rare person in his generation, or in any generation, and Terre Haute should be proud of him."[26]

On the following Tuesday, Jan Arnett, an administrator in Student Affairs at Indiana State University in Terre Haute, had a sudden urge to attend Robert Greenleaf's memorial service. She had read his work but never met him. "I simply knew I had to be there," she said. "I didn't know why."[27] She drove to Callahan's Funeral Home at 25th and Wabash, just a few miles from where Bob was born, and slipped into the room for the 10:00 a.m. service. Not many people were there, and those who were had come from some distance. In the Quaker tradition, those present were invited to say a few words if the spirit moved. Alan Rankin, the former President of ISU, who had been introduced to Bob by Jim Morris of the Lilly Endowment, made a few brief, gracious, heartfelt remarks, and others stood and said their remembrances. It was a simple, dignified ceremony, just right for the man.

Before the service, the three children decided to place the urn with Esther's ashes in the coffin with her Bobby. It remains there today, close to his heart.

Then, on that chilly, raspy, rainy day, the small group of family and friends traveled to the Highland Lawn Cemetery and sloshed through the wet ground, their black umbrellas adding color to the landscape. They gathered around the gravesite—Ed Ouelette, who was in the Carleton classroom with Bob when Professor Helming made his famous remark; Bob Lynn, who challenged Bob's thinking about religion; Sister Joel Read; Mac Warford; Jim Tatum; Larry Spears; Susan Wisely and others from the Lilly Endowment—they all had their stories of time with Bob. "It felt right, peaceful," said Jan Arnett. "It was where we were all supposed to be." A granddaughter sang an alleluia by Mozart, the coffin was lowered, and then there was a moment of awkwardness. Newcomb, in a spontaneous gesture, suggested they all bow as a way of saying goodbye. Every person in the tent put his or her hands together and made a deep Buddhist bow toward the open grave. Thus ended the service, but not Robert K. Greenleaf's influence.[28] That would continue.

EPILOGUE

Exactly ninety-eight summers after Robert Greenleaf first saw light, I drove to Terre Haute on another cloudy, humid July day to see what remained of his time there. His birth house at the corner of 11th Street and Lafayette was gone. The home at 1021 South 21st, where Bob watched Halley's comet, was replaced years ago by a sturdier structure, one with electric lights and indoor plumbing. I never found the three adjacent houses where George, Burchie, and June lived their final days, forever together, forever separated. The wonderful people at the Vigo County Historical Society, fellow travelers on the high roads of history's adventures, had never heard of Robert K. Greenleaf.

I knew one place where I could find evidence—Highland Lawn Cemetery, east on the Old National Road. Entering the gothic gate, I drove to Section 15, walked through fragrant new-mown grass to Lot 223, and found Burchie, George, and June, lying in that order. June was still diminished, her headstone half the size of her parents'. Not more than 100 yards south, in Section 17, Lot 588, Grave 3, I stumbled upon Robert Kiefner Greenleaf's marker. It was half-covered with grass clippings, barely raised above the ground. I had walked by it four times before noticing it. I knelt to read the inscription:

Robert Kiefner Greenleaf

1904–1990

Teacher, Philosopher

Servant-Leader

"Potentially a good plumber; ruined by a
sophisticated education."

RKG

I straightened up and looked around to get my bearings. Bob's final resting place was lovely, peaceful, but also within sight and sound of Route 40, a road historically important to America's doers and seekers, connecting far Eastern and Western horizons. A fitting backdrop for this life.

A hill occupies the center of Robert Greenleaf's section in the restful 1884 cemetery, but Bob's gravesite is not on the summit. He reposes in a spot down-slope, where he can be present but not draw attention to himself.

He always wanted it that way.

Afterword: The Living Legacy of Robert K. Greenleaf

Larry C. Spears
President & CEO
The Robert K. Greenleaf Center for Servant Leadership

I. A PERSONAL REMEMBRANCE OF ROBERT K. GREENLEAF

"Robert Greenleaf takes us beyond cynicism and cheap tricks and simplified techniques into the heart of the matter, into the spiritual lives of those who lead."

PARKER PALMER,
AUTHOR OF *The Courage to Teach* AND OTHER BOOKS

On September 20th, 1990 I had my one-and-only encounter with Bob Greenleaf, which occurred just nine days before his death. I had been appointed as the new director of The Greenleaf Center in February of 1990. Several planned trips were scheduled and postponed throughout the spring and summer, due to Bob's strokes and related health matters.

At that time, the future of servant leadership, and of The Greenleaf Center, seemed not nearly as strong as it is today. Awareness of Greenleaf's writings was still mostly word-of-mouth, and there were a few people who had voiced doubts to me as to the likelihood of The Greenleaf Center continuing after his passing. I was also aware of Bob Greenleaf's own concerns as to his legacy, and so as I planned for what turned out to be our one-and-only morning together, I sought to share with him my vision and insights into what I believed was a brighter future still to come for the organization that carried his name. I felt in my bones that servant leadership was about to blossom all over the world as a result of the many seeds that he and others had sown in the preceding 20 years, and I shared my ideas with him as to how I thought The Greenleaf Center could be of greater help in nurturing those seeds and many more in the future.

In addition to trying to reassure him about the future legacy of his work and his writings, I had also brought dozens of letters that I had received from people who had shared with me just how great an influence servant leadership and Bob's writings had been to them. With those twin hopes in mind to reassure Bob as to his future legacy and to remind him of the positive difference that he had already had in the world, I drove out from Indianapolis to Kennett Square, Pennsylvania and to the Crosslands Retirement Center.

Immediately prior to visiting with Bob, I spent a half hour talking with Lisa Sweeney, the social worker who frequently read to him. She told me a bit about his recent life there; how his weakening physical condition and multiple strokes had caused him great frustration and had seriously limited his ability to speak; how he loved listening to classical music; and a bit about his personality traits. Ms. Sweeney mentioned that he was one of the most unassuming people she had ever met, and she recounted a story that seemed illustrative of his extremely modest nature: Bob Greenleaf had supposedly once been asked by a new resident at Crosslands what kind of work he had done in the past. Greenleaf, a man of remarkable accomplishments and an active professional life that lasted sixty years, had simply responded by saying, "I worked in an office."

Walking into Bob's room, I found him sitting in his wheelchair and facing the window. He turned his head and smiled, and said "hello." I sat down in a nearby chair and introduced myself. As I did, I noticed on his sunny windowsill several pictures, including a picture of my two sons, James and Matthew, which I had sent to him along with a birth announcement about Matthew's arrival into the world two months earlier. Matthew Spears had been born on the same date as Bob's own birthday—July 14th (Bastille Day!). I picked up the picture and turned it toward him. He smiled at me and slowly said, "nice children."

Robert Greenleaf had been concerned in past years about the continuation of both the servant-leader concept and the Greenleaf Center. In a letter from the mid-1980s he wrote, "My major concern for the

Greenleaf Center is for its future. I may be hanging up my sword any day now, and I would like to feel the work I have done to encourage building greater integrity into our many institutions will be continued and enlarged in new directions." It was important for me to share some of the positive things that had occurred at the Greenleaf Center since arriving a few months earlier—and to convey my own sense of the on-going revitalization of the Robert K. Greenleaf Center.

Bob had not seen the Center's new office in Indianapolis; however, we visually walked around it through a series of black-and-white photographs that I had taken for this purpose. I described the area and building where we were located at that time, and I showed him the half-dozen literature cabinets filled with hundreds of copies of his books, essays, and videotapes. Bob was clearly moved by this visualization of our office, and he stared for a long time at a photo of a lithograph ("Terms of Light") created by his wife, Esther, which still hangs on a wall in my office.

Greenleaf tenderly examined photocopies of a series of ten display advertisements that I had recently put together, and which had been placed in various magazines. As Bob heard about the significance of this project—and particularly when he was told that his ideas and writings would be reaching a new audience of over a half-million readers through the advertisements in these publications—he chuckled and said, "good work." I then read to Bob some heartfelt and laudatory letters and messages that I had received from a dozen different people, including: Jude Dougherty, Dean of The Catholic University in America, Washington, D.C.; Tom Kessinger, President of Haverford College, Haverford, Pennsylvania.; Ed Ouellette, Bob's life-long friend from Evansville, Indiana, who had named his son Robert Greenleaf Ouellette; Ladislas Rice, a British businessman in London, England; Harold Miller, management consultant and another longtime friend of Bob from Winnetka, Illinois; Richard Hunt, Harvard University, Cambridge, Massachusetts, and others. As I finished reading these letters and good wishes, a look of amazement swept across his face. Bob seemed profoundly touched by hearing these expressions of appreciation from others who had, in turn, been touched by him and his writings. As Quakers, both Bob and I found great meaning in silence together, and so we sat quietly together for some time before he whispered, "I don't know what to say."

There was, of course, nothing that he needed to say. It was I who had come to do the saying on behalf of many of us—to remind him of the rich legacy that he has left each of us—and to simply thank him for his life's work. I told him of my own appreciation of the opportunity to serve as the Greenleaf Center's own servant-leader. Bob listened as I also told him of the hundreds of people whom I had already met by that time who had been profoundly influenced by his writings on the servant-leader concept. I said to him that I believed that his ideas were likely to become increasingly influential in the coming years. He stared intently for a few moments, and then gave a relaxing sigh.

Our single meeting on that sunny Thursday morning in September was of great importance to me, personally. Bob's son, Newcomb, has suggested that it may also have been of considerable importance to Bob as well, providing him with a reminder of his positive legacy to the world, and of the many lives that he touched for the better during his 86 years— as well as communicating the increasing vibrancy of the organization which bears his name, and which he had founded twenty-six years earlier as the Center for Applied Ethics. Newcomb Greenleaf has said that he believes that following that meeting his father was at last able to let go of any remaining concerns that he may have had, and assume a greater sense of peacefulness. I like to think that was the case, and I know that for me, our single encounter just days before his death provided me with a palpable sense of inspiration and purpose that has guided my own work ever since.

I stood up and took Bob's hand in mine, and thanked him for our time together. He smiled and said, "Thank you, Larry." As I walked out of his room in Crossland's Firbank East Wing I turned around for one final look. Bob had picked up the Greenleaf Center's latest newsletter and was slowly turning the page.

II. WHY SERVANT LEADERSHIP MATTERS

"I have found Robert Greenleaf's writings to be
among the most original, useful, accessible
and moral on the topic of leadership."

WARREN BENNIS
Author of *On Becoming a Leader* and Other Books

Since Bob Greenleaf's death, we have witnessed an unparalleled explosion of interest and practice of servant leadership. In many ways it can be said that the times are only now beginning to catch up with Robert Green-leaf's visionary call to servant leadership. Greenleaf's thinking tran-scended the old arena of leadership techniques and helped to move our thinking toward the deepening wisdom of servant-based leadership. This emerging model is based on trust, teamwork and community; it seeks to involve others in decision making; it is strongly based in ethical and car-ing behavior, and attempts to enhance the personal growth of workers while improving the caring and quality of our many institutions.

It is important to stress that servant leadership is *not* a "quick-fix" ap-proach. Nor is it something that can be quickly instilled within an institution. At its core, servant leadership is a long-term, transformational approach to life and work—in essence, a way of being—that has the potential for creating positive change throughout our society.

CONTEMPORARY APPLICATIONS
OF SERVANT LEADERSHIP

1. SERVANT LEADERSHIP AND ORGANIZATIONS

Servant leadership crosses all boundaries. Today it is being applied by peo-ple working within a wide variety of organizations: for-profit businesses, not-for-profit corporations, churches, universities, health care organiza-tions, and foundations. Each institution adapts Greenleaf's ideas to not only fit their own culture but help transform it. Nothing could have made Robert Greenleaf happier than to see the ongoing evolution of his ideas since 1990.

- An increasing number of for-profit companies have adopted servant leader-ship as part of their corporate philosophy or as a foundation for their mis-sion statement. Among these are The Toro Company (Minneapolis, Minnesota), Synovus Financial Corporation (Columbus, Georgia), Service-Master Company (Downers Grove, Illinois), The Men's Wearhouse (Fre-mont, California), Southwest Airlines (Dallas, Texas), and TDIndustries (Dallas, Texas), to name but a few. These and other institutions are also busy developing the skills and capacities in their employees which Greenleaf advocated: listening, consensus decision making, persuasion, lifelong learn-ing, participatory research, exposure to ideas from the humanities, shared power, and full accountability. It turns out these are some of the same capaci-ties required for related management and leadership approaches such as continuous quality improvement and systems thinking. In an age marked by conspicuous corporate scandals, servant leadership offers the refreshing notion that profit, important as it may be, is not the only purpose of a business; it also exists to create a positive impact on its employees and community.

■ Religious leaders from the full spectrum of traditions have recognized that the ideas of servant leadership resonate with the history and mission of their faith. Christian churches are using servant leadership as a way to give fresh meaning to parish and congregational missions, to engage in church renewal, and to develop members as servants in the wider community. Several independent organizations rooted in Christian values are applying servant leadership to the journey of faith. Chief among these are: The Servant Leadership School (Washington, D.C.), The Institute for Servant Leadership (Asheville, North Carolina), and The Center for Faithwalk Leadership (Augusta, Georgia). None of this is surprising. Catholic sisters were the first to respond to Greenleaf's essay *The Servant as Leader* when it was published in 1970. But servant leadership also applies to other faith traditions. Newcomb Greenleaf, for example, teaches workshops on the connections between servant leadership and Buddhist thought. And both Jewish and Islamic practitioners of servant leadership have commented to me over the years that they have found Greenleaf's writings and their own faith literature to be mutually reinforcing.

■ Servant leadership has influenced many noted writers, thinkers, and leaders. Max DePree, former chairman of the Herman Miller Company and author of *Leadership Is an Art* and *Leadership Jazz* has said, "The servanthood of leadership needs to be felt, understood, believed, and practiced." And Peter Senge, author of *The Fifth Discipline,* has said that he tells people "not to bother reading any other book about leadership until you first read Robert Greenleaf's book, *Servant Leadership.* I believe it is the most singular and useful statement on leadership I've come across." In recent years, a growing number of leaders and readers have "rediscovered" Robert Greenleaf's writings through books by DePree, Senge, Covey, Wheatley, Autry, and many other popular writers.

2. SERVANT LEADERSHIP AND BOARD GOVERNANCE

A second major application of servant leadership is its pivotal role as the theoretical and ethical basis for "trustee education." Greenleaf wrote extensively on servant leadership as it applies to the roles of boards of directors and trustees within institutions. His essays on these applications are widely distributed among directors of for-profit and nonprofit organizations. In his essay *Trustees as Servants* Greenleaf urged trustees to ask themselves two central questions: "Whom do you serve?" and "For what purpose?"

Servant leadership suggests that boards of trustees need to undergo a radical shift in how they approach their roles. Trustees who seek to act as servant-leaders can help to create institutions of great depth and quality. Over the past decade, one of America's largest grant-making foundations (Lilly Endowment Inc.) has sought to encourage the development of programs designed to educate and train not-for-profit boards of trustees to function as servant-leaders. The noted board governance author/consultant/theorist John Carver includes servant leadership as the foundation for his Policy Governance Model.

3. SERVANT LEADERSHIP AND LOCAL COMMUNITIES

The third application of servant leadership concerns its deepening role in community leadership organizations across the country. A growing number of community leadership groups are using Greenleaf Center resources as part of their own education and training efforts. Some have been doing so for more than twenty years.

M. Scott Peck, who has written about the importance of building true community, says the following in *A World Waiting to Be Born:* "In his work on servant-leadership, Greenleaf posited that the world will be saved if it can develop just three truly well-managed, large institutions— one in the private sector, one in the public sector, and one in the nonprofit sector. He believed—and I know—that such excellence in management will be achieved through an organizational culture of civility routinely utilizing the mode of community."

4. SERVANT LEADERSHIP AND EDUCATION

The fourth application involves servant leadership in experiential education and academic programs.

- During the past thirty years experiential education programs of all sorts have sprung up in colleges and universities—and, increasingly, in secondary schools, too. Experiential education, or "learning by doing," is now a part of most students' educational experience. Around 1980, a number of educators began to write about the linkage between the servant-leader concept and experiential learning under a new term called "service-learning." Among other educational institutions, the National Society for Experiential Education (NSEE) emphasizes service-learning as one of its major program areas. In 1990 NSEE published a massive three-volume work called *Combining Service and Learning: A Resource Book for Community and Public Service (Jane C. Kendall and Associates, Editors)*, which brought together numerous articles and papers about service-learning—several dozen of which discuss servant leadership as the philosophical basis for experiential learning programs.

■ A second educational application of servant leadership concerns its use in both formal and informal education and training programs. This is taking place through leadership and management courses in colleges and universities, as well as through corporate training and development programs. A number of undergraduate and graduate courses on management and leadership incorporate servant leadership within their course curricula, and some colleges and universities now offer specific courses on servant leadership. In the area of corporate education, many management and leadership consultants now utilize servant leadership materials as part of their ongoing work with corporate development programs, including U.S.Cellular, TDIndustries, and the Singapore Police Department. Through internal training and education, institutions are discovering that servant leadership can truly improve how business is developed and conducted, while still successfully turning a profit.

5. SERVANT LEADERSHIP AND THE GROWTH OF INDIVIDUALS

A fifth application of servant leadership involves its use in programs relating to personal growth and transformation. Servant leadership operates at both the institutional and personal levels. For individuals it offers a means to personal growth—spiritually, professionally, emotionally, and intellectually. It has ties to the ideas of M. Scott Peck *(A World Waiting To Be Born)*, Parker Palmer *(The Active Life)*, Ann McGee-Cooper *(You Don't Have to Go Home from Work Exhausted!)*, and others who have written on expanding human potential. A particular strength of servant leadership is that it encourages everyone to actively seek opportunities to both serve and lead others, thereby setting up the potential for raising the quality of life throughout society.

6. SERVANT LEADERSHIP AND MULTICULTURALISM

For some people, the word *servant* prompts an immediate negative connotation, due to the oppression that many people—particularly women and people of color—have historically endured. For some, it may take a while to accept the positive usage of this word *servant*. Those who are willing to dig deeper understand the inherent spiritual nature of what is intended by the pairing of *servant* and *leader*. The startling paradox of the term *servant leadership* often serves to prompt new insights.

In an article titled, "Pluralistic Reflections on Servant-Leadership," noted Latina leadership consultant Juana Bordas has written: "Many women, minorities and people of color have long traditions of servant leadership in their cultures. Servant leadership has very old roots in many of the indigenous cultures. Cultures that were holistic, cooperative, communal, intuitive and spiritual. These cultures centered on being guardians of the future and respecting the ancestors who walked before." There is a growing body of literature on servant leadership by people of color, and internationally by many non-Western writers and teachers.

Women leaders and authors are writing and speaking about servant leadership as a twenty-first century leadership philosophy that is most appropriate for both women and men to embrace. Patsy Sampson, former president of Stephens College in Columbia, Missouri, is one such person. In an essay on women and servant leadership she writes: "So-called (service-oriented) feminine characteristics are exactly those which are consonant with the very best qualities of servant-leadership."

III. GREENLEAF'S GREATEST LEGACY: THE GREENLEAF CENTER FOR SERVANT LEADERSHIP

"I congratulate the Greenleaf Center for its invaluable service to society, and for carrying the torch of servant-leadership over the years."

STEPHEN R. COVEY, AUTHOR, THE 7 HABITS OF HIGHLY EFFECTIVE PEOPLE

Robert Greenleaf's greatest institutional legacy is undoubtedly his establishment in 1964 of The Center for Applied Ethics, renamed the Robert K. Greenleaf Center in 1985. Over a twenty-five year period from 1964 to

1989, Bob Greenleaf made his greatest and most lasting contributions to the world through the not-for-profit organization which he founded. Throughout this most important quarter of a century of Bob Greenleaf's life, The Greenleaf Center provided him with the organizational structure from which he wrote and published, pursued a series of grant-funded research-and-writing projects: and, through which he further shared his wisdom as a lecturer, consultant, and facilitator with numerous institutions.

Bob Greenleaf was a paradoxical man, and it should come as no surprise that this element of paradox would find expression within both his attitude and approach to even this very organization which he founded. Throughout the first twenty-five years of The Greenleaf Center's existence, Bob Greenleaf, the self-proclaimed student of how things get done in organizations, consciously chose to maintain the Center as a hip-pocket organization to support his own work. In the early years he was the sole staff person for the Center. Eventually he did hire a part-time assistant to help in responding to orders for his essays. And in the 1980s, as his declining health began to overtake him, the Center had two part-time directors, Dick Broholm (1984–88) and Kate Crane (1988–1990). However, I believe that Bob Greenleaf knew all too well the challenges that come with growing-and-sustaining even small organizations (fundraising, personnel issues, fiscal management, board relations, public relations, programs, etc.), as well as his own limitations-and-strengths, and that Bob very deliberately chose to keep the organization intentionally small and in service to those things which he felt he could do best.

While this clearly worked quite well for Bob Greenleaf during the first twenty-five years of The Greenleaf Center's existence, it also meant that by 1989 when Bob could no longer continue to work, The Greenleaf Center found itself in the unenviable position of having no existing programs or services (other than the sale of Bob's own essays and books), no real savings to fall back upon, limited staff leadership, and no significant sources of revenue capable of sustaining even the very small organization that it was at the time. The Center's financial support that year came almost entirely in the form of a $70,000 operational grant which had been given to it by Lilly Endowment. In 1989, Lilly Endowment had given the Greenleaf Center a three-year operational support grant which came with the message that this would be the last grant of its kind to the Center. This grant was made with the clear understanding that The

Greenleaf Center would have to find a way to make it on its own in the future, if that was even possible.

The combination of Bob's "second" retirement from The Greenleaf Center in 1989 (his "first" retirement had come when he left AT&T after thirty-eight years to establish The Center in 1964) and the final "operational" grant from Lilly Endowment prompted the Center's board to make a series of decisions. Two of the board's major decisions were moving The Greenleaf Center from the Andover Newton Theological School in Newton, Massachusetts to Indianapolis, Indiana, and hiring its first full-time director. The choice of Indianapolis as a new base for The Greenleaf Center occurred for two reasons:

First, because of Bob Greenleaf's long affiliation with Lilly Endowment, and the Endowment's many grants to Indiana organizations encouraging trustee education, Bob's writings on servant leadership, and especially his essay, "Trustees as Servants," came to be known as an important source of wisdom literature in Indiana. There was a built-in audience for his writings.

Second, when Bob was told that it might be in the Center's best interests to relocate, he replied that all things being equal he would like to see the Greenleaf Center move to his home state of Indiana. And so, in November of 1989 the Greenleaf Center's board began to advertise in several publications for a director.

I came to the Center through what I believe was an incredible example of synchronicity-in-action. In the Fall of 1989 my wife, Beth, learned that we were expecting a second child. We had been happily living-and-working in Philadelphia for a dozen years, but this news caused us to begin thinking about moving back to our home state where our children could be closer to their grandparents and other relatives. I called the circulation office of *The Indianapolis Star*, and arranged to begin receiving the Sunday edition of the paper by mail as a source of job notices. As luck would have it, the first Sunday paper I received contained what turned out to be the last of three postings advertising The Greenleaf Center's search for a new director.

As I read the description, I couldn't believe how close a match the position description was with my own skills and interests. We were also both Quakers, and I had first encountered Bob Greenleaf's writings on servant leadership in 1982 while working at *Friends Journal*, a magazine of The Religious Society of Friends. Throughout the 1970s and 80s Bob had published a half-dozen articles in *Friends Journal*, and I had been taken by his persuasive ideas on servant leadership. Between the position description, my prior awareness of Bob Greenleaf and servant leadership, and certain similarities in our backgrounds (both of us having grown up in Indiana; both of us having moved to large Eastern cities after college—Bob to New York City, myself to Philadelphia; both of us having spent a good deal of our professional and personal time in various kinds of writing; and both of us being somewhat strong-willed introverts who preferred to work "behind-the-scene" whenever possible), the confluence of The Greenleaf Center's relocation and need for a director, coupled with my own personal desires and interests, immediately seemed like a perfect match.

Eventually I was offered, and accepted, the role of executive director for The Greenleaf Center. One month later we moved from Philadelphia back to Indiana, and I shepherded the relocation of the Greenleaf Center's office from Newton Center, Massachusetts to Indianapolis.

The details of how I worked to first stabilize and then build the Center's operations are best left to another time, but they encompassed a broad range of innovative elements of organizational growth—creating revenue sources, raising public awareness, establishing marketing plans, creating the means and vehicles for individual and organizational support, establishing relationships with many different people, working with our own board, developing grant proposals linked to sustainable endproducts, establishing a certain entrepreneurial, "can-do" spirit, and being open to the notion of figuratively walking through a number of doors that opened up in ways that could not have been predicted. In the years since then the Greenleaf Center has been able to establish—and grow—numerous earned revenue streams in support of its mission, and it has succeeded in attracting a succession of project-focused grants from Lilly Endowment, the W.K. Kellogg Foundation, the William Penn Foundation, and others.

Another critical decision that I made in the early months of 1990 involved my making a fundamental commitment to doing all that I could to ensure that The Greenleaf Center would continue to hold at its core work the original servant leadership ideas and writings by Bob Greenleaf, while simultaneously establishing an equally strong commitment to expanding his servant leadership ideas in new directions, and encouraging the emergence of many new "voices" of servant leadership These twin commitments have been profoundly crucial for the significant growth of The Greenleaf Center ever since.

Now in our 40th year, The Greenleaf Center is an international, not-for-profit educational organization that seeks to encourage the understanding and practice of servant leadership. The Center's mission is to fundamentally improve the caring and quality of all institutions through servant leadership.

In recent years, The Greenleaf Center for Servant Leadership has experienced tremendous growth and expansion, with programs that now include: the worldwide sales of more than 130 books, essays, and videotapes on servant leadership; a research-and-publications effort through which we have produced and published dozens of new resources on servant leadership since 1990; a worldwide membership program involving individuals and institutions; a servant-leader speakers bureau; a variety of tailored workshops and seminars; a reading-and-dialogue program; and our annual International Conference on Servant Leadership. A number of notable Greenleaf Center members have spoken at our annual conferences, including James Autry, Peter Block, Max DePree, Stephen Covey, Meg Wheatley, M. Scott Peck, and Peter Senge, to name but a few.

The Greenleaf Center now encompasses offices located in Australia/New Zealand, Canada, Japan, Korea, the Netherlands, the Philippines, Singapore, South Africa, the United Kingdom, and at its global headquarters in Indianapolis, Indiana. Servant leadership books and essays have been translated into more than a dozen different languages. Bob Greenleaf's key essay, *The Servant as Leader*, is now available in Arabic, Chinese, Czech, Dutch, English, French, Japanese, Russian, Spanish, and Turkish editions. Our books have also been translated into Korean, Bahasa Indonesian, and other languages.

Life is full of curious and meaningful paradoxes. Servant leadership is one such paradox that has slowly but surely gained hundreds of thousands of adherents. The seeds initially planted by Bob Greenleaf over thirty-five years ago have begun to sprout in many institutions, as well as in the hearts of many who long to improve the human condition. Don Frick's fine biography of Robert Greenleaf is a welcome addition to the growing body of literature on servant leadership, and it serves to underscore the paradoxical nature of Bob Greenleaf, the man. Of course, the creations of people (paintings, music, books, ideas, organizations, etc.) generally have the benefit of being perceived as a completed end-product, and thus appear to be "finished" in a way that we generally understand and find satisfying. As human beings, we all have our own strengths and weaknesses, and our lives are inevitably messier than any of our creations. What I find so inspirational about Bob Greenleaf's life is that he eventually came to understand both his conscious and unconscious mind to the degree that he was able to learn and grow as a person, and then to find ways to synthesize his ideas into what we now call "servant leadership." In so doing, he has influenced several generations of seekers and has inspired many of us in our shared goal of creating a better, more caring society.

What a rare legacy to leave behind, and through a life lived extraordinarily well.

For more information on servant leadership resources
and programs contact:
The Greenleaf Center for Servant Leadership
921 E. 86th Street, Suite 200
Indianapolis, IN 46240
Phone: 317-259-1241
Fax: 317-259-0560
Website: www.greenleaf.org

Larry C. Spears has served as President & CEO of The Robert K. Greenleaf Center for Servant Leadership since 1990. During the 1970s and 80s Larry also worked with the Greater Philadelphia Philosophy Consortium, The Philadelphia Center, and *Friends Journal*. He is the editor/co-editor of nine books on servant leadership, which now include five posthumously-published books of essays by Robert K. Greenleaf, plus four anthologies on contemporary practices of servant leadership: *Practicing Servant-Leadership* (with Michele Lawrence), 2004; *The Servant-Leader Within: A Transformative Path* (with Hamilton Beazley and Julie Beggs), 2003; *Servant Leadership, 25th Anniversary Edition*, 2002; *Focus on Leadership: Servant-Leadership for the 21st Century* (with Michele Lawrence), 2002; *The Power of Servant-Leadership*, 1998; *Insights on Leadership: Service, Stewardship, Spirit and Servant-Leadership*, 1998; *On Becoming a Servant-Leader* (with Don Frick), 1996; *Seeker and Servant* (with Anne Fraker), 1996; and *Reflections on Leadership: How Robert K. Greenleaf's Theory of Servant Leadership Influenced Today's Top Management Thinkers*, 1995. Over the past 25 years Larry has published several hundred articles that have appeared in a variety of books and other publications. He serves as series editor for the *Voices of Servant-Leadership Essay Series*, published by The Greenleaf Center, and the founder and senior editor of The Greenleaf Center's quarterly newsletter, *The Servant Leader*. He is a longtime member of the Association of Fundraising Professionals. Larry is both a "conceptualizer" and "operationalizer" with three decades of experience in organizational leadership, entrepreneurial development, and non-profit management, and he has conceived and written dozens of successful grant projects over the years that total several million dollars. For more information on servant leadership contact The Greenleaf Center, 921 E. 86th St., Suite 200, Indianapolis, IN 46240; phone: 317-259-1241; or online at www.greenleaf.org.

Larry C. Spears
President & CEO, The Robert K. Greenleaf
Center for Servant Leadership

A Servant Leadership Primer

P eople who first hear the phrase *servant-leader* naturally ask "What does it mean?" Fair enough, but be warned that it is a catchy term with big arms that can embrace multiple meanings. Dozens of writers have tried their hand at decoding Greenleaf. Nearly all of their bullet point lists are right, as far as they go, but none are complete. Perhaps this is as it should be because Greenleaf was not a bullet-point kind of thinker, and perhaps no such list could be complete. Still, a short introduction to the basics of servant leadership should be useful in understanding Robert Greenleaf's life, just as his biography should illuminate his writings. The short primer that follows uses Greenleaf's own words as much as possible.

WHO AND WHAT IS A LEADER?

For openers, begin with a leader—any leader. Greenleaf says a leader is one who "goes out ahead and shows the way . . . He says, 'I will go, follow me!' when he knows that the path is uncertain, even dangerous."[1] The leader is open to inspiration, but "the leader needs more than inspiration . . . He initiates, provides the ideas and the structure, and takes the risk of

337

failure along with the chance of success."[2] The leader always knows the goal and "can articulate it for any who are unsure. By clearly stating and restating the goal the leader gives certainty and purpose to others who may have difficulty in achieving it for themselves. . . . The word *goal* is used here in the special sense of the overarching purpose, the big dream, the visionary concept, the ultimate consummation which one approaches but never really achieves."[3]

People follow leaders because they believe leaders "see more clearly where it is best to go."[4] In that sense, followers make the leaders. Hitler was a leader, but his vision of where to go was ethically warped. Still, he could not have accomplished what he did without followers who not only believed in his goal, but coerced unbelievers into followership.

How does one "see more clearly where it is best to go?" Through foresight. "Foresight is the 'lead' that the leader has. Once he loses this lead and events start to force his hand, he is leader in name only. He is not leading; he is reacting to immediate events and he probably will not long be a leader."[5] Machiavelli knew this. Here is his advice to princes who wished to survive, quoted by Greenleaf in a modern paraphrase. "Thus it happens in matters of state; for knowing afar off (which it is only given a prudent man to do) the evils that are brewing, they are easily cured. But when, for want of such knowledge, they are allowed to grow so that everyone can recognize them, there is no longer any remedy to be found."[6]

By this definition a leader can be moral or amoral, kind or cruel. Mother Teresa, Winston Churchill, and Ivan the Terrible were all leaders. In defining servant leadership, Greenleaf takes the common notion of heroic leadership (known in leadership circles as "The Great Man" theory) and turns it on its head.

WHO IS A SERVANT-LEADER?

Greenleaf's first servant writing was titled "The Servant as Leader," not "The Leader as Servant." Greenleaf explains the difference:

> The servant-leader *is* servant first . . . It begins with the natural feeling that one wants to serve, to serve *first*. Then conscious choice brings one to aspire to lead. That person is sharply different from one who is leader first, perhaps because of the need to assuage an

> unusual power drive or to acquire material possessions. For such it will be a later choice to serve—after leadership is established. The leader-first and the servant-first are two extreme types. Between them there are shadings and blends that are part of the infinite variety of human nature. . . The difference manifests itself in the care taken by the servant-first to make sure that other people's highest priority needs are being served.[7]

Even though motives are critical to one's identity as a servant-leader, personal qualities are not enough. The "best test" of a servant-leader is one of sheer pragmatism, based on mostly-observable outcomes.

> The best test, and difficult to administer, is: do those served grow as persons; do they, *while being served,* become healthier, wiser, freer, more autonomous, more likely themselves to become servants? *And,* what is the effect on the least privileged in society; will he benefit, or, at least, will he not be further deprived? [8]

Neither Greenleaf's definition of a servant-leader nor his best test requires one to hold a formal leadership position. What matters is what we do in "our little corner of the world"— as Greenleaf often said—and why we are doing it. In his workshops, Richard Smith, a former colleague at the Greenleaf Center and a thoughtful Greenleaf scholar, teaches that servant leadership "turns leadership into a territory," a field of action in which various people can operate depending upon their individual abilities and capacities to serve the mission of the enterprise and the people who make it all happen.

SKILLS AND CAPACITIES
OF THE SERVANT-LEADER

Few of the skills and capacities of a servant-leader are taught in schools. If they are, they are often reduced to formulas.

Listening is the premier skill, even though Greenleaf sees it as more than a skill. "Listening might be defined as an attitude toward other people and what they are attempting to express."[9] "I have a bias about this," he writes, "which suggests that only a true natural servant automatically responds to any problem by listening first. When he is a leader, this disposition causes him to be *seen* as servant first. This suggests that a non-servant who wants to be a servant might become a *natural* servant through a long arduous discipline of learning to listen, a discipline sufficiently sustained that the automatic response to any problem is to listen first."[10] "Listening isn't just keeping quiet; and it isn't just making appropriate responses that indicate one is awake and paying attention," says Greenleaf. "Listening is a healing attitude, the attitude of intensely holding the belief—faith if you wish to call it thus—that the person or persons being listened to will rise to the challenge of grappling with the issues involved in finding their own wholeness."[11]

Servant-leaders *use power ethically, with persuasion as the preferred mode.* Persuasion "involves arriving at a feeling of rightness about a belief or action through one's own intuitive sense . . . The act of persuasion, thus defined, would help order the logic and favor the intuitive step. But *the person being persuaded* must take that intuitive step alone, untrammeled by coercive or manipulative stratagems of any kind."[12] [Italics added] Greenleaf recognized that there were times when manipulation, and perhaps even coercion, were in order, but only when it involved the well-being of others or institutional survival, not for the purpose of inflating one's ego. Persuasion is not easy. It is, "on a critical issue, a difficult, time-consuming process. It demands one of the most exacting of human skills."[13]

When possible, a servant-leader seeks consensus in group decisions. "Consensus is used in its commonly understood meaning of unanimity or general agreement in matters of opinion, as opposed to taking a vote," says Greenleaf. "[Individuals] either accept the decision as the right or best one, or they agree to support it as a feasible resolution of the issue. . . the individual's position is intuitively derived in the absence of any coercive pressure to conform." To nurture consensus, a servant-leader must be able to: (1) deeply understand the issue under consideration and articulate it clearly and succinctly, (2) listen, (3) "decide when it is feasible to begin to search for consensus. This may be early or late in the discussion. . ." and (4) decide when it is feasible to adjourn to speak privately with remaining holdouts, realizing that "[holdouts] may be of great value, but they may function best as lone workers or in groups that operate by majority rule."[14]

A servant leader practices foresight. We have already seen that foresight is a core skill for all leaders. For servant-leaders, Greenleaf believes that foresight is the central ethic of leadership.

> The failure (or refusal) of a leader to foresee may be viewed as an ethical failure; because a serious ethical compromise today (when the usual judgment on ethical inadequacy is made) is sometimes the result of a failure to make the effort at an earlier date to foresee today's events and take the right actions when there was freedom for initiative to act. . . .
>
> By this standard a lot of guilty people are walking around with an air of innocence that they would not have if society were able always to pin the label 'unethical' on the failure to foresee and the consequent failure to act constructively when there was freedom to act.[15]

One need not look far to see how short-term thinking and lack of foresight have led to business failures, bankrupt government policies, and individual ruin. In fact, Greenleaf believed prudent foresight could have gone a long way toward saving AT&T from its breakup.

Greenleaf's view of how one achieves foresight was somewhat nontraditional. Imagine time as a line drawn from the dim past to the infinite future. *Now* is but one point on the line, a point which moves incessantly towards the future like a tireless rabbit chasing a carrot just out of reach. Here is the nontraditional part—imagine a flashlight beam focused on *now*, moving with the action. The beam is most intense at the present moment, but it also illuminates part of the past and the future. "*Now* includes all of this," says Greenleaf, "all of history and all of the future. As I view it, it simply gradually intensifies in the degree of illumination as this moment of clock time is approached."[16] Knowing history helps us understand patterns of the past. Foresight, based on intuition, can help us tentatively understand and predict patterns of the future. Paradoxically, one must live fully in the *now*, with high awareness of conscious and non-conscious realities and potentials, to access information about the future. Given these conditions, everyone can learn the art of foresight.

A servant-leader *uses language* in a way that avoids the "closed verbal worlds" of narrow disciplines or cults. Specifically, he or she "must have facility in tempting the hearer into that leap of imagination that connects the verbal concept to the hearer's own experience. The limitation on language, to the communicator, is that the hearer must make that leap of imagination . . . Many attempts to communicate are nullified by saying too much."[17]

The art of *withdrawal* serves leaders who love intense pressure as well as those who do not. For both kinds of leaders, we can assume the intention is to be performing at one's optimum, a state which Greenleaf defines as "that pace and set of choices that give one the best performance over a lifespan." To reach optimum performance "out there" in the world, a servant-leader, paradoxically, goes "in here," seeking the quiet which allows deep wisdom and intuition to emerge. "That sounds great, but you should see my schedule!" many will object. Greenleaf suggests another skill to enable withdrawal. "The ability to withdraw and reorient oneself, if only for a moment, presumes that one has learned the art of *systematic neglect*, to sort out the more important from the less important—and the important from the urgent—and attend to the more important . . ."[18] [Italics added]

A servant-leader practices *acceptance and empathy*.

> The servant as leader always empathizes, always accepts the person but sometimes refuses to accept some of the person's effort or performance as good enough.[19]
>
> It is part of the enigma of human nature that the 'typical' person—immature, stumbling, inept, lazy—is capable of great dedication and heroism *if* he is wisely led. Many otherwise able people are disqualified to lead because they cannot work with and through the half-people, who are all there are. The secret of institution building is to be able to weld a team of such people by lifting them up to grow taller than they would otherwise be.[20]

Conceptualizing is an ability that requires more than verbal skills. Greenleaf called it the prime leadership talent. The conceptualizer has "the ability to see the whole in the perspective of history—past and future—to state and adjust goals, to evaluate, to analyze, and to foresee contingencies a long way ahead. . . The conceptualizer, at his or her best, is a persuader and a relation builder."[21] By contrast, much of management is accomplished through the skills of "operators," who have "the ability to carry the enterprise toward its objectives in the situation, from day to day, and resolve the issues that arise as this movement takes place." Organizations need the skills of both operators and conceptualizers. The latter are often passed over for promotion in this can-do world, but they "usually emerge when an organization makes a strong push for distinction."[22]

Servant-leaders nurture community. "Living in community as one's basic involvement will generate an exportable surplus of love which the individual may carry into his many involvements with institutions which are usually not communities: businesses, churches, governments, schools."[23] Community is diminished when its members limit their liability for each other. It is enhanced when "the liability of each for the other and all for one is unlimited, or as close to it as it is possible to get."[24] Unlimited liability. Strange words in a society where individuals and institutions seek to limit liability, words judged as unwise to many a lawyer's ear. Still, it is a requirement of love, which is something we say we want more of in private and public life. "As soon as one's liability for another is qualified *to any degree,* love is diminished by that much."[25]

A servant-leader chooses to lead. The enemy is "Not evil people. Not stupid people. Not apathetic people. Not the 'system.' Not the protesters, the disrupters, the revolutionaries, the reactionaries . . . *In short, the enemy is strong natural servants who have the potential to lead but do not lead, or who choose to follow a non-servant.*"[26] [Italics are Greenleaf's.] Followers will appear—will, in fact, make the leader—"because [servant-leaders] are proven and trusted as servants."[27]

SERVANT LEADERSHIP IN THE WORLD

In his 1972 essay *The Institution as Servant* which was directed to businesses, universities, and churches, Greenleaf expands the idea of an individual servant-leader by suggesting that institutions should also function as servants.

> This is my thesis: caring for persons, the more able and the less able serving each other, is the rock upon which a good society is built. Whereas, until recently, caring was largely person to person, now most of it is mediated through institutions—often large, complex, powerful, impersonal; not always competent; sometimes corrupt. If a better society is to be built, one that is more just and more loving, one that provides greater creative opportunity for its people, then the most open course is to *raise both the capacity to serve and the very performance as servant* of existing major institutions by new regenerative forces operating within them.[28] [Italics are Greenleaf's.]

One might ask how such a thing is possible, or if it is even desirable. Greenleaf makes the case that "with the present level of education, and the extent of information sources, too many people judge our institutions as not meeting the standard of what is reasonable and possible in their service."[29] He points his finger at three culprits: trustees who don't care enough for their institutions and the people in them, institutions organized around the idea of a single chief, and lack of trust.

He claims that trustees—board members—are the "prime movers in institutional regeneration" when they accept full responsibility for the fate of the organization, ask the right "big picture" questions that lead to clear institutional goals and strategic plans, and employ staff answerable only to the board.[30]

In place of a single chief—a heroic figure who wields king-like power from the top of the organizational pyramid—Greenleaf suggests an organizational structure based on the ancient Roman notion of *primus inter pares*, "first among equals." Greenleaf explains: "What is proposed here for the top leadership team of large institutions is a shift from the hierarchical principle, with one chief, to a team of equals with a *primus* (a "first"), preceded by the change in trustee attitude and the role necessary to assure its success."[31]

As for trust, board members and everyone else in the organization should hold the institution "in trust," but they must also trust each other. "This must come first," says Greenleaf. "Trust is first. Nothing will move until trust is firm."[32]

In his third essay, *Trustees as Servants* (1974), Greenleaf expands on how trustees can exercise a servant role, becoming more proactive rather than reactive, closely overseeing operational use of power without micromanaging, operating by consensus in their own proceedings, gathering their own information, employing a trustee coach, and claiming their own power.

> Having power (and every trustee has some power) one *initiates* the means whereby power is used to serve and not to hurt. *Serve* is used in the sense that anyone touched by the institution or its work becomes, because of that influence, healthier, wiser, freer, more autonomous, more likely themselves to become servants . . . What shall one do, as a trustee who is aware of this necessity, if one finds that

> one cannot persuade one's fellow trustees to accept such an obliga-
> tion, and if one does not foresee the possibility of doing so in a
> reasonable period? *My advice is to resign.*[33] [Italics are Greenleaf's.]

In later years, Greenleaf suggested an Institute of Chairing be established to prepare people to chair boards—and other groups—using the
strategies of *primus inter pares* and consensus decision making. He eventually concluded that organizations that train religious leaders could be the
levers to change society if they taught the skills, capacities, and strategies
necessary for servant-leaders to operate in the wider world. If ritual leaders of churches, synagogues, and mosques modeled and taught such
ideas, and demanded distinction of their own religious institutions, the
ripple effect could change our society into one which was more serving. It
was an idea with which virtually no one agreed.

Bob Greenleaf had much more to say about how servant leadership
could operate in business, education, foundations, churches and the society at large—those resources are annotated in the bibliography—but the
basics are to be found in his first three essays: *The Servant as Leader*, *The Institution as Servant*, and *Trustees as Servants*. These writings comprise the
first three chapters of the Paulist Press book *Servant Leadership* (1977 and
2002).

Mindmap of Robert K. Greenleaf's Thought

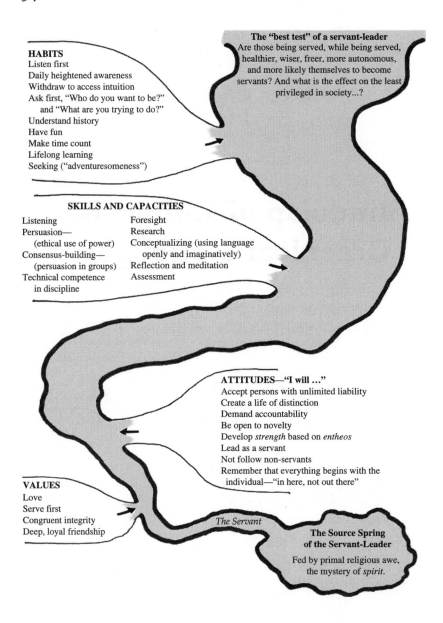

HABITS
Listen first
Daily heightened awareness
Withdraw to access intuition
Ask first, "Who do you want to be?"
    and "What are you trying to do?"
Understand history
Have fun
Make time count
Lifelong learning
Seeking ("adventuresomeness")

The "best test" of a servant-leader
Are those being served, while being served, healthier, wiser, freer, more autonomous, and more likely themselves to become servants? And what is the effect on the least privileged in society...?

SKILLS AND CAPACITIES

Listening
Persuasion—
    (ethical use of power)
Consensus-building—
    (persuasion in groups)
Technical competence
    in discipline

Foresight
Research
Conceptualizing (using language
    openly and imaginatively)
Reflection and meditation
Assessment

ATTITUDES—"I will ..."
Accept persons with unlimited liability
Create a life of distinction
Demand accountability
Be open to novelty
Develop *strength* based on *entheos*
Lead as a servant
Not follow non-servants
Remember that everything begins with the
    individual—"in here, not out there"

VALUES
Love
Serve first
Congruent integrity
Deep, loyal friendship

The Servant

**The Source Spring
of the Servant-Leader**

Fed by primal religious awe,
the mystery of *spirit*.

Copyright 2004, Don M. Frick. From: *Robert K. Greenleaf: A Life of Servant Leadership*. (San Francisco: Berrett-Koehler) 2004. Permission is granted to reproduce this page.

Timeline of Robert K. Greenleaf's Life

July 14, 1904	Robert Kiefner Greenleaf born in Terre Haute, Indiana.
1908–1921	George Greenleaf takes Bob along to his workplace and meetings of the city council, school board, and machinist's union. They make educational visits to factories, machine shops, repair facilities, and municipal works. Bob notices father's ability to "see things whole" while diagnosing and repairing machines.
1910–1913	Attends Montrose Methodist Episcopal Church. Impressed by young minister, Rev. John Benson.
1913	George Greenleaf acts as community trustee, takes over relief efforts after massive flood and tornadoes.
1915	George Greenleaf joins in testifying against Mayor Donn Roberts and other municipal officials in "the biggest election fraud in American history."
1917	Uncle John Parkhurst exposes Bob to the "world outside the working class environment." Introduces him to astronomy at Yerkes Observatory in Wisconsin.
1918–1922	Attends Wiley High School. Is popular, sociable, president of senior class.

1918–1924	Works at shoe store, machine and electrical firm, and construction company. Decides he does not want to "run things" as a manager.
1923	Looks through telescope at Mount Wilson observatory. "I shook with awe and wonder at the majesty of all creation," he reports. "This primitive unstructured feeling . . . is to me the source of religious feeling at its greatest depth."
1923–1924	Attends Rose Polytechnic Institute, studies math and engineering. Supports effort to get deceptive president of school fired.
1924–1926	Attends Carleton College, Northfield, Minnesota to study astronomy.
	Active in behind-scenes work in school plays. Takes lead in getting Glee Club director replaced. College hijinks land him in President's office. Becomes disillusioned with astronomy and university education. After hearing comment from Professor Oscar C. Helming, makes vocational decision to work with a big organization to change it from inside.
1926–1929	Hired by AT&T Ohio Bell subsidiary. In Toledo and Cleveland Greenleaf works his way up from "groundman" to Supervisor of Technical Training, responsible for the skills development of hundreds of employees. Develops innovative approach to teaching algebra to the unschooled and begins developing foremen through group processes.
1929	Transferred to AT&T headquarters in Manhattan with broad portfolio to consult and conduct research in all phases of personnel. First assignment is to investigate hiring policies and assessment techniques.
	Discovers author E. B. White and is influenced by White's ability to "see things whole."
1930	Meets and does research with Johnson O'Connor, pioneer in testing for human potentials.
	Begins national travel and consulting for AT&T. Always takes the train because, "I like my solitude."

1931	Meets and marries the artist and architect Esther Hargrave, beginning a lifelong love story. They attend the (Unitarian) Community Church of New York and become friends with its minister, John Haynes Holmes.
	Meets Eugene R. Bowen, becomes involved in the Cooperative Movement.
1932	Meets Mary Arnold, a leader in the Cooperative Movement. Greenleafs live in a Manhattan cooperative.
1934	Bob and Esther take a delayed honeymoon and learning trip to Europe where they sightsee, hike, and study modern architecture, Grundtvig's Folk Schools of Denmark and the Cooperative Movement.
	Outlines his philosophy of education in a series of wide-ranging letters to Dr. Donald Cowling.
1935	In speech titled "Industry's Means for Personality Adjustment." Greenleaf says, "A search for the capabilities and possibilities in people is gradually supplanting the search for their limitations. It is a more optimistic philosophy."
	Greenleafs move to Mt. Kisco. Their neighbors Levi Hollingsworth Wood and his sister Carolena interest them in Quakers. Join Society of Religious Friends. Bob and Esther begin intense study of Quaker history and practice.
	First child, Elizabeth, is stillborn.
	Bob and Esther write for Cooperative League publications.
1937	Newcomb Greenleaf is born.
1939	John Lovejoy Elliot of the New York Society for Ethical Culture invites Bob to serve with Eleanor Roosevelt on the Good Neighbor Committee and help relocate European refugees. Elliot impresses Bob as "the starter of useful work."
	Anne Greenleaf is born, contracts a hospital infection, and dies within one week.

Attends weeklong conference where he becomes better acquainted with original Hawthorne Studies researchers, including Fritz Roethlisberger, William Dickson, and Elton Mayo. Greenleaf already knows Hawthorne Plant managers.

Sometime during the 1930s Greenleaf (1) meets and takes courses from Alfred Korzybski, founder of modern general semantics and (2) begins developing a management course which was later known in its printed form as "Management Ability."

1940   Taking what he has learned from the Hawthorne "counselors" and Quaker practice, Greenleaf develops a course in listening called "Talking With People."

1941   Elizabeth (Lisa) Greenleaf born at home. Mother and child are healthy.

The Greenleafs move to Short Hills, New Jersey, plant a large organic garden and eventually keep bees.

1943   Madeline Greenleaf born.

1942–1945   Receives secret clearance, works closely with War Communications Board to protect vital AT&T personnel and facilities during wartime.

Begins using persuasion and consensus decision making in his AT&T work. Conducts his own experiments in cultivating heightened awareness.

"Around the age of forty" Greenleaf gets the idea of preparing to be useful in old age, even though he does not know the goal of his preparation. Broadens his reading and personal contacts with top thinkers.

1946   Reads about the OSS assessment work during the war and initiates a long-term plan to adapt it to industry. Invites prominent psychologists and social researchers to speak with AT&T executives.

1947   Attends the founding meeting of National Training Labs in Bethel, Maine. Later he co-facilitates a "T-Group" but is quickly disillusioned with what he believes is cult-like attention given to Kurt Lewin, who died before the Bethel meeting.

1948	Is assigned responsibility for AT&T personnel research.
1950–1957	Faculty member of the Graduate School of Credit and Financial Management at Dartmouth College.
1951	First visits the Wainwright House in Rye, New York and becomes involved in the Laymen's Movement.
1952	Suggests the creation of two new organizations: the Yokefellow Institute and the Earlham Institute for Executive Growth.
1953	Writes his "hole in the hedge" philosophy.
1954	Bob and Esther develop the Receptive Listening Course for Wainwright House, which would offer a version of the course for many years. They evolve the course from its business roots to a group-facilitated journey of spiritual exploration.
1953–1958	Takes on responsibility for the Bell Humanities Program. Six universities would eventually offer some version of the in-residence program which exposed executives to the humanities.
1953–1964	Is involved in developing and delivering the Management Objectives Program (an offshoot of the Bell Humanities Program) and the Bell System Executive Conference, a four-week course focused on business-related issues.
1956	Hires Douglas Bray to design, staff, and deliver the first AT&T assessment program. Eventually AT&T's success leads to thousands of corporate assessments centers around the world.
	Assists Thomas Watson, Jr. in reorganizing IBM.
1958–1960	Engages in Jungian-based "dream work" with Dr. Ira Progoff and Dr. Martha Jeager.
1958	First experience with LSD—then a legal substance—under the direction of Gerald Heard and a medical doctor.

	Begins writing a book titled *The Ethic of Strength*, which he completes seven years later but was only published after his death.
1957–1964	Trustee of the Russell Sage Foundation, New York. Other activities during this period included:
	1962–1963: Visiting lecturer at Harvard Business School and the Sloan School of Management, MIT.
	1962–1964: Consultant to Ford Foundation Public Affairs Program.
	1963: Consultant to National Council of Churches to develop a program for education of church executives.
	1964: First trip to India as a consultant to the Ford Foundation's South Asia Program. Helps organize India's first school of administration set up after India's independence. Bob and Esther make a total of six trips to India between 1964 and 1971.
September, 1964	Retires from AT&T. Organizes the Center for Applied Ethics as a nonprofit umbrella organization to support his consulting and writing activities.
1964–1978	Dozens of consultancies. A partial list includes:
	1965–1971: Member, Overseers's Visiting Committee for Harvard Divinity School.
	1966: Consultant to the Committee on Structure of the American Institute of Certified Public Accountants, Inc.
	1967–1974: Consultant to the president and trustees of the Sloan School of Management, MIT.
	1968–1969: Special consultant on continuing education to the President of Dartmouth College.
	1968: Faculty member, Salzburg Seminar in American Studies.
	1968: Lecturer, Dartmouth Alumni College.
	1967–1968: Consultant, Prescott College. In 1968 Greenleaf coins the phrase "servant-leader" after a

consultancy at Prescott College which he termed a "miserable failure."

1968: Executive in Residence, School of Business, Fresno State College.

1969–1970: Consultant to Fondacion Giovanni Agnelli, Turin, Italy.

1969–1970: Consultant to Douglas Williams Associates on a project examining causes of student unrest at Cornell University.

1972–1985: Consultant to the Lilly Endowment. Meets Robert Wood Lynn and is deeply influenced by Lynn's thinking about religious institutions.

1973–1977: Consultant to the Mead Corporation.

1973: Olsson Professor of Business Ethics in the School of Business Administration at the University of Virginia.

1974–1978: Consultant to the Hill Family Foundation (later renamed the Northwest Area Foundation).

1976–1983: Consultant to the Sisters of Mercy Health Corporation.

1970	Bob and Esther move to the "dream home" they built in Peterborough, New Hampshire.
1970–1974	Publication of Greenleaf's most important essays: *The Servant as Leader* (1970), *The Institution as Servant* (1972), and *Trustees as Servants* (1974).
1977	Bob and Esther move to Crosslands, a Quaker-related retirement facility at Kennett Square, Pennsylvania.
	Paulist Press publishes the book *Servant Leadership: A Journey into the Nature of Legitimate Power and Greatness*.
1984	Bob suffers his first stroke.
	The Center for Applied Ethics changes its name to the Robert K. Greenleaf Center for Servant Leadership.

1988	First national Symposium on Servant Leadership is held in Atlanta. Bob attends by speakerphone.
February 22, 1989	Esther Greenleaf dies.
September 29, 1990	Robert K. Greenleaf dies.

NOTES

Abbreviations and permissions

AT&T   Courtesy of AT&T Archives

CCA   Used by permission of the Carleton College Archives

DP   Used by permission of DePauw University and Indiana United Methodism Special Collections of DePauw University

FTL   Used by permission of the Franklin Trask Library, Andover Newton Theological School

RKGC   Used by permission of the Robert K. Greenleaf Center for Servant Leadership, Indianapolis.

NTL   Courtesy of NTL Institute Archives

E.B. White's correspondence to Robert K. Greenleaf is used by permission of the E.B. White Estate.

PREFACE

1. RKG, *The Servant as Leader* (Indianapolis: Greenleaf Center for Servant Leadership, 1970, 1991), 1.

2. *Ibid.*, 34.

3. RKG, "An Interview with Robert K. Greenleaf by Joseph J. Distefano, December, 1985," RKGC.

INTRODUCTION

1. Stephen Covey, *Insights on Leadership: Service, Stewardship and Servant Leadership* (New York: John Wiley & Sons, 1998), xiv–xv.

2. Warren Bennis, Interview with Larry C. Spears, 2003, RKGC.

3. William Strunk and E. B. White, *The Elements of Style*, 4th ed. (New York: Macmillan Publishing Company, 1979), 34–35.

4. John C. Hodges and Mary E. Whitten, *Harbrace College Handbook*, 7th ed. (New York: Harcourt Brace Jovanovich Inc., 1972), 184.

5. RKG, *The Servant as Leader*, 6.

INTRODUCTION TO SERVANT SECTION

1. RKG, *Seeker and Servant: Reflections on Religious Leadership* (San Francisco: Jossey-Bass, 1996) 46, 48.

CHAPTER 1

1. Albert Camus, *Resistance, Rebellion and Death* (New York: Alfred A. Knopf, Inc., 1961), 272.

2. RKG, Distefano interview, RKGC. Greenleaf's description of his experiences at Prescott and his coining of the phrase "servant-leader" are based on his conversations with Dr. Distefano, his interviews with Dianne Bullard and Fred Myers, and autobiographical notes.

3. The Dartmouth lectures are available in RKG, *On Becoming a Servant Leader* (San Francisco: Jossey-Bass, 1996), 287–338.

CHAPTER 2

1. Theodore Dreiser, *A Hoosier Holiday* (Bloomington, Indiana: Indiana University Press, 1997), 429–432.

2. *Terre Haute Morning Star*, 14 July, 1904, 1.

3. Dorothy Weinz Jerse and Judith Stedman Calvert, *Terre Haute: A Pictorial History* (St. Louis, MO: G. Bradley Publishing, 1993), 23.

4. *Ibid.*, 110–113.

5. *Ibid.*, 77.

6. "Carrie Nation Spoke," *Terre Haute Morning Star*, 14 July, 1904.

7. RKG, *My Life With Father* (Newton Centre, MA: Robert K. Greenleaf Center, 1988), 4.

8. Newcomb Greenleaf, telephone interview with the author, 22 August, 2002.

9. RKG, "Autobiographical Notes," FTL, Box 1.

10. Jerse and Calvert, *op. cit.*, 77.

11. RKG, *My Life With Father*, 5.

12. *Ibid.*

13. *Ibid.* Also, RKG, "Narrative of my Life And Work After Age 60," FTL, Box 1.

14. Miriam Z. Langsam, "Eugene Victor Debs, Hoosier Radical," *Gentlemen from Indiana: National Party Candidates 1836–1940* (Indianapolis: Indiana Historical Bureau, 1997), 285.

Five days after the Canton speech, Debs was arrested under the Federal Espionage Act. At trial, he made an eloquent two-hour statement which concluded with the assertion that freedom of speech was at stake. It was futile because the jury was hostile to Debs. With an average age of over 70 and a hefty average net worth of $50,000 to $60,000—large for those days—the jurors thought this young radical was a *bona fide* traitor, dangerous to the survival of the United States. See also the official website for the Eugene V. Debs Foundation: <http://www. eugenevdebs.com/> (4 August, 2003).

15. John Bartlow Martin, *Indiana: An Interpretation* (Bloomington: Indiana University Press, 1947, 1992), 153.

16. *Ibid.*, 287.

17. RKG, *My Life With Father*, 6.

18. James Whitcomb Riley, "Regardin' Terry Hut," *The Complete Poetical Works of James Whitcomb Riley* (Bloomington: Indiana University Press, 1993), 374.

19. RKG, "Early Autobiographical Notes," FTL., Box 1.

20. *Ibid.*

21. RKG, *My Life With Father*, 10.

22. *Ibid.*, 3.

23. RKG, "Early Autobiographical Notes," FTL, Box 1.

24. *Ibid.*, 4.

25. RKG, *My Life With Father*, 3.

26. *Ibid.*, 4.

CHAPTER 3

1. RKG, *My Life With Father*, 11.

2. *Ibid.*, 4.

3. In 1851, Hoosier Sarah Bolton wrote the famous poem, "Paddle Your Own Canoe," part of which reads: Nothing great is lightly won,/Nothing won is lost, Every good deed, nobly done/ Will repay the cost./Leave to Heaven, in humble trust/All you will to do./But if succeed, you must/Paddle your own canoe.

4. All genealogical information comes from "Our Greenleaf Lineage," an unpublished manuscript by Newcomb Greenleaf, 2001.

5. RKG, *My Life With Father*, 4–5. Also, RKG, "Narrative of My Life and Work After 60," FTL, Box 1.

6. *Ibid.*, 13.

7. Marylee Hagan, "Introduction," Clifton H. Bush, *The Incumbent* (Indianapolis: Skyward Entertainment, 1996), iv.

8. "Vote Fraud Case Opens Today," *Indianapolis Star*, 15 March, 1915, 1, 5.

9. Marylee Hagan, *op. cit.*, iv.

10. RKG, *My Life With Father*, 6–7.

11. David Hawes, ed., *The Best of Kin Hubbard: Abe Martin's Sayings and Wisecracks, Abe's Neighbors, His Almanack, Comic Drawings* (Bloomington: Indiana University Press, 1984), 14.

12. Marylee Hagan, *op. cit.*, iv.

13. "Roberts Ousted by 7–3 Vote," *Indianapolis Star*, 25, April, 1915, 1, 3.

14. RKG, *My Life With Father*, 7.

15. "Calamity Dazes Storm Victims in Terre Haute," *Indianapolis Star*, 25 March, 1913, 1, 13.

16. RKG, *My Life With Father*, 2.

17. *Ibid.*, 2–3.

18. *Ibid.*, 7.

19. *Ibid.*, 7–9.

20. *Ibid.*, 12.

21. "Greenleaf to Battle to Hold School Job," *Terre Haute Tribune*, 16 October, 1918, 1.

22. "Greenleaf Petition Attacked in Court," *Terre Haute Tribune*, 24 October, 1918, 1.

23. "What Could Judge Cox Have Meant?" *Terre Haute Tribune*, 14 February, 1919, 1.

24. RKG, *My Life With Father*, 11.

25. *Ibid.*, 12.

26. *Ibid.*, 18–19.

27. RKG, "Narrative of My Life and Work After Age 60," FTL, Box 1.

28. RKG, *My Life With Father*, 1.

CHAPTER 4

1. RKG, *Seeker and Servant*, 289–290.

2. Peter Vaill, interview with author, June 14, 1997.

3. RKG, *My Life With Father*, 9.

4. Jerse & Calvert, *Terre Haute, A Pictorial History*, 145.

In later years, Robert Greenleaf joined the Quakers but he was probably not influenced by exposure to the Friends during his childhood. Even though the Quakers were among the earliest participants in Terre Haute's religious life, by 1915 there were no meeting houses in the city.

5. Minutes of the Southern Indiana Annual Conference, 1913. DP.

6. RKG , *My Life With Father*, 9.

7. *Ibid.*

8. John Baughman, "United Methodism in Indiana." Presented at the Inaugural Program of the South Indiana Conference United Methodist Historical Society DePauw University, 26 April 27, DP.

9. Circuit riders began regular visits to Terre Haute in 1824. and they were a tough breed who lived out of their saddles, "Protestant 'soldiers of the cross' who vied with the priest-missionary of the Catholic faith in courage, tenacity, intrepidity and fidelity to convictions." (Jerse & Calvert, *op cit.*, 145.)

10. Baughman, *op. cit.*

11. *Ibid.*

12. Minutes of the Southern Indiana Annual Conference, 1908, DP.

13. *Ibid.*

14. *Ibid.*

15. Until fairly recently, Methodist ministers served short pastorates, often no more than three to five years. The idea was that, by moving clergy around and removing the choice of minister from local congregations, the pastor would be free

to "preach the Gospel" and take unpopular stands without fear of losing his or her job. In recent years, the United Methodist Church has become more flexible in decisions about the location and timing of pastoral moves.

16. RKG, *My Life With Father*, 9.

17. RKG, *The Servant as Leader*, 7. "The best test, and difficult to administer, is: do those served grow as persons; do they, *while being served*, become healthier, wiser, freer, more autonomous, more likely themselves to become servants? *And*, what is the effect on the least privileged in society; will he benefit, or, at least, will he not be further deprived?

18. *Ibid.*, 8.

19. *Ibid.*, 7. "The servant-leader is *servant* first—as Leo was portrayed. It begins with the natural feeling that one wants to serve, to serve *first*. Then conscious choice brings one to aspire to lead."

20. See William James, *Varieties of Religious Experience*, (Charmichael, CA: Touchstone Books, 1997).

For many Protestants, a conversion experience is *sina qua non* to call oneself a Christian. During the Vietnam war a friend of the author asked his draft board for a 4-D draft classification, which would exempt him from the draft while he attended seminary. The board members, who all belonged to Protestant denominations that saw a conversion experience as the only proof of a true Christian, required him to submit the exact year, day and time of day when he was "converted." Only after months of tense correspondence filled with quotes from sources ranging from the Gospels to ancient and contemporary theologians did the board reluctantly grant him his 4-D exemption. Today he is a pastor and seminary professor.

21. Peter Drucker, "Introduction." *On Becoming a Servant Leader*, xi–xii.

22. A few of the *metanoia* moments reported by Robert Greenleaf included his decision to work in a large organization and serve from within, a determination to "prepare for old age," and the moment he had his insight about the phrase "servant-leader."

23. RKG, *Seeker and Servant*, 5.

24. RKG, *Seeker and Servant*, 9.

25. *Ibid.*, 18.

26. RKG, *My Life With Father*, 10.

27. A widely used textbook on Indiana history, *Indiana: The Hoosier State* outlines three possible origins of the word Hoosier. (p. ix) John B. Martin, in *Indiana: An Interpretation* claims that the first Hoosiers to whom the term applied favored the "husher" source because it implied strength. (p. 8) To prepare for a radio program in 1980, the author discovered the connection to the Celtic word from Dr. George Geib, head of the History Department at Butler University. For that same program, the author interviewed three former Indiana governors and found no common agreement on the origin of the word "Hoosier."

28. Ralph Gray, *Gentlemen From Indiana: National Party Candidates 1836–1940* (Indianapolis: Indiana Historical Bureau, 1987), vii.

29. Clifton Phillips, *Indiana In Transition: 1880–1920* (Indianapolis: Indiana Historical Bureau and Indiana Historical Society, 1968), 503.

30. See Davis S. Hawes, ed. *The Best of Kin Hubbard: Abe Martin's Sayings and Wisecracks, Abe's Neighbors, His Almanack, Comic Drawings* (Bloomington: Indiana University Press, 1984).

31. Also see James H. Madison's discussion of Indiana's canal mess in *The Indiana Way, A State History* (Bloomington: Indiana University Press, 1986), 82–86. During its first forty years, the state was fairly progressive, especially in regard to public works. In 1836, the General Assembly voted for a massive improvement project in roads, railroads, and canals which would cost ten million dollars. The resulting budget gap was filled by optimism. As it turned out, prudence would have been a better choice. The state put most of its eggs in the canal basket at precisely the wrong time in history. A national depression played havoc with financial projections, railroads eventually won the transportation derby, and Indiana was stuck with hundreds of miles of unfinished or unprofitable canals. By 1847, the *interest* on Indiana canal bonds was ten times the state budget. The state was forced to default on half of its obligations. The other half was paid in Wabash and Erie Canal stock, which proved worthless, even though this canal (which ran through Terre Haute) was eventually finished and saw considerable traffic during the 1840s and 1850s.

32. James Madison, *op. cit.*, xiv. "Hoosiers have never been all alike. Yet there has been a dominant Indiana way—a tradition of individual freedom and responsibility, of intense interest in politics, of wariness of government, particularly when it is located at a distance or is preparing to tax, of attachment to small-town and rural values of community identification and pride, of friendliness and neighborliness. These are American traditions, too, but nowhere are they more firmly rooted and more fully respected. Theirs is the most American of states, Indianans have often claimed. And if other states or regions do not share these traditions it is they who are atypical, not Indiana.

33. James Madison, *op. cit.*, 117.

34. The Delaware, Miami and Potawatomi were the largest Native American groups in Indiana. The Kickapoo and Wea lived along the Wabash River from Terre Haute to Lafayette, and the Shawnee lived southeast and northeast of Terre Haute.

35. James Madison, *op. cit.*, 201. Also see Madison's portrayal of Governor Morton pp. 98–105.

36. Jerse & Calvert, *op. cit.*, 34.

37. The article by Peter Wyden in the February 11, 1961 issue of *Saturday Evening Post* reads, in part.

"I had spent less than a day in Terre Haute, Indiana, when it became apparent to me that the town was—well, let's say unusual. In a decorous little night club on the main street, which is also U.S. Highway 40, I watched customers straining in concentration over a whirling roulette wheel. Farther downtown I climbed a short flight of steps right into a booming bookie joint. At other stops utterly respectable citizens assured me that there weren't 'over a dozen' brothels operating any more. They were convinced that Terre Haute (pop. 71,851), the somber, tranquil-appearing seat of Vigo County. . . really was a fine city—except for just a few flaws.

High water, unemployment—these are hardships which can be met, other cities have done so . . . but what can be done for a city enfeebled by apathy. . . Bluntly speaking, folks there don't give a hoot."

38. Jerse & Calvert, *op. cit.*, 64.

CHAPTER 5

1. RKG, "Narrative of my Life and Work During 1920s," FTL, Box 1.

2. Storrs B. Barrett, "John A. Parkhurst," *Popular Astronomy* No. 325, 1924.

3. *Ibid.*

4. *Ibid.*

5. RKG, *My Life With Father*, 14.

6. RKG, *Notes* dated October 3, 1954. FTL, Box 1.

7. RKG, "Narrative," FTL, Box 1.

8. *Ibid.*

9. *The Red Pepper,* 1922. (Terre Haute, Indiana, Wiley High School).

10. RKG, "Early Autobiographical Notes," FTL, Box 1.

11. RKG, *My Life With Father*, 13.

12. RKG, "Early Autobiographical Notes," FTL, Box 1.

13. RKG, *My Life With Father*, 14.

14. RKG, "Narrative," FTL, Box 1.

15. RKG, *My Life With Father*, 15–16.

16. RKG, "Autobiographical Notes," FTL, Box 1.

17. RKG, *Seeker and Servant*, 288.

18. RKG, "My Work With Foundations and Other Autobiographical Notes," FTL, Box 1.

19. RKG, "Narrative," FTL, Box 1.

20. *Ibid.*

21. *Ibid.*

CHAPTER 6

1. RKG, correspondence to Dr. John Nason, November 7, 1966. CCA, M-6.

2. Delevan Leonard, *The History of Carleton College: Its Origin and Growth, Environment and Builders* (Chicago: Fleming H. Revell Company, 1904), 201–202.

3. For a comprehensive story of Carleton College's history, see: Eric Hillerman and Diana Anderson, *Carleton College: Celebrating 125 Years* (Northfield, MN: Carleton College, 1991), CCA.

4. Mark Greene, former Archivist at Carleton, recounts the history of the Goodsell observatory on a series of web pages. See: http://www.acad.carleton.edu/curricular/PHYS/Astro/index.html (3 March, 2004).

5. *Carletonian*, 10 February, 1926.

6. *Carletonian*, 13 February, 1926.

7. Robert Greenleaf academic transcription, CCA.

8. RKG, *Ages 20–40: What I Did With Those Years*. FTL, Box 1.

9. *Carletonian*, 12 December, 1925.

10. RKG, "Ages 20–40: What I Did With Those Years," FTL, Box 1.

11. RKG, "Notes," dated 3 October, 1954, FTL, Box 1.

12. *The Algol* (Northfield, MN: Carleton College, 1924–1925), 217.

13. David Perter & Merrill Jarchow, eds, *Carleton Remembered: 1909–1986*, (Northfield, MN: Carleton College, 1987), 17.

14. Leal Headley & Merrill Jarchow, *Carleton: The First Century* (Northfield, MN: Carleton College, 1996), 344.

15. *Carleton: The First Century*, 345.

16. *Carletonian*, 6 December, 1924.

17. Ed Ouelette, interview by the author and Anne Fraker, Evansville, Indiana, 19 June, 1996, RKGC.

18. Ed Ouelette, interview by the author and Anne Fraker, Evansville, Indiana, 4 December, 1992, RKGC.

19. Ed Ouelette, interview by the author and Anne Fraker, Evansville, Indiana, 19 June, 1996, RKGC.

20. *Ibid*.

21. RKG, *Lifestyle of Greatness*, (Northfield, MN: Carleton College, 1966), 2.

22. RKG, "Notes," dated October 3, 1954. FTL, Box 1.

23. *Ibid*.

24. Ed Ouelette, Interview by the author and Anne Fraker, Evansville, Indiana, 4 December, 1992, RKGC.

25. *Ibid*.

26. Undated entry. Journal: 1940–1943. RKG Archives.

27. Ed Ouelette, Interview by the author and Anne Fraker, Evansville, Indiana, 4 December, 1992, RKGC.

28. O. C. Helming, *The Church and the Industrial Problem*, (Chicago: Chicago Church Federation, 1919), CCA.

29. *Carletonian*, 22 October, 1924.

30. O. C. Helming, "Ethics and Economics," Reprinted from *Religious Education*, 1932, 7. CCA 58A.

31. *Ibid*.

32. Helming, *The Church and the Industrial Problem*, 1919. CCA.

33. *Ibid*.

34. Helming correspondence quoted in 13 June, 1921 response from Sheldon. CCA 58A.

35. Sheldon correspondence to Cowling,13, June 1921. CCA 58A.

36. Cowling correspondence to Sheldon, 16 June, 1921. CCA 58A.

37. Sheldon correspondence to Helming, 18 June, 1921. CCA 58A.

38. RKG, "Ages 20–40: What I Did With Those Years," FTL, Box 1.

39. RKG, "Narrative," FTL, Box 1.

40. RKG, "Journal, 1940–1943," Undated entry. FTL, Box 1.

41. RKG, "Ages 20–40: What I Did With Those Years," FTL, Box 1.

42. Ed Ouelette, Interview by the author and Anne Fraker, Evansville, Indiana, 19 June, 1996, RKGC.

43. RKG, "Ages 20–40: What I Did With Those Years," FTL, Box 1.

44. *The Algol*, 1925–1926, 75.

INTRODUCTION TO SEEKER SECTION

1. RKG, *Seeker and Servant: Reflections on Religious Leadership*, 288.

CHAPTER 7

1. RKG, *On Becoming a Servant Leader*, 235–236.

2. RKG, "Autobiography of an Idea," FTL, Box 1.

3. RKG, "Notes on Aspirations," FTL, Box 1.

4. RKG, "Autobiography of an Idea," FTL, Box 1.

5. RKG, "Ages 20–40: What I Did With Those Years," FTL, Box 1.

6. George Greenleaf correspondence to RKG, 3, December, 1926, Greenleaf family.

7. W. L. Eastman correspondence to RKG, 22 December 1926, Greenleaf family.

8. George Greenleaf correspondence to RKG, 3 December, 1926, Greenleaf family.

9. Greenleaf describes his first weeks at AT&T in various writings. This version was taken from RKG, *Ages 20–40: What I Did With Those Years*. FTL, Box 1.

10. *Ibid.*

11. *Ibid.*

12. RKG, Distefano interview, RKGC.

13. John Brooks, *Telephone: The First Hundred Years*. (New York: Harper & Row, 1976) 114.

14. *Ibid.*

15. *Ibid.*, 69.

16. *Ibid.*, 84.

17. *Ibid.*, 125.

18. Ibid., 131–132.

19. *Ibid.*, 135.

20. *Ibid.*, 136.

21. *Merriam Webster's Collegiate Dictionary*, 10th ed. (Springfield, MA, Merriam-Webster Inc., 1993), 267.

22. RKG, *On Becoming a Servant Leader*, 244.

23. RKG, Distefano interview, RKGC.,

24. *Ibid.*

25. RKG, *On Becoming a Servant Leader*, 239.

26. RKG, Distefano interview, RKGC.

27. *Ibid.*

28. RKG, "Autobiographical notes" 3 October, 1954. FTL, Box 1.

29. RKG, *On Becoming a Servant Leader*, 237.

30. RKG, "Ages 20–40: What I Did With Those Years" FTL, Box 1.

31. *Ibid.*

32. RKG, correspondence to Dr. Donald Cowling, 25 May, 1934. CCA, M-4.

CHAPTER 8

1. RKG, correspondence to Dr. Donald Cowling, 12 December, 1935. CCA, M-4.

2. John Brooks, *Telephone: The First Hundred Years* (New York: Harper & Row, 1976), 19–20.

A short portrait of Forbes and other AT&T board members appeared in September 30, 1930 issue of *Fortune* (Vol. 11, No. 3).

3. "World's Biggest Corporation," *Fortune*, 30 September, 1930, (Vol. 11, No. 3), 38.

4. John Kenneth Galbraith, *The Great Crash: 1929* (New York: Houghton Mifflin, 1955), 66.

5. *Ibid.*, 84.

6. David K. Fremon, *The Great Depression in American History* (Berkeley Heights, N.J.: Enslow Publishers, 1997), 5.

7. Galbraith, *op cit.*, 141–142.

8. Elizabeth (Lisa) Greenleaf-Miller interview by the author, New Haven, Connecticut, 17 December, 2000.

RKG's daughter Lisa says that "She [Esther] must have felt a mystical sense of destiny. She didn't say that but I think she must have felt that—a very strong feeling that this was it. And, if you could imagine the volcanic energy that existed between the two of them that played itself out in everything they did . . . well, the two of them could have taken on the world."

9. *Ibid.*

10. Newcomb Greenleaf, interview by the author, Indianapolis, Indiana, 4 June, 1997.

11. Lisa Greenleaf, interview by the author, New Haven, Connecticut, 17 December, 2000. "Mother was fairly close to her own mother, so it's likely her parents had advance warning of the wedding."

12. RKG, *My Life With Father*, 18.

13. Lhote often defended his ideas in *Nouvelle Revue Française*. Robert Rosenblum in his *Cubism and the Twentieth Century Art* has called Lhote "the official academician of Cubism," even though he disliked Lhote's "transformation of the intuitive classicism of Cubism into a system of stringent rules. . ." Robert

Rosenblum *Cubism and the Twentieth Century Art*. (New York: Harry N. Abrams, 1976), 182.

14. Lisa Greenleaf, interview by the author, New Haven, Connecticut, 17 December, 2000. The Mozart-Beethoven insight comes from daughter Lisa Greenleaf. "You know, she was a Libra, which is an air sign. She was Gemini rising, which is an air sign. And, her moon was Aquarius. So, she was up there. She was Mozartian. Very light; very light touch. But, she had her own defenses which were . . . very hard to get behind. . . .You could only tell something was going wrong by looking at her eyes. Bob's eyes were more from the Beethovian, dark side. More tumultuous, bringing stuff up out of the darkness."

15. *Ibid*.

16. *Ibid*.

17. RKG, "Open Discussion" with Dianne Bullard and Fred Meyers, 1986," RKGC, transcription 0550S.

18. *Ibid*.

19. Newcomb Greenleaf, interview by the author, Indianapolis, Indiana, 4 June, 1997.

20. Lisa Greenleaf, interview by the author, New Haven, Connecticut, 17 December, 2000.

21. Madeline Greenleaf Jaynes, interview by the author, New York, NY, 16 December, 2000.

22. Lisa Greenleaf, interview by the author, New Haven, Connecticut, 17 December, 2000.

23. RKG, Distefano interview, RKGC.

24. RKG, *My Debt to E. B. White* (The Robert K. Greenleaf Center for Servant Leadership, 1987), 5.

25. E. B. White, *Charlotte's Web* (New York: Harper & Row Publishers, 1952). Reprinted in RKG, *My Debt to E. B. White*, 22.

26. RKG, *My Debt to E. B. White*, 22.

27. E. B. White, "A Slight Sound at Evening," *Essays of E. B. White* (New York: Harper & Row, 1977). Reprinted in RKG, My *Debt to E. B. White*, 7.

28. RKG, Distefano interview, RKGC.

29. "Maitland Seminar Covers Life Styles, Social Changes," *Carletonian*, 25 September, 1969.

The group, officially called The Research and Development Seminar on Careers and Lifestyles, met twice daily from September 3–17 for two and a half hour sessions. Participants were requested to read several recommended books and pamphlets, watch ten films, and read twenty-six articles which were distributed in the course of the sessions. Greenleaf was one of four outside speakers who made presentations.

30. RKG, *My Debt to E. B. White*, 16.

31. "Maitland's Seminar Presents Manifesto," *Carletonian*, 30 October, 1969.

The "manifesto" had twelve points. Several insisted that college education be made more experiential, connecting classroom work to individual goals and the larger society. College dormitories should be remodeled to allow smaller living groups of true communities, and provide quarters for some faculty members to live in dorms. Evaluations should go beyond simple letter grades. Students should be allowed to customize their own majors, following departmental guidelines. An approved program could allow students to integrate their new learning by helping teach courses, and encourage upper classmen to assist as academic advisors to freshmen and sophomores. One of the more interesting suggestions was, "The freshman year must be viewed in terms of presenting the broadest disorientation from the basically anti-educational expectations of college life aroused by the American secondary school system."

Even though several recommendations were more trivial, like "College policies must allow for more spontaneity," the manifesto's statement of purpose reflects an overall vision of wholeness and service. "Carleton should exist less to equip students for a specific occupation than to develop a sense of their broader 'careers' in the world. The total Carleton experience should give graduates a sense of the basic worth and interdependence of human lives and the conviction that their self-interest necessarily encompasses the well-being of others. Yet, competition for individual success and the divorce of academic and non-academic life have become the staple of education at Carleton and throughout America today."

32. "Maitland Seminar Covers Life Styles, Social Changes," *Carletonian*, 25 September, 1969.

33. RKG, *My Debt to E. B. White*, 16.

34. E. B. White correspondence to RKG, 8 October, 1969, FTL. Bob sent a copy of his essay and White's response to several friends. In the margin, he wrote: "I am glad that I got it too him before his final illness hit him."

35. E. B. White correspondence to RKG, 22 April, 1984. FTL, Box 5.

36. Paul Sprecher, "John James Holmes," *Dictionary of Unitarian and Universalist Biography*, <http://www.uua.org/uuhs/duub/articles/johnhaynesholmes. html> (28 July, 2003).

The Unitarian and Universalist Biography project provides a concise Holmes biography. Holmes withdrew his ministerial membership in the American Unitarian Association in 1918 after the AUA voted to withhold financial support from any church whose minister opposed the war. Holmes then tried to withdraw his Church of the Messiah from the AUA. His congregation refused to withdraw affiliation with the AUA but did agree to change the name to the Community Church of New York. In many ways, the Community Church presaged today's non-denominational community church phenomenon. Holmes was also one of the first people to discover Mahatma Gandhi. In 1921 he preached a sermon about Gandhi titled, "The Greatest Man in the World."

37. In his essay *The Servant as Gradualist*, found in the book *Seeker and Servant: The Private Writings of Robert K. Greenleaf*, 67–68 Greenleaf writes, "I learned early to be a gradualist, and I was not aware that I was different from the norm. It was just my natural way of working . . . Gradualism, as I see it, is more a disposition than a method. One is comfortable with a slow pace and accepts taking opportunities

when they come, rather than trying to batter down offending walls that are not ready to give way."

38. Richard Wrightman Fox, "Reinhold Niebuhr's 'Revolution'," *The Wilson Quarterly*, Autumn, 1984.

Greenleaf's generation was described in Dr. Fox's article. "Born between the early years of the century and the end of World War I, that group was too young to have been demoralized by the disillusionment that followed the Treaty of Versailles. Many kept their hopeful assumptions about man and society. . ." The Depression caused grave doubts, but fascism, the Nazi-Soviet pact and World War II completed the disillusionment.

39. RKG, Distefano interview, RKGC.

40. *Ibid.*

41. RKG, "Open Discussion" interviews, RKGC, transcription 0550S.

42. In the Acknowledgement section of *Teacher as Servant* Greenleaf writes, "With gratitude for my mentors; those who, by their examples as servants and through their concern for my growth as a serving person, helped create this book." Mary Ellicott Arnold is listed first. See RKG, *Teacher as Servant*. (New York: Paulist Press, 1979), 7.

43. Rusty Neal. *Brotherhood Economics: Women and Co-operatives in Nova Scotia.* (Cape Breton: UCCB Press, 1998), 127.

44. See Mary Ellicott Arnold and Mabel Reed, *In the Land of the Grasshopper Song: Two Women in the Klamath River Indian Country in 1908–1909.* (Lincoln: University of Nebraska, 1980).

45. Rusty Neal, *op. cit.*, 127.

In 1928 Father Moses Michael Coady and Father J.J. ("Jimmy") Tompkins founded the Antigonish Cooperative Movement as an outgrowth of the Extension Department of St. Francis Xavier University. The Antigonish Movement combined adult education and economic development. Coady urged impoverished Nova Scotians to "Shape your own destiny!" He believed universities should go to the people and saw to it that St. Francis Xavier "generated materials and organizational structures oriented to the social and economic development of the exploited fishing, farming and industrial communities of the region." See: Daniel Schugurensky, "1928: University Extension for Social Change: The Antigonish Movement," *History of Education: Selected Moments of the 20th Century* <http://fcis.oise.utoronto.ca/~daniel_schugurensky/assignment1/1928antigonish.html> (27 July, 2003).

See also: Anne McDonald Alexander, *The Antigonish Movement: Moses Coady and Adult Education Today.* (Toronto: Thompson Educational Publishing, 1998).

46. Lisa Greenleaf, E-mail to author, 22, May, 2003.

47. Holger Begtrup, Hans Lund, Peter Manniche, *The Folk High Schools of Denmark and the Development of a Farming Community* (London, Oxford University Press, 1929), 3.

48. *Ibid.*, 25.

49. *Ibid.*, 78.

50. *Ibid.*, 81.

51. *Ibid.*

52. *Ibid.*, 82.

53. *Ibid.*, 84.

54. *Ibid.*, 85.

55. II Corinthians, 3:17.

56. Holger Begtrup, Hans Lund, Peter Manniche, *op. cit.*, 86.

57. RKG, *The Servant as Leader*, 24.

58. Holger Begtrup, Hans Lund, Peter Manniche, *op. cit.*, 100.

"[Grundtvig] believed that "the Spirit" was the moving power in all forms of life; but his conception of spirit was by no means narrow, and he spoke about natural law in human life in plain and direct terms. He always tried to speak to the very souls of his pupils, and the young people felt that his clear blue eyes penetrated into the depths of their inner life. He considered the acquisition of external knowledge as quite secondary, believing that a young man with an awakened and clarified inner life could easily acquire the information he needed in his daily occupation. The aim of the high-school was to approach the soul of the pupils through "the living word" and thus awaken a life which would never stop growing. Kold [one of the famous Folk High School teachers . . . ed.] said that his especial task was to enliven the young people rather than to enlighten them."

59. RKG, *The Servant as Leader*, 24.

60. John R. Barton, "How Danish Farmers Work Together," address given before a convocation of students at the University of Wisconsin, 12 December, 1934, FTL, Box 6.

61. In March 1936 Esther wrote an article titled "Let the Package Tell the Story" for *Consumers' Cooperation*, a national magazine for cooperative leaders. In May 1938 Greenleaf wrote an article for the same publication titled, "Cooperative Education in Sweden." Greenleaf's 1935 pamphlet, ghostwritten for Eugene R. Bowen, was titled "Sweden: Land of Economic Opportunity," and was published by *The Cooperative League, New York*. FTL, Box 16.

62. RKG correspondence to Dr. Donald Cowling, Dec. 12, 1935. CCA, M-4.

63. RKG, *Life's Choices and Markers* (Indianapolis: The Greenleaf Center for Servant Leadership, 1984), 4–5.

CHAPTER 9

1. RKG, *Journal*, 30 August, 1940. FTL, Box 1.

2. John Brooks, *Telephone: The First Hundred Years*, 190.

3. *Ibid.*, 188.

4. *Ibid.*, 191.

5. *Ibid.*, 192. John Brooks writes, "In a larger sense, the maintained dividend prepared the way for the future. By keeping faith with its stockholders in bad times, AT&T assured their loyalty in better times to come, and that loyalty, in the form of new investment, would translate into more and better telephone service. . . .

(The manner in which it was handled) led directly to the rise in the total of AT&T stockholders, in the years after World War II, to the previously unthinkable figure of three million."

6. RKG, "Open Discussion" interviews, RKGC, transcription 0550S.

7. Katherine M. H. Blackford, M.D. and Arthur Newcomb, *The Right Job: How to Choose It and Keep It*, Vol. I & II. (New York: The Reviews of Reviews Corporation, 1924), 62.

8. RKG discusses the Holmes course in his "Open Discussion" interviews, RKGC, transcription 0550S.

9. Whittier Merton Holmes, *Descriptive Mentality From the Head, Face, and Hand*. (Philadelphia: David McMay, 1899).

10. RKG, "Open Discussion," 16–17. RKGC.

11. See "A History of The Highlands Ability Battery," <http://www.high-landsco.com/about_history.php> (17 June, 2003). The Highlands Company (Atlanta and New York) is one of a number of contemporary companies that offer aptitude testing that traces origins to O'Connor's original work.

12. For more on Johnson O'Connor, see: George Wyatt, "Johnson O'Connor: A Portrait from Memory" on the Johnson O'Connor Research Foundation website: <www.jocrf.org.> (7 May, 2003). Wyatt's short portrait quotes an article by O'Connor called "Taking a Man's Measure" in the June, 1931 issue of *Atlantic Monthly* (page 12) which expressed a position on research with which Bob Greenleaf would have concurred. "The application of science to the study of man must be inspiring, not disheartening, strengthening, not weakening; must aim first to prove to each individual that he possesses a unique combination of abilities, one which the world has perhaps never seen before, and one which he can use to new purposes, to create new things, new thoughts; and, having convinced him of his own strengths, must then show him in what practical, concrete ways he can best use his particular combination of characteristics." A refined version of O'Connor's tests are still offered by the Johnson O'Connor Research Foundation, and have been taken by people as diverse as high school students, a future President of the United States, and G. Gordon Liddy.

13. RKG, "Open Discussion," RKGC, transcription 0427S.

14. RKG correspondence to Dr. Donald Cowling, 12 December, 1935. CCA, M-4.

15. *Ibid.*

16. *Ibid.*

17. RKG, correspondence to Donald Cowling, 12 December, 1935, FTL, Box 7.

18. *Ibid.*

19. RKG, *On Becoming a Servant Leader*, 181–182.

20. See Douglas McGregor's management classic, *The Human Side of Enterprise* (New York: McGraw Hill, 1960). McGregor described two contrasting theories of workers and management. Managers who hold to Theory X believe workers are essentially lazy and need to be closely monitored and motivated with rewards and punishments. In fact, in Theory X, workers prefer direction. Theory Y managers

believe that work holds—or could hold—intrinsic meaning for workers. Workers are capable of self-direction in pursuit of the company's goals, are more creative and intelligent than Theory X managers believe, capable of accepting responsibility and responding to intrinsic as well as extrinsic rewards.

Much of McGregor's thinking was based on Abraham Maslow's needs satisfaction model of human motivation, culminating in the "self-actualized" person. All the humanistic management thinkers of the 1950s and 1960s also owed a debt to the brilliant social psychologist Kurt Lewin.

21. RKG, *On Becoming a Servant Leader*, 181.

22. Rosabeth Moss Kanter, "Preface," *Mary Parker Follett—Prophet of Management*, ed. Pauline Graham (Boston: Harvard Business School Press, 1995), xiv.

In his Introduction to this book, a collection of Follett's writings from the 1920s, Peter Drucker lists four of her key contributions. (1) The use of "constructive conflict" to understand the other's view and make it work for both parties. (2) Management as a generic activity of all organizations, including government. (3) Management as a "function" not a "tool box." (4) ". . .nothing can work unless it is based on a functioning civil society—that is, on citizens and citizenship." (page 8) In that same book, Pauline Graham recasts Drucker's fourth point as a kind of self-governing principle that applies to business organizations as well as democratic government. "Follett was advocating the replacement of bureaucratic institutions by group networks in which the people themselves analyzed their problems and then produced and implemented their own solutions." (page 17) Mary Parker Follett died in 1933.

23. See Frederick Winslow Taylor, *The Principles of Scientific Management*. (New York: Harper & Brothers, 1911). For a friendly review of Taylor's work and impact written about the time Follett was making her mark in the business world, see Richard Feiss, "The Life of Frederick W. Taylor," *Harvard Business Review*, October 1924. Vol. III, Number 1, 86.

24. RKG, *Servant Leadership*, 257.

25. RKG correspondence to Dr. Donald Cowling, 25 May, 1934, CCA, M-4.

26. *Ibid.*

27. RKG, *Servant Leadership*, 258.

28. RKG correspondence to Dr. Donald Cowling, May 25, 1934. CCA, M-4.

29. Dr. Donald Cowling correspondence with RKG, 15 November, 1934, CCA, M-4.

30. RKG correspondence to Dr. Donald Cowling, 10 December, 1934, CCA, M-4.

31. *Ibid.*

32. Internal correspondence from Lindsey Blaynay, Dean of the College, to Dr. Cowling, 9 January, 1935, CCA, M-4.

33. Internal correspondence from Leal A. Headley to President Donald Cowling, 2 November, 1935, CCA, M-4.

34. RKG correspondence to Dr. Donald Cowling, 12 December, 1935, CCA, M-4.

35. *Ibid.*

At the end of this expansive letter, Greenleaf summarized his points in a long paragraph which uses more abstract language than much of the letter: "Gradually shift the administrative emphasis from the formal curriculum to the important aspects of the program which are outside of the curriculum. Gradually lessen the requirements for formal classroom study and diminish, wherever possible, the stress upon false incentives. Extend the activity of the college to a wider sphere of influence and bring more of the broader community interests to the campus. Provide a dynamic and continuous educational leadership and leaven the faculty and the student body with a wider diversity of experience. Subordinate scholarship and academic attainment to the development of a well rounded personality. Through informal conferences with faculty members, bring them into closer relationship with community problems. Slowly but positively work for the development of a pervasive and dynamic spirit of adventure and conquest into new frontiers. So interweave the life on the campus with the life of the community that the distinction of the college on the hill will melt away and so that the aristocracy of formal learning will be transformed into a more democratic relationship with the common knowledge of the community."

36. All quotes are from RKG's correspondence to Dr. Donald Cowling, 12 December, 1935, CCA, M-4.

37. RKG, "Journal, 1940–1943," undated entry, FTL, Box 1.

38. RKG, *Servant Leadership*, 259–260.

39. RKG, *Servant Leadership*, 255.

40. RKG, "Ages 40–60: What I Did With Those Years," FTL, Box 1.

41. *Ibid.*

42. Madeline Greenleaf Jaynes, interview by the author, New York, NY, 15 December, 2000.

43. RKG, "Open Discussion" interviews, RKGC transcription 0550S.

44. Lisa Greenleaf, interview with author, 16 December, 2000.

45. RKG, "Open Discussion" interviews, RKGC, transcription 0550S, 19.

CHAPTER 10

1. RKG, "Untitled on Society of Friends," FTL, Box 11.

2. "Biographical Sketch of L Hollingsworth Wood." L Hollingsworth Wood Papers, 1903–1953. Haverford College Archives.

3. RKG. Untitled on Society of Friends. RKG Archives, Box 14, Folder 7.

4. William C. Braithwaite, *The Beginnings of Quakerism* (Cambridge, MA, Cambridge at the University Press, 1955), 2.

5. *Ibid.*, 30.

6. Elizabeth Braithwaite Emmott, *The Story of Quakerism.* (London: Headley Brothers, 1932), 15.

7. *Ibid.*, 16.

8. Braithwaite, *op. cit.*, 32.

9. George Fox, from his *Journal*, i, 8, as quoted in Braithwaite, 34.

10. *Ibid.*, 36.

11. Emmott, *op. cit.*, 125.

12. Braithwaite, *op. cit.*, 139.

13. Rufus Jones, *The Faith and Practice of the Quakers* (London: Methuen & Co., 1949), 31.

14. *Ibid.*, 34–35.

15. B. A. Robinson, (2002) "Religious Society of Friends." <http://www.religioustolerance.org/quaker.htm> (7 March, 2003).

16. Braithwaite, *op. cit.*, 26.

17. Emmott, *op. cit.*, 86.

18. RKG, *Seeker and Servant*, 77.

19. "Approaches to God: Worship and Prayer," *Quaker Faith & Practice* (London: The Yearly Meeting of the Religious Society of Friends (Quakers) in Britain, 1995), paragraph 2.89, <http://www.qnorvic.com/quaker/qfp/QF&P_02.html> (19 January, 2003).

20. RKG, *Seeker and Servant*, 77.

21. *Ibid.*, 77–78.

22. John Woolman, *The Journal of John Woolman and a Plea for the Poor* (New York: Corinth Books, 1961), 15. This is a reprint of the John Greenleaf Whittier Edition Text which was originally published in 1871. The First Edition of Woolman's *Journal* was published in 1774.

23. Frederick B. Tolles, "Introduction," *The Journal of John Woolman and a Plea for the Poor*, vii–viii.

24. John Woolman, *Journal*, 22.

25. *Ibid.*, 26.

26. RKG, *Seeker and Servant*, 26.

27. John Woolman, *Journal*, 50.

28. *Ibid.*, 52.

29. Frederick B. Tolles, "Introduction," *The Journal of John Woolman and a Plea for the Poor*, viii.

30. RKG, *The Servant as Leader*, 12–13.

31. RKG, "Open Discussion" interviews, RKGC, transcription 0550S.

32. RKG, *Servant Leadership*, 81–82.

33. Newcomb Greenleaf, interview by the author, Indianapolis, Indiana, 4 June, 1997.

34. A short biography of John Lovejoy Elliot can be found on the website of the American Ethical Union, <http://www.ethicalculture.org/neac/elliott-black/ebalist.html> (17 March, 2003).

35. RKG, Distefano Interview, RKGC.

36. RKG, correspondence with Terri Thal, 19 September, 1967. FTL, Box 2.

37. *Ibid.*, 13–14.

38. John Lovejoy Elliott, "Spiritual Discoveries," in *The Fiftieth Anniversary of the Ethical Movement 1876–1926*. Can be accessed online at the American Ethical

Union website, <http://www.ethicalculture.org/uer/elliott1.html> (3 April, 2003).

39. Greenleaf's "best test" for a servant-leader is found in the 1970 essay *The Servant as Leader*, which is also the first chapter of the 1977 book *Servant Leadership*. "The best test, and difficult to administer, is: Do those served grow as persons? Do they, *while being served*, become healthier, wiser, freer, more autonomous, more likely themselves to become servants? *And*, what is the effect on the least privileged in society; will they benefit, or, at least, not be further deprived?" RKG, *Servant Leadership*, 13–14.

40. Felix Adler, "An Address by Dr. Felix Adler, May 10, 1931, On the Occasion of the Fifty-Fifth Anniversary of the founding of the Ethical Movement," can be accessed online at the American Ethical Union website < http://www.aeu.org/adler4.htm> (9 January, 2003).

41. RKG, *Journal, 1940–1943*, 3 August, 1941. FTL, Box 1.

42. *Ibid.*, 31 August, 1940.

43. RKG, "Open Discussion" interviews, RKGC, transcription 0550S.

44. Newcomb Greenleaf, E-mail to the author, 29 May, 2003.

45. Newcomb Greenleaf, interview by the author, Indianapolis, Indiana, 4 June, 1997.

CHAPTER 11

1. RKG, *On Becoming a Servant Leader*, 36.

2. RKG, "Open Discussion" interviews, RKGC, transcription 0550S.

3. RKG, "Journal, 1940–1943," 2 September, 1941. FTL, Box 1.

4. RKG, "Open Discussion" interviews, RKGC, transcription 0550S.

5. RKG, "Open Discussion" interviews, RKGC, transcription 0436S.

6. *Ibid.*, 2–3.

7. RKG, *On Becoming a Servant Leader*, 129.

8. RKG, "Open Discussion" interviews, RKGC, transcription 0427S.

9. United States Department of Agriculture. "Honey Bees." <http://gears.tucson.ars.ag.gov/beebook/sec1/sec1.html> (10 June, 2003).

10. RKG, *On Becoming a Servant Leader*, 11.

11. Newcomb Greenleaf interview by the author, Indianapolis, Indiana, 6 June, 2003.

12. RKG. *On Becoming a Servant Leader*, 32–33.

13. *Ibid.*, 36–37.

14. *Ibid.*, 37.

15. *Ibid.*, 38.

16. *Ibid.*, 38–39.

17. RKG, *Life's Choices and Markers* (Indianapolis: The Robert K. Greenleaf Center, 1984), 5–6.

This pamphlet is a reprint of a commencement address given via videotape to graduates of Alverno College in Milwaukee in the spring of 1984.

18. Even though Greenleaf often repeated the story of the impact Davis's article had on him "around the age of forty," the evidence is solid that he did not read the piece until 1953. First, Elmer Davis was Director of the Office of War Information (OWI) from 1941 to 1945. (Bob's fortieth year was in 1944.) Davis still made occasional radio addresses, but his main job was to coordinate information given out to the public. Second, in one description of Davis's article, Bob mentioned that Davis was in his sixties at the time and was having health problems. Elmer Davis was sixty years old in 1950, and began showing health problems in the next few years.

Davis did write an article called "Grandeurs and Miseries of Old Age" in the July 1953 issue of *Harper's Magazine*, which was reprinted in the 1954 book *But We Were Born Free*. Davis called the piece an "annoyed reaction" to a previous *Harper's* article that was a "well-intended, but in my opinion fallacious, endeavor to persuade people who are getting older that all is for the best in the best of all possible worlds. I wish it were." The article he was responding to was titled "The Magnificence of Age" by Catherine Drinker Bowen, which appeared in the April 1953 issue of *Harper's*. In it, Bowen wrote about the astounding elderly people she met in the course of researching *Yankee From Olympus*, her biography of Justice Oliver Wendell Homes. Davis did accurately quote Bowen's line that "luck being equal, whether a man at eighty finds himself reaping the harvest or the whirlwind depends on how he has spent his forties and thirties and twenties" but went on to say that "luck is not equal," but Davis's piece was much darker than Bob remembered.

Bowen's article, on the other hand, was right down Bob's alley. She quoted Goethe, "The youth had best take care of what he desires, for in old age he shall have it," and finally, this: "But of all Holmes's eloquent sayings, the one I like best was written at eighty-three in a letter to a young Chinese law student in Washington named Wu: 'If I were dying my last words would be: 'Have faith and pursue the unknown end.' No young person could have said that."

19. RKG, "Open Discussion" interviews, RKGC, transcription 0550S.

CHAPTER 12

1. RKG, *On Becoming a Servant Leader*, 215–216.

2. "A Good Man is Hard to Find," *Fortune*, March 1946, Vol. XXXIII, no 1, 92. See also the OSS's own version of how their assessment program started: The OSS Assessment Staff, *Assessment of Men: Selection of Personnel for the Office of Strategic Services* (New York: Rinehart & Company, Inc., 1948), 3.

Even though the OSS developed its own procedures for assessment, their staff reported that the overall methods "were first used on a large scale by Simoneit, as described in *Wehrpsychologie*, and the German military psychologists, and after them by the British."

3. *Ibid.*, 13.

Although the commander wrote the memo after the assessment unit began operation, the people he referred to had not gone through OSS assessment.

4. *Fortune, op. cit.*, 92.

5. *Ibid.*, 93.

6. *Ibid.*, 3.

7. *Ibid.*, 8.

8. The various tests—and ruses—used with recruits are described in detail in *Assessment of Men*, but Greenleaf specifically mentioned the OSS's calculated effort to get people drunk in his videotape *Assessment*, (Indianapolis, Robert K. Greenleaf Center, 1986).

9. OSS Assessment Staff, *Assessment of Men: Selection of Personnel for the Offices of Strategic Services* (New York: Rineheart & Co., 1948), 451.

10. RKG, *Assessment* videotape. RKGC.

11. Harold P. Mold, "An Executive Development Program." *Personnel Journal*, May, 1948. Vol. 28, No. 1.

12. *Ibid.*, 3.

13. In *Telephone, The First Hundred Years*, author John Brooks called president Leroy Wilson "a rate-getter through negotiations with regulatory agencies . . . Within the company, Wilson was known as a driving nonstop worker with a strong strain of abrasiveness and ruthlessness. Slick-haired, and handsome in a forceful way, he was widely known to lead a chaotic life . . .," 230.

14. RKG, *Assessment* videotape, RKGC.

15. Douglas Bray, *Formative Years in Business: A Long-Term AT&T Study of Managerial Lives* (Melbourne, FL: Krieger Publishing Company, 1974), 59.

16. Newcomb Greenleaf, "Reflections on Robert K. Greenleaf," *Reflections on Leadership*, 318–319.

17. J. F. Parrish, "Acknowledgment," *Management Ability* (Pacific Telephone, no date of publication), RKGC Archives, Joseph Distefano Collection.

18. RKG, *Management Ability*, 2.

19. *Ibid.*, 4–25.

20. J. F. Parrish, June 17, 1970 correspondence with RKG. FTL, Box 2.

21. G. T. Bowden and R. K. Greenleaf, *Bell Humanities Program*. (Indianapolis: The Robert K. Greenleaf Center), 4. No date is given in the pamphlet, but it was originally published in the 1980s by the Greenleaf Center when it was located in Newton Centre, MA. *Bell Humanities Program* is, in turn, a reprint of a paper co-authored by Bowden (who was Greenleaf's colleague in AT&T's Personnel Relations department) and Greenleaf titled, "The Study of the Humanities as an Approach to Executive Development," AT&T, Corporate Collection, 140 10 01.

Chester Barnard went on to become president of New Jersey Bell Telephone in 1927. In 1948 he retired from AT&T to become president of the Rockefeller Foundation. He lectured frequently at Harvard Business School and wrote two important books, *The Functions of the Executive* and *Organization and Management*. In *Bell Humanities Program* (pp. 4–5) Greenleaf wrote about Barnard, "One wonders now, considering the range and magnitude of the major policy questions confronting the Bell System in his time, why a person of Mr. Barnard's intellectual stature was not brought into one of the key vice presidencies of AT&T where his imagination and conceptual powers might have contributed greatly to the advancement of the whole System."

22. G. T. Bowden and R. K. Greenleaf, *Bell Humanities Program*, 5.

23. Peter Siegle, *New Directions in Liberal Education for Executives*. (Chicago: Center for the Study of Liberal Education for Adults, c. 1958), AT&T, C. 127 05 02, L. 79.

24. G. T. Bowden and R. K. Greenleaf, *Bell Humanities Program*, 19.

25. *Ibid.*, 1–2.

26. Peter Siegle, *op. cit.* 9–10. Mr. Markle's remarks were quoted from "How Can We Broaden the Telephone Man's Horizon?" *Bell Telephone Magazine*, Autumn, 1955.

27. G. T. Bowden and R. K. Greenleaf, *op. cit.*, 18.

28. Douglas Williams Associates, "Summary: Interview Study of Northwestern Program," 1957. AT&T, C. 127 05 02, L. 79.

29. RKG, "Open Discussion" interviews, RKGC, transcription 0467S.

30. Douglas Williams, correspondence with Anne Fraker, 16 November, 1992. RKGC.

31. *Ibid.*

32. G. T. Bowden and R. K. Greenleaf, *op. cit.*, 25.

33. Cleo F. Craig "Big Business and the Community." This speech was ghost-written by Robert Greenleaf and delivered at the Annual Meeting of the Life Insurance Association of America, New York, December 8, 1954. It was reproduced in a Bell System pamphlet titled *Big Business and the Community*, 1954. AT&T, Corporate Collection, 127 04 01.

34. "Bell Systems Executive Conference, 1955–1956–1957," a 1957 AT&T internal report, AT&T, Corporate Collection, 141 08 02.

35. *Ibid.*

36. *Ibid.*, 26.

37. Douglas Bray and Ann Howard, *Managerial Lives in Transition: Advancing Age and Changing Times* (New York: Guildford Press, 1988), x.

38. Douglas Bray gives a brief history of his early experiences at AT&T, in the article "Centered on Assessment," found on the website of The International Congress on Assessment Center Methods, <http://www.assessmentcenters.org/pages/centeredonassess.html> (13 July, 2003).

39. The Management Progress Studies variables were fully evaluated at the initial assessment then again eight and twenty years later. The variables, as reported in *Formative Years in Business* (18–20) included:

1. Scholastic Aptitude
2. Oral Communication Skill
3. Human Relations Skills
4. Personal Impact
5. Perception of Threshold Social Cues
6. Creativity

7. Self-Objectivity

8. Social Objectivity

9. Behavior Flexibility

10. Need Approval of Superiors

11. Need Approval of Peers

12. Inner Work Standards

13. Need Advancement

14. Need Security

15. Goal Flexibility

16. Primacy of Work

17. Bell System Value Orientation

18. Realism of Expectations

19. Tolerance of Uncertainty

20. Ability to Delay Gratification

21. Resistance to Stress

22. Range of Interests

23. Energy

24. Organization and Planning

25. Decision Making

Dr. Bray's longitudinal research lasted twenty-five years. Along the way he published several monographs about the work at AT&T. In 1974 his landmark book *Formative Years in Business: A Long-Term A.T. and T. Study of Managerial Lives* was released, summarizing decades of findings. In 1970, he co-founded Development Dimensions International to market assessment center materials. In 1988 Dr. Bray also co-authored with Ann Howard *Managerial Lives in Transition: Advancing Age and Changing Times*. In 1991 his book *Working with Organizations and Their People: A Guide to Human Resources Practice* (New York: Guilford Press) was released. As of 2003 he was Chairman of the Board Emeritus for Development Dimensions International.

40. RKG Videotape, *Assessment*, RKGC.

41. Douglas Bray, telephone interview by the author, July 10, 2003.

42. In Chapter 8 of *Formative Years in Business*, Bray and his co-authors summarized nine dimensions which emerged from the MPS study: Occupational, Ego Functional, Financial-Acquisitive, Locale-Residential, Marital-Familial, Parental-Familial, Recreational-Social, Religious-Humanism, and Service. These, in turn, were correlated to describe two emerging "life themes," Enlargers and Enfolders.

For a more detailed account of Greenleaf's contributions to assessment work, see "The Assessment Legacy of Robert Greenleaf," an essay by Jeff McCollum and Joel Moses available from the Greenleaf Center in Indianapolis.

43. G. A. Pennock, "Industrial Research at Hawthorne," *Personnel Journal*, Vol. VII, No. 5, April, 1930, 299.

44. *Ibid.*, 311.

45. Walter V. Bingham, "Management's Concern with Personnel in Industrial Psychology," *Harvard Business Review*, October 1931, Vol. X, No. 1.

46. Ongoing findings from the Hawthorne studies were published in journals beginning in the late 1920s, but the 1939 publication of *Management and the Worker* (Cambridge, MA: Harvard University Press) by Fritz J. Roethlisberger and William J. Dickson brought widespread attention.

47. To be fair, researchers since the Hawthorne studies have reevaluated a number of original conclusions. For example, in 1978, R. H. Franke, & J. D. Kaul, J.D. published "The Hawthorne experiments: First statistical interpretation" in *American Sociological Review* and concluded that replacing mediocre workers with more disciplined and productive ones, and factoring in the pressure to keep one's job because of the Depression during the experiments accounted for the majority of variation. "Social science may have been too ready to embrace the original Hawthorne interpretations since it was looking for theories or work motivation that were more humane and democratic," say Franke and Kaul (42, 623–643). Other researchers have noted that increased productivity due to the "Hawthorne Effect" subsides when the novelty wears off. See also Henry A. Landsberger's 1958 book *Hawthorne revisited. Management and the Worker: its critics, and developments in human relations in industry.* (Ithaca, N. Y., Cornell University).

48. William J. Dickson & F.J. Roethlisberger. *Management and the Worker*, 596–597.

49. *Ibid.*, 591.

50. *Ibid.*, 599. Roethlisberger and Dickson note that the counselor "stands outside of the network of relations in which the individual supervisor or worker spends his working days. He can thus look at this system of relations objectively, and he is in a good position to see the various problems arising in these relations and ways in which they may be remedied." (p. 601) On the following page, they also describe the counselor as a kind of social historian.

51. RKG. *The Servant as Leader*, 10.

52. Greenleaf made these comments in his essay "Growth Through Groups," which he wrote for the *Receptive Listening Course Leadership Manual.* Bob and Esther helped develop the course for the Wainwright House in Rye, New York in the early 1950s.

53. William J. Dickson & F.J. Roethlisberger. *Management and the Worker*, 598. The history of the counseling experience is recounted in Roethlisberger and Dickson's 1966 book *Counseling in an Organization: A Sequel to the Hawthorne Researches.* (Boston, Division of Research, Graduate School of Business Administration, Harvard University). The number of counselors mentioned in the book was quoted by MIT Chairman Howard W. Johnson who reviewed the Hawthorne studies in a paper titled "The Hawthorne Studies: The Legend and the Legacy" at the symposium, *Man and Work in Society* on the fiftieth anniversary of the Hawthorne studies, November 12, 1974. Greenleaf, an old friend of Johnson's, told Fred Myers and Diane Cory that he wrote the address for Johnson and it was delivered unchanged. "Open Discussion" interviews, RKGC, transcription 0443S.

54. Howard W. Johnson, "The Hawthorne Studies: The Legend and the Legacy." FTL, Box 16.

55. F. J. Roethlisberger, *Management and Morale* (Cambridge, MA: Harvard University Press, 1941), 8.

56. *Ibid.*, 11.

57. RKG, "Human Relations Research in the Bell System: Talk before Field Study Group of School Administrators" was given at the AT&T New York headquarters, 20 February, 1948. RKGC Archives, Joseph Distefano Collection.

58. *Ibid.*

59. *Ibid.*

60. *Ibid.*

61. Michael Quinn Patton, *Utilization-Focused Evaluation*, 3rd ed. (Thousand Oaks, CA: SAGE Publications, 1997), 22.

Supporting Dr. Patton's conclusion is another vivid example of participatory research leading to wide acceptance of results, one with which the author is personally familiar. Years ago a major plant and animal products company was in the final stages of testing a revolutionary new herbicide. The small, controlled scientific studies were completed but larger trials were necessary. One employee had the idea of teaching growers (farmers) enough about scientific observation and record-keeping to prove the efficacy—or failure—of the product. Bucking broad opposition from his own company's scientists who believed growers were not up to the task, he enlisted farmers around the country to try the product and trained them to keep careful records, which they did with meticulous detail.

The product was successful in widespread trials and researcher-growers were pleased to participate in ad campaigns which touted the effects of the herbicide, *and* the fact that they—ordinary farmers—had helped prove those effects in legitimate scientific trials. The herbicide quickly became the top-selling product in its category but many of the company's internal researchers never forgave the employee who made it all happen. He did not have a Bob Greenleaf at the higher levels to support his approach. His career was stifled and never recovered.

62. RKG, *On Becoming a Servant Leader*, 214.

In this chapter, Greenleaf describes in some detail his justification and protocol for a two-person research team approach to research.

63. *Ibid.*, 208.

64. *Ibid.*

65. *Ibid.*, 214–215.

66. "Bell Labs: More Than 50 Years of the Transistor," Lucent Technology website: <http://www.lucent.com/minds/transistor/> (4 February, 2003).

See also <http://www.bell-labs.com/history>.

67. There are several good histories of Bell Labs, but Bob personally knew the many of the early employees and got a first-hand account of its founding. Like so many enduring efforts within AT&T, it all started with Theodore Vail. In 1986, Bob told his version of the story.

Once Vail had taken over, he had a census made of all the people who were tinkering with the system. It was a very poorly working system, and there were people around who were just tinkering with it. He had a census made of these people and found he had five-hundred-fifty of them scattered all over the business. So, he made a very radical move. He brought these people all together in one place and we had the first Bell Laboratories. At first, it was first just part of Western Electric, and I think it was in Chicago or Hawthorne. (RKG, "Open Discussion" interviews, RKGC, transcription 0427S.

In 1926, on the fiftieth anniversary of the invention of the telephone, each of the original five-hundred members of the Bell Labs' staff was given a replica of the first Bell Telephone. One of them was a man who later became Bob's boss and when he died, his widow gave the phone to Bob. One day Bob and Newcomb hooked it up and it still worked. It was one of Bob's prized possessions.

68. Newcomb Greenleaf, interview by the author, 7 June, 2003.

CHAPTER 13

1. RKG, "Hole in the Hedge" notes dated October 3, 1954. Later in the document Greenleaf indicates these are notes for a spiritual biography. FTL, Box 1.

2. Douglas Williams correspondence to Anne Fraker, 16 November, 1992. RKGC Archives.

3. Newcomb Greenleaf, interview by the author, Indianapolis, Indiana, 4 June, 1997.

4. Douglas Williams correspondence to Anne Fraker.

5. RKG, "Open Discussion" interviews. RKGC, tape 5 of 8 (no transcription number given).

6. RKG note dated 3 October, 1954, FTL, Box 1.

7. Douglas Williams correspondence to Anne Fraker, 16 November, 1992, RKGC.

8. RKG, "Open Discussion" interviews, RKGC, transcription 0427S.

9. RKG, "Age 40–60: What I Did With Those Years," FTL, Box 1.

10. "PROCEEDINGS: The Third Air Staff Management Development Conference 26 March 1953, The Pentagon." RKGC Archives, Center for Executive Development Collection.

11. RKG, "Age 40–60: What I Did With Those Years," FTL, Box 1.

12. Miriam Lewin, "Kurt Lewin: Social Psychologist," *Lewin's Legacy/Lewin's Potential: Next Step for Group Process, Consultation and Social Justice: A Source Book* (Alexandria, VA: NTL Institute), 9–10. This collection of essays is based on an NTL 50th Anniversary Event in Bethel, Maine, July 7–9, 1997. NTL.

13. *Ibid.*, 11–12.

14. Roger Evered, "An Exploration of the Origins of Lewinian Science," *Lewin's Legacy/Lewin's Potential*, 46.

15. *Ibid.*, 42.

Evered goes on to write: "Alfred Marrow, a close personal friend of Lewin for the last 13 years of Lewin's life, sums up Lewin with these words. 'Perhaps the word that describes Lewin more realistically than any other is playful—in the most significant sense of the word. That is, work was most fun for him when it was hardest. He had a zest for searching and seeking—working a problem this way, working it that way, turning it upside down, inside out, left to right, right to left. He communicated a sense of enjoyment, in the spirit of one wanting to share his play with others."

16. Henry W. Riecken, "Theory-Based Practice in Human Relations: Two Lewinian Concepts," *Lewin's Legacy/Lewin's Potential*, 212.

17. RKG, Distefano interview, RKGC.

18. The author well remembers his first T-Group experience his first year of graduate school in 1968. I was placed in the group with no knowledge of T-Groups, their history or purpose. In the first session, group members sat silent for ten minutes. Finally, I could stand it no longer. "Why are you doing this to us?!!" I blurted out, even though the trainer had "done" nothing. I learned that inauthentic and habitual behaviors, suppressed emotions and prejudices soon saw the light of day in an intense T-Group experience.

19. RKG, Distefano Interview, RKGC.

20. William B. Wolf, "The Enigma of Kurt Lewin's Impact on Management, Management Consulting and O.D." *Lewin's Legacy/Lewin's Potential*, 443.

21. RKG, "Age 40–60: What I Did With Those Years," FTL, Box 1.

22. *Ibid.*

Others learned from the T-Group experience too. Even though the movement spurred increased understanding of group formation and team-building, all the effects were not constructive. For example, T-Groups sometimes encouraged a level of disclosure which was inappropriate for work settings. When participants were ordered to participate, they were less likely to experience positive changes than when the motivation was intrinsic. Finally, T-Groups could be very effective in encouraging emotional expression and battering down personal defenses but not so helpful in the long-term process of rebuilding one's psyche. Many of the learnings from T-Groups were incorporated into the emerging field of Organizational Development, where they were used to address more traditional business needs of meeting goals and objectives and building purposeful teams.

23. The most recent edition of *Science and Sanity: An Introduction to Non-Aristotelian Systems and General Semantics* (5th Edition, 1995) is published and distributed by the Institute of General Semantics, Brooklyn New York. In 2001 IGS also released the 2nd Edition of Korzybski's 1921 book, *Manhood of Humanity: The Science and Art of Human Engineering*.

24. For an excellent short article on the basics of Korzybski's thought, see "General Semantics: An Introduction to non-Aristotelian Systems" on the website of the Institute of General Semantics: <http://www.general-semantics.org/Institute/AK_intro.shtml> (5 November, 2002).

25. RKG. Distefano interview, RKGC.

One can speculate on reasons why Greenleaf did not personally "connect" with Korzybski, but it is possible that he had some disagreement with Korzybski's thought. Bob, the person who wrote, "Not much happens without a dream," believed in the power of imaginal language. Furthermore, he learned from George

Greenleaf that "keeping your word" was synonymous with personal integrity—which meant that language *about* oneself and the reality *of* oneself were identical in that instance.

26. RKG "Hole in the Hedge," FTL, Box 1.

27. *Ibid.*

28. *Ibid.*

29. RKG, "Age 40–60: What I Did With Those Years," FTL, Box 1.

30. James R. Newby, *Elton Trueblood: Believer, Teacher, and Friend* (San Francisco: Harper & Row, 1990), 68.

Newby writes, "[*The Predicament of Modern Man*] had the enthusiastic support of Reinhold Niebuhr who called it 'an able and profound analysis of the spiritual situation of our time.' Norman Vincent Peale wrote, 'A powerful book. One hundred and five pocket sized pages of common sense. Convincingly shows that only the gospel can save our decaying society.'"

31. *Ibid.*, 69.

32. D. Elton Trueblood, *While It Is Day: An Autobiography* (New York: Harper & Row, 1974), 69.

33. "Facilities," website of Wainwright House, <http://www.wainwright. org/facilities.htm> (19 July, 2003).

34. RKG "Hole in the Hedge," FTL, Box 1.

35. D. Elton Trueblood, *While It Is Day: An Autobiography,* 105–107.

36. James R. Newby, *op. cit.,* 89.

37. D. Elton Trueblood, *Alternative to Futility* (New York: Harper & Row, 1949), 73.

38. James R. Newby, *op. cit.,* 90–91.

39. D. Elton Trueblood (1974) *While It Is Day: An Autobiography*, 108–109.

40. *Ibid.*, 114–116.

41. *Ibid.*, 113.

42. *Ibid.*, 116–117.

43. Jim Beier, Director of Institute for Executive Growth Director, correspondence to Larry Spears, 19 June, 2000, RKGC, Executive Training Program Collection.

44. RKG, "Memorandum, Proposed Management Development Program at Earlham College," 1954. RKGC, Executive Training Program Collection.

45. Robert N. Huff, correspondence to Robert K. Greenleaf, March 5, 1954. RKGC, Executive Training Program Collection.

46. "Management Training, Schedule for Visiting Lecturers," Memo to RKG from Earlham College, 1954–1955. RKGC Executive Training Program Collection.

47. James Beier, "The Earlham Institute for Executive Growth," *The Earlhamite,* July 1967, 18.

48. "Facilities," website of Wainwright House, <http://www.wainwright. org/facilities.htm> (22 July, 2003).

49. RKG, "Open Discussion" interviews, RKGC, transcription 0427S.

50. *Ibid.*

51. RKG, "Some Rough Notes on Growth Through Groups," *Receptive Listening Course Leadership Manual.* (Rye, New York: Wainwright House) Unpublished document. There were several versions of the Leadership Manual and this was not the first. The most recent books and articles quoted in this version date to 1957. RKGC.

52. *Ibid.*

53. *Ibid.*

54. *Ibid.* Even though Esther Greenleaf's name does not appear as the author of the article which describes the purpose of creative art activities in the manual, in private interviews—especially "Open Discussion"—Bob acknowledged her full participation. Apparently they wrote these pieces together.

55. Paolo J. Knill and Helen Nienhaus Barba and Margo N. Fuchs, *Minstrels of Soul: Intermodal Expressive Therapy* (Toronto: Palmerston Press, 1995), 140.

56. RKG, "Age 40–60: What I Did With Those Years," FTL, Box 1.

57. *Ibid.*

58. *Ibid.*

59. *Ibid.*

60. Mitchell K., "Self Supporting," part of a series of short articles about the history of Alcoholics Anonymous on the about.com website: <http://alcoholism.about.com/library/blmitch10.htm> (23 July, 2003).

61. *Alcoholics Anonymous*, 2nd ed. (New York: Alcoholics Anonymous World Services, Inc., 1955), 568. This is the famous "Big Book," the basic text for AA.

62. *Ibid.*, 567.

63. RKG, *Servant Leadership*, 221.

64. RKG, "Age 40–60: What I Did With Those Years," FTL, Box 1.

65. RKG, "Open Discussion" interviews, RKGC.

66. RKG, transcript of audiotaped conversation with Gerald Heard, dated 1958, RKGC.

67. RKG "Age 40–60: What I Did With Those Years," FTL, Box 1.

68. See Laurens van der Post. *A Mantis Carol* (New York: Morrow, 1976).

69. See Laurens van der Post *The Voice of the Thunder*, 1993. Also: Laurens van der Post, *A Walk With A White Bushman: In conversation with Jean-Marc Pottiez* (New York: William Morrow 1986).

70. Margaret Wheatley, address at the 1999 International Conference on Servant Leadership. RKGC Archives.

71. "Menninger develops management, leadership innovations," *Important Dates and Achievements*, <http://www.menningerclinic.com/about/history.html.> (1, November, 2003).

72. RKG autobiographical notes. "Age 40–60: What I Did With Those Years," FTL, Box 1.

73. *Ibid.*

74. *Ibid.*

75. *Ibid.*

76. William Wolf contributed to the book *Rhythmic Functions in the Living System.* (New York: New York Academy of Sciences, 1962). His endocrinology

textbook was *Endocrinology in Modern Practice Edition*, 2d ed. (Philadelphia: W. B. Saunders Company, 1939).

77. RKG, "Age 40–60: What I Did With Those Years," FTL Box 1.

78. RKG, "Notes Greenleaf made on talks by Dr. William Wolf." FTL, Box 12.

79. At the time Greenleaf met him, Heschel had already published dozens of German articles in various languages and several books which were reaching an English-speaking audience beyond the Jewish community. They included: Heschel, Abraham Joshua. *The Earth is the Lord's: The Inner World of the Jew in East Europe* (NY: H. Schuman, 1950).

_____. *The Sabbath: Its Meaning for Modern Man* (NY: Farrar, Straus & Giroux, 1952).

_____. *Man is Not Alone: A Philosophy of Religion* (NY: Farrar, Straus & Giroux, 1951).

_____. *Man's Quest for God: Studies in Prayer & Symbolism* (NY: Scribner, 1954).

_____. *God in Search of Man: A Philosophy of Judaism* (NY: Jewish Publication Society of America, 1955).

80. Edward K. Kaplan and Samuel H. Dresner, *Abraham Joshua Heschel: Prophetic Witness* (New Haven: Yale University Press, 1998). ix.

81. *Ibid.*, 47.

82. RKG, *Servant Leadership*, 254.

83. Abraham Joshua Heschel, *The Earth is the Lord's: The Inner World of the Jew in East Europe* (New York: H. Schuman, 1950), 28.

84. Kaplan and Dresner, *op. cit.*, 160.

85. Abraham Joshua Heschel, Quoted in Kaplan and Dresner, 152.

86. Abraham Joshua. Heschel, *Who Is Man?* (Stanford, CA: Stanford University Press, 1965), 76–77.

87. Kaplan and Dresner, *op. cit.*, 164.

88. Abraham J. Heschel, *The Prophets: An Introduction* (New York: Harper & Row, 1962), xii. This book is Volume I of II, which together constitute a 1969 paperback reprint of the first half of Heschel's original book *The Prophets*.

89. Greenleaf's prime example of withdrawal to make room for *awareness* and creative insight is the story of Jesus answering those who would stone an adulterous woman. He recounts the scene in *The Servant as Leader*, 20. "They cry, 'The *law* says she shall be stoned; what do *you* say?. . . He [Jesus] sits there writing in the sand—a withdrawal device. In the pressure of the moment, having assessed the situation rationally, he assumes the attitude of withdrawal that will allow creative insight to function."

90. RKG, *Servant Leadership*, 250–254.

91. *Ibid.*, 250.

92. RKG, Distefano interview, RKGC.

CHAPTER 14

1. Meister Eckhart, *The Cloud of Unknowing*, trans. Ira Progoff, (New York: Dell Publishing, 1957), 62.

2. Abraham Joshua Heschel, *Who Is Man?*, 109.

3. See "Friends Conference on Religion and Psychology Conference Programs, 1943–2002," complied by Richard A. (Dick) Bellin, June, 2002. <http://www.quaker.org/fcrp/fcrphistory.pdf> (30 August, 2003).

4. See Morelle Smith, *Journeys In and Out of Time: The Life and Writing of Anais Nin*, <http://www.lunatica.pwp.blueyonder.co.uk/SAA/Documents/Anais_Nin/Anais_Nin.htm> (8 August, 2003).

5. RKG, "Open Discussion" interviews, RKGC, transcription 0550S.

6. In an interview published in *Psychology Today*, Ira Progoff remembered meeting Greenleaf in 1957. Progoff, however, does not appear on the program until the following year. See Robert Blair Kaiser, "The Way of the Journal," *Psychology Today*, March, 1981.

7. *Ibid.*

8. *Ibid.*

9. During the 1960s Dr. Progoff began to formalize a process of keeping journals that allowed ordinary people to be honest about where they were in their lives and look at fresh emotional, spiritual and career possibilities. See Progoff's *At a Journal Workshop: The Basic Text and Guide for Using the Intensive Journal*, (New York: Dialogue House Library, 1975), and *The Practice of Process Meditation* (New York: Dialogue House, 1980).

10. Ira Progoff,. *The Death and Rebirth of Psychology*. (New York: Julian Press, 1956), 254–255.

11. Robert Blair Kaiser, *op. cit.*

12. Dr. Glenn Mosley telephone interview by the author, 3 September, 2003. Dr. Mosley worked with Ira Progoff as a colleague for three years. According to Mosley, Progoff believed that a dream would "interpret itself" if one immersed oneself into the imagery. Progoff also thought that important themes were revealed through series of dreams, with each series lasting as long as three months. The connections between individual dreams in a series held rich meaning. Through dreams, God could give guidance if one asked three questions: (1) What does the dream say about where I am in my life now? (2) What do similar dreams say about where I am in my life now? (3) What am I anxious about right now? For Progoff, anxiety indicated a "pregnancy" of coming experiences.

13. Kathy Juline, "An Interview with Ira Progoff." Originally printed in *Science of Mind* magazine. July, 1992. Accessed online from <http://www.intensive-journal.org/Progoff/frame.htm> (8 August, 2003).

14. All dream material transcribed from handwritten papers: "Dreams" (c.1958–1962) FTL, Box 1. Transcriptions of RKG's dream notebooks are part of the collection of the Robert K. Greenleaf Center for Servant Leadership Archives.

15. Dr. Glenn Mosley telephone interview by the author, 3 August, 2003.

16. Carl Jung, *C. G. Jung Speaking*, W. McGuire, and R. F. C. Hull, eds. (Princeton, NJ: Princeton University Press, 1987), 296.

17. C. S. Hall and V. J. Nordby, eds. *A Primer of Jungian Psychology* (New York: New American Library, 1973), 46–47.

18. RKG, "Dreams (c.1958–1962)." FTL, Box 1. Quote also appears in *Insights on Leadership*, 357.

19. RKG, *Seeker and Servant*, Anne T. Fraker and Larry C. Spears, eds. (San Francisco: Jossey-Bass, 1996), 103. The chapter quoted is titled "An Opportunity for a Powerful New Religious Influence," which was included in "A New Religious Mission," an earlier paper Greenleaf was working on at the time of his squirrel dream.

20. Nicholas Murray, *Aldous Huxley: A Biography* (New York: St. Martin's Press, 2002), 252.

21. *Ibid.*, 252–253. Quoted from Christopher Isherwood, *Christopher and His Kind* (London: Eyre Methuen,1977), 81–82.

22. For a complete bibliography and short biography of Gerald Heard, visit his official <website at http://www.geraldheard.com/index.htm> (6 June, 2000).

23. RKG, Distefano interview, RKGC.

24. Gerald Heard, transcript of audiotaped conversation with RKG and Gerald Heard, 1958 RKGC.

25. Gerald Heard, *The Eternal Gospel* (New York: Harper & Brothers, 1946), 6.

26. Ira Progoff, *The Practice of Process Meditation: The Intensive Journal Way to Spiritual Experience* (New York: Dialogue House, 1980) 10.

27. *Ibid.*, 14.

28. RKG, Distefano interview, RKGC.

29. John Cashman, *The LSD Story* (Greenwich, CN: Fawcett Publications, 1966), 30–31.

30. See Edward M. Brecher, chapter 48, "Hazards of LSD Psychotherapy," *Licit and Illicit Drugs; The Consumers Union Report on Narcotics, Stimulants, Depressants, Inhalants, Hallucinogens, and Marijuana -Including Caffeine* (New York: Little Brown and Company, 1972).

31. Aldous Huxley, *The Doors of Perception* (New York: Harper & Row, 1954), 22–23.

32. *Ibid.*, 156.

33. Dr. Sidney Cohen wrote one of the popular classics to examine the effects of LSD: *The Beyond Within: The LSD Story* (New York: Atheneum, 1965).

"Under [the influence of psychedelic drugs] episodes of psychotic disorganization are certainly possible. In other instances they have induced an experience of psychic integration which has been called identical with the spontaneous religious experience by people who have known both states. Mental disorganization results in a psychosis; a creative reorganization underlies the visionary state. Should this state, entered into with or without chemical aid, also be call insanity? It would seem more appropriate to differentiate it and call it *unsanity* in view of the constructive solutions that can arise from it. " 61–62.

34. RKG, Distefano interview, RKGC.

35. Madeline Greenleaf Jaynes, Interview by the author, New York, NY, 15 December, 2000.

36. Lisa Greenleaf, interview by the author, New Haven, Connecticut, 16 December, 2000.

37. Madeline Greenleaf Jaynes, interview by the author, New York, NY, 15 December, 2000.

38. A 1963 law required investigators to turn stocks of LSD over to the federal government by 1965. "The first federal criminal sanctions against LSD were introduced in the drug Abuse Control Amendments in 1965. . . These amendments were modified in 1968: possession became a misdemeanor, and sale a felony. Individual states determined penalties, although most adopted the federal classification system." See Leigh A. Henderson and William J. Glass, *LSD: Still With Us After All These Years* (Fan Francisco: Jossey-Bass, 1994), 41–42.

39. RKG, Distefano interview, RKGC.

40. *Ibid.*

41. See Laura Huxley's book *This Timeless Moment* (Berkeley, CA: Celestial Arts, 2000).

42. See: David E. Kahn as told to Will Oursler, *My Life With Edgar Cayce* (New York: Doubleday & Company, 1970), 203–204.

43. See: Sidney Cohen, "Lysergic Acid Diethylamide: Side Effects and Complications," *Journal of Nervous and Mental Diseases*, 130 (January, 1960), 30–40.

CHAPTER 15

1. RKG, *On Becoming a Servant Leader*, 338.

2. Stephen Barrett, M.D. and Victor Herbert, M.D., J.D. (September 17, 2001) "Some Notes on Carleton Fredericks," <http://www.quackwatch.org/11Ind/fredericks.html> (8 July, 2003).

3. Newcomb Greenleaf, interview by the author, Indianapolis, Indiana, 4 June, 1997.

4. Madeline Greenleaf Jaynes, Interview by the author, New York, NY, 16 December, 2000.

5. *Ibid.*

6. Newcomb Greenleaf, *Reflections on Leadership*, 318.

7. Madeline Greenleaf Jaynes, Interview by the author, New York, NY, 16 December, 2000.

8. *Poems, Stories, Drawings by Elizabeth, Madeline and Newcomb Greenleaf.* (Milburn, New Jersey: Cella Press, 1946). Used by permission of the Greenleaf family.

9. Madeline Greenleaf Jaynes, Interview by the author, New York, NY, 16 December, 2000.

10. Lisa Greenleaf, interview by the author, New Haven, Connecticut, 17 December, 2000.

11. Lisa Greenleaf, telephone interview by the author, October 3, 2003.

12. *Ibid.*

13. Newcomb Greenleaf, "Reflections on Robert K. Greenleaf," *Reflections on Leadership*, 314–315.

14. *Ibid.*

15. "Fascinating facts about the invention of Erector Sets by A.C. Gilbert in 1913." *The Great Idea Finder*, <http://www.ideafinder.com/history/inventions/erectorset.htm> (July 8, 2003).

16. Newcomb Greenleaf, interview by the author, Indianapolis, Indiana, 4 June, 1997.

17. Lisa Greenleaf, interview by the author, New Haven, Connecticut, 17 December, 2000.

18. Newcomb Greenleaf, interview by the author, Indianapolis, Indiana, 7 June, 2003.

19. RKG first wrote down his "hole in the hedge" philosophy in an untitled note dated October 3, 1954. FTL, Box 1.

20. Newcomb Greenleaf, interview by the author, Indianapolis, Indiana, 4 June, 1997.

21. Madeline Greenleaf Jaynes, interview by the author, New York, NY, 15 December, 2000.

22. Lisa Greenleaf, telephone interview by the author, 12 October, 2003.

23. Newcomb Greenleaf, interview by the author, Indianapolis, Indiana, 4 June, 1997.

24. *Ibid.*

25. Newcomb Greenleaf, *Reflections on Leadership*, 315.

26. *Ibid.*

27. Lisa Greenleaf, interview by the author, New Haven, Connecticut, 16 December, 2000.

28. Parker Palmer, "Foreword," *Seeker and Servant*, xi.

29. Lisa Greenleaf, interview by the author, New Haven, Connecticut, 16 December, 2000.

30. RKG, "Open Discussion" interviews, RKGC, transcription 0443S.

CHAPTER 16

1. This talk, titled "A Concept of Vitality," was the first of three speeches RKG wrote for AT&T President Kappel which comprise the series *Vitality in a Business Enterprise* delivered in April, 1960 at the McKinsey Foundation Lectures at the Graduate School of Business, Columbia University. AT&T. These were compiled into a book with Kappel listed as the author. See: Frederick Kappel, *Vitality in a Business Enterprise* (New York: McGraw-Hill, 1960).

2. RKG, "Open Discussion," interviews, RKGC, transcription 0443S.

3. *Ibid.*

4. RKG, "Open Discussion" interviews, RKGC, transcription 0446S.

5. RKG, "Open Discussion" interviews, RKGC, transcription 0443S.

6. See Peggy Noonan, *What I Saw at the Revolution: A Political Life in the Reagan Era* (New York: Random House, 1990).

7. A good example of Greenleaf's consistent promotion of human growth can be seen in a 1957 document he prepared for the exclusive use of Bell System employees titled *Present Implications of A Forward Look at Management Development*.

In it, he linked managers' growth *as persons* (intellectual curiosity, new learning, heightened awareness, risk-taking, balance of family and other responsibilities) to performance in their jobs, all in an age of accelerating change. Greenleaf described the developmental growth challenges of different adult lifecycles then offered fifteen concrete suggestions on how the company could support sustained growth. AT&T, Collection 127 05 02, Location 79.

8. Most of the structural elements in Greenleaf's ghostwritten speeches are found in the second lecture he penned for President Kappel in the series *Vitality in a Business Enterprise*. The title of that lecture was "Goals That Build the Future," and was delivered on April 28, 1960. AT&T.

9. Cleo F. Craig "Big Business and the Community." This speech was ghostwritten by Robert Greenleaf for AT&T President Craig and delivered at the Annual Meeting of the Life Insurance Association of America, New York, 8 December, 1954. It was reproduced in a Bell System pamphlet titled *Big Business and the Community*, 1954. AT&T, Corporate Collection, Location 127 04 01.

10. RKG, ghostwriter for Frederick R. Kappel, Lecture III, "The Spark of Individuality," delivered May 12, 1960 found in the book *Vitality in a Business Enterprise*. AT&T.

11. *Ibid.*

12. Kappel, *op cit.*, Lecture II. "Goals that Build the Future."

13. Kappel, *op cit.*, Lecture I. "A Concept of Vitality."

14. The entire manuscript of *The Ethic of Strength* was first published as Part One of *On Becoming a Servant Leader*, 13–99.

15. *Ibid.*, 13.

16. *Ibid.*

17. *Ibid.*, 27.

18. *Ibid.*, 33.

19. *Ibid.*, 81.

20. *Ibid.*, 99.

21. "Education and Maturity" was first presented as a talk before the faculty and students of Barnard College at their Fifth Biennial Vocational Conference, 30 November, 1960. It was most recently published as a chapter in: RKG, *The Power of Servant Leadership*, Larry C. Spears, ed. (San Francisco: Berrett-Koehler, 1998), 61–76.

22. RKG, *The Power of Servant Leadership*, 62.

23. *Ibid.*, 62.

24. *Ibid.*, 64.

25. *Ibid.*, 65.

26. *Ibid.*, 75.

27. Greenleaf's 1963 manuscript was titled: *Robert Frost's* Directive *and the Spiritual Journey*. It has been out of print for many years, but was included as the chapter "An Inward Journey" in the book *Servant Leadership*, pp. 315–328.

28. RKG, *The Power of Servant Leadership*, 318.

29. *Ibid.*, 327.

30. RKG correspondence to "B," 22 May, 1962, FTL, Box 2.

31. RKG, "Open Discussion" interviews, RKGC, transcription 0550S.

32. RKG, "Open Discussion" interviews, RKGC, transcription 0470S.

33. Warren Bennis, interview by Larry C. Spears, 2003, RKGC.

34. Peter Vaill, interview by the author, Indianapolis, Indiana, 9 June,1997.

35. RKG, 28 January, 1974 correspondence with the editor of *Business Week* in response to an article which the magazine had recently published entitled "Why Scientists take Psychic Research Seriously." FTL, Box 2.

36. All quotes are from correspondence from RKG to George Baker, Dean of Harvard Business School. No date is given in the letter, but it was written in the late spring or early summer following the 1962–63 academic year. FTL, Box 2.

37. *Ibid.*

38. RKG, Distefano interview, RKGC.

39. RKG, "Notes on Visits to Schools of Administration and a Concluding Observation," 1963, RKGC Archives, Joseph Distefano Collection.

40. *Ibid.*

41. *Ibid.*

42. Joseph J. Distefano completed his M.B.A. from Harvard and an M.A. and Ph.D. in social psychology from Cornell. He went on to a distinguished career as an international business and management expert. See his biographical sketch in the pamphlet *Tracing the Vision and Impact of Robert K. Greenleaf* (Robert K. Greenleaf Center for Servant Leadership, 1988).

43. Joseph J. Distefano, *Tracing the Vision and Impact of Robert K. Greenleaf*, 26.

44. See Chapter 17 of this book for the story of Greenleaf's contribution to the Staff College at Hyderbad.

45. RKG, *On Becoming a Servant Leader*, 241.

46. RKG, "Autobiography: Narrative of Life and Work After Age 60," FTL, Box 1.

47. RKG, "Open Discussion" interviews, RKGC, transcription 0550S. RKGC.

48. RKG, "Open Discussion" interviews, RKGC, transcription 0436S. RKGC.

49. Douglas Williams correspondence, 16 November, 1992, RKGC.

50. RKG, "Open Discussion" interviews, RKGC, transcription not numbered.

51. RKG, "Autobiography: Narrative of Life and Work After Age 60." FTL, Box 1.

52. William Sharwell, telephone interview by the author, 29 July, 1999.

53. RKG, "Open Discussion" interviews, RKGC, transcription not numbered.

54. Newcomb Greenleaf, interview by the author, 6 June, 2003.

LEADER SECTION NOTES

CHAPTER 17

1. RKG, "Autobiography: Narrative of Life and Work After Age 60." FTL, Box 1.

2. *Ibid.*

3. Besides Greenleaf, original incorporators included James Luther Adams, Joseph F. Fletcher, Charles P Price, J. Leslie Rollins, and John E. Soleau.

4. Center for Applied Ethics, Inc. "Agreement of Association," The Commonwealth of Massachusetts. Executed 10 September, 1964. RKGC Archives.

5. The "Covering Note" is found in the first book of minutes for the Center for Applied Ethics, Inc. No date is given but the preface indicates the proposal was provided by the Provisional Committee for a Center for Applied Ethics, which suggests it is the product of the Greenleaf's preliminary proposal he developed with Dr. Joseph Fletcher during the period 1962–63. RKGC Archives.

6. *Ibid.*

7. Dr. Vernon Alden, telephone interview by the author, 22 August, 2002.

8. *Ibid.*

9. Vernon R. Alden, *Speaking for Myself: The Personal Reflections of Vernon R. Alden* (Athens, Ohio: Ohio University Press, 1997), 5.

10. *Ibid.*, 4.

11. Comments from participants in the Ohio Fellows Reunion were made to the author in Athens Ohio, 23 November, 2002.

12. RKG, "The Next Three Years." A parenthetical note by Greenleaf says, "Written in the summer of 1967 from notes used in a talk to freshmen of Ohio University who had applied for appointment as Ohio Fellows, Athens, Ohio, April 1967." FTL, Box 9.

13. *Ibid.*

In 1968 the Center for Applied Studies (the name of the organization had been changed in January, 1968) published this talk under the title, "Have You a Dream Deferred" and sent it to eleven-hundred college presidents. They received fifty-five replies. The Greenleaf Center eventually published the essay and it is included in: RKG, *The Power of Servant Leadership*, Larry C. Spears, ed. (San Francisco: Berrett-Koehler, 1998), 93–110.

14. Dr. Vernon Alden, telephone interview by the author, 22 August, 2002.

15. Ken Blanchard, "Foreword," *Focus on Leadership*, Larry C. Spears, ed., (New York: John Wiley & Sons, 2002), ix.

16. Kenneth Blanchard, interview by the author, Indianapolis, Indiana, 5 June, 2003.

17. Kenneth Blanchard, *Focus on Leadership*, x.

18. Kenneth Blanchard, interview by the author, 5 June, 2003.

19. Joseph Fletcher, *Situational Ethics: The New Morality* (Philadelphia: Westminster Press. 1966), 17.

20. *Ibid.*

21. Kenneth Blanchard, interview by the author, 5 June, 2003.

22. Kenneth Blanchard, *Focus on Leadership*, xii.

23. Dr. Vernon Alden, telephone interview with the author, 22 August, 2002.

24. RKG, "My Work in India," 1983, FTL, Box 1.

25. *Ibid.*

26. *Ibid.*

27. *Ibid.*

28. *Ibid.*

29. For a full description of current consulting activities, see the Administrative Staff College of India's website. "Consultancy Activity," <http://www.asci.org.in/cor_com/consultancy.html> (20 August, 2003).

30. RKG correspondence to Sr. Joel Read, 1981, FTL, Box 3.

31. RKG, "My Work in India," FTL, Box 1.

32. *Ibid.*

33. *Ibid.*

34. *Ibid.*

35. *Ibid.*

36. *Ibid.*

37. *Ibid.*

38. Douglas Williams, correspondence to Anne Fraker, 16 November, 1992 RKGC.

39. Madeline Greenleaf Jaynes, interview by the author, New York, NY, 15 December, 2000.

40. James McSwiney, telephone interview by the author, 5 February, 2004.

41. William H. A. Carr, *Up Another Notch: Institution Building at Mead* (Dayton, Ohio, The Mead Corporation, 1989), 40.

42. Carr, *op. cit.*, 73.

43. *Ibid.*, 57.

44. *Ibid.*

45. Robert K. Greenleaf, *Teacher as Servant: A Parable* (Indianapolis: Robert K. Greenleaf Center, 1987), 35.

46. James McSwiney, telephone interview by the author, 5 February, 2004.

47. John W. Nason correspondence to Robert K. Greenleaf, July 15, 1966. FTL, Box 2.

48. RKG, *Servant Leadership*, 250.

49. Carleton College News Bureau, news release (no headline) dated 28 May, 1969, CCA, M-8.

50. Call Report, 12 June, 1985. CCA, M-9.

51. Memo from Wallace Remington, Class Agent '26, 1986, CCA, M-9.

52. See the text of all five talks from the "Leadership and the Individual" lecture series in: RKG, *On Becoming a Servant Leader*, 285–339.

53. *Ibid.*, 327.

54. *Ibid.*, 328.

55. John W. Garner, "The Antileadership Vaccine," Annual Report of the Carnegie Corporation of New York (New York: Carnegie Corporation, 1965), 3–12.

56. RKG, *On Becoming a Servant Leader*, 330.

57. *Ibid.*, 332.

58. *Ibid.*, 302.

59. *Ibid.*, 303.

60. *Ibid.*, 303–305.

61. *Ibid.*, 306.

62. *Ibid.*, 306.

63. *Ibid.*, 308.

64. *Ibid.*, 310.

65. *Ibid.*, 338.

66. Bernard M. Bass, *Bass & Stogdill's Handbook of Leadership: Theory, Research, and Managerial Applications*, 3rd ed. (New York: The Free Press, 1990), 6.

67. RKG, "Open Discussion" Interviews, RKGC.

CHAPTER 18

1. RKG, *Servant: Leader & Follower*. (New York: Paulist Press, 1978), 3–4.

2. RKG, "President's Report," Center For Applied Studies, Inc. 29 November, 1968. RKGC.

3. RKG, "Proposed Resolution to be considered at the March 31, 1967 meeting of the Trustees of The Center for Applied Ethics," RKGC.

4. The Center's 1969 financial report, for example, lists seven students who received stipends for summer study. In this case, these were radical Cornell students who met with Greenleaf and others to talk about current tensions and how universities could be better structured to serve students. The students produced their own report on the matter.

5. RKG. Distefano interview, RKGC.

6. *Ibid.*

7. RKG. Distefano interview, RKGC.

8. *Ibid.*

9. Quote is from the original 1970 version of *The Servant as Leader* which has been reprinted in: RKG, *The Servant-Leader Within: A Transformative Path*, Hamilton Beazley and Julie Beggs and Larry C. Spears, eds. (New Jersey: Paulist Press, 2003), 33.

10. *Ibid.*, 34.

11. *Ibid.*, 34–35.

12. *Ibid.*, 35.

13. *Ibid.*, 40.

14. *Ibid.*, 41.

15. *Ibid.*, 43. In 1972 Greenleaf removed the language about pyramidal structures from *The Servant as Leader* but included it in *The Institution as Servant*.

16. *Ibid.*, 50–52.

17. *Ibid.*, 44.

18. *Ibid.*, 69.

19. *Ibid.*

20. RKG, "President's Report," Center For Applied Studies, Inc. March 23, 1970," RKGC.

21. RKG, Distefano interview, RKGC.

22. *Ibid.*

23. *Ibid.*

24. Robert Wood Lynn, telephone interview by the author, 30 August, 1999.

25. Robert Wood Lynn, correspondence to Anne Fraker, 27 November, 1995, RKGC.

26. Kenneth Blanchard, interview by the author, Indianapolis, Indiana, 5 June, 2003.

27. Bill Bottum, correspondence with the author, April, 2003.

28. RKG, "Open Discussion" interviews, RKGC, transcription 0427S.

29. *Ibid.*

30. Ashley Cheshire, *Partnership of the Spirit: The Story of Jack Lowe and TDIndustries.* (Dallas: Taylor Publishing Company, 1987), 127.

31. RKG, "Open Discussion" interviews, RKGC, transcription 0443S.

32. RKG, *Servant Leadership,* 13–14.

33. *Ibid.,* 8.

34. RKG, correspondence to Norm Shawchuck, July, 1982. FTL, Box 4.

35. RKG. Distefano interview, RKGC.

36. *Ibid.*

37. RKG, *Robert Frost's* Directive *and the Spiritual Journey* (The Nimrod Press, Boston, 1963), 5.

38. Douglas Williams, correspondence to Anne Fraker, 16 November, 1992. RKGC.

39. James E. Perdue, 6 April, 1977 correspondence with Hugh Lally, Paulist Press. Used by permission of James E. Perdue.

40. RKG, "Open Discussion" Interviews, RKGC.

41. RKG, *Servant Leadership,* 49.

42. *Ibid.,* 53–65.

43. *Ibid.,* 63.

44. *Ibid.,* 67.

45. *Ibid.,* 84–85.

46. RKG, Distefano interview RKGC.

47. One prominent effort to implement *primus inter pares* can be seen in the Housing Facilities Department at the University of Michigan in Ann Arbor. Their organizational chart—which reflects actual rather than theoretical functions—looks like a kaleidoscope, with lines joining interconnecting circles.

In the 1990s the author once sat in on a meeting with a group of middle managers who worked for a multinational corporation and noticed it was being run by a *primus inter pares* model; decisions were made by consensus. When he asked the designated leader where she learned the technique, she said, "I'm a floor chief at my manufacturing plant. Unless it's an emergency, I can't just order people around. I'd be fired. We all participate in reaching consensus on important decisions." I then asked, "Where did you learn how to do that?" She shrugged. "Oh, some Quakers came down and taught us."

48. RKG, *Servant Leadership,* 94.

49. *Ibid.,* 100.

50. *Ibid.*, 103–104.

51. For thoughtful reflections and stories about how Greenleaf's view of trusteeship can be realized in organizations, see Richard Broholm and Douglas Johnson, *A Balcony Perspective: Clarifying the Trustee Role.* (Indianapolis: The Robert K. Greenleaf Center, 1993).

52. RKG, *Servant Leadership*, 116.

53. Macolm Warford, interview by the author, Lexington, Kentucky, 9 September, 1999.

54. RKG, interview by Ann McGee-Cooper. RKGC.

55. *Ibid.*

56. *Ibid.*

57. Parker Palmer, interview by the author, Madison, Wisconsin, 17 August, 1998.

58. Parker Palmer, presentation at 2002 International Conference for Servant Leadership in Indianapolis, Indiana, June, 2002.

59. *Ibid.*

60. RKG, interview by Ann McGee-Cooper, RKGC.

61. *Ibid.*

62. *Teacher As Servant* has recently been made available in its entirety in *The Servant-Leader Within: A Transformative Path.*

63. Correspondence from John Goldberg to RKG, undated c. 1975, FTL, Used by permission.

64. RKG, correspondence to Jaxon and Arlene Tuck, 28 January, 1982, FTL, Box 4.

65. RKG "My Work in India," FTL, Box 1.

66. *Ibid.*

67. *Ibid.*

68. RKG, correspondence to Loren Mead, 2 August, 1982. FTL, Box 4.

69. *Ibid.*

70. See the Center for Creative leadership website: <http://www.ccl.org/capabilities/history.htm> (15 August, 2003).

71. Joann Lynch, interview by the author, Indianapolis, Indiana, 21 June, 1999.

72. *Ibid.* "Bob was very quiet, very unassuming, down to earth, just a good guy. He was very deep, a good honest value, but he didn't flash it around. In many ways I think that's a common observation that I, and others, had of Mr. Eli."

73. RKG, *Servant Leadership*, 214.

74. "Prudence and Creativity" is reprinted in the book *Servant Leadership*, 210–217.

75. RKG, *Servant Leadership*, 212.

76. Jim Morris, interview by the author, Indianapolis, Indiana, 28 June, 1999.

CHAPTER 19

1. RKG, *The Power of Servant Leadership*, 163.

2. Macolm Warford, interview by the author, Lexington, Kentucky, 9 September, 1999.

3. Susan Wisely, interview by the author, Indianapolis, Indiana, 21 June, 1999.

4. RKG, correspondence to Bob Lynn, 9 March, 1982. FTL, Box 4.

5. Correspondence from the Rt. Rev. David E. Richards to RKG, 26 December, 1978. Used by permission.

6. RKG, "Open Discussion," FTL.

7. Definitions excerpted from *Merriam Webster's Collegiate Dictionary*, Tenth Edition. (Springfield, MA: Merriam-Webster, Inc., 1993).

8. RKG, *On Becoming a Servant Leader*, 324.

9. For the full text of "Note on the Need for a Theology of Institutions" see *Seeker and Servant, Reflections on Religious Leadership*, 191–198.

10. *Ibid.*, 191.

11. *Ibid.*, 192.

12. Correspondence from The Rt. Rev. C. Charles Vache to RKG, 23 January, 1980. Used by permission.

13. Dick Broholm, former Director of the Center for Applied Ethics, has headed up an multi-year effort to develop a theology of institutions. You can download working papers and reports from: <www.seeingthingswhole.org>

14. RKG, *The Servant as Religious Leader*, 11.

15. *Ibid.*, 15.

16. *Ibid.*, 42.

17. RKG, correspondence to Jan Erteszek, 21 January, 1981, FTL, Box 3.

18. For a more complete description of Greenleaf's logic model of how seminaries have the potential for affecting societal change, see Professor Joseph Distefano's *Tracing the Vision and Impact of Robert K. Greenleaf*, available from the Greenleaf Center in Indianapolis.

19. Bob Lynn, telephone interview with the author, 20 August, 1999.

20. Macolm Warford, interview by the author, Lexington, Kentucky, 9 September, 1999.

21. Susan Wisely, interview by the author, Indianapolis, Indiana, 21 June, 1999.

22. *Reflections on Leadership*, 271.

23. Bill Bottum, interview by the author, Ann Arbor, Michigan, 21 July, 1999.

24. For a full account of the details of T&B's transformation into a trusteed corporation, see: Carl Rieser, *The Trusteed Corporation: A Case Study of the Townsend & Bottum Family of Companies*. (Indianapolis: The Greenleaf Center, 1987).

25. Bill Bottum, interview by the author, Ann Arbor, Michigan, 21 July, 1999.

26. RKG, "Open Discussion" interviews, RKGC, transcription 0443S.

27. Sister Joel Read, telephone interview by the author, 13 November, 1997.

28. *Life's Choices and Markers* is available from The Robert K. Greenleaf Center in Indianapolis.

29. Bennett Sims, telephone interview by the author, 2 August, 1999.

30. *Ibid.*

31. *Ibid.*

32. See Bennett J. Sims, *Servanthood: Leadership for the Third Millennium* (Boston: Cowley Publications, 1997).

33. Bennett Sims, telephone interview by the author, 2 August, 1999.

34. *Ibid.*

35. *Ibid.*

36. Newcomb Greenleaf, interview by the author, Indianapolis, Indiana, 4 June, 1997.

CHAPTER 20

1. RKG, *On Becoming a Servant Leader.* 272.

2. *Ibid.*, 275.

3. *Ibid.*, 275, 276–280.

4. RKG, undated memo, FTL, Box 1.

5. *Ibid.*

6. Bob Lynn, telephone interview by the author, 30 August, 1999.

7. *Ibid.*

8. "Greenleaf Center Timeline: 1964–2002," compiled by Larry C. Spears. 26 October, 2002, RKGC.

9. May 20, 1986 report to Greenleaf Center Board, RKGC.

10. Diane Cory, interview by the author, Indianapolis, Indiana, 8 June, 2003.

11. James McSwiney, telephone interview by the author, 5 February, 2004.

12. "Greenleaf Center Timeline: 1964–2002," compiled by Larry C. Spears. 26 October, 2002, RKGC.

13. RKG, interview by Ann McGee-Cooper. RKGC.

14. Jim Tatum, telephone interview by the author, 1 August, 1999.

15. *Ibid.*

16. RKG, "Autobiography of an Idea," FTL, Box 1.

17. RKG. Distefano interview, RKGC.

18. *Ibid.*

19. Parker Palmer, interview by the author, Madison, Wisconsin, 17 August, 1998.

20. Madeline Greenleaf Jaynes, interview by the author, New York, NY, 15 December, 2000.

21. RKG, "Old Age; The Ultimate Test of Spirit—An Essay on Preparation" in *The Power of Servant Leadership*, 268–269.

22. *Ibid.*, 264.

23. Lisa Greenleaf, telephone interview with the author, 3 August, 2003.

24. "Esther Hargrave Greenleaf: Artist, 84," *New York Times*, 23 February, 1989. Esther's obituary describes her as a painter, printmaker and ceramicist. "Mrs.

Greenleaf taught art history at Cooper Union and the University of Minnesota, her alma mater. She exhibited in the Dartmouth College Gallery and the Cambridge Art Association's Symphony Hall Show in Massachusetts." Esther was survived by Bob, her three children, a brother, sister, and seven grandchildren.

25. Descriptions of the last days of Bob and Esther are compiled from in-person and telephone interviews by the author with all three children.

26. *The Servant Leader*, (newsletter of the Greenleaf Center for Servant Leadership in Indianapolis) Winter 1990–91. RKGC.

27. Jan Arnett, interview with author, 8 December, 1997. Parts of the description of the memorial are also taken from Ms. Arnett's guest column in the *Terre Haute Journal of Business*, 2 June, 1997.

28. Descriptions of graveside service are taken from author's interviews with Jan Arnett, Larry Spears, Newcomb Greenleaf and Mac Warford.

APPENDIX I NOTES

A SERVANT LEADERSHIP PRIMER

1. RKG, *The Servant as Leader* (Indianapolis: Greenleaf Center for Servant Leadership, 1970, 1991), 8.

2. *Ibid.*

3. *Ibid.*, 9.

4. *Ibid.*, 8.

5. *Ibid.*, 18.

6. *Ibid.*, 17.

7. *Ibid.*, 7.

8. *Ibid.*

9. RKG, *On Becoming a Servant-Leader*, (San Francisco: Jossey-Bass, 1996), 70.

10. RKG. *The Servant as Leader*, 10.

11. RKG, *On Becoming a Servant-Leader*, 95.

12. *Ibid.*, 129.

13. *Ibid.*, 14.

14. RKG, *On Becoming a Servant-Leader*, 141–143.

15. RKG. *The Servant as Leader*, 16.

16. RKG, *On Becoming a Servant-Leader*, 317.

17. RKG. *The Servant as Leader*, 11.

18. *Ibid.*, 12.

19. *Ibid.*, 12–13.

20. *Ibid.*, 13–14.

21. RKG, *On Becoming a Servant-Leader*, 217.

22. *Ibid.*

23. RKG, *The Servant as Leader*, 29.

24. *Ibid.*

25. *Ibid.*

26. *Ibid.*, 34–35.

27. *Ibid.*, 4.

28. RKG, *The Institution As Servant* (Indianapolis: Greenleaf Center for Servant Leadership, 1972, 1976), 1.

29. *Ibid.*, 6.

30. *Ibid.*, 6–8.

31. *Ibid.*, 12.

32. *Ibid.*, 34.

33. RKG, *Trustees as Servants* (Indianapolis: Greenleaf Center for Servant Leadership, 1974, 1991), 37.

Bibliography

WRITINGS BY ROBERT K. GREENLEAF

Greenleaf, Robert K. "Abraham Joshua Heschel: Build a Life Like a Work of Art." *Friends Journal*, 1973, *19(15), 459–460.*

—. "Achieving increased operating effectiveness: through training." *Planning for Peak Production*, Production series no. 197. New York: American Management Association, 1951.

—. *Advices to Servants*. Indianapolis: The Greenleaf Center, 1991.

—. "The Art of Knowing." *Friends Journal*, 1974, 20(17).

— . with Bowen, G. T. *Bell Humanities Program*. Indianapolis: The Greenleaf Center, 1972.

—. "Business Ethics—Everybody's Problem." *New Catholic World*, 1980, 223, 275–278.

—. "Choose the Nobler Belief."*AA Grapevine*, 1966, 23(5), 27–31.

—. "Choosing Greatness." *AA Grapevine*, 1966, 23(4), 26–30.

—. "Choosing to be Aware."*AA Grapevine*, 1966, 23(1), 26–28.

—. "Choosing to Grow."*AA Grapevine*, 1966, 23(2), 11–13.

—. "Community as Servant and Nurturer of the Human Spirit. "*Resources for Community-Based Economic Development*, 1986, 4, 9–11.

—. "Creative, Realistic Leaders." *Managers for the Year 2000*, ed. William H. Newman. Englewood Cliffs, NJ: Prentice-Hall, 1978, 99–104.

—. *Education and Maturity*. Indianapolis: The Greenleaf Center, 1988.

—. "Education and the Art of Knowing." *Friends Journal* (October 1974).

—. "Exploring the Paradox of Servant as Leader." (Videotape). Indianapolis: Greenleaf Center, 1984.

—. "A Forward Look at Management Development." Ann Arbor: Bureau of Industrial Relations, University of Michigan, 1958.

—. "The Foundation Trustee." *The Journal of Philanthropy*. (July / August, 1973), 30–34.

—. *Have You a Dream Deferred?* Indianapolis: The Greenleaf Center, 1988.

—. *The Institution as Servant*. Indianapolis: The Greenleaf Center, 1976.

—. "Is it More Blessed to Give than to Receive?" *Friends Journal* (May 1, 1976): 267–268.

—. *The Leadership Crisis*. Indianapolis: The Greenleaf Center, 1978.

—. *Life's Choices and Markers*. Indianapolis: The Greenleaf Center, 1986.

—. *Life With Father*. Greenleaf Center for Servant-Leadership, Indianapolis, 1988.

—. *Mission in a Seminary: A Prime Trustee Concern*. Indianapolis: The Greenleaf Center, 1981.

—. *Management Ability*. Pacific Telephone. (No date)

—. "A Mission for Us." *Christian Laymen*, 14 (November–December, 1955): 5–6.

—. *My Debt to E. B. White*. Indianapolis: The Greenleaf Center, 1987.

—. *My Life With Father*. Greenleaf Center for Servant-Leadership, Indianapolis, 1988.

—. "Now is the Time to Build Anew." *Friends Journal* (May 15, 1973): 292–293.

—. *Old Age: The Ultimate Test of Spirit*. Indianapolis: The Greenleaf Center, 1987.

—. *On Becoming a Servant Leader*. San Francisco: Jossey-Bass, 1996.

—. "On Evaluation." (Videotape) Indianapolis: Greenleaf Center, 1984.

—. "Overcome Evil with Good." *Friends Journal*, 1977, 2 3(10), 292–302.

—. *The Power of Servant Leadership*. San Francisco: Berrett-Koehler Publishers, 1998.

—. "The Problem and Challenge for Social Institutions." *Journal of Current Social Issues*, 10 (Winter 1971–1971): 4–5.

—. "Prudence and Creativity: A Trustee Responsibility." *The Journal of Philanthropy*. (May/June 1974): 28–32.

—. *Robert Frost's "Directive" and the Spiritual Journey*. Boston: Nimrod Press, 1963.

—. *Seeker and Servant*. San Francisco: Jossey-Bass, 1996.

—. *Seminary as Servant*. Indianapolis: The Greenleaf Center, 1988. Servant Leadership. New York: Paulist Press, 1977.

—. *The Servant as Leader*. Indianapolis: The Greenleaf Center, 1991.

—. "The Servant as Leader." *Journal of Religion and the Applied Behavioral Sciences*, Winter 1982, 3, 7–10.

—. The *Servant as Religious Leader*. Indianapolis: The Greenleaf Center, 1983.

—. *Servant: Leader & Follower*. New York: Paulist Press, 1978.

—. *Servant Leadership: A Journey into the Nature of Legitimate Power and Greatness*. Ramsey, N.J.: Paulist Press. 1977.

—. *Servant: Retrospect and Prospect*. Indianapolis: The Greenleaf Center, 1980.

—. *Spirituality as Leadership*. Indianapolis: The Greenleaf Center, 1988.

—. *Teacher as Servant: A Parable*. Indianapolis: The Greenleaf Center, 1987.

—.*The Servant-Leader Within: A Transformative Path*. New Jersey: Paulist Press, 2003.

—. "The Trustee: The Buck Starts Here." *Foundation News* 14 (July/August 1973): 30–34.

—. "The Trustee and the Risks of Persuasive Leadership," *Hospital Progress*, 1978, PP. 50–52, 88.

—. "Trustee Traditions and Expectations." *In The Good Steward: A Guide to Theological School Trusteeship*. Washington, D.C.: Association of Governing Boards of Universities and Colleges, n.d.

—. *Trustees as Servants*. Indianapolis: The Greenleaf Center, 1990.

—. "Trustees Consider a Hypothetical Case" *Association of Governing Boards of Universities and Colleges* (March 1974): 14–19.

—. "Two More Choices." *AA Grapevine*, 1966, 2 3(3), 22–23.

———

"A Good Man is Hard to Find." *Fortune*, March 1946, Vol. XXXIII, no 1, 92.

Adler, Felix. "An Address by Dr. Felix Adler, May 10, 1931, On the Occasion of the Fifty-Fifth Anniversary of the founding of the Ethical Movement," 1931. Accessed October 19, 2002 from the World Wide

Web at The American Ethical Union website: http://www.aeu.org/adler4.html.

Administrative Staff College of India Website. "Consultancy Activity," http://www.asci.org.in/cor_com/consultancy. html. Accessed August 20, 2003.

Alexander, Anne McDonald. *The Antigonish Movement: Moses Coady and Adult Education Today*. Toronto: Thompson Educational Publishing, 1998.

Alden, Vernon R. *Speaking for Myself: The Personal Reflections of Vernon R. Alden*. Athens, Ohio: Ohio University Press, 1997.

Barnhard, John D., Carmony, Donald F., Nichols, Opal M., Weicker, Jack E. *Indiana: The Hoosier State*. New York: Harper & Row, 1963.

Barton, John R. "How Danish Farmers Work Together." Address given before a convocation of students at the University of Wisconsin, December 12, 1934.

Barrett, Stephen M.D. and Herbert, Victor, M.D., J.D. "Some Notes on Carleton Fredericks." September 17, 2001. Retrieved July 8, 2003 from the World Wide Web: http:// www.quackwatch.org/11Ind/fredericks.html.

Baughman, J. *United Methodism in Indiana*. Presented at the Inaugural Program of the South Indiana Conference United Methodist Historical Society DePauw University April 27, 1996.

Beier, James. "The Earlham Institute for Executive Growth." *The Earlhamite*, July 1967.

"Bell Labs: More Than 50 Years of the Transistor." Accessed May 27, 2003 at the Lucent Technology site: http://www. lucent.com/minds/transistor/.

Begtrup, Holger and Lund, Hans and Manniche, Peter. *The Folk High Schools of Denmark and the Development of a Farming Community*. London, Oxford University Press, 1929.

"Biographical Sketch of L Hollingsworth Wood." L Hollingsworth Wood Papers, 1903, 1953. Haverford College Libraries—Special Collections. Accessed from World Wide Web April 18, 2003. http://www.haverford.edu/library/ special/aids/wood/#genealogy

Blackford, Katherine M. H. and Newcomb, Arthur. 1924. *The Right Job: How to Choose It and Keep It, Vol. I & II*. New York: The Reviews of Reviews Corporation, 1924.

Bowen, Catherine D. "The Magnificence of Age." *Harper's*, April, 1953.

Braithwaite, William C. *The Beginnings of Quakerism*. Cambridge: Cambridge at the University Press, 1955.

Bray, Douglas W. *Formative Years in Business: A Long-Term A.T. and T. Study of Managerial Lives*. Melbourne, FL: Krieger Publishing Company, 1974.

—. *Working with Organizations and Their People: A Guide to Human Resources Practice*. New York: Guilford Press, 1991.

Bray, Douglas W. and Howard, Ann. *Managerial Lives in Transition: Advancing Age and Changing Times*. New York: Guilford Press, 1988.

Brecher, Edward M. *et. al.* "Hazards of LSD Psychotherapy," *Licit and Illicit Drugs; The Consumers Union Report on Narcotics, Stimulants, Depressants, Inhalants, Hallucinogens, and Marijuana -Including Caffeine*. New York: Little Brown and Company, 1972.

Brooks, John. *Telephone: The First Hundred Years*. New York: Harper & Row, 1976.

Cashman, John. 1966. *The LSD Story*. Greenwich, CN: Fawcett Publications. 1966.

Cheshire, Ashley. *Partnership of the Spirit: The Story of Jack Lowe and TDIndustries*. Dallas: Taylor Publishing Company, 1987.

Cohen, Sidney. "Lysergic Acid Diethylamide: Side Effects and Complications." *Journal of Nervous and Mental Diseases*, 130. January, 1960, 30–40.

—. *The Beyond Within: The LSD Story*. New York: Atheneum, 1965.

Craig, Cleo F. "Big Business and the Community." *Business and the Community*, Pamphlet. New York: The Bell System,1954.

Davis, Elmer. *But We Were Born Free*. Westport, CT: Greenwood Publishing Group,1971.

DiStefano, Joe. *Tracing the Vision and Impact of Robert K. Greenleaf*. Indianapolis: Greenleaf Center, 1990.:

Doris, George. "General Semantics: An Introduction to non-Aristotelian Systems." Accessed from the World Wide Web on June 1, 2002 from the website of the Institute of General Semantics: http://www.general-semantics.org/Institute/ GD_AKGS. shtml.

Dreiser, Theodore. *A Hoosier Holiday*. Bloomington: Indiana University Press, 1997.

Eggleston, Edward. *The Hoosier Schoolmaster*. New York: Hart Publishing Co., 1996.

Elliot, John L. "Spiritual Discoveries," in *The Fiftieth Anniversary of the Ethical Movement 11876–1926*. New York: D. Appleton, 1926.

Evans, Charles. *Friends in the Seventeenth Century*. Philadelphia: Friends Book Store, 1876.

"Fascinating facts about the invention of Erector Sets by A.C. Gilbert in 1913." Revision December 13th, 2002. The Great Idea Finder. Retrieved July 8, 2003 from the World Wide Web: http://www.ideafinder.com/history/inventions/erectorset.htm.

Feiss, Richard. "The Life of Frederick W. Taylor," *Harvard Business Review*, October 1924. Vol. III, Number 1.

Fletcher, Joseph. *Situation Ethics: The New Morality*. Philadelphia: Westminster Press, 1966.

Follett, Mary P. *Parker Follett—Prophet of Management*. Boston: Harvard Business School Press, 1995.

Fox, Richard W. "Reinhold Niebuhr's 'Revolution'." *The Wilson Quarterly*, Autumn, 1984.

Franke, R. H. & Kaul, J. D. published "The Hawthorne Experiments: First Statistical Interpretation." *American Sociological Review*, 1978.

Fremon, David K. *The Great Depression in American History*. Berkeley Heights, NJ: Enslow Publishers, 1997.

Galbraith, John K. *The Great Crash: 1929*. New York: Houghton Mifflin Company, 1955.

Garner, John W. "The Antileadership Vaccine," Annual Report of the Carnegie Corporation of New York. New York: Carnegie Corporation, 1965.

Gordon, John S. *The Business of America*. New York: Walker Publishing Co., 2001.

Gray, Ralph D., Ed. *Gentlemen From Indiana*. Indianapolis: Indiana Historical Bureau, 1977.

Greenleaf, Elizabeth and Greenleaf, Madeline and Greenleaf, Newcomb. *Poems, Stories, Drawings by Elizabeth, Madeline and Newcomb Greenleaf*. Milburn, New Jersey: Cella Press, 1946.

Greenleaf, Newcomb. "Our Greenleaf Heritage." Unpublished manuscript.

Hawes, David S. *The Best of Kin Hubbard: Abe Martin's Sayings and Wisecracks, Abe's Neighbeors, His Almanack, Comic Drawings*. Bloomington: Indiana University Press, 1984.

Headley, Leal A. & Jarchow, Merrill E. *Carleton: The First Century*. Northfield, MN: Carleton College, 1996.

Heard, Gerald. *The Eternal Gospel*. New York: Harper & Brothers, 1946.

—. *The Five Ages of Man: The Psychology of Human History*. New York: Crown Publishing Group, 1960.

—. *Is God in History? An Inquiry into Human and Prehuman History in Terms of the Doctrine of Creation, Fall and Redemption*. New York: 1950.

—. *Is God Evident? An Essay Toward a Natural Theology*. Harper, 1948.

—. *The Creed of Christ: An Interpretation of the Lord's Prayer*. Monograph, London: Religion Book Club, 1944.

—. *Training for the Life of the Spirit*. New York: Crown Publishing Group, 1960.

—. *Man the Master*. New York: Crown Publishing Group, 1941.

Helming, O. C. Pamphlet, *The Church and the Industrial Problem*. Pamphlet, Chicago: Chicago Church Federation, 1919.

—. "Ethics and Economics." *Religious Education*, April, 1932.

Henderson, Leigh A. and Glass, William J. *LSD: Still With Us After All These Years*. San Francisco: Jossey-Bass, 1994.

Heschel, Abraham J. *The Earth is the Lord's: The Inner World of the Jew in East Europe*. NY: H. Schuman, 1950.

—. *The Sabbath: Its Meaning for Modern Man*. NY: Farrar, Straus & Giroux, 1952.

—. *Man is Not Alone: A Philosophy of Religion* NY: Farrar, Straus & Giroux, 1951.

—. *Man's Quest for God: Studies in Prayer & Symbolism*. NY: Scribner, 1954.

—. *God in Search of Man: A Philosophy of Judaism* NY: Jewish Publication Society of America, 1955.

—. *The Prophets: An Introduction*. New York: Harper & Row, 1962.

Hesse, Hermann, *The Journey to the East*. New York: The Noonday Press, 1992.

—. *The Glass Bead Game (Magister Ludi)*. New York : H. Holt, 1990.

Hillerman, Eric and Anderson, Diana. *Carleton College: Celebrating 125 Years*. Northfield, MN: Carleton College. 1991.

Holliday, Rev. F. C. *Indiana Methodism*. Cincinnati: Hitchcock and Walden, 1873.

Holmes, Whittier M. 1899. *Descriptive Mentality From the Head, Face, and Hand*. Philadelphia: David McMay, 1899.

Huxley, Aldous. *The Doors of Perception and Heaven and Hell*. New York: Harper & Row, 1954.

Huxley, Laura. *This Timeless Moment*. Berkely, CA: Celestial Arts, 2000.

Important Dates and Achievements, "Menninger develops management, leadership innovations." Accessed from the World Wide Web, November 1, 2003, from: http://www. menningerclinic.com/about/history.html.

James, William. *The Varieties of Religious Experience*. Carmichael, CA: Touchstone Books, 1997.

Johnson, H. "The Hawthorne Studies: The Legend and the Legacy." Presented at the symposium, *Man and Work in Society*, November 12, 1974.

Juline, Kathy. "An Interview with Ira Progoff." Originally printed in *Science of Mind* Magazine. July, 1992. Accessed online from http://www.intensivejournal.org/Progoff/ frame.htm on August 8, 2003.

Jung, C. G. McGuire, W. and R. F. C. Hull, Eds. *C. G. Jung Speaking*. Princeton, NJ: Princeton University Press, 1987.

—. C. S. Hall and V. J. Nordby, Eds. *A Primer of Jungian Psychology*. New York: New American Library, 1973.

Kahn, David E., *My Life With Edgar Cayce*. New York: Doubleday & Company, 1970.

Kaiser, Robert B. "The Way of the Journal." *Psychology Today*, March 1981.

Kleiner, Art. *The Age of Heretics: Heroes, Outlaws, and the Forerunners of Corporate Change*. New York: Doubleday/Currency, 1996.

Knill, Paolo J., Barba, Helen N., Fuchs, Margo N. *Minstrels of Soul: Intermodal Expressive Therapy*. Toronto: Palmerston Press, 1995.

Korzybski, Alfred. *Science and Sanity: An Introduction to Non-Aristotelian Systems and General Semantics* (5th Ed.). Brooklyn, NY: Institute of General Semantics, 1995.

—. *Manhood of Humanity: The Science and Art of Human Engineering* (2nd Ed.). Brooklyn, NY: Institute of General Semantics, 2001.

Landsberger, Henry A. *Hawthorne revisited. Management and the Worker: Its Critics, and Developments in Human Relations in Industry*. Ithaca, N. Y., Cornell University, 1958.

Lewin, Miriam. "Kurt Lewin: Social Psychologist," *Lewin's Legacy/Lewin's Potential: Next Step for Group Process, Consultation and Social Justice: A Source Book*. Alexandria, VA: NTL Institute, 1997.

Markle, John II. "How Can We Broaden the Telephone Man's Horizon?" *Bell Telephone Magazine*, Autumn, 1955.

McGregor, Douglas. *The Human Side of Enterprise*. New York: McGraw Hill, 1960.

Mitchell K. "Self Supporting," Website: http://alcoholism. about.com/ library/blmitch10.htm. Accessed July 23, 2003.

Mold, Harold P. "An Executive Development Program." *Personnel Journal,* May, 1948. Vol. 28, No. 1.

Myers, Fred (Producer). *Robert K. Greenleaf, Servant-Leader.* (Videotape). Greenleaf Center, 1988.

Murray, Nicholas. *Aldous Huxley: A Biography.* New York: St. Martin's Press, 2002.

Noonan, Peggy. *What I Saw at the Revolution: A Political Life in the Reagan Era.* New York: Random House, 1990.

The OSS Assessment Staff, 1948. *Assessment of Men: Selection of Personnel for the Office of Strategic Services.* New York: Rinehart & Company, Inc., 1948.

Patton, Michael Q. *Utilization-Focused Evaluation, 3rd Ed.* Thousand Oaks, CA: SAGE Publications, 1997.

Pennock, G. A. "Industrial Research at Hawthorne," *Personnel Journal,* Vol. VII, No. 5, April, 1930.

Progoff, Ira. *At a Journal Workshop: The Basic Text and Guide for Using the Intensive Journal.* New York: Dialogue House Library, 1975.

—. *The Practice of Process Meditation.* New York: Dialogue House, 1980.

—. *The Death and Rebirth of Psychology.* New York: Julian Press, 1956.

—. *The Practice of Process Meditation: The Intensive Journal Way to Spiritual Experience.* New York: Dialogue House, 1980.

Jerse, Dorothy Weinz and Judith, Stedman Calvert. *Terre Haute: A Pictorial History.* St. Louis: G. Bradley Publishing, 1993.

Jones, Rufus M. *The Faith and Practice of the Quakers.* London: Methuen & Co., 1949.

Kaplan, Edward K. and Dresner, Samuel H. *Abraham Joshua Heschel: Prophetic Witness.* New Haven: Yale University Press, 1998.

Leonard, Delavan. *The History of Carleton College: Its Origin and Growth, Environment and Builders.* Fleming H. Revell Company, Chicago, 1904.

Madison, James H. *Eli Lilly: A Life, 1885–1977.* Indianapolis: Indiana Historical Society, 1989.

—. *The Indiana Way: A State History.* Bloomington: Indiana University Press, 1986.

Martin, John B. *Indiana: An Interpretation.* Bloomington: Indiana University Press, 1992.

McGregor, Douglas. *The Human Side of Enterprise.* New York: McGraw Hill, 1960.

Meister Eckhart, translated by Ira Progoff, *The Cloud of Unknowing.* New York: Dell Publishing, 1957.

Morrow, Barbara O. *From Ben-Hur to Sister Carrie: Remembering the Lives and Works of Five Indiana Authors*. Indianapolis: Guild Press of Indiana, Inc., 1995.

Neal, Rusty. *Brotherhood Economics: Women and Co-operatives in Nova Scotia*. Cape Breton: UCCB Press, 1998.

Newby, James R. *Elton Trueblood: Believer, Teacher, and Friend*. San Francisco: Harper & Row, 1990.

Phillips, Clifton. Indiana *In Transition: 1880–1920*. Indianapolis: Indiana Historical Bureau & Indiana Historical Society, 1968.

Porter, David H. & Jarchow, Merrill E. (Eds.) *Carleton Remembered: 1909–1986*. Northfield, MN: Carleton College, 1987.

Rieser, Carl. *The Trusteed Corporation: A Case Study of the Townsend & Bottum Family of Companies*. Indianapolis: The Greenleaf Center, 1987.

Riley, James Whitcomb, *The Complete Poetical Works of James Whitcomb Riley*. Indiana University Press, Bloomington, 1993.

Robinson, B. A. (2002) "Religious Society of Friends." Religious Tolerance. org, November 19, 2002. Accessed from World Wide Web on February 15, 2003. http://www.religioustolerance.org/quaker.htm

Roethlisberger, Fritz J. *Management and Morale*. Cambridge, MA: Harvard University Press, 1941.

Roethlisberger, Fritz J. and Dickson, William J. *Management and the Worker*. Cambridge, MA: Harvard University Press, 1939.

—. *Counseling in an Organization: A Sequel to the Hawthorne Researches*. Boston, Division of Research, Graduate School of Business Administration, Harvard University, 1966.

Rosenblum, Robert. *Cubism and the Twentieth Century Art*. New York: Harry N. Abrams, Inc., 1976.

Schugurensky, Daniel. "1928: University Extension for Social Change: The Antigonish Movement" from *History of Education: Selected Moments of the 20th Century* Accessed from the World Wide Web, July 27, 2003. http://fcis.oise.utoronto.ca/ ~daniel_schugurensky/assignment1/ 1928antigonish.html.

Siegle, Peter. *New Directions in Liberal Education for Executives*. Chicago: Center for the Study of Liberal Education for Adults, 1958.

Sims, Bennett J. *Servanthood: Leadership for the Third Millennium*. Boston: Cowley Publications, 1997.

Smith, Morelle. "Journeys In and Out of Time: The Life and Writing of Anais Nin." http://www.lunatica.pwp.blueyonder. co.uk/SAA/Documents/Anais_Nin/Anais_Nin.htm Accessed August 8, 2003.

Smith, Rev. I. *Reasons for Becoming a Methodist*. New York: Carleton & Porter, 1850.

Spears, Larry C. Ed. *Insights on Leadership: Service, Stewardship and Servant Leadership*. New York: John Wiley & Sons, 1998.

Spears, Larry C., Ed. *Reflections on Leadership: How Robert K. Greenleaf's Theory of Servant-Leadership Influenced Today's Top Management Thinkers*. New York: Wiley, 1995.

Spears, Larry C. and Lawrence, Michele, Eds. *Focus on Leadership: Servant Leadership for the 21st Century*. New York: Wiley & Sons, 2002.

Sprecher, Paul. "John James Holmes." *Dictionary of Unitarian and Universalist Biography*. Accessed June 17, 2003. Website address: http://www.uua.org/uuhs/duub/articles/johnhaynesholmes.html.

Strunk, William and White, E. B. *The Elements of Style, Third Edition*. New York: Macmillan.

Taylor, Frederick W. *The Principles of Scientific Management*. New York: Harper & Brothers, 1911.

The Red Pepper. Terre Haute, IN: Wiley High School, 1922.

Troyer, Byron L. *Yesterday's Indiana*. Miami: E. A. Seemann Publishing, 1975.

Trueblood, Elton D. *While It Is Day: An Autobiography*. New York: Harper & Row, 1974.

—. *The Predicament of Modern Man*. New York: Harper & Bros., 1944.

—. *Alternative to Futility*. New York: Harper & Row, 1949.

United States Department of Agriculture. "Honey Bees." Accessed from the World Wide Web, March 1, 2002. http://gears.tucson.ars.ag.gov/beebook/sec1/sec1.html.

Vanausdall, Jeanette. *Pride & Protest: The Novel in Indiana*. Indianapolis: Indiana Historical Society, 1999.

van der Post, Laurens. *A Mantis Carol*. New York: Morrow, 1976.

—. *The Lost World of the Kalahari*. New York: Harcourt Brace Jovanovich, 1977.

—. *Heart of the Hunter*. New York: Harcourt Brace Jovanovich, 1980.

—. *A Walk With A White Bushman: In conversation with Jean-Marc Pottiez*. New York: William Morrow, 1987.

Walton, Joseph. *Incidents Concerning the Society of Friends*. Philadelphia: Friends Books Store, 1897.

Wesley, John. *The Journal of John Wesley*. Chicago: Moody Press, 1952.

White, E. B. *Charlotte's Web*. New York: Harper & Row Publishers, 1952.

—. *Essays of E. B. White*. New York: Harper & Row, 1977.

Whitney, Janet. *John Woolman: American Quaker*. Boston: Little, Brown and Co., 1942.

Woodman, Charles M. *The Present Day Message of Quakerism*. New York: The Pilgrim Press, 1915.

Woollen, William W. *Biographical and Historical Sketches of Early Indiana*. Indianapolis: Hammond & Co., 1883.

Woolman, John. The *Journal of John Woolman and a Plea for the Poor*. New York: Corinth Books, 1961.

"World's Biggest Corporation," *Fortune*, September 30, 1930, Vol. 11, No. 3.

Williams Associates. "Summary: Interview Study of Northwestern Program." Unpublished manuscript, 1957.

Wolfe, William. *Endocrinology in Modern Practice Edition*, 2d ed. Philadelphia: W. B. Saunders Company, 1939.

Wyatt, George. "Johnson O'Connor: A Portrait from Memory" on the Johnson O'Connor Research Foundation website: www.jocrf.org. Accessed from the World Wide Web August 17, 2003.

FURTHER READING: BOOKS AND ESSAYS ABOUT APPLICATIONS OF SERVANT LEADERSHIP

Besides the books listed in the bibliography, there are scores of other publications about the applications of servant leadership for individuals and institutions. Many of them are available from the Greenleaf Center's website: www.greenleaf.org. Following is a small sample.

Autry, James A. *The Servant Leader: How to Build a Creative Team, Develop Great Morale, and Improve Bottom-Line Performance*. New York: Prima Publishing, 2001.

Broholm, Richard & Johnson, Douglas. *A Balcony Perspective: Clarifying the Trustee Role*. Indianapolis: The Robert K. Greenleaf Center, 1993.

Guillory, William A. *The Living Organization—Spirituality in the Workplace*. Salt Lake City: Innovations, 1997.

McGee-Cooper, Ann, and Gary Looper. *The Essentials of Servant Leadership: Principles in Practice*. Waltham: Pegasus Communications, 2001.

Melrose, Ken. *Making the Grass Greener on Your Side: A CEO's Journey to Leading by Serving*. San Francisco: Berrett-Koehler, 1995.

Turner, William B. *The Learning of Love: A Journey Toward Servant Leadership*. Macon, GA: Smith & Helwys, 2000.

Williams, Lea E. *Servants of the People: The 1960s Legacy of African American Leadership*. New York: St. Martin's Press, 1996.

Young, David S. *Servant Leadership for Church Renewal*. Scottdale: Herald Press, 1999.

Index

About the Author

Don M. Frick co-edited, with Larry Spears, the book On *Becoming a Servant-Leader* (1996) and contributed chapters to *Reflections on Leadership* (1995), and *Insights on Leadership* (1998). He has conducted workshops on the theory and practice of servant leadership for numerous for-profit and nonprofit organizations, with audiences ranging from educators to managers to community leadership professionals. Don has designed and written servant leadership curricula for Sterling College, the Servant-Leader Development Center, and several business organizations, and is in demand as a public speaker.

As an entrepreneur, Don created his own business in order to live a mission that touches lives and affects organizations in positive ways through communications activities. He has written and produced hundreds of training programs, films, videos, and web-based interactive products for some of America's top corporations, created broadcast programs for outlets like The History Channel, and is founder of an award-winning radio series about Indiana history called *The Nineteenth State*, which is represented in the collection of the Museum of Television and Radio in New York City. He has written four continuing education books for the insurance industry, including one about ethics for insurance professionals, and managed departments for several organizations, including a university.

In addition to writing and consulting activities, Don teaches speech and communications at the college level. He holds a Bachelor's degree from Eastern Illinois University, a Master of Divinity from Christian Theological Seminary, and is currently pursuing a Ph.D. in Leadership and Organizational Studies at The Union Institute and University in Cincinnati.

Don traces his interest in Robert Greenleaf to a day in 1986 when he first read the essay *The Servant as Leader*. As he studied Greenleaf's life, he found someone who cultivated eclectic interests, sought to understand his personal shadows, was extremely competent in his profession but also comfortable with mystery and paradox. Greenleaf had much to teach him, and the world. "I am constantly amazed by the wide applications of Bob Greenleaf's wisdom," says Frick. "For example, one of his least-known aphorisms is 'means *determine* ends.' That is an important thought for an old communicator like me. In a letter to a sick friend, Greenleaf wrote that 'One does not do right in order to become a saint. Rather one becomes a saint in order to know what is right, what one should do, and to gain the courage and strength to do it.' That is an important thought for everyone."

Berrett-Koehler Publishers

B errett-Koehler is an independent publisher of books and other publications at the leading edge of new thinking and innovative practice on work, business, management, leadership, stewardship, career development, human resources, entrepreneurship, and global sustainability.

Since the company's founding in 1992, we have been committed to creating a world that works for all by publishing books that help us to integrate our values with our work and work lives, and to create more humane and effective organizations.

We have chosen to focus on the areas of work, business, and organizations, because these are central elements in many people's lives today. Furthermore, the work world is going through tumultuous changes, from the decline of job security to the rise of new structures for organizing people and work. We believe that change is needed at all levels— individual, organizational, community, and global—and our publications address each of these levels.

To find out about our new books,
special offers,
free excerpts,
and much more,
subscribe to our free monthly eNewsletter at

www.bkconnection.com

Please see next pages for other books
from Berrett-Koehler Publishers

Spread the word!

Berrett-Koehler books are available at quantity discounts for orders of 10 or more copies.

Robert K. Greenleaf
A Life of Servant Leadership
Don M. Frick

Hardcover
ISBN 1-57675-276-3
Item #52763 $29.95

To find out about discounts for orders of 10 or more copies for individuals, corporations, institutions, and organizations, please call us toll-free at (800) 929-2929.

To find out about our discount programs for resellers, please contact our Special Sales department at (415) 288-0260; Fax: (415) 362-2512. Or email us at bkpub@bkpub.com.

Subscribe to our free e-newsletter!
To find out about what's happening at Berrett-Koehler and to receive announcements of our new books, special offers, free excerpts, and much more, subscribe to our free monthly e-newsletter at www.bkconnection.com.

Berrett-Koehler Publishers
PO Box 565, Williston, VT 05495-9900
Call toll-free! **800-929-2929** 7 am-9 pm EST

Or fax your order to 1-802-864-7626
For fastest service order online: **www.bkconnection.com**